WEBSTER'S DICTIONARY OF
USAGE and STYLE

ROY H. COPPERUD

THE REFERENCE GUIDE FOR
PROFESSIONAL WRITERS ♦ REPORTERS ♦ EDITORS
TEACHERS AND STUDENTS

Introduction by J. R. Wiggins
Former Editor of *The Washington Post*

AVENEL BOOKS
New York

This 1982 edition is published by Avenel Books, distributed by
Crown Publishers, Inc., by arrangement with Hawthorn Properties,
a division of E.P. Dutton, Inc.

Manufactured in the United States of America

Library of Congress Cataloging in Publication Data

ISBN: 0-517-385686

h g f e d c b a

Introduction

Writing is deficient as an art form, Brancusi once said, because it can be looked at from only one direction. And that was a great deficiency in the mind of the sculptor who grew more and more fascinated with the different aspects in which his figures might be viewed when mounted on their revolving platforms.

Roy H. Copperud, in *Webster's Dictionary of Usage and Style*, has a Brancusi-like way of looking at words and construction and style. He does not look upon the written language from one direction alone, but from many directions. He is not content to examine usage or arrangement in one light only. He is not satisfied to know the origins of meaning alone. He is not willing to settle for the judgment of a single authority. He is tolerant of changing preferences. He is friendly to innovation and invention. He is impatient with pedantry and dogmatism. He is basically permissive in his willingness to accept new meanings, once-scorned constructions or words, popular alterations in fusty rules.

Yet his mind is not so open that everything runs out at both ends. He has standards. But they are the standards dictated by logic and by common sense, by good taste, by a sound ear, and by a reverence for clarity and coherence. This man has a view of style and usage that comes from looking at writing from more than one direction. The sentence which comes before him for judgment is in a court disposed to be friendly and tolerant and inclined to credit good intentions. If it is a serious and sincere attempt to get an idea from the mind of a writer into the mind of a reader, it will be dealt with in a kindly manner—whatever rules and regulations have been violated in the process. But the

5

sentence that begins with nothing to say and ends by saying it badly is before a hanging judge. And this really is fair enough. To have an idea and to care so little about it as to put it into English that is unintelligible is worse than contempt of court. It is self-contempt. And that deserves to be severely punished.

This book will not be of any use to persons who do not wish to write well; but to professional writers and others who really wish to write in a way that can be understood, it will prove an invaluable guide. Its value to a writer does not lie in any claim to infallible authority. The reporter and author who turn to Copperud will find him definite enough, precise enough, and unequivocal enough in all those areas where the weight of precedent and usage is so confirmed as to leave no room for debate. In the infinitely more numerous cases where there is real doubt and difference, the writer is more likely to find a discussion than a decision. But the discussion will be one that helps the writer make his own selection, his personal compromise between following a rule and making an exception to it.

What professional writers will like about this book is the evidence on every page that Mr. Copperud cares about writing. No one can go far into this text without discovering that he greatly cares, or without caring a little more himself about the right choice of word and structure required to convey with the greatest clarity, force, and simplicity the subject matter at hand.

The great virtue of a dictionary of usage and style written from such a point of view is that its utility does not depend upon total agreement with the opinions of the author. If you come to this book to confirm your judgment or opinion, you may be gratified to discover that you have a confederate of like mind; you may be dismayed to find that you have a worthy opponent. No matter. You will profit from exposure to a fresh analysis of the problem of usage involved. You will have your ear improved and your taste sharpened by frequent reference to these pages. Copperud invites argument more than agreement. You will leave your consultation with him either with a different opinion of usage, or with a better-informed reason for sticking to your opinion. Either way is a comfort to those who really are anxious to say a thing well.

Even with such reliable guides to usage as common sense and a good ear, of course, one can get into plenty of trouble. Many will differ with Copperud in some of his preferences. No matter. This book will make you think about it and you will not go thoughtlessly all out in either direction without any reflection. Ear and intellect will be sharpened by the exercise. If you remain in some uncertainty you will be comforted by Copperud's reassurance that the reading public does manage to extract meaning from diverse usage and style.

Those who are less knowledgeable technically than Copperud will be much comforted by his insistence that a sentence "sound right." He is quite correct when he says: "If a sentence doesn't sound right it isn't any good, whether the infinitive is split, rewoven, braided, or sawed in half." Unfortunately it may not be any good even if it does sound right. And this is where good books on style and usage make their contribution. The ear that is cultivated and improved by frequent exposure to good writing, by repeated exercise in the careful use of the language, by recurrent resort to the opinions of thoughtful and serious lexicographers becomes a much more reliable gauge of usage. It is the difference between the trained and the untrained ear. The ear cannot be expected to be a discriminating guide if conditioned by continuous bad usage and never exposed to a type-high check that will show if it is right. It is the training of much good usage against which is laid the frequent test of good counsel that produces an ear upon which the writer can rely.

Permissive as Copperud is generally, he is pretty hard on those who have a blind aversion to split infinitives or an unreasoning objection to separating the parts of a verb even when this produces a better sentence. A writer's own preferences may survive the Copperud doctrine; but the editor who consults these pages will hold that pencil a little longer before unsplitting all the infinitives and marrying the parts of all compound verbs. In this respect, at least, Copperud is on the side of the reporters in that long war between writers and editors. But the writers get their lumps, too.

This is the kind of book that every writer will be proud to own—but not as proud as he was before he bought it. If he is candid, he will be discomfited to find how many of the examples of bad usage in this book have crept into his own daily writing. The neat little exercises by which the clichés are laid bare, the stereotoypes uncovered, and the redundancies exposed will give pain to all those who have the wit to recall and the candor to admit their own writing foibles. The pain, it is to be hoped, will linger. It is simply astonishing how many bad writing habits can be accumulated in a relatively short writing lifetime. Coming up against one of Copperud's bad examples is like hitting a boulder with a walking plow. It is downright jolting to discover that you have fallen into expressions that have no basis in logic or language. It is dismaying to see how frequently the plainest dictates of good sense and taste can be forgotten in the haste of careless writing. And as this text makes abundantly clear, haste really is no excuse. It is more swift and efficient to write plainly and simply.

It is quite clear that enough has been put into this book to make it an item of value to any writer. The way that the individual writer can get out of this book the good that has been put into it may not be as self-evident. This is called *Webster's Dictionary of Usage and Style* but it should not be used solely as a reference work. The writer who wishes to get full value out of such books should double-track his use of them. It is worthwhile to go straight through this book. The plot may not be absorbing but any person who is a professional writer could find few more profitable ways to spend a couple of evenings. And the project should not be rushed. It should be read through with much thought and reflection. It should be gone over with appropriate pauses at those painful parts that remind the reader of his own writing weaknesses. This journey will be the more profitable if the pilgrim is equipped with dictionary and encyclopedia. Be prepared to give Copperud an argument. (You don't have to like *Webster's Third International* if you do not wish to like it!) But take this exercise seriously. To show you are in earnest it might be well to take a few notes about which you wish to write—and challenge—the author.

After you have given the book this kind of decent and respectful attention, *then* put it on your reference shelf. You will find it far more helpful once its contents have been recommended to you by this sort of exercise. In the daily examination of their own writing or of the writing of others, writers and editors will find this book one to which they will resort frequently, if they have been willing to take the pains to become reasonably familiar with its contents and at home in its format and arrangement.

This is not the sort of book on writing that is going to turn out a generation of writers who sound like Copperud. If it is consulted carefully and frequently it ought to help turn out a generation of writers who sound like themselves—when they are writing clearly and carefully.

J. R. WIGGINS
Former editor of
The Washington Post

Washington, D.C.

Preface

The best a dictionary like this can do is to develop the user's critical faculty. If he becomes sensitive to inaccuracies, redundancies, unnecessary complexities, and slipshod constructions, he will forestall most of these lapses unaided. His writing will gain in precision and effect far more from an acute critical sense than from any attempt at remembering a mass of details.

My purpose is to offer the reader information on which to base an intelligent choice of language, to encourage precision, and to discourage excess. The first aim of this book is that he who writes should subordinate everything to the ease of the reader, while conveying exactly, unmistakably, and—if possible —engagingly what he intends.

I have tried to avoid hairsplitting, but this is a matter of opinion, like the acceptability of a borderline cliché. The error whose correction one person regards as hairsplitting may be viewed by another as an outrageous boner.

Usage is a matter of taste. Since taste is notoriously arbitrary, and usage is perpetually in flux, no one can expect to find a work on the subject that he agrees with on every point. One sophisticated enough to consult a book of this kind should have confidence in his ability to weigh its counsel critically. He should be ready to reject it if he is not convinced of its validity.

No encompassing agreement exists among even the most discriminating writers concerning usages that are beyond the pale. What one condemns and shuns, another will employ freely and without apparent awareness that it has been criticized—or, sometimes, with deliberate disregard for what he considers pedantry or superstition. Announced principles are more conservative than practice—even the practice of the severest critics.

11

The point at which a new usage wins acceptance is also a matter of opinion. Decisions about it are useful only if the one making them is reasonably receptive to change and is not resolved to die with the notions he acquired in grammar school. The unyielding man who lives long enough will cut himself off entirely from communication with his fellows. Insistence on going against usage that has widespread acceptance on a cultivated level often results in failure to convey exactly what is intended, and sometimes in misunderstanding.

Comments on usage merely indicate how language is being used at the time. This fact is easy to ascertain by looking into earlier works on the subject. Some of this advice will still be pertinent, but some of it will have become quaint or amusing, and some of it meaningless. Writing has grown strikingly simpler and more informal in the last generation or so. Many of the horrible examples cited in earlier works are so complex one's impulse now is to ignore the moral they are intended to point and wonder instead why the thing was not set down more simply to begin with.

The book contains no invented errors nor imagined confusions; the examples have been taken from published material. Nor have lapses been dealt with unless they occur with some regularity. A book based on one-time errors would have no end and no point. Commonly published misspellings are given, not because the correct versions are hard to find in a dictionary, but because reminders are always useful. The misspeller will not go in search of such words, of course, but the assumption is that he may encounter them in looking up other entries or in browsing. References to *Webster* in the text refer to the Merriam-Webster family of dictionaries; other works are specifically identified.

I am indebted to Jerome H. Walker, executive editor of *Editor & Publisher*, for the interest and encouragement that brought my "Editorial Workshop" column in that magazine into existence. The column has served as the basis for two books, *Words on Paper* (Hawthorn, 1960) and this one, and has given me many advantages and satisfactions, including hundreds of kind and instructive letters from readers throughout the country and abroad.

I am indebted also to my wife, Mary, for typing the manuscript and for other help in putting the book together; most importantly for steadfast reassurance in sieges of self-doubt and flagging confidence.

The responsibility of a writer to his readers is memorably stated in a collection of Cambridge University lectures by Sir Arthur Quiller-Couch, entitled *On the Art of Writing* (used by permission from G. P. Putnam's Sons, Copyright 1961):

> You have been told, I daresay often enough, that the business of writing demands *two*—the author and the reader. Add to this what is equally obvious, that the obligation of courtesy rests first with the author, who invites the séance, and commonly charges for it. What follows, but that in speaking or writing we have an obligation to put ourselves into the hearer's or reader's place? It is *his* comfort, *his* convenience, we have to consult . . .
>
> All reading demands an effort. The energy, the good-will which a reader brings to the book is, and must be, partly expended in the labour of reading, marking, learning, inwardly digesting what the author means. The more difficulties, then, we authors obtrude on him by obscure or careless writing, the more we blunt the edge of his attention: so that if only in our own interest—though I had rather keep it on the ground of courtesy—we should study to anticipate his comfort.

ROY H. COPPERUD

Washington, D.C.

List of Major Articles

The following is a list of important entries, both expressions and subjects. Word entries in the book are set in boldface, lower-case letters; subject entries are in small, bold capitals. Only a few of the nearly two thousand entries are given here.

Abbreviations
Ad Lingo
Alphabetical Designations
Appositives
as, like
Attribution
Boldface Type
both
Capitalization
"Clean Copy"
Clichés
Collectives
Colloquialisms
Colon
Comma
Commandments, Sequence of
Communist, Socialist
Comparison of Adjectives
consider
contact
continual, continuous
Contractions
cop
culture, cultured
Dangling Participles
Dash

Democrat, -ic
desegregation, integration
Diacritical Marks
Dictionaries
Dr.
due to
Editorial (and Royal) We
Ellipsis
Euphemisms
ex-
Exclamation Point
False Comparison
feel
Fused Participle
Gerund Construction
gobbledygook
he, she; his, her
Hyphens
Infinitives
Italics
Itemized Paragraphs
*journalese, journalism, jour-
  nalistic*
Leapfrog
Letters to the Editor
Meaning

LIST OF MAJOR ARTICLES/

—A—

a, an *An* before words beginning with *h* (*an hotel, an historic event*) is now an affectation in the United States. It was formerly the practice to use *an* before unaccented *h*'s. In 1909, crotchety Ambrose Bierce wrote, "The contrary use in this country comes of too strongly stressing our aspirates." Too bad, old boy, it's all over now; our aspirates have aspired and are beyond aspersion. Some exceptions remain: *heir, honest, honor,* and *hour,* in which the *h*-sound is not merely unstressed but vanished. There will always be some Uriah Heeps around saying "an 'umble," however. Expressions like *an habitual* tend to indicate to the American reader that the *h* is not to be sounded. Instead of achieving the elegance aimed at, such affectations impart a kind of Cockney flavor. One halmost hexpects to find the missing *h*'s prefixed to the words that start with vowels.

An before words beginning with *u* or *eu* (*an utopia, an eulogy*) is a related peculiarity. These words in fact begin with a consonant sound, *y,* and call for *a.* It is hard to pronounce *an eulogy* and, by the same token, faintly irksome to read it.

Webster speaks of expressions like *an union* as often employed by British writers. As far back as 1926, however, that British oracle on usage, Fowler, advised against the locution and at the same time called *an humble* "meaningless & undesirable."

A is mistakenly used instead of *an* before figures, initials, and even words that begin with vowel sounds. Instances: *a $800 salary, a RCA contract, a Amazonian feat.* The figures 100, 1,000, and 1,000,000 are read *one hundred, one thousand, one million,* not simply *hundred, thousand, million.* Those who have never taken note of this write such things as "It was a journey of *a* 100 miles" and "He bought *a* 1,000 tankloads of oil." English-speaking people learn to put *a* before consonant sounds and *an* before vowel sounds when they learn to talk, and most people are grown before they become aware what the distinction is. Few lack the right instinct in this matter, although some of them are breaking into print. See also *Appositives*.

a- Solid as a prefix: *amoral, achromatic, atonal*, etc.

a poor thing. . . . See *Misquotation*.

ABBREVIATIONS It is considered improper to abbreviate the month without the date (*He left last Dec.*, as against *He left last December*, or *last Dec. 21*) ; or to abbreviate the state without the city (*The factory is in Ala.*, as against *The factory is in Alabama*, or *in Mobile, Ala.*).

Nor should proper names be abbreviated by anyone but their owners: *Wm.* for *William, Robt.* for *Robert* and the like. When a clipped form of a proper name is used it is not regarded as an abbreviation and does not take a period: *Ed.* is properly *Ed* for *Edward, Edmund, Edwin*, etc.

The urge to dispense with what might well be omitted does not seem to have touched the use of periods after *Mr., Mrs.,* and *Dr.* in most editing. Yet there is a trend in this direction, especially in books, and more especially in British usage. Here's how it looks: "Dr Livingston, I presume?" Not so bad, really. This practice follows Fowler's ingenious though generally unobserved dictum that abbreviations that begin and end with the same letters as the words they stand for should be written without periods.

Most publications use the *Postal Guide* as their authority for abbreviations of state names. It specifies *N. Dak.* and *S. Dak.,* not *N. D.* and *S. D.*; *N. Mex.*, not *N. M.*; *Nebr.* rather than *Neb.*; *Oreg.*, rather than *Ore.* (but who ever uses *Oreg.*?) ; *Calif.* and *Colo.*, not *Cal.* and *Col.*, for evident reasons; *Pa.*, not *Penna.* The frequent *Wisc.* is not sanctioned; it's *Wis.* Nor is *Wn.* acceptable; it's *Wash.* The *Postal Guide* recognizes no abbreviations for *Alaska, Idaho, Hawaii, Maine, Ohio*, or *Utah*. See also *Alphabetical Designations; lb., lbs.*

abdomen, belly, stomach *Stomach* once meant only the internal organ; genteelly, the part of the torso beneath the belt was and still is the *abdomen. Belly* was once a workaday word, but somehow many now regard it as vulgar or erotic, and it is generally avoided except by those with a sure command of language. Since *abdomen* is somewhat technical, *stomach* has become the common expression for *belly* while it continues to serve as the name of the internal organ. See also *Euphemisms*.

about Often used redundantly with figures spanning a range: "The victims were described as about 45 to 50 years old." *as 45 to 50 years old.*

It is a superstition that *about* is improper in the sense *on, around*: "beaten about the head and shoulders." The *Oxford Universal Dictionary* cites Tennyson: "My crown about my brows."

about to See *not about to.*

above Unsettling to some in reference to what has gone before in printed or written matter, if what is referred to is not actually on the same page. It can be avoided by such expressions as *referred to* or *previously mentioned.*

abrasions See *Technical Terms.*

abstract Despite some criticism, the word is standard and in wide use as a noun referring to paintings: "A number of abstracts were hung in the otherwise representational exhibit."

ACCENT MARKS See *Diacritical Marks;* formed on the typewriter, see *Typewriter Tricks.*

acceptable Sometimes misused for *receptive.* "The natives of this area are acceptable to Christianity" does not say what the writer intended. He wanted to describe them as ready to sign up, but instead gave the impression they had passed some kind of entrance examination.

accidentally, accidently Webster now recognizes the second form, but it is seldom seen and is likely to be considered a misspelling.

accompanist, accompanyist The second form is more often spoken than written and probably is considered a harmless error by some who hear it. Both forms are actually standard, but the second is seldom seen in print, perhaps because it is awkward and is also likely to be considered a mistake.

according to   See *Misleading Attribution* under *Attribution.*

accordion   Often misspelled *accordian.*

accumulative, cumulative   Interchangeable; Fowler found the first giving way to the second. Now a reverse movement seems under way, although *cumulative* is generally preferable.

accuse (with, of); accused   People are increasingly being accused *with* crimes, rather than *of* them, as they should be.
   Characterizations like *the accused murderer* and *the suspected spy* are unjustified, damaging, and perhaps actionable. More judicious: *the person accused of murder, the woman suspected of spying.*

accustomed   Takes *to*, not *with: accustomed to luxury.*

ACRONYM   Applies only to abbreviations that form words, not to any alphabetical abbreviation. *Jato* (for *jet-assisted take-off*) is an acronym; *FHA* (for *Federal Housing Administration*) is not.

act, action   *Action* often appears where it seems *act* or something else belongs. The consensus of authorities is that the choice between *act* and *action* is based less on rule than on what sounds right in the context. Of course, anyone accused of misuse of one or the other will say that his choice sounded right to *him.* A sentence about some kids who had emptied their piggy bank to pay their father's traffic fine read "The judge dug into his pocket and reimbursed the children after learning of their action." This may not go against everyone's grain, but the word should have been *act;* or, less stiltedly, the sentence might have read *after learning what they had done.* But after pondering the authorities' pronouncements, it is impossible to arrive at any satisfactory distinction in the usage of *act* and *action* that clearly tips the scales either way in this instance. Generally, however, *action* refers to the doing, and *act* to the thing done; beyond this, an act is usually something single, whereas an action may be made up of more than one part.

actual, actually   People often seem thunderstruck by their own perspicuity. This may account for the presence of *actual* and *actually* where they give an uncalled-for impression of "You won't believe this, but that's what happened." For example "No sooner had the Reds appeared than they were actually pelted with tomatoes." *Actually* is required only to point out the contrast between actuality and something else. When there is no such contrast, there need be no *actually*.

The following examples are open to criticism on this basis:

"The President has become so concerned over leaks from the National Security Council and the Cabinet that he has actually cut down on the number of officials attending the meetings." He wasn't merely pretending to cut down on them?

"The stocks were sold at prices above actual market prices." Better: "above the market."

"Economic activity for March might be up a point when the figures are in. Actually, this is the encouragement economists have been waiting for." Maybe those economists were suspected of waiting for some other kind of encouragement, but the context gave no such indication.

"Only two of the persons present actually spoke." What were the others—ventriloquists' dummies?

Actually (it must be contagious) the word is being used as an unnecessary intensive, and like all such, it plays the writer false by taking away, instead of adding, force. Porter G. Perrin writes that intensives "may be used for a just emphasis, but they usually suggest an oral stress and are often out of place in writing. Too many of them suggest the schoolgirl style."

A.D. It's wrong to write of *the tenth* (or any other) *century* A.D., even if it is done all the time. The reason is that A.D. stands for *anno domini* (the year of our Lord), and anyone knows a century is not a year. The tendency to regard A.D. as the opposite, for all practical purposes, of B.C. may prove irresistible, however. The really large view, incidentally, has been achieved by the historian, Arnold Toynbee, whose scope spans so many centuries he feels constrained to designate events of his own life as having taken place in "A.D. 1907" and "A.D. 1903." As indicated by Mr. Toynbee's usage, A.D. properly precedes the year; B.C. follows it.

ad So generally used and so convenient that aspersing it in favor of *advertisement* is pedantry.

AD LINGO The admen gain their sometimes bizarre, sometimes amusing effects by making the old college try. Effort in

21

writing is preferable, even if it misfires, to the automatic repetition of stereotypes.

The first thing that comes to mind when faults of advertising prose are discussed is the widely reprobated slogan, "Winston tastes good, like a cigarette should." The fact is that the rule against *like* as a conjunction has seen its best days, and the R. J. Reynolds Tobacco Co. really did nothing very heinous. (See *as, like.*)

It is intriguing the way *better* and *older,* which began life as comparatives, are verging toward the positive. Certain products, we are informed, are to be found in the *better* stores. Not the *good* stores, mind you, nor the *best,* but the *better* ones. We must admit that the adwriters have invested *better* with a mysterious toniness that even *best* somehow now lacks.

The comparative that seems suspended in the air is a common advertising device. Old Hospice Beer, the admen insist, is so much *more* refreshing. More refreshing than what? Than competing beers, presumably.

Automobiles, homes, and people are never *old* in the ads; they are merely older, though cars generally take a specialized descriptive: *older-* (or *early-*) *model.* (A not-so-old car is a *late-model* one.) Who would buy a home baldly conceded to be *old?* Thus older fills the admen's bill, even if it does not meet the requirements of logical expression.

It is perhaps antisocial these days to speak of people as *old;* in the ads and often elsewhere they are often *older people.* This expression has been enthusiastically adopted by journalists, who have nothing to sell but writing, but whose squeamishness is nevertheless notorious. If *old* is too harsh an adjective to apply to people, how about *Time*'s favorite noun, *oldsters?* That euphemism, *senior citizens,* is distasteful to many. (See also *Comparison of Adjectives.*)

Einstein, with his fourth dimension, was a piker compared with the adwriters, who extol bread, for instance, that is as many as eight *ways* better. If Elizabeth Browning had been a huckster, she might have written:

> How do I love that soap?
> Let me count the ways . . . .

add an additional   A common and careless redundancy.

added fillip   In such constructions as "He gave the investigation an added fillip," *added* is redundant unless there was a previous fillip.

additionally   The hard way to say *also*: "Additionally, Kuznetsov had acquired three houses and two cars." *Kuznetsov had also acquired.*

adequate   A euphemistic counter word of the reviewing profession, employed in damning faintly. When the critic says that a performance was adequate, he generally believes it was something less than equal to the occasion and should realize the reader senses this.

adhere   One's risibility may be touched when he reads that someone *adheres* to a style of presentation, a plan of study, or whatever. Such a plan, it seems, would be printed on flypaper. This is not an out-and-out bastardization of the word, however. As Fowler points out, the British speak of *giving in adhesion to* (i.e., backing) a political party, for example, but he frowns on the form *adhere to* in this sense. To avoid a suggestion of the ludicrous while losing nothing, it may be well to write of *following* a plan of study, *supporting* a party, and *obeying* the rules.

adjacent   Takes *to,* not *of*: "The store is adjacent of the Lincoln Avenue School." *to.* See also *contiguous* for comparison with *adjacent* and *adjoining.*

ADJECTIVES   See *Modifiers; Comparison of Adjectives.*

adjust, readjust   *Adjust* means bring into position, or into a proper relation. The necessary shift may be in any direction. *Readjustment* is in great favor as a euphemism for *pay raise.* Pay rates can indeed be adjusted, to bring them in line with those for comparable work elsewhere, for example, but only if the change may be in either direction. If only increases (or cuts) are under consideration, it is more explicit and thus better to say so. The writer who told of a readjustment of milk-inspection areas might better have said *realignment* or *rearrangement.*

administer, administrate   Synonyms, and equally reputable, although *administrate,* an Americanism, is newer and less common, and may be regarded by some as unnecessary beside *administer.*

admission, admittance   The terms are usually interchangeable.

admit   Unsuitable in attribution unless there is reason to suggest what is undesirable or concealed, or response to a challenge: "Clark admitted he had been working on the plan to restore the neighborhood for several years." None of the conditions cited applied here, as shown by the context; the writer simply used *admitted* as a random variant for *said*, but he made it sound as if the hapless neighborhood restorer were owning up to a misdeed. See *Attribution*.

admit to   "He also admitted to previous conversations with the suspect." *admitted*. See *confess to*.

ad nauseam (to the point of nausea)   Often misspelled *ad nauseum*.

Adolf, Adolph, Josef, Joseph   The first name of Stalin is sometimes given *Josef*, sometimes *Joseph*. Transliteration from the Cyrillic alphabet is involved, and both forms must be considered acceptable. *Webster's New Collegiate Dictionary* gives *Joseph*, together with the strict transliteration *Iosif*.
  Adolf, as in Hitler, is something else again. *Adolf* is what his name was, not Adolph, the version often given. The spelling is the same in German as in English; both languages use the Roman alphabet.

adopt a wait-and-see attitude   An overblown way of saying *wait and see*, as is *adopt a hands-off policy* for *keep hands off*. Journalese clichés.

advance   Redundant with *warning, planning*. Sometimes wrongly displaces *advanced: advance writing classes. advanced*.

ADVERBS   See *Modifiers;* wrongly hyphened, see *Hyphen*.

adverse, averse (to)   *Adverse* (which means *hostile, unfavorable, antagonistic*) is often misused for *averse* in such expressions as "She was not adverse to a drink before dinner despite her puritanical upbringing." *averse. Averse* means *having a dislike for;* in America it takes *to* and in Britain *from*.

advise   Objectionable and inexact when *say* or *tell* or *inform* will serve. "The complainant was advised by the city councilman that plans for remodeling the clubhouse have been prepared. " *told, informed*. See *Attribution*.

adviser, -or Insistence on *adviser* in preference to *advisor* is one of the more fanatical prescriptions in many stylebooks. Perrin points out that *adviser* is now changing to *advisor* by analogy with *advisory*, and it seems likely that *advisor* is now predominant. But both are standard.

ae-, e- The Latin diphthong *ae*, once a joined character (a ligature), has been almost entirely abandoned in favor of *e* in such words as *esthetic* (*aesthetic*), *encyclopedia* (*encyclopaedia*), *estivate* (*aestivate*), *anesthetic* (*anaesthetic*).

aeroplane, airplane *Aeroplane* used to be fairly common in America, but it has been displaced by *airplane*. Meanwhile, Britain has clasped *aeroplane* to its breast, so that now the forms are as distinctive as *tire* and *tyre*.

affect, effect The confusion of these words is so common they might be expected to have become interchangeable, but there is no sign of this. To *affect* is to have influence upon, as "The moon *affects* lovers"; to *effect* is to accomplish, as "A merger was *effected*." "About 500 ocean-going vessels are effected by the strike." *affected*.

affiliated (associated, identified) with Dear to the hearts of society-page writers and many others, who cannot bring themselves to say *works for* or *belongs to*.

affirmative, negative "He replied in the affirmative" and "Her answer was negative" are pompous ways of writing "He said yes" and "She said no." Favorite pretensions among the military, especially.

afford In the sense *provide* (or any other sense) does not take *with*: *afford some protection* (not *afford with*).

affray The word has a technical legal sense, but it is used indiscriminately, in sports and other news stories, for *fight, contest, game*, and the like.

aforesaid Legalese; inappropriate to nonlegal contexts.

Afrikaner, Afrikander *Afrikaner* is the term applied to a South African of Boer descent. *Afrikander*, sometimes described as the British term, is said by John Gunther in *Inside Africa* to be an old-fashioned form applied now only to a breed of cattle.

after   See *following*.

age, aged   Expressions like *at age 65* and *children aged 9 to 12* sound actuarial and old-fashioned, respectively. The usual forms are *at the age of 65, 65 years of age* (or *old*), *children 9 to 12 years old*. Simply *at 65* and *children 9 to 12* are also standard. See also *elderly*.

agenda   Though this is the Latin plural of *agendum*, for ordinary use the fact is now only of historical interest. *Agenda* is now almost invariably singular in English: "Eighteen items made up the agenda"; "This is the agenda" (not *these are*). Inevitably, *agendas* has become a legitimate plural.

aggravate   The time has come to concede that the word may mean *annoy, irritate* as well as *make worse* or *increase*. Herman Melville and Carl Sandburg are cited by Webster as having used *aggravate* in the first sense. "Continual questioning aggravated his impatience" illustrates the sense *increase*. "The President is completely satisfied with his new house except for one aggravation—the pigeons" illustrates the sense *annoyance*. The examples also show that the context prevents any confusion. Fowler indignantly rejected *annoy* for *aggravate*, but the *Oxford Universal Dictionary* gives *exasperate* for *aggravate*, and *the action of irritating* for *aggravation* (qualified as *familiar*, which describes most writing these days).

ago   Should be followed by *that*, not *since*, which is redundant: "It is only 10 years ago since the treaty was signed." *ago that*.

ah, aw   The time has come to strike a blow against the confusion in the lands of *ah*s and *aw*s. Agreement is general that *ah* denotes relish or approval, or sometimes comprehension, and *aw* indicates remonstrance, disgruntlement, or protest. To many something like " 'Ah, shucks,' said the boy," seems to represent a baffling conflict of emotions.

While we are dealing with the subarticulate, let us consider *uh-huh* (meaning *yes*) and *huh-uh* (meaning *no*). The use of these expressions in writing is small, to be sure. But there seems to be confusion here, too. *Webster's New International Dictionary* lists *uh-huh* but omits the converse, *huh-uh*, though of course it is just as prevalent. The occasional renderings *hunh-unh, unh-unh*, and the like seem open to the objection that they are not phonetic, if indeed they are pronounceable at all. *Unh-unh*, especially, seems liable to interpretation as either *yes* or *no*.

ahold   Dialectal for *hold*, with *get* or *take*: "I'd like to get ahold of that information." *get hold*.

aid, aide   Loosely interchangeable in the sense of *assistant*. *Aide* has been retained in military connections, however, and more or less also in diplomacy and nursing. Newspaper headlines would be less ambiguous if *aide* were used invariably as the noun.

ain't   Do you look down your nose at people who say *ain't*? You may feel you have good reason to, considering how that word was impressed on us in school as the leading example of bad English. *Ain't* is a contraction of *am not* and no doubt owes its popularity to the fact that it is easier to say. It developed from another contraction, *an't*, which went out of circulation a long time ago, in the unaccountable way words have.

If *ain't* had continued to be used only for *am not*, it might never have fallen into disrepute, for some authorities today consider it acceptable in that sense. In one construction, there is no substitute for *ain't* that does not seem equally objectionable. That construction is the question "Ain't I?" The strictly grammatical way of expressing this is "Am I not?" but that sounds a little too stilted for most of us. Some say, instead, "Aren't I?", but this has a distinctly feminine overtone, and most men and many women will reject it.

Ain't is at its worst when it displaces *isn't* or *hasn't*, as in "He ain't" or *aren't* or *haven't*, as in "We ain't." In such uses *ain't* is unquestionably one of the marks of the uneducated, like such errors as "He don't" and "We wasn't." The fate of *ain't*, which at least has a small claim to respectability as a contraction of *am not*, seems to be hanging in the balance. Time and again reports come from conventions of linguists to the effect that *ain't* is gaining ground. The news is always reported in a startled tone, however.

air   Unexceptionable for *broadcast* and, indeed, a felicitous synonym. Webster cites "programs that will be aired in the future." *Air* may be ambiguous in newspaper headlines, however, where the word also means *expose, discuss, explore*.

a la mode   not *ala; a la Hollywood, a la mode*. The French accent over *a* has been pretty much abandoned. See *Diacritical Marks*.

alas, poor Yorick. . . . See *Misquotation.*

alibi Sometimes criticized in the sense *an excuse* on the basis that the Latin meaning is *a plea of having been elsewhere.* The *Oxford Universal Dictionary,* a conservative work, has admitted it, however, in the sense *an excuse.* Lawyers are likely to be jealous of the technical senses of words like *privilege* and *alibi,* which have gone into general use and picked up extended meanings.

align, aline Both versions are in use, but the first is by far the commoner.

all- Hyphenated as a prefix: *all-round, all-out, all-seeing,* etc.

all-around, all-round Some say that *all-round* is preferable (*an all-round* [*-around*] *athlete*) but both versions are in wide use and the distinction is footless.

allege, -d, -dly It is a widespread delusion in journalism that the use of *alleged* or one of its derivatives, for example in relating the statements in a police report, confers immunity from libel. *Alleged* has a nice legal ring, however, and this would probably keep it in use even if everyone were convinced it offers no protection.

Alleged is often used redundantly: "The suspect was indicted for alleged perjury." An indictment is an accusation, and consequently it would be for perjury, not alleged perjury. This is also true of a charge; people are charged with offenses, not alleged offenses. The charge is itself an allegation. "He was charged with alleged burglary" is nonsense.

Alleged is the adjective, *allegedly* the adverb: "This book lets us look through the eyes of an alleged unbiased lawyer." *allegedly,* unless it is intended to say he is an alleged lawyer. See also *suspected.*

all is (are) not See *not, not all.*

all of *Of* should not be coupled with *all* if *of* can be done without. Whether *of* is dispensable is obvious, as in *all* [*of*] *the papers, all* [*of*] *the money.* The personal pronouns (*me, us, you, him, her, it, them*) require it: *all of it, all of us, all of them.* Other pronouns, including demonstratives (*all this, all these, all those*) and possessives (*all its fur, all our dealings*), like any noun (*all the time, all the cars*) do not.

allow of *Of* is unnecessary with *allow;* this usage is out of fashion. The same is true concerning *of* with *permit.*

allude, refer To *allude* to is to suggest without naming the thing specifically; to *refer* to is to name it specifically.

allusive, elusive, illusive *Allusive* (usually with *to*) means *in reference:* "The remark was *allusive* to the Bible." *Elusive* means *hard to catch:* "The rabbit is *elusive.*" *Illusive* means *illusory* (the more common word) or *deceptive:* "Mirages are *illusive.*"

all power corrupts. . . . See *Misquotation.*

all right, alright *Alright* may some day establish itself as acceptable, but the correct form remains *all right.*

all that *All that* for an emphatic *that, very, a great deal,* and the like is a fad, apparently imported from Britain: "The novel hasn't been around very long, and there's no reason to believe it will be around all that much longer." *that much, very much. All that* in this sense is an affectation in America; in Britain it may be different.

all-time record See *Record.*

all together, altogether *All together* means in a *group,* as "We will go *all together*"; *altogether* means *entirely,* as "The idea is *altogether* ridiculous." *In the altogether,* a colloquialism meaning *naked,* is sometimes ludicrously rendered *in the all-together:* "The article described a scandalous Hollywood party at which the actor cavorted *in the all-together.*" See also *au naturel.*

almost Often wrongly hyphenated, like adverbs ending in *-ly: an almost-open break.* It is unnecessary to indicate, by means of the hyphen, that *almost* and *open* form a unit modifier; *almost,* as an adverb, cannot modify anything but the adjective *open. An almost-automatic response; almost-limitless power;* omit the hyphens. See also *much, sometimes.*

almost, more, less (better, worse, etc.) Flat contradictions in terms and thus nonsense. A condition is either almost, equal, or more; it cannot be two at once. *Almost* and *more* taken together, if they mean anything, cancel each other out precisely on the line of equality. "The whole orchestra is used with almost more than the composer's usual adroitness." What did the writer really mean? More adroitness? No, not quite. Less? No, more than that. The composer's usual adroitness? We can only guess, not having been taken fully into the writer's confidence. "Direct intervention, if it had been successful, would have been almost less harmful than failure." *Perhaps less harmful* would have made the sense aimed at and missed.

Boswell quoted Johnson as saying "The chaplain . . . could tell me scarcely anything" and then commented in a footnote, "It has been mentioned to me by an accurate English friend, that Dr. Johnson could never have used the phrase *almost nothing*, as not being English; and therefore I have put another in its place. At the same time, I am not quite convinced it is not good English. For the best writers use the phrase *'little or nothing'*; i.e., almost so little as to be nothing." See also *times, less*.

along with   See *together with*.

ALPHABETICAL DESIGNATIONS   If there is a prize for the most irritating form of cryptography, it should go to the little trick of reducing the name of an unfamiliar organization or agency to initials after its first appearance. The press associations consider this great stuff, but to many readers it is confusing, exasperating, and unnecessary. After the upsurge of alphabetical agencies in Roosevelt days, some of them (AAA, NRA, FHA, CCC) became so familiar that writers took to using the abbreviations without spelling out the names even once. Some thoughtful editor, to jog the memories of readers, directed that the names of such agencies be given in full the first time in each story and followed by the abbreviation: *Federal Housing Administration* (*FHA*).

Use of the abbreviation alone thereafter is fine, for agencies as well known as the FHA. But the thing has gone full speed into reverse. Instead of helping the reader with the names of organizations whose abbreviations are relatively familiar, the press-association reporters (and their sedulous apes on newspapers) use the device to fabricate new and baffling abbreviations for organizations that are all but unknown.

"A security board has found doubt of the loyalty of an official of the International Monetary Fund (IMF). The finding was made after a hearing by the International Organizations Employees Loyalty Board (IOELB). Because the IMF is an international body, the IOELB worked in cooperation with foreign agencies."

It's bad enough when only one such abbreviation figures in a story, but when there are more, we have confusion compounded. Readers have to fumble back to the beginning for the key every now and then, meanwhile cursing the diabolical cleverness of the abecedarian who encoded the names. But you don't want to repeat unwieldy titles, you say? You don't have to. Just use a key descriptive that the reader will recognize instantly. This is less complicated, and may be less fun. But the reader will like it.

In the example cited, the International Monetary Fund might have been referred to, after having been named once, as *the fund.* The International Organizations Employees Loyalty Board could have become *the loyalty board,* or even just *the board,* instead of *the IOELB.*

The practitioners of alphabetism know no shame. They will start out with the translated version of a foreign name, for example *General Confederation of Labor,* and in going on will use an abbreviation based on the original (CGT for Confédération Générale du Travail). This is a game for polyglots, devised by stupes.

There is a place, of course, for FHA, ICC and other abbreviations that are widely known. Every town has its own handful that everyone recognizes, and they are very useful, especially for headlines. But the writer who converts Associated Society of Locomotive Engineers and Firemen into ASLEF belongs in the acrostics department.

already existing Redundant; *existing.*

also As a conjunction ("The automobile needs repair; also it must be repainted") *also* is not in good odor. Usually the trouble can be corrected by adding *and,* substituting *moreover, in addition, besides,* or by shifting the position of *also* to make it function as the adverb it is. "A typical picnic menu includes wieners, buns, beer, also potato salad." *and* or *and also.* "Also, the general situation needs to be re-evaluated." "The general situation *also* needs to re-evaluated" or *"In addition* [or *Besides*], the general situation. . ." "Also, the plans of officials to be helpful were often frustrated." *In addition, Besides,* or "The plans . . . *also* were often frustrated."

It may be taken as a rule of thumb that *also* at the beginning

31

of a sentence or clause is probably wrong, except in such constructions as *"Also* on the agenda are . . ."* where *also* is used as an adverb but has been taken out of its normal position: *". . . are *also* on the agenda."*

"These bills propose funneling federal money into the cost of elementary school facilities. Also to provide loans to colleges and universities." There are two offenses here; one is the use of *also* as a conjunction and the other is the disregard of parallelism: "These bills propose funneling . . . and *also* providing. . ."

altar, alter   Sometimes confused in spelling; the *altar* is the church structure; *alter* is the verb meaning *to change.*

alternate, alternately; alternative, alternatively   *Alternate,* as an adjective, means *in turns; first one and then the other. Alternative,* on the other hand, involves a choice. An alternate course of action is interchanged with another; an alternative course is a substitute.

The idea that *alternative,* as a noun, is a choice between two things and no more is pedantry. "Several alternatives confronted the diplomat" is correct.

Alternate as a noun referring to a person means *substitute.*

although, though   The Second Edition of *Webster's Unabridged,* now superseded by the Third, described *although* as originally more emphatic than *though,* and as preferred by many writers ". . . to introduce a fact as distinguished from a supposition, and in formal style." This caveat is absent from the Third Edition, and all other current dictionaries equate *though* with *although.* The choice between them now depends on rhythm or on the formality of the context.

aluminum, aluminium   The second is the British preference.

alumnus, alumni, alumna, alumnae   Most Latin terms that come into common use acquire sensible English plural forms, but there is no sign of it in this instance, perhaps because *alumnuses* would be clumsy. Thus care is required to use these terms correctly. *Alumnus* is the masculine singular, *alumni* the plural; *alumna* the feminine singular; *alumnae* the plural. *Alumni* is applied to mixed groups of graduates (*the alumni of the university*). *Alumni* is substandard for the singular: "He is an alumni of the state university." *alumnus.*

32

A.M., P.M.   Often used redundantly in constructions that otherwise indicate the half of the day; *6* A.M. *this morning, 9* P.M. *tonight.* The meaning of A.M. is *ante meridiem, before noon;* P.M. means *post meridiem, after noon.* Pretty elementary, to be sure, but the frequent misuse of these indicators in the manner illustrated shows that their meanings are not kept in mind.

am to, are to, is to   See *Misleading Infinitives* under *Infinitives.*

amass   Best used in reference to a great quantity; in the sense *accumulate* or *score points,* it is a beloved counter word of sportswriters.

ameliorate   "Kennan set himself the job of ameliorating the singleminded fascination that the Soviet problem holds for Americans." Mrs. Malaprop rides again. *Ameliorate* means *improve,* and anyway, it's bookish. What this writer really meant is a question; *mitigating* or *counteracting,* possibly.

American   A sporadic and useless debate is waged whether the term has been unjustifiably monopolized by inhabitants of the United States. Canadians as well as Latin Americans, it is argued, have just as good a license to it, since they too live on the American continents.

All this is sophistry, however; what counts is what people generally understand by the term. It stretches more easily over Canadians than over the rest. Unfortunately, there is no other convenient expression to describe residents of the U.S.; if there is any room for doubt, *American* will not be exact enough but in this case the writer will avoid it anyway. Only the unreasonable and hypersensitive will complain that the use of the term is unfairly restrictive, for this did not happen by design any more than the confusing dual application of the term *Indian.*

The United States is more exact than *America* in reference to the nation, but the issue is not clear-cut here either, for *America* has been enshrined in paeans (*America; America the Beautiful; God Bless America*) that are unhesitatingly understood to apply to the United States.

amok   See *amuck,* etc.

among, amid   *Among* is generally used with plurals: *among my friends, among the audience, among the trees.* Properly its object should be a plural (*friends*) or a collective (*audience*). With singular nouns, *amid* is preferable: *amid the wreckage, amid the confusion*. This principle is not invariable, however; *among the news was an obscure item about the abdication* is unexceptionable, perhaps because *news* suggests a variety of items, and is in a sense a collective, or maybe even a plural. *Amongst* is quaint, and *amidst* is reaching that state. See also *between, among*.

among them   *Among them* in constructions like "He has accompanied numerous artists, among them Tito Schipa and John Charles Thomas . . ." is not followed by a comma.

amount   Not good usage in reference to what is countable or readily measurable: "A large amount of people." *number*.

AMPERSAND (&)   Proper in the names of businesses that use it themselves: *Wellington & Co.* Fowler used it abundantly in text, and also in the form *&c.* (for *et cetera*), presumably to save space, but perhaps also to assert his individuality. It would be a convenience if *and* might be universally replaced by the ampersand, but such a departure would outrage traditionalists. As for saving space, devices like this and the studied use of abbreviations, for example in street addresses, accomplish little.

amphibian   The journalese variant for *frog*. See also *Variation*.

amuck, amok, berserk   *Amuck* is generally preferred to *amok*. The word comes from the Malayan *amoq*, meaning *furious*. *Amuck* is stronger than *berserk; amuck* connotes murderousness, *berserk* (from Berserkers, wild Norse warriors of mythology) merely means *enraged*.

ANACHRONISM   Not merely a contradiction, but a misplacement in *time*, as is evident to those who take note of the root *chron* (*chronometer, chronological*, etc.). The novelist, for example, who had Queen Victoria watching television would have committed an anachronism. "The cell warder is played by an actor with a British accent. But since the action is supposed to take place in Hungary, this casting seems a bit anachronistic." *inconsistent* or *inappropriate*.

analogy, analogous   Sometimes misspelled *analagy, analagous*.

analysis Takes *of;* "an analysis on government information policies." *of.* See *on.*

and At the beginning of a sentence, and followed by comma, see *Comma After Conjunctions* under *Comma.*

and also Generally redundant; *and.*

and (but) which, and (but) who The consensus appears to be that *and which* and *and who* (as well as *but which* and *but who*) are permissible only after *which* or *who,* respectively, a principle that can be defended as desirably emphasizing parallel construction. Fowler cited exceptions that he considered permissible, but his reasoning is tortuous, and his general conclusion favors the principle stated here. Partridge agrees with this principle, and it is observable that careful writing follows it. Often, however, *and which* and *and who* are used where *which* or *who* or *and* alone would be smoother.

"Life has two strikes on children deserted by their parents and who never experience the love and home life adoptive parents can give them." *who have been deserted by their parents and never experience* or *who have been deserted . . . and who.*

"Most Italians believe that the loot, known as the Dongo Treasure, and which has been valued at $32 million . . ." *Dongo Treasure, which has been valued* or *which is known as . . . and which is.*

"Production of European-type grapes, which are grown almost exclusively in California and Arizona, and which account for most of this year's crop. . . ." This conforms with our rule but *and account for* is simpler.

"Most men entering their eighty-ninth year and who have won wealth and fame might be content to sit back at ease." *who are entering . . . and have.*

"Fritz Weaver, who played Hamlet last summer, and who is one of the most versatile actors in the American theater, is shockingly believable as the haunted weakling." *summer and is one.*

In summary, it may be said that nearly all Fowler's examples are disagreeably involved or quaint to the modern ear, and would likely be stated today in ways that would not cause the *and which* problem to arise.

But who, which occur in similar constructions: "The Copts are a forgotten people but who made interesting contributions to art." *people, who made* or *people, although they made.*

and I quote   In writing, a pomposity when quotation marks set off the quoted matter.

and/or   Objectionable to many, who regard it as a legalism.

anent   This archaism makes for hoary humor. Some spell it *annent,* and thus unconsciously make it funnier.

anoint   Often misspelled *annoint.*

another   *Another* with a number is sometimes criticized: "Eighteen persons were summoned as witnesses, and *another* six were interrogated." The reason given for the criticism is that *another* means *one more of the same kind;* thus it would be correct only if the second figure were the same as the first. This does not stand up against dictionary definitions of *another,* however, one of which is "distinct, or different, from the one considered." Leaving out *another* makes the sentence ambiguous, and all in all the criticism seems captious. See also *other.*

antagonist   See *protagonist.*

ante-   Solid as a prefix: *antedate, anteroom, antemarital,* etc. But *ante-Norman* (followed by a capital).

anti-   Generally solid as a prefix: *antiwar, antitrust,* etc. But *anti-American* (followed by a capital) and *anti-intellectual* (to avoid doubling the *i*). The hyphen may be desirable to avoid creating a word with a strange look, such as *antilabor, antibias.*

anticipate   *Expect* is not a dirty word, but many have washed it out of their vocabularies and substituted the more orotund *anticipate.* The absence of *expect* and its displacement by *anticipate* is, in fact, one of the most conspicuous earmarks of pretentiousness. *Anticipate* does not mean the same thing as *expect,* however, and alert writers distinguish between them. *To expect* is simply to look ahead to, but *to anticipate* has the sense of seizing time by the forelock, of preparing or being prepared in some way for what is to come.

In "Agricultural officials anticipate production will be about the same as last year" we have the work of one who could not settle for a simple *expect,* which is what the sentence calls for.

"The principal anticipated normal attendance" is wrong or right, depending on whether he did something in expectation of it. Probably he *expected*.

This writer made the right choice: "The collection date was set a week earlier this year in *anticipation* of an increased workload." *Expectation* might have passed muster, but *anticipation* is precise.

"The woman said she was pregnant and anticipating a child within two months." Madam, leave those calculations to your doctor.

The ad that ballyhooed a film as "The most anticipated motion picture of our time" was an unintentional example of truth—the awful truth, that is—in advertising.

"An anticipating audience was treated to a delightful program." *eager, expectant*.

If you're too tired to decide which you need, use *expect*. *Anticipate* is seldom required, and with *expect* you'll seldom be wrong.

Some hold that *anticipate* is appropriate for *await eagerly*. But this is only a delusion that grows out of misuse. This sense is not supported by the observable practice of careful writers.

antidisestablishmentarianism This word now seems to have been disestablished as the longest one in the language, and let's be glad of it. Millions must have grown sick of hearing it announced as such by those who are enchanted with useless information. But even if the king is dead, the customary cry, "Long live the king!" sticks in the throat. The reason for this is that the new king is *pneumonoultramicroscopicsilicovolcanokoniosis*. Forty-five letters, as against twenty-eight in the old one. It's a disease—like going around telling people about *antidisestablishmentarianism*. Other candidates, however, have been announced by dictionary-makers.

any and all A redundant pomposity. "Any and all efforts to remove the statue will be resisted." Either *any* or *all* or neither will do.

any more Critics of *any more* in a positive sense may be drawing too hard a line. Literary idiom allows it in heightening a contrast, and not merely with an explicit negative. A writer in *Word Study* cited as an example of dialectal use the sentence: "Any more, it's hard to find a good glass of beer." The only exceptionable thing about this is the word order; not even a purist would demur at: "It's hard to find a good glass of beer *any more.*" Both versions imply a contrast with times when a good glass of beer was easy to find. The following, on the other hand, are examples of truly dialectal, and thus objectionable, use: "They certainly have good television programs any more" and "One can get terribly discouraged just by reading the newspapers any more." It may be that a contrast was intended here, but *any more* cannot indicate it unassisted; the presence of some such negative modifier as *hard* in the sentence about the beer, or *hardly,* as in "We *hardly* see her *any more,*" or *seldom,* as in "Wells are *seldom* dug *any more*" is required. In other words, *any more* cannot be used in an unqualifiedly positive statement. Webster gives *anymore,* but no other authority does, and the one-word form is noticeably shunned in careful writing.

anyone, anybody *Anybody* is one word in reference to a person; *anyone* is likewise one word in most connections, except in such constructions as *Any one of the crowd will testify.*

any other See *other.*

anyway, anyways, any way The first is an adverb meaning *nevertheless, at any rate* or *in any way whatever* ("We'll go *anyway*"; "The tools were scattered around *anyway*"); *any way* are adjective and noun, and when preceded by a preposition must be two words ("We did not understand him in *any way*"—not *anyway,* since an adverb cannot be the object of a preposition). "We are entitled to defend ourselves anyway we can." *any way. Anyways* is backwoods for *anyway,* and on a par with *nohow.*

apologize, apologise The second is the British preference.

APOSTROPHE See *Possessives; Plurals.*

apparent Often used misleadingly: "The man died of an apparent heart ailment." Ambiguous; was a heart ailment apparently the cause of death, or was it only a psychosomatic illness that proved fatal? Reason will tell us the former is the sense intended. Even so, exact statement is a good thing to practice: "A heart ailment apparently was the cause of death."

appear Often ambiguous with an infinitive. It is to be avoided in sentences like "The budget was approved after no one *appeared* to protest," which can be taken to mean either that no protesters appeared, or that statements made about the budget apparently were not protests. See also *Infinitives*.

appendix, appendices, appendixes Either *appendices* (the Latin form) or *appendixes* is correct. But probably *appendixes,* the Anglicized and thus the more comfortable form, is driving the other out.

APPOSITIVES

Punctuation There is a marked tendency to drop the commas that we were taught should set off appositives. This may be a conscious bent toward a new usage, or merely a reflection of ignorance. One may set it down to ignorance in something like this: "He has been married to his wife Ethel for twenty-six years. Their daughter, Eve, is married to a Harvard man." If this writer was out to do away with the commas around appositives, why drop them from *Ethel* and use them with *Eve?* The constructions are identical. (Eve was, of course, the only daughter.)

Rare appositives are technically restrictive and do not take commas: *My son Barry* (distinguished from my other son, John); an only son would be *My son, Barry.* Others are *Ivan the Terrible, William the Conqueror,* and the like. Omission of commas from other appositives usually occurs in writing that shows other signs of carelessness.

The intrusion of commas and the articles *a* and *an* within certain appositive constructions can raise doubt whether one or two persons are being referred to. "The publication will be edited by Dr. Willy Nilly, executive secretary of the conference, and a member of the faculty." Dr. Nilly is both secretary and faculty member, but the sentence may leave the impression that the faculty member is someone else. Omit the comma after *conference* and the *a* before *member.*

Misrelated Appositives Grammarians have been so preoccupied with the dangling participle they have taken little notice of another kind of misplaced modifier. This error grows out of a common appositive construction.

"Until recently a resident of San Carlos, Peaches' real name is Mrs. Ralph Willson." It was Peaches herself, and not her real name, that was a resident of San Carlos. The basic fault here may be the attempt to jam unrelated material together into one sentence. Still, all this can be said grammatically: "Until recently a resident of San Carlos, Peaches is known formally as Mrs. Ralph Willson."

"A devout, old-fashioned Moslem, his concubines are numbered by the hundreds." The fault is evident; a possible cure is "A devout, old-fashioned Moslem, he numbers his concubines by the hundreds."

"A widow of seventy, her health is poor." The woman herself, not her health, is the widow of seventy. *A widow of seventy, she is in poor health.*

Dangling adjectival phrases are somewhat similar. "Tiny and slender, Yuomi's straight hair is clipped close in the trademark of a nurse." Tiny, slender hair? *"Tiny and slender, Yuomi wears her hair straight and clipped close. . ."*

"Now forty-four years old, his assignments have taken him around the world." Forty-four-year-old assignments will not gladden the heart of the editor. *"Now forty-four years old, he has had assignments that have . . ."*

"At thirty-five, the people of France made Poujade the undisputed master of the fourth largest party in their National Assembly." It was Poujade, and not the people of France, who was thirty-five. *"The people of France made Poujade, at thirty-five, the undisputed master . . ."*

"Now sixty-eight, he and his second wife live in a Colonial-style house." The writer here was led astray by a compound subject—not *he* alone, but *he and his second wife.* Husband and wife could have been the same age, but were not, and the descriptive was intended to apply only to the husband. The correction that suggests itself is recasting in some such form as *"Murgatroyd, now sixty-eight, and his second wife live . . ."*

"Now a widow, she and her husband moved to New York in 1956." The way this sentence stands both the woman and her husband together are characterized as *a widow.*

appraise, apprise *Appraise* means *set a value on,* as "appraise a house"; *apprise* (usually with *of*) is a highfalutin way of saying *inform, tell,* or *notify,* as "apprise him of danger" and "apprise us of the circumstances." "I don't care to comment," the lawyer said, "until I have been properly appraised of the conditions." *apprised.*

APPROXIMATIONS See *Figure at Beginning of Sentence* under *Numbers.*

apropos   Takes *of*, not *to:* "This is apropos to the controversy." *of*.

apt, liable, likely.   *Apt* and *likely* are so often used interchangeably in the sense of *prone to* that it may seem like quibbling to draw a distinction: "It's *apt* [likely] to be cold on the pier." Quibblers, however, tend to preserve *likely* for this sense and to use *apt* to mean *fit, suited,* or *to the point*: "His reply was sarcastic, but it was *apt*." *Liable* is often used loosely for *likely:* "At this rate, we are *liable* to win the award." Discriminating use generally applies *liable* only to what is undesirable: "An overheated radiator is *liable* to explode." *Liable* is also used in the sense of *exposed to legal action*: "If a stair is broken, the householder may be *liable*."

arbitrate, mediate   Sometimes confused. An arbitrator's decision is binding; a mediator merely attempts to help disputants come to an agreement. He has no authority.

arc, arch   Something needs to be done about the verb forms *arced* and *arcing,* but it's hard to say what. The verb *arc,* from which they come ("The power will *arc* across the lines"; "The demented assassin tried to *arc* his grenade close to the low ceiling, toward the ministers' bench") is pronounced *ark,* but the conventions of pronunciation would ordinarily soften the *c* in *arced* and *arcing.* This makes it seem as if the pronunciation should be *arsed* and *arsing,* which, of course, is not merely wrong but unseemly. Dictionaries give *arcking,* which solves the problem, as a variant spelling, but this form is never used. By attempting to discourage the use of *arc* as a verb in this technological age, one would only be making an *arce* of himself. The answer in many contexts may be *arch*.

aren't I   See *ain't*.

arithmetical, geometrical   Often inaccurately used with *progression* and *ratio.* An arithmetical progression is a sequence that grows by addition of the same quantity; 2, 4, 6, 8, for example, in which the quantity added is 2. A geometrical progression grows by multiplication by the same quantity; for example, 2, 4, 8, 16, in which the multiplier is 2.

armed with   Often used ineptly. One who is armed has a weapon —a gun, a club, perhaps only a pop bottle. It would be quibbling to boggle at a figurative extension of this use; a lawyer going forth to do battle in court might be referred to as armed with facts. But *armed with* somehow has become an automatic substitute for *possessing, prepared with, carrying,* and other more suitable expressions. Considering the bellicose connotation of *armed with,* it is surely inappropriate to speak of a man as winning new friends by being armed with a wide smile, or of a father going to visit his children armed with boxes of new toys.

around, round   *See all-around, all-round.*

arrest   Some assume that an arrest consists in the mere act of being halted by an officer of the law. This assumption apparently results from confusion of differing senses of *arrest.* One of those senses is simply *to stop,* as when we say, "The hurtling boulder *was arrested* by a crevasse." The legal sense is something else again; it is "to take or keep in custody." In law violations, of course, the legal definition is the one that must apply.

In the popular mind, the word *arrest* produces an image of some unfortunate being marched off to the jug. This does not happen in the mere issuance of a ticket, and when that act is described as an arrest the suspect suffers an undeserved indignity. It is just as easy, more accurate, and not unjustly derogatory to say that the suspect was given a summons or a ticket, or was cited.

artful, artistic   *Artful* means *devious* or *crafty,* like Dickens' Artful Dodger. *Artistic* means *possessing the quality of art,* as "an artistic arrangement of flowers" and "artistic ability."

article   Often misleadingly applied to short pieces, particularly editorials, signed regular columns, and letters to the editor. An article is a piece of nonfictional prose that does not fall into some more specific category like those mentioned. *Story* is often applied to newspaper pieces, especially narrative accounts, but the term (usually in the form *news story*) is perhaps somewhat more common within journalism than among the public, which tends to favor *article* or *news article.* See also *piece.*

ARTICLES   See *a, an; the; appositives.*

as As a preposition, unnecessary after such words as *named, appointed, elected*: "He was appointed as vicar" might as well be "He was appointed vicar."

As should be used with care in attribution; it identifies the writer with the statement, and thus is a form of editorializing. "As he explained in this office last week, the technique of flying had been the big thing for too long." The effect of this is "We [the writer or the publication or both] agree."

See also *as, like; as, since*.

as . . . as; so . . . as; not so . . . as These pairs sometimes give difficulty. "He likes to be known as philosopher as much as a theologian" lacks an essential *as*. With the construction filled out, it would be "He likes to be known as a philosopher as much as as a theologian." The third *as* is required to complete the comparison, and the fourth is a preposition that is needed with *theologian* just as much as the first one is needed with *philosopher*. As revised, of course, this sentence is impossible; it might be called half-*as*'d in spite of its abundance of *as*'s. The only cure here is recasting: "He likes to be known equally as a philosopher and as a theologian."

"The critic said the play was as good or better than last season's hits." Another omitted *as*, but this one can be slipped in without difficulty: "as good *as* or better than."

The idea that *so* is required with *not*, rather than *as* ("The moon is not *so* large as it was last night") has no grammatical basis. The sentence as quoted is correct, but so is "not *as* large as"; indeed, this is more natural. In a positive statement, the preferable pair is *as . . . as*, not *so . . . as:* "This leader is likely to run the show *as* [not *so*] long as he lives."

as follows, as follow The idiom is *as follows;* we should not be misled into *as follow* by the fact that a series of items ensues: "The tools used by the mason are as follows: the trowel, the plumb-line, the level, and the groover."

as good or better See *as . . . as*.

as if See *as, like*.

as is, as are (than is, than are), etc. The trick of making a comparison by putting *as* or *than* in front of a misplaced verb is both artificial and unnecessary. "The defendant—as did everyone in the courtroom—knew the verdict was coming." Clumsy and unnatural. *The defendant, like everyone else in the courtroom, knew . . .*

"He is not pessimistic, as are the Democratic lieutenants in the House and Senate." Not only clumsy but ambiguous; *unlike Democratic lieutenants.*

"The poorer states are on the whole making a greater effort to support their schools than are the richer states." Smoother: *than the richer states are.*

"The President is probably as popular as was his predecessor after his first month in office." *as his predecessor was after.*

"The citizen should recognize in this organization an extreme mentality that is potentially as dangerous as is that of Communism." Drop the second *is.* An elliptical construction, as in this example and the next two, reads better. It's no sin to omit a clearly understood verb.

"Obviously the people of the United States are as anxious as are the people of Russia for peace and friendship." Drop the second *are.*

"He is far less committed than is his opponent by the mistakes and omissions of the past." Drop the second *is.*

"To make a hero out of this senator as did the President and his aides is to reduce politics to the lowest common denominator." *as the President and his aides did.*

"On the central issues the secretary is just as far away from the platform as is his party." *as his party is.*

The use of *as did, as was* and the like is something of a fad, perhaps. On the other hand, it may be merely another aspect of the dread of using *like,* even when it is called for, or of a fear of ending a sentence comfortably on a verb like *is* or *are.*

as, like *Don't use* like *as a conjunction.* How many ages hence this conjunctional injunction will go ringing down the windy corridors of grammatical right and wrong would be hard to say. The odd thing is that, while the rule itself is still marching down the main street as proudly as a drum major, actual practice is increasingly drifting off into side alleys.

To apply this rule, it is necessary to know what a conjunction is. This is often the parting of the ways. Observation shows that the sternest followers of the rules don't fully understand what many of them mean. Of this much they are sure: *like* has a curse on it, and is to be avoided whenever possible. This approach produces some strange contortions. What disturbs many is the use of *like* in sentences like these:

"He said the movies are not going to stand still like they have for twenty-five years."

"She walked to the altar like she said she would."

Note that the groups of words introduced by *like* have subjects and verbs; that is, they are clauses. *Like*, under strict application of the rule, is correctly used only to introduce words or phrases: "He ate like a beast" and "She trembled like a leaf." The same principle applies to *like* for *as if*: "The Kremlin has been making noises like [strictly, *as if*] it wants such a meeting."

Like is poaching more and more on the preserves of *as*, and few warrants are being sworn out. What often makes the distinction seem artificial is that the examples quoted last may be thought of as possessing implied verbs. If these verbs are expressed, the phrases become clauses, and *as* is required under the rule to introduce them: "He ate *as* a beast eats" and "She trembled *as* a leaf does."

A useful rule of thumb was propounded by Frank O. Colby:

"If *as, as if, as though* make sense in a sentence, *like* is incorrect. If they do not make sense, *like* is the right word."

This rule is easy to use, as will be found by making some trial substitutions. But Mr. Colby said he had given up as a lost cause the fight against *like* as a conjunction. So have other authorities.

Now, will you join in a brief excursion out the window with those who are so terrified by *like* that they won't use it even when it's right? First, we have the *as with* aficionados, who write: "The helicopter, as with the horseless carriage of an earlier day, is here to stay." There is a place for *as with*, but the one belonging to *like* is not it.

"The offense was relatively trivial, as with going barefoot to a black-tie affair." *like*.

As with has its uses, where neither *like* nor *as* will do: "The best course, *as with* so many things, lies somewhere in between."

Then there are those who would walk a mile, not just for a Camel, but to evade *like*: "The unique plane stands on the ground in a manner similar to a camera tripod." *like*.

"He said the scientist, just as any other citizen, has the right to petition the government." *like*.

"Editors, as inventors, are creative people." Not only wrong but misleading; the writer was not speaking of editors in some supposed capacity as inventors, but intended, the context showed, a comparison: "Editors, *like* inventors, are creative people."

"Mrs. Nelson, as all who grew up on the island, has never spent a day in school." *like.*

One of the biggest fusses in the history of usage was stirred up by a slogan of the R. J. Reynolds Tobacco Co.: "Winston tastes good, like a cigarette should." Reynolds no doubt rubbed its hands gleefully over the extra attention its colloquial use of *like* attracted.

Grammarians would agree that Reynolds was well within the pale of informal usage. Shakespeare, John Dos Passos, *The New York Times,* and H. L. Mencken are among those cited by Rudolf Flesch in *The Art of Readable Writing* as *like*-likers. *Like* for *as* still will not pass muster in *formal* writing, whatever that is. But it is astonishing that such an uproar should have been created by its use in ads aimed at the lowest common denominator.

Porter G. Perrin, the author of *Writer's Guide and Index to English,* pretty well sums up the views of grammarians when he says *like* as a conjunction "is obviously on its way to becoming generally accepted and is a good instance of a change in usage, one that we can observe as it takes place."

How did the ultrafastidious feel when they read Liggett & Myers' "Live modern—smoke an L&M"? If they had to be critical, *modern* as an adverb is worse than *like* as a conjunction. Here, again, the choice of words no doubt was made with great care, to strike a homey, down-to-earth note.

Criticizing the ad men for things like these is like criticizing Joel Chandler Harris for not having had Uncle Remus talk the King's English, or Finley Peter Dunne for having allowed Mr. Dooley an uncommon liberty with syntax. See also *similarly to.*

as, since   *As* in the sense *since* or *because* is avoided in careful writing; partly, perhaps, because sometimes it may be confused with *as* in the sense of *during the time that,* but mostly because it grates on the well-tuned ear, a not unimportant organ when it comes to words.

"As the door was locked, he turned and walked away" is ambiguous, for *as* may be understood as meaning either *during the time that* or *because.* Even when there is no real ambiguity, *as* for *because* is objectionable because it creates a momentary uncertainty.

"Porter's design is called the Revised Springfield, as he made it while living in Springfield, Mass.," is improved by exchanging *as* for *because*—and perhaps even more by removing the comma.

as is well known See *of course.*

as of Properly used in a more or less technical sense to indicate a particular time: "*As of* the first of the month, your bank balance was $137.45"; "He will rank as major *as of* January 15." It is, however, a legalism, and easily sidestepped, by those who object to it, with other prepositions: "*On* the first of the month. . . ."; "He will rank as major *from* January 15." *As of now* is undesirable as an intensification of *now; right now* or *at present* is preferable: "*Right now* his chief interest is philately."

as regards See *regard.*

assay, essay To assay is to analyze; ore is assayed to determine its metal content. To essay is to attempt. "He recently assayed the role Clarence Darrow in a movie." *essayed*; the reference is to the actor who played the part, not to the critic who evaluated the performance.

associated with See *affiliated with.*

assure *Assure* takes an object; no ifs, ands, or buts. Thus "The United States, the President assured, will always be willing to discuss the question" sounds off-balance because it flouts idiom. The President was assuring *somebody*, not just doing it in thin air. "The President had assured the troops would not be sent into the city." Somewhat ambiguous, besides being awkward; he did not assure the troops, but assured a senator identified in the context. See also *remind.*

ASTERISK (*) The commonest of the devices for referring the reader to a footnote; its misuse in advertising (referring, often, to nothing, and deceitfully placed simply to attract special attention to the word it is set beside; or sometimes referring to a note placed *above* the text) has put readers on guard when they encounter the mark in such surroundings.

The place for the asterisk ("little star") is after the word or phrase being designated, like other footnote indicators; not before, as is sometimes thought. It is placed at the beginning of the footnote. *Asterisk* is often mispronounced, and consequently misspelled, *asterik*. The correct version will be remembered by those who have heard the following:

> Mary bought an aeroplane
> Among the clouds to frisk
> Now wasn't she a plucky girl
> Her little * ?

astronomical Overworked and often inappropriately used to convey the idea of large quantity: "The odds against detection in the act are astronomical." Overstated; *great*.

as though Mushmouthed for *if*: "These costs would be far less than as though one of the districts undertook the project alone." *than if*.

as to See *whether or not*.

as to why Verbiage: "An official explanation as to why . . ." *why*.

as well as Phrases beginning thus are not set off by commas in modern usage: "The pictures, as well as the text, pointed out our civic features." *pictures as well as the text pointed*. See also *together with*.

as with see *as, like*.

at, in see *in, at*.

at about Use one or the other, as appropriate, not both together: *at 9 o'clock, about 9 o'clock*.

athletic, athletics See *-ic, -ics*.

at present, at the present time Usually the long way around for *now*. See also *presently*.

attacked In the sense *sexually assaulted*, a newspaper euphemism. Reports like this are not uncommon: "The woman's arm was broken, her ear cut off, and her cheek slashed, but she had not been attacked."

at the rear of Usually excessive for *behind*.

attorney   Not necessarily a lawyer, but merely someone who has been authorized to act for another; that is, who has been given power of attorney. In the U.S., however, *attorney* is nearly synonymous with *lawyer*. More than that, *attorney* has become the genteel word for *lawyer*. Thus most lawyers prefer to be referred to as attorneys, and newspapers, almost always sedulously deferential in these matters, cater to this preference. There are lawyers who unpretentiously advertise themselves as such on their shingles, however, and there are also newspapers that shun on principle any word intended to confer a specious dignity. See also *lawman*.

attractive   "What an attractive girl!" is now the standard tribute. Not *beautiful, lovely, handsome, pretty, bonny, comely, fair, beauteous, pulchritudinous,* or *good-looking*. Words often change in sense and force, and this seems to be happening to *attractive*. Strictly speaking, an attractive girl is not necessarily a pretty one, but one who attracts. It cannot be denied, however, that there is a connection between beauty and attraction. It seems questionable whether *attractive* as a synonym for *beautiful* or *pretty* is more than a fad. People who choose their words carefully, at any rate, appear to be reserving *attractive* for the idea of attraction, which may not include beauty.

   Attractive, in fact, is a rather tame substitute for *pretty* or *beautiful*. Women, who seem fondest of using it, may be choosing the word subconciously as a means of giving credit where due with one hand, and at the same time watering it down with the other. *Beautiful, pretty, lovely,* and *good-looking* are still holding on, however. *Handsome* may be properly applied to a woman as well as to a man, contrary to the ideas held in some quarters, but it suggests elegance rather than beauty. *Comely* and *fair* now have an old-fashioned sound.

ATTRIBUTION   One of the most pervasive problems of journalism has to do with the question Harold Ross, the editor of *The New Yorker,* is said to have asked sometimes about cartoons submitted for publication: "Who's talking?" The newsman's word for this problem is *attribution*.

   Troubles with attribution probably have their root in police and court stories, where the danger of libel is greatest. The young reporter quickly learns that damaging statements must be ascribed to the authorities, or to privileged documents. The danger, both moral and legal, of aspersing someone on one's own say-so is impressed on him so unforgettably that he comes to think of attribution as a virtue, rather than a necessary evil.

Like other principles slavishly followed, the need for attribution carries writers overboard, even in police stories. Here is an example: "Highway patrolmen said the car skidded 80 feet before striking the truck, which, they said, was parked on the shoulder." Can anyone reasonably hold that the first *said* will not alone easily carry the weight of all that follows?

It sounds silly to attribute innocuous bits of general information, but one widely followed school of thought insists on attributing *everything* in police stories. "The lake is about 20 miles from Podunk and about 12 miles in circumference, the officers reported." This suggests to the reader that the publication carrying the information has no confidence in any part of it. Such supercaution might easily result in "The sun rose on schedule, according to the investigator."

Stories about crimes in which no arrest has been made hardly need more than one citation of the source, for an unnamed burglar or whatever cannot be libeled. Similarly, the fact of an arrest is a matter of public record, and ought to need no qualification. Consider "Officers George Hamilton and Walter Schroeder said the dancer was arrested on a charge of indecent exposure." Another factor enters here: kowtowing by reporters, and even newspapers, to the police. Where this is practiced, the names of the arresting officers are invariably worked into the account, and sometimes the facts of a brief report are overshadowed by unnecessary references to the source of the information. See also *allege.*

Inversion in Attribution Such forms as *said he, declared she, questioned Mr. Smith,* inverting the word order in a desperate attempt at variety, in place of *he said, she declared, Mr. Smith questioned,* are tiresome and a damning admission by the writer, as Fowler commented, that he is in fear of boring his readers.

Misleading Attribution Attribution has become such a mania that newswriters sometimes end by putting reverse English on what they are trying to say. In this way they unintentionally associate themselves (or their newspapers) with statements they really want to hang exclusively on the speaker. A number of commonly and carelessly used expressions imply that what is being quoted, directly or indirectly, is the fact. *Pointed out* is one of them: "The senator has an ugly record of broken promises, his opponent pointed out." The effect of this is that the writer (or the newspaper) concurs in the accusation. Even if they do, such acquiescence has no place in the news columns.

Similar impressions are created by *as* with the attributive verb ("as he said") and by *admitted, noted, conceded, explained,* and *cited the fact that.* "A young TV comedian admitted in New York that all funnymen are sick and desperately in need of psychoanalysis." The effect here is not so much that the writer agrees as that the speaker is conceding a generally accepted fact. There was no occasion for *admitted,* because the point of view being expressed was a novel one, at least at the time.

Other bits of heedlessness can unintentionally convict, as, "The couple were indicted as spies by a federal grand jury but have denied their guilt." That hapless *their* assumes the couple are guilty.

There is also such a thing as winking at the reader and saying, by implication, "Take this guy with a grain of salt." That is what the use of *according to* does. When that expression does not cast a shadow on the credibility of the speaker, it may merely sound nonsensical, as in "The Rev. John Jones will ask the invocation, according to the chairman." It is usually preferable to have the speaker *report* or *announce,* instead of using the *according to* formula. *Said he believes,* instead of either *said* or *believes,* may also erect a small BEWARE sign, in that it may imply the speaker is not necessarily to be taken at his word.

Disclose and *reveal* are appropriate only in reference to that which has been concealed. It's stupid, when you stop to think about it, to write of the time of a dinner as disclosed, or the name of a Rotary Club speaker as revealed. Once again, *report* and *announce* are more suitable.

Sometimes attribution, though called for, is doubled. "The secretary and his associates were criticized for what the committees said were 'political and other considerations.' " Either *what the committees said* or the quotation marks should suffice. "Truman told reporters that his memoirs will explain what he said was the part Eisenhower played in the incident." Here *what he said was* indicates unnecessary caution. In giving the substance of reports and the like, it seems superfluous to tack *the report said* or something of the kind onto every sentence, unless the material is questionable or damaging.

Advise, contend, and *claim* are sadly overworked and at the same time inexactly used in attribution. *Advise,* as in "The meeting will be postponed, he advised," is journalese at its worst. *Contend* is suitable only where there is contention or disagreement, and *insist* only where there is insistence. *Claim* may be excusably bent out of shape in headlines in the sense of *say* or *assert*, but in text, where there is no such space problem, it is questionable in that sense. ("The informant claimed he did not know the name of his source.") *Stress* and *emphasize* are suitable only where there is indeed stress or emphasis.

Much hinges on the choice between *as* and *for* in certain attributive constructions. To say that a man was criticized *for* committing perjury is to imply that the perjury was committed. To say that a man was criticized *as* committing perjury, on the other hand, places the burden of proof on the critic.

"Said" and Its Variants Said and its relations, both rich and poor, pose a problem. Not many years ago it was the custom to use *said* with the first of a series of quoted statements. Next came *asserted,* then perhaps *averred, asseverated* (seldom resorted to, because nobody was sure what it meant), *declared,* and of course that old standby, *stated.* These and perhaps a few others, such as *opined,* were enough to see the writer through a typical interview. If not, it was considered legal to start over again with *said,* the theory being that the reader would not realize by that time that he was getting a warmed-over word. The point was not to use *said* or any of the others twice, or anyway, not twice in succession. The substitutes were dropped in automatically, as if they all meant exactly the same thing. No consideration was given the possibility that one or another might be the most appropriate with a given quotation.

There is abundant evidence that the *said* problem is with us still. A distinguished editor, citing an example of a poor choice of a substitute that resulted in a misleading, not to say damaging, statement, said (or perhaps declared): "There never was a verb better than *said.*" This enthusiasm, while understandable under the circumstances, may have been excessive.

The best word is probably different for every quotation. It may be *said,* it may be *roared,* it may be *mumbled.* Whatever it is, it is always the *exact* word. Errors in choice of words are regrettable, but it does not seem likely that the best purpose is going to be served by arbitrarily damming off part of the language and condemning ourselves to the use of a single overworked and flavorless expression.

Here are some expressions that can stand duty for *said*, when appropriate:

Admitted, admonished, affirmed, agreed, avowed, barked, begged, bellowed, called, chided, contended, cried, croaked, declaimed, demanded, disclosed, drawled, emphasized, entreated, exclaimed, hinted, implored, insisted, maintained, mumbled, murmured, muttered, pleaded, proclaimed, proposed, rejoined, retorted, roared, scolded, shouted, shrieked, yelled, wailed.

Some of these words, of course, can lead to trouble if used improperly or indiscreetly. Others are unquestionably touchy: *grumbled, insinuated, prated, ranted, spouted, stammered, whined, whimpered.* All these are uncomplimentary to the speaker, but they may be called for in an accurate account.

Even for the timid, however, there are a number of innocuous substitutes that will make for less stodgy writing: *added, announced, answered, asserted, commented, continued, declared, observed, remarked, replied, reported, responded, returned, stated. Stated,* it may be remarked, is overworked, and conveys a tone of formality that is usually unsuitable.

Utterance by Proxy The purported utterance of words by smiling, frowning, grimacing, laughing, and other methods is frequently criticized:

"Romance seems to be out of fashion these days," he grimaced.

"I'd rather work from the neck up," the actress smiled.

"This equipment is not included in the budget," the auditor frowned.

This is a cute trick, and may be only a fad that will have its day and cease to be. In a way, it appears to be an extension of what Ruskin deplored as the pathetic fallacy—ascribing lifelike acts to inanimate things, as in having the sun smile. But Ruskin's criticism is usually regarded as footless carping.

Those who choose to use this device must be prepared to defend themselves against the logical, though perhaps hairsplitting and pedantic, complaint that words cannot be formed by smiling, frowning, and the like. In any event, it is harmless, since no one is really misled, and those who consider it absurd are free to write *he said, grimacing; she said, smiling;* and *he said, frowning.* Fowler traced this idiosyncrasy back to Meredith, dubbing it "a circumvention system for 'said so-&-so.'"

Speech Tags Quotations should not be broken into awkwardly for the attribution, or what is sometimes called the speech tag:

"I," the producer said, "will not accept this responsibility." This not only interrupts at an undesirable place, but also lays meaningless stress on *I*. Some people consider this clever.

"We have never," the curator of birds said, "had any previous complaint about our pelicans biting people." The writer fancied, perhaps, that his awkward insertion of the speech tag enhanced the humor of the remark.

Insertion of speech tags in every paragraph of a continuing quotation is excessive and annoying, even though some stylebooks prescribe it:

" 'The toughest place to cross is the Southwest,' one of the leaders of the expedition said.

" 'Towering mountains and the distances between communities pose particular problems,' [he said]." The bracketed tag should be omitted. One attribution in a continuing quotation is enough.

Only a nitwit will need to be reminded who is talking, and only another will refuse the reader credit for enough intelligence to remember. The quotation marks are there for a purpose, and they can fulfill it unassisted. See also *Quotation; as.*

If a quotation runs to more than one paragraph, the quotation marks are left off the ends of the paragraphs except the last, but are used at the beginning of each quoted paragraph. The same rule applies to parentheses enclosing matter that continues beyond one paragraph.

audience By derivation, an audience would be listeners only, as *a concert audience, a radio audience.* But much of our language has come a long way from its origins. *Audience* now properly designates a group of spectators as well.

au naturel It is hardly necessary to resort to French to say *naked,* but if it must be, at least it should not be misspelled *au natural.* See also *all together, altogether; naked, nude.*

auspices The phrase *under the auspices of,* commonly used to describe simple sponsorship of an event by an organization, sounds pompous. *Auspices* has to do with "protection, patronage, and care," and derives from the superstition of good omens deduced from the flight of birds. In such circumstances as "the bazaar will be under the auspices of the Young People's League," it is less pretentious and more direct to say "the Y.P.L. will *sponsor* [or *give* or *hold*] the bazaar."

authentic, genuine Fowler gave up on attempting to lay down a hard distinction here; the words now apply interchangeably to mean *not a fake.*

author Not in the best standing as a verb ("The book was authored by an expert in the field"). The consensus is still that books are *written,* not *authored.*

authoritative Sometimes misspelled *authorative, authoratative.*

automation, mechanization Automation does not mean simply the substitution of machinery for hand labor; it refers, rather, to the automatic control of machines. A thermostatically controlled heating system is an example of automation; a mechanical coal stoker that does the job of a man is not. Automated factories have devices that regulate their own operation, although, ultimately, somewhere there must be a man to check on and regulate the regulators.

average, median, mean *Average* is often loosely interchanged with *median* and *mean.* The average of a group of quantities is their sum divided by the number in the group; the average of 6, 10, 14 and 2 (which add up to 32) is 8 (32 divided by 4). The median of a set of quantities is that above which and below which an equal number of quantities occur; if the median pay rate is $3.40, there are as many rates higher than $3.40 as lower. The mean, in ordinary use, is the midpoint; the mean temperature on a day when the maximum was 90 and the minimum 60 would be 75. These generalities will not satisfy the statistician, who makes such distinctions as mean average, median average, and mode average. But then he is not liable to the confusions pointed out here either. What the layman generally means by *average,* and what is defined thus here, is to the expert the *mean average.*

avoid *Avoid* frequently usurps the place of *prevent.* To avoid is to keep away from, as in "The horse veered to avoid the tree," whereas to prevent is to keep from happening, as in "The dam prevents the snow-melt from escaping." A company headed its interoffice communication blanks with the advice, "Avoid Verbal Orders." Any employee who took this literally, however, was asking to be fired. Another example: "The firemen fought to avoid flying sparks setting fire to neighboring roofs." *prevent.* What can be avoided is already in existence, like the

55

tree; what can be prevented is not. *Avoid* is the equivalent of *sidestep*.

aw   See *ah, aw*.

away back   See *way back,* etc.

aweigh   See *under way*.

awful.   *Awful* no longer means only *awe-inspiring;* in common parlance it means *terrible* (itself something of a perversion) or *dreadful*. It may yet be necessary, however, to spell the word *aweful* to restore it to its original sense, as one writer did in referring to "The *aweful* powers of the presidency." Thus does the wheel of corruption come full circle.

awhile, a while   *While* is a noun as considered here and *awhile* is an adverb. This means that *for a while* is the equivalent of *awhile,* and that "We loafed for *a while*" and "We loafed *awhile*" are correct, but "We loafed for *awhile*" is incorrect. This distinction is often disregarded.

awoke, etc.   *Awoke, awakened, awaked, wakened, woke* are all equivalent and all standard.

ax, axe   *Axe* is the British preference.

—B—

baby boy, girl   Often objected to in references to births on the ground that *baby* is redundant.

back yard   Whether an expression should be rendered in one word rather than two (*airbase* vs. *air base, payroll* vs. *pay roll*) is an academic question, fit only for the deliberations of those who have nothing better to do than compile lists of exceptions for stylebooks. Decisions on such matters usually reflect only opinions, often wrongheaded ones insofar as they resist dictionaries, on how far the evolution from two words to one has progressed in specific cases.

But it seems that something valid may be said against the frequent amalgamation of *back yard* into one word. When this is done, convention appears to dictate that the pronunciation should be *back*yard. But equal stress is usually laid on each syllable; this would seem to call for the preservation of *back yard* as two words. The defense, if any, of *backyard* ought to justify *frontyard*, but *frontyard* is unknown.

The same logic applies to *home town* vs. *hometown*. A case can be made out, however, for both *backyard* and *hometown* when they are used as modifiers (*a backyard incinerator, a hometown hero*) because then the stress shifts to *back* and *home*.

bad, badly   See *feel bad, badly*.

bad off   Subliterate. "The town isn't as bad off as many of us like to think in our bluer moments." *badly off*.

badly, painfully hurt (injured)   Use of the adverbs (*badly, painfully*) is sometimes criticized on the ground that no injury is either good or painless, and thus the modifiers are superfluous. This is pedantry of a peculiarly wrongheaded kind; *badly* in this case is equivalent to *severely*; *painfully* serves a similar purpose.

bail, bale   *Bail* means dip water out of, or post a bond; *bale* means tie in a bundle. Boats and prisoners are *bailed*; hay is *baled* (made into bales).

balance   In the sense *rest* or *remainder*, best left to accountants. One stylebook, however, curiously discourages the use of *rest* as well as *balance* in this sense. This would make of Shakespeare's poignant line, "The remainder is silence." "One hundred of the ships were of British registry and most of the balance were Greek and Lebanese." *rest, others*.

balding   Some say there is no such word, but if not, how does it find its way into print, and in reputable surroundings? These critics appear to reason that *bald* is an adjective, and that to make a verb form like *balding* from it is illegitimate. There is a verb *balden*, however, meaning to grow bald, although it is little used. Presumably *baldening* is a legal form of *balden*, and so *balding* may be merely a compression of *baldening*. In any event, *balding* (*Bald and balding politicians usually keep their hats on when their pictures are taken*) fills a need. Dictionaries have been reluctant to admit *balding* despite its frequency in the press, but the newest of them now do. Whether a word is in dictionaries or not reflects only its newness, not its usefulness or reputability. After all, dictionaries never invent and announce new words; they merely report on what is already in existence.

band, orchestra   See *orchestra, band.*

bank, banker   Carelessly and improperly applied to savings and loan associations and their officials, which operate under different laws from banks. People who place their money in such associations are correctly known as shareholders, not depositors; they are investors and share in ownership. Bank depositors are creditors and in case of liquidation receive all their money before the shareholders get anything. These may seem like technicalities but savings and loan associations are very sensitive to the distinctions, and regularly chide publications that neglect to make them. In some states it is illegal to refer to savings and loan institutions as banks.

With respect to another sense of *bank,* the left and right banks of a river are determined by imagining oneself as facing in the direction the water flows.

banquet   Unduly sumptuous for *dinner* as used to describe most such occasions today. The word has been discouraged to the extent that it is now generally regarded as pretentious, together with *repast* and *collation.*

bar, saloon   The changes in American drinking habits and attitudes have been accompanied by changes in the words used for the places where drinking is done. Before Prohibition, which took effect in October, 1919, the place for public drinking was a saloon and nothing else. Its chief characteristics were swinging doors, a free lunch, and a clientele that was almost exclusively male. Those were the days when a boy could be sent out with a bucket to fetch some beer.

Saloon, just a neutral designation at one time, was successfully associated by the dry, or pre-Prohibition, interests with disreputability, low-lifes, "Father, dear Father, come home with me now," and all that sort of thing. Perhaps because of this propaganda, *saloon* is now undignified if not rough, and there are states where its use to designate a place of business is prohibited by law. On the other hand, its revival by the legal gambling resorts of Nevada, prompted perhaps by its Old West flavor, had a refreshing effect.

In spite of its low estate at present, *saloon* has a more or less distinguished ancestry. It developed from the French *salon*, meaning a reception room or hall, especially in a palace or great house. Later the term was applied to the gatherings of literati and other intellectuals conducted by French ladies of fashion in such rooms.

Saloon at one time had other applications than to a drinking place. People once spoke of the dining saloon aboard a ship, for example (it is now *salon*). By the time Prohibition was repealed in 1933 *saloon* was in such bad odor that its general revival was out of the question, especially from the standpoint of businessmen who opened bars. A great effort was made to popularize the term *tavern* for this purpose, but it never really caught on except in the names of establishments. When used otherwise, it seems to be equated with *beer joint*.

Cocktail lounge is rather specialized, calling to mind a somewhat tony place, more likely to be frequented by women. But the word-of-all-work for a drinking establishment today seems to have become *bar*, which is equally and neutrally applicable up and down the scale.

barbecue, barbeque Both forms are standard but the first is predominant and also closer to the generally assumed derivation (from the American-Spanish *barbacoa*).

barbiturate Often misspelled *barbituate*.

basically The correct form; *basicly* is unrecognized, although both *incidently* and *incidentally* are now accepted.

base, bass *Bass* (deep-toned) is pronounced *base* but not spelled that way. "The adventure had the nation all but wired to its communication systems, listening for the next base-voiced announcement." *Bass-*, unless the voice was ignoble. It's always *bass* in musical connections: *basses, bass viol, bass clarinet, bass clef*.

B.C. See *A.D.*

be advised As used in business correspondence, a Victorian pomposity ("Be advised that nothing of the sort is contemplated.") The simple statement, omitting *be advised*, is preferable.

because   See *as; reason is because.*

behalf   The question sometimes arises whether *on* or *in* is correct with *behalf* (*on my behalf; in my behalf*). Partridge, following the *Oxford English Dictionary*, holds that confusion here leads to the loss of a useful distinction. *On behalf*, strictly, means *as the agent*, or *instead of:* "Since I was unable to appear, he reported on my behalf" (that is, *in my place*). *In behalf* means *in the interest* or *for the benefit of:* "She put in a good word in my behalf" (that is, *to my credit*). It may as well be conceded, however, that the loss of which Partridge complains is irretrievable. *On* and *in* are used indiscriminately with *behalf*, and both *on* and *in behalf* are nearly always used to mean *in the interest of*. Different wording is used for *as the agent*, or *instead of*, because *on* or *in behalf* no longer convey this sense explicitly.

being that, being as how   Quaint and wordy for *since* or *because*.

belabor   A curious defiance of idiom occurs in the expression *belabor a point*. The generally accepted and correct version is *labor a point*. *Labor* in this connection means to work out with effort or in detail, or to elaborate. *Belabor*, on the other hand, means to stroke blows upon; belaboring is what one would use a shillelagh for. So it is plain that one could only blunt a point by belaboring, rather than laboring, it. Those who speak of belaboring a point do have history on their side, for *belabor* once meant to work carefully at. Yet idiom now calls for *laboring* a point or question.

believe   See *feel.*

bells   Those who essay to give a salty flavor to things by saying *six bells* instead of *six o'clock* are drifting off course. Bells formerly were sounded on shipboard to divide four-hour watches into half-hour intervals, so six bells would be eleven o'clock, three o'clock, etc.

belly   See *abdomen.*

belong to   See *affiliated with.*

belt out (a song)   A cliché.

berserk   See *amuck, amok.*

benedict *Benedict*, for *newly married man*, is society-page lingo, like *justweds*. (Strictly, it should be *Benedick*, from the character in *Much Ado About Nothing*.)

benefit of clergy The expression has two distinct senses: sanction of the church, generally by means of the marriage ceremony; and the ancient privilege of the clergy to be tried in their own courts.

beside, besides *Beside* means *at the side of:* "We stood beside the canyon." *Besides* means *in addition to*: "Besides the lecture there was a concert."

bet, betted Both are standard for the past tense of *bet* ("She bet fifty dollars at the track") but *betted* is obsolescent.

better See *Ad Lingo; Comparison of Adjectives.*

between, among No one would use *among* with only two objects. ("Among you and me") but there is a misguided though prevalent idea that *between* cannot be correctly used with more than two: "Agreements were reached *between* six nations." The proper use of *between* does not depend on the number of objects but on whether they are being considered in pairs. Even this is open to question as an absolute rule; the *Oxford English Dictionary* specifies that *between* may be used of relations between two or more things.

  And, not *to* or *or*, follows *between* in such constructions as "Reporters on Florida newspapers were receiving between $40 to $150 weekly." *and*. "Between six to ten trials of the apparatus were made." *and*.

between each Illogical; *each* is singular and *between* denotes a position before one and after another. "Between each inning the vendors peddled soda pop." *Between (the) innings*.

bi- In such expressions as *biennial(ly)* and more especially *bimonthly* and *biweekly*, *bi-* has become ambiguous, no matter what the dictionaries say. It is safer to make it *every two years (months, weeks)* or *twice a year (month, week)*, or *semiannual(ly)*, *semimonthly*, *semiweekly*, as appropriate.

  Bi- is solid as a prefix: *biaxial, bicameral, bilateral, bipartisan,* etc.

bid Many and bitter are the complaints against the misuse and fancied misuse of *bid*. Most of the criticized instances occur in newspaper headlines, but as is the way in journalism, headlinese tends to seep into text, where there is not the excuse of tight space. The commonest uses of *bid* as a verb are in the senses *command* or *direct* (*bid them leave*), *say* (*bid farewell*), or *offer* (*bid on a contract, bid two no trump*). As a noun, a bid is an offer (*the low bid*), an attempt (generally with *for: a bid for election*) and, colloquially, an invitation (*a bid to the prom*).

It is the use of *bid* as a verb in the sense *attempt* that generally raises objections: "Navy Flight Bids to Save Russian." In this headline the exact sense would be given by *tries; bid* in the sense *try* or *attempt* is, as we have noted, objectionable. The word would never be used this way in text. Headlines, to be sure, have their exigencies, and *tries* is longer than *bids* in any size of type. But *bids* is often used when there is space to spare for *tries*, reflecting the headline writer's devotion to journalese even when he can avoid it. Note also "Scientist Predicts Next Bid in 4 Weeks." *Predicts Next Try* would have been better, though *Try* is slightly longer than *Bid*. *Bid* as a noun is ambiguous without *for*; we do not know whether the scientist is predicting an experimental attempt or a bid on a contract. Here too the idea would never have been expressed this way in text. The gist of all this: do not use *bid* for *try* or *attempt* as either noun or verb unless you are willing to risk ambiguity and criticism. If *try* or *tries* will not fit, recast.

The past tense of *bid* in the senses *command, direct, say, tell* is *bade* (pronounced *bad*): "We bade them welcome." It is always *bid* in the sense *offer:* "Last year the firm bid on nine projects."

bid in The expression has a nice technical flavor, which perhaps causes it to displace *bid*. They are not synonyms, however; that flavor is not for nothing. Bidding in is topping a bid on behalf of the owner of the property.

billion All the more regrettably in these days when the term has come into such common use, it means different things in the United States, France, and Germany, on the one hand, and Britain and its imitators in linguistic matters, on the other. The American billion is a thousand million; the British, a million million. The American *billion* is the British *milliard*. The disparity persists throughout the names of other large numbers ending in *illion:* trillion, quadrillion, quintillion, etc. Both systems are set forth in detail in a table accompanying the entry *number* in *Webster's Unabridged, Third Edition.*

birthday anniversary   Some stylebooks insist that one can have only one birthday—the day on which he was born—and that recurrences of the date must be his *birthday anniversary.* This notion is unsupported by either dictionaries or usage, but it does illustrate what often goes on in the heads of the compilers of the stylebooks. When they raise their voices in congratulatory song, it is presumably with "Happy birthdayanniversary to you."

bivalve   The journalese variant of *clam* or *oyster.*

blacken acres   Journalese, invariably encountered in reports of forest fires.

blame for, on   *Blame for* is right, *blame on* wrong, declaim the pedants. Not so; the forms are equally acceptable. The construction of the sentence (*They blamed me for it; I blamed it on him*) sometimes determines the choice. When either will go they are interchangeable.

blink the fact   "Democratic politicians aren't blinking at the fact that his popularity gives them a slight chance of recapturing the legislature." The idiom is *blink the fact,* not *blink at.* One blinks *at* a strong light; *not to blink* (the usual form of the expression) means take into account.

bloc, block   The first is a political grouping: *the Communist bloc; a bloc of bipartisan votes. Block* sometimes appears in this sense.

blond, blonde   Formerly distinctive masculine and feminine forms for the noun, but *blonde* now is neglected. ("The sailors had a couple of blonds on their arms.") Fowler thought *blond* should displace *blonde,* and in this instance it appears his advice is being followed.

blood, sweat, and tears   See *Misquotation.*

boast   In statements like "Such clubs now number more than a thousand and boast assets in the millions," *boast* is nothing to brag about. The imputation of boasting is no compliment, and the writer usually makes it undeservedly. Journalese. See also *brag on.*

boat   The idea that *boat* cannot be applied to a seagoing vessel but only to a small open craft is a naval fetish. In the technical sense, *ship,* as a large vessel, is opposed to *boat. Boat,* however, is acceptably established in casual references to ocean liners and otherwise.

boatswain   Readers of tales of the deep are familiar with the rendering *bosun* for *boatswain,* but in the Navy, at least, the favored pronunciation is *boatson.* Yet *forecastle* is said the way the fictioneers have it (*fo'c'sle*).

bogey, bogie   The first is the preferred form for the golf term (whose meaning is a hole shot in one over par) and also for a goblin or specter (as in *bogeyman*).

BOLDFACE TYPE   Visual variety is often introduced into printed matter by using boldface paragraphs, sometimes indented, at intervals. This practice seems thoroughly objectionable. Boldface unavoidably denotes emphasis, and even though it is used solely to create an interesting appearance, there is no way to make this clear to the reader. Consciously or subconsciously assuming that emphasis is intended, he often is nonplused to find paragraphs of no special import set in black type.

On the other hand, consider the boldfacing of paragraphs to convey emphasis and not as a typographical device. This, like such tricks as setting sentences and paragraphs in capitals, insults the intelligence of the reader because it seizes him by the ear and says, in effect, "Pay attention. This is important." He will resent being managed in such fashion. The reader who has no intelligence is unlikely anyhow to discern the importance of what is being thrust at him in this way. In newspapers, this applies with greater force to editorials than to news stories. If boldface (or, for that matter, capitals) is necessary to supply emphasis, the editorial is poorly written.

The visual effect of boldface interspersed in running text is undesirable regardless of its purpose. It gives a page a spotty, untidy appearance. Most publications edited with discrimination eschew boldface for either emphasis or variety. Short boxed items set entirely in boldface are a different case. In that instance there is at least no likelihood of misconstrued emphasis.

boost   Overblown and journalese for *increase, raise.*

born, borne   *Born* is sometimes used where *borne* is called for as the past and participle of the verb *bear* that means carry (*the burdens were borne patiently*). "Helicopter-born commando troops were landed." *-borne,* unless their mothers were helicopters.

-borne, the suffix, as distinguished from part of a compound, as in *helicopter-borne,* is normally solid: *airborne, waterborne,* etc. See also *nee.*

bosom, breast, etc.   It was a sad thing to see a loathsome nice-Nellyism employed by a nationally known theater critic, a man whose prose is usually notable for unflinching directness. He reported an episode in which the "false bosoms" were torn from the dress of an actress. *False bosoms* is certainly going the long way around to avoid *falsies.* Everyone knows what falsies are, and there seems to be no other reason than prissiness for sidestepping the term.

Bosom for *breasts* is a genteelism that seems to have emanated from the world of brassiere advertising. *Bosom* is, indeed, the equivalent of *breast* (in distinction to *breasts*) but both *bosom* and *breast* are applicable equally to men and women in designating what is otherwise known as the chest. We have all read of children being pressed to the bosom, and of a dagger being plunged into the breast. *Bosom* and *breast,* however, in these strict senses, tend to be literary, if not poetic. In any event, they are asexual.

Breasts may be too explicitly anatomical for many purposes, and it is likely that *bosom* will continue to be widely used in that sense. *Bust* was once popular, though never reputable, in this connection, but now seems to have fallen into disuse. *Busts,* of course, is beyond the pale. It is only to be expected, perhaps, that the powerful urge to cover up the thing itself should affect the language chosen to describe it, or them.

both   Often redundantly used with such words as *equal, alike, agree, together. Both* indicates duality, or twoness, which is established by such words as those cited. "They are both equally deadly" and "Both are equally liberal" should be *They are equally deadly* and *They are equally liberal.* "Both appeared together in a new Broadway show" should be *They appeared together.* "Both agreed" is unsuitable if the agreement is reciprocal; *they agreed.* "Both looked alike" is illogical; *They* *looked alike.* Fowler noted that *both* with *as well as* is ungrammatical. The exegesis is not simple, but the construction offends the ear; "Both students as well as teachers protested the ruling" should be *Students as well as teachers* or *Both students and teachers. Both* in constructions of this kind should always be paired with *and,* never with *but.* "The story prompted both a slow but methodical investigation" is impossible; "The story prompted a slow but methodical investigation."

"Soon both sides had joined forces." With each other, presumably, but this would be explicit in "Soon the sides had joined forces."

Both is sometimes misused for *each:* "Both seemed to have blamed his martyrdom on the other." *Each seemed;* or, somewhat loosely, *their martyrdom.*

Both is often misplaced ahead of prepositions: "She was considering childbirth both as a woman and an obstetrician." *as both;* the reason is that *as* here is a preposition controlling both *woman* and *obstetrician;* the structure is not clear with *both as.*

"Foreign policy, both under the present and preceding administrations. . . ." *under both.* "But leftover passions both in the North and the South made it unlikely." *in both.* "I have heard the question asked both by Caucasians and Negroes." Wrong order, and *by* need not be repeated: *by both Caucasians and Negroes.*

"Plans for improvements were discussed both from the standpoint of utility and beautification of the city." Here as in the similar examples *both* should stand as close as possible to the nouns (*utility* and *beautification*) it links as a conjunction. *from the standpoint of both utility and beautification.* See also *either.*

-bound Solid as a suffix: *earthbound, heavenbound,* but hyphenated with proper names: *Europe-bound, Chicago-bound.* It can be ambiguous, for it may mean either headed for or restricted by (e.g., *snowbound*).

boundary Often misspelled *boundry.*

bovine The journalese variant for *cow.* See also *Variation.*

boy Use of this term to address or refer to Negroes regardless of age is an indignity. It is comparable, in a way, to the pronunciation *nigra* for *Negro.*

BRACKETS Brackets [ ] are not parentheses ( ) in a different shape; they are used to set off material inserted by an editor or someone other than the writer. The term is loosely applied to parentheses, but it does not seem sensible to create unnecessary confusion in this way. See also *Parentheses; Typewriter Tricks*.

brag, brag on *Brag* is acceptable as a noun (*his brag and bluster*) but it has a dialectal twang when used in reference to a specific statement rather than in a general sense, as in "We resented his brag that he was the son of a general." *boast*. *Brag on* is distinctly dialectal: "He liked to brag on his ancestors." *brag about*.

Brahms In the possessive, the name of this composer often emerges in forms like "Brahm's *Requiem*." *Brahms'*.

breach, breech Like *affect* and *effect*, often confused. In their commonest senses as nouns, a breach is a place that has been broken open (*a breach in the dike*), and a breech is the back end of a gun. As a verb, *breach* means break open (*breach a cask*). *Breech* as a verb has no current sense, though it once was used to mean put pants (breeches) on.

break, broke It has been seriously argued that "Mrs. Jones broke her leg" is improper and absurd unless she did so deliberately. This is good, unmistakable idiom, however. See also *suffer, sustain, receive;* and *had*.

breakthrough, break through One word as a noun; often erroneously *break-through* or *break through*: "An important scientific *breakthrough*." As a verbal, however, the phrase is proper: "They will *break through* some day."

breast See *bosom, breast*.

bridelet A curiosity employed on some society pages for a recent bride. The expression has no standing and fills no need, since *bride* itself ceases to be applied once the bloom is off the nuptials.

bring, take Opposites in the sense that *bring* indicates motion toward the speaker or agent, and *take* motion away from him. *Webster's Dictionary of Synonyms* cites as illustrations of their use: "a mother asks a boy setting out for school to *take* a note to the teacher and to *bring* home a reply; a farmer *takes* his cattle to the market and *brings* back a supply of sugar, flour, and fresh meat." The indifferent use of *bring* and *take* is so prevalent, however, that the distinction may be on the way out.

Britain   See *Great Britain.*

Britisher, Briton   *Britisher* carries a hint of derision or at least chaffing that *Briton* does not.

broadcast, broadcasted   Both forms are acceptable as the past tense ("The Coast Guard broadcast a warning of heavy seas") but, as in the analogous case of *forecast, forecasted,* those who prize economy will prefer the first.

brother, sister   Fraternal cant in reference to members of an organization, and therefore unsuitable except among the members themselves, who have chosen to address or refer to each other in this way. The mannerism apparently originated in fraternal orders as a means of affirming the strong bond supposedly existing among members. It was enthusiastically taken up by labor unions. It is a hypocritical and simpleminded device that nevertheless has been adopted by some unions of white-collar and quasi-professional workers.

browse   Sometimes misspelled *brouse.* Which suggests the gymnasium that had a sign in the window reading, "Come in and bruise around."

brunet, brunette   As with *blond, blonde,* the first was formerly the masculine and the second the feminine form. *Brunet* is now often applied to women (Webster no longer recognizes a sex distinction here), but *brunette* continues in wider use than *blonde.*

bugger   Widely enough known in the sense of *sodomite* to be offensive in its alternate sense as a term of affection ("a cute little bugger"). The word in this sense, although it will be understood as it is meant (without a sexual connotation), is coarse, and coming from a woman may mark her as either raffish or ignorant. *Bugger* as a verb ("bugger the works") suffers from the unsavory associations of *bugger* in its sexual sense.

bulk of   A bootless variant of *most of*.

bullet, cartridge, shell   *Bullet* is often misused for *cartridge;* the bullet is what becomes the slug when a rifle cartridge is fired. The cartridge comprises both the bullet and the shell, which holds the explosive charge. A round is the ammunition for a single shot; that is, a cartridge. *Shell* is interchangeable with *cartridge* in reference to rifle ammunition and is the usual term for shotgun ammunition.

burglary   Means breaking and entering. One should distinguish between it and *robbery,* taking away by force or threat; *theft,* taking what belongs to someone else; and *holdup,* which is essentially the same as robbery but involves the use of a weapon. Under the common law, burglary is not committed unless entry is gained forcibly into a dwelling at night with intent to commit a felony. This concept, or substantial parts of it, has been enacted as statutes by some states.

burst, bust   *Burst* is good English and *bust* not so good for *break open,* except in expressions like *bronco busting* and *trust busting.* The past tense of *burst* is *burst* or *bursted.*

BUSINESS ENGLISH   There is really no such thing, although books have been published with the term in their titles. Insofar as the language of business differs from standard expression (like "Yours of the 12th inst. received and contents noted") it is non-English. Vigorous efforts have been put forth by business establishments in recent years to make their communications more lucid and thus improve efficiency. An essential part of such efforts should be discarding the idea that business expression should exhibit peculiarities. *Pidgin English* came from *business English*—something to think about.

bust, busts   See *bosom, breast.*

but, but that, but nevertheless, but however   When *but* occurs before one of a pair of adjectives, the *but*-phrase should not be set off by commas: "Residents of this area have now had two annoying, but instructive, false alarms." *annoying but instructive false* . . . Nor should *but* at the beginning of a sentence be set off by a comma: "But, the instructions were incomplete."
  But cannot do its job of indicating a contrast when it begins

successive clauses or sentences: "But the storm continued through the night, but the river did not rise dangerously." *Though the storm continued, the river . . .*

But that sometimes sticks in the craw of the critical, in such sentences as "I do not doubt but that society feels threatened by homosexuality." Technically, *but* is excessive here. Yet usage by good writers as well as those not so good has earned it a respectable place.

But nevertheless is redundant; use one or the other. This applies also to *but however*.

buy The aspersion of *buy* as a noun ("This car was a good buy") is the work of those remarkably out of touch with the facts of usage. It is recognized by *Webster, The American College Dictionary*, and the *Oxford Universal Dictionary*, among others.

by- Usually solid as a prefix: *byplay, bylaw, bypath;* but *by-line, by-product, by-election*.

by means of Usually redundant for *by* or some other preposition alone: "The fish are caught by means of a net." *in* or *with*.

by the same token To be avoided unless the user can convince himself he knows what it means. Usually *similarly* will do as well and more economically.

by way of being A fancy phrase of indeterminate and perhaps no meaning: "European industry is by way of being as sophisticated technologically as our own." European industry either is or is not as sophisticated; the writer should not confuse us as to his intention with *by way of being*, which may suggest *becoming, ostensibly, apparently*, and other things.

—C—

caesarian See *cesarean*.

Cal., Calif. The *Postal Guide*, the authority in such matters, gives *Calif. Cal.*, especially in longhand, may be misread *Col.*, although *Colo.* is the correct abbreviation for *Colorado*.

calculate Dialectal in the sense *expect, assume:* "I calculate it will rain."

caliber, calibre Designations of the caliber of rifles and pistols should be preceded by decimal points (.22 caliber, .45 caliber) since they indicate hundredths of an inch; *Caliber* is the preferred spelling in the U.S.

callous, callus The thickening of the skin is either form, but usually *callous* (formerly only *callus*). The adjective meaning *unfeeling* is *callous*: "His callous attitude is infuriating." In this sense *calloused* is unnecessary and unusual ("This may seem a somewhat calloused observation"). *callous*. Either *calloused* or *callused* is the term for *having calluses.*

Calvary, cavalry Sometimes carelessly or ignorantly confused. Calvary was the place of the Crucifixion; cavalry are troops mounted on horses, a vanishing breed except for ceremonials.

campus Years ago it was unheard of to apply the term to anything but a college or institution of similar rank. More recently, however, high schools, especially in the West, have developed layouts resembling college campuses, and the expression has been inevitably applied to them. To resist this on the ground that they are only secondary schools is surely a form of snobbery, even if it does set the college graduate's teeth on edge and the old school tie aflutter.

can, may The old rule was that *can* should be used for the possible, and *may* to ask permission: "Can he beat the record?"; "May I look at your watch?" But the feeling for this distinction is being lost, for *can* is being used to ask permission with no lack of politeness.

candelabra Another Latin plural (of *candelabrum*) that has been Anglicized into a singular. This gives rise to a new plural form, *candelabras*. Both *candelabra* as a singular and *candelabras* as its plural are now standard.

candor and frankness This redundant pair occurs often: "We appreciate the candor and frankness with which you have expressed your views." One or the other, not both at once. *Candour* is the British spelling.

canine The journalese variant for *dog*. See *Variation.*

cannot   One word is preferable to *can not*.

can't hardly   A double negative, and not standard. See *hardly*.

canvas, canvass   Canvas is heavy cloth; to canvass means, usually, to go from door to door soliciting.

capacity   A pomposity in such contexts as "What is his capacity?" Translation: "What is his job?" "What is his capacity?" is sometimes answered with an estimate in liquid measure, such as "One quart at a time," and deserves to be. This use is like that of *affiliated with* for *belongs to*.

capital, capitol   The capital is the city and the capitol is the building.

CAPITALIZATION   Questions of capitalization are closely involved with names and titles. Apart from its use in those conventions we all agree on, as in starting a sentence, capitalization is mainly a device for conferring status. It is a form of tipping the hat, of shouting "huzza," or, in certain instances, of bending the knee. It has nothing to do, ordinarily, with meaning. We know that new york is New York just as certainly with or without the capitals, and that nelson d. rockefeller is the same scion of wealth we recognize in upper case.

Probably no other mechanical practice shows such divergent and confused treatment as capitalization. Things are made worse by the fact that some publications are possessed by delusions of grandeur concerning matters of opinion about style. Two newspapers in the same town may refer to the *City Hall* and the *city hall*, respectively, but the reader gets the sense as quickly from one as from the other. Furthermore, he does not notice the difference.

Nothing much can be said for or against differing schools of thought on these matters. Consistency within a given publication is the most that can be hoped for, but even this is made all but impossible by rules that prescribe capitals only part way through a hierarchy; that is to say, the kind of style that calls for *Pope, Cardinal, Archbishop*, but *prothonotary, monsignor, priest*; *Abbot, Prior*, but *monk, novice, friar*; or, to eschew the ecclesiastical, *Chief of Police, Captain, Lieutenant*, but *sergeant, patrolman*; or even *Federal, State*, but *city, county*.

The capitalization of *president*, in reference to the president of the United States, is almost universal in newspapers, although they do not ordinarily capitalize the word in other connections. The treatment of such references as *king, queen,* and *general* appears to depend on the amount of reverence the editor feels for the offices. It would be unheard of for a British or Canadian newspaper not to capitalize *queen* in reference to the queen of England. It would be equally unlikely for a public-relations man to lower-case *company* in reference to his own company.

The two great cults of capitalization are known as the Up Style and the Down Style. The schism is based mainly on a difference in the treatment of generic terms, that is, *Mississippi River* vs. *Mississippi river.* But it manifests itself in other ways too: *Pope* vs. *pope, Spring* and *Summer* vs. *spring* and *summer, Diesel* vs. *diesel,* and so forth. Idiosyncrasies like the Down Style, especially as it applies to generic terms, are thought by those practicing it to make for breezy, informal readability. This is a commendable goal, but it is questionable whether the Down Style assists it. Addiction to the Down Style often accompanies some of the stuffiest, most turgid writing this side of a government (Government?) report.

Now to rush in and announce some conclusions on this confused subject:

1. The Up Style is preferable to the Down Style because it is what is taught in school and is more widely used.

2. But even practitioners of the Up Style should make a stab at some reasonable consistency. This would prevent such divided usage within hierarchies as that noted above.

3. To cut down the stylebook to reasonable size, the same prescription as in other stylistic problems is offered: Let *Webster,* or whatever dictionary you use, be your guide.

The ignorant approach to capitalization is to capitalize terms that seem unfamiliar. For example, an article about animals identified the Chamois as a goatlike Antelope. The wolf was denied the dignity of upper case. Not exotic enough, apparently. Yet the accolade of capitalization was accorded to Beagle. In fact, chamois, antelope, wolf, and beagle are all common nouns. Most questions of capitalization, disregarding arbitrary stylistic prescriptions, may be resolved by consulting a dictionary, although these works are not as forthright on the subject as we might wish. Most desk dictionaries, including the *Webster Collegiate, Webster's New World,* the *Standard College,* and *American College* dictionaries, indicate capitalization by capitalizing entries. The *Oxford English Dictionary* evades the issue by capitalizing *all* entries. The Third Edition of *Webster's Unabridged* lower-cases them all, but does specify *cap* or *usu cap*. This device is much less convenient for the user than capitalizing the entry.

CAPTIONS   See *Pictures*.

capture   In connection with sports events, especially, a sadly bruised variant of *win*.

car   The criticism is still occasionally heard that *car* is improper, or at least undesirable, for *automobile*. This notion may have grown from a fear of confusing references to streetcars, railroad cars, and automobiles. It may once have had merit, but now is pedantry. *Car* means *automobile* unless the context indicates otherwise. *Auto* is fully acceptable.

carat, caret   The first is the unit of weight for precious stones and metals, and the second is the mark (∧) used to indicate an insertion in written or printed material. *Carat* is sometimes spelled *karat*.

cardiac   See *heart attack*.

career, careen   Often confused. *To career* is to go at top speed, or to swerve from side to side of the path; *to careen* is to heel, lean, or sway. A horse might career but could never careen; an automobile or boat might do either or both.

care of   The abbreviation is c/o, not %.

case   See *redundancy*.

casket, coffin   *Casket* originally was a euphemism for *coffin*, and its use in that sense is still criticized by those who have neglected to notice that the word is no longer used in any other sense in modern parlance. A euphemism ceases to be one when people are not conscious of it.

catch (caught) fire   The form of the idiom; not *catch on fire*.

category   Often a pomposity for *class*, which should be used, as the less technical term, if it will fit.

Catholic   See *Roman Catholic*.

74

cause   It is redundant to say *cause is due to*: "The cause of the flood was due to heavy rain in the foothills." *the cause was,* or *the flood was due to.* See also *due to. Caused from* is a common example of the offenses against idiom that spring from a wrong choice of preposition; correctly, *caused by.*

cease   Pretentious where *stop* or *quit* will do. "Cease your lamentations" is highfalutin these days for "Stop crying."

celebrant, celebrator   Strictly, a celebrant is one who performs a religious ceremony, such as a priest who conducts a mass, and a celebrator is one who celebrates, as on New Year's Eve. The distinction is tenuous, however, and of dubious value. It may already have been done in by the widespread, if heedless, preference for *celebrant* in both senses.

'cello, cello   The apostrophe is unnecessary and rather old-fashioned.

cement, concrete   Technically, cement is the powder that, together with water and sand or gravel, is used to make concrete. Like many technical terms that have gone into common use, however, *cement* has lost its distinctiveness. *Cement sidewalks* is common, and so are similar uses. The context always shows, anyway, whether the reference is to the powder or the finished product (*eighteen sacks of cement; a cement bird bath*). *Concrete* is never misapplied to the powder. See also *portland.*

cemetery   Often misspelled *cemetary.*

censor, censure   Often confused. Ours is a waspish age, unhappily, that grows increasingly full of both. To censor is essentially to prohibit; to censure is to condemn. A book, for example, that is censored is forbidden to be sold or circulated, or parts of it that are adjudged objectionable may be cut out. Censoring is also the act of reviewing something (a book, a movie, mail) to discover whether it contains something objectionable.

Censure is merely expression of disapproval—strong disapproval, to be sure. It does not involve prohibition or suppression, as censorship does.

Censor is sometimes used where *censure* is meant. It may be helpful to remember that people may be censured but not censored. Writings, speeches, and other forms of expression may be either censored (prohibited in whole or in part) or censured (condemned).

center   Center logically takes *in, on,* or *upon,* but *about* and *around* are so widely in use that only pedants quibble over this point, since nothing of consequence hinges upon it.

CENTS   The decimal point should not be used with the symbol: .20¢ is not twenty cents but two-tenths, or twenty hundredths, of a cent. This is not really likely to be misunderstood, but it is likely to be considered stupid.

CENTURIES   Confusingly designated by a number one higher than seems right at first glance; 1865 was in the nineteenth century, 1963 in the twentieth, etc.

ceremonial, ceremonious   What is ceremonial pertains to a ceremony (*ceremonial wine*); what is ceremonious is marked by ceremony (*a ceremonious manner, tone of voice, gesture*).

certain   Often ambiguously used. "If there was a fixed agenda this system could not work. Instead the conference would be bound to negotiate one certain proposal." *Assured?* No, *particular* or *specific,* which would have been preferable. Another kind of lapse: "This little town has a certain, awkward fame." Not *definite* but *unspecified;* the construction is an idiom. *Certain* modifies both *awkward* and *fame: a certain awkward fame* (no comma).

cesarean, caesarean, etc.   The operation known as cesarean section, to effect delivery by cutting through the walls of the abdomen and uterus, is commonly supposed to have taken its name from the legend that Julius Caesar, like Macduff,

> was from his mother's womb
> Untimely ripp'd,

but this is disputed. It has also been held that the term comes from the Latin *caesus,* which in turn derives from the verb *caedere,* to cut.

At any rate, the preferred spelling now, and the one generally used in medical circles, is *cesarean.* The terminations *-ean* and *-ian* are both acceptable, but *-ean* tends to be favored for the operation and *-ian* for the adjective meaning *pertain-*

ing to Caesar (Caesarian ambition). It has been the tendency for some time not to capitalize the name of the operation no matter how spelled.

chafe, chaff   To chaff is to make fun of good-naturedly; to chafe is to irritate, literally or figuratively. A man's wrists might be chafed by handcuffs, or he might be chafed by chaffing. The participles are *chaffing* (for *chaff*) and *chafing* (for *chafe*), and the past tenses are *chaffed* and *chafed*. "The mayor was chaffing at his confinement in the hospital." *Chafing*, unless he was making light of it. *Chafe* rhymes with *safe, chaff* with *laugh*.

chain reaction   This expression, a gift from the atomic physicists, is what Fowler would have called a popularized technicality. As pointed out by *Winners and Sinners, The New York Times* critique, "*Chain reaction* does not mean a great quantity; it means a process in which a cause produces an effect that in turn becomes a cause, and so on." Thus a flood of telephone calls to the police, prompted by an explosion, would not be a chain reaction unless the calls were self-multiplying.

chair, chairman   *Chair* as a verb meaning *serve as chairman of* is distasteful and unnecessary in spite of its popularity on the society pages, where some other questionable verbs, such as *host,* find a haven. "Mrs. Adams *chaired* the meeting" carries an alarming suggestion of *attacked with a chair*. If this is too farfetched, in any event *chaired* accomplishes nothing that *presided at, led,* or *directed* does not. *Chairman* as a verb is equally ungainly: "Smith chairmanned the meeting." *presided at.*

This term has the additional disadvantage of uncertainty over spelling. There are choices of *chairmaned, chairmanned,* and *chairmaning, chairmanning,* but they all look wrong.

chaise longue   *Chaise longue* (pronounced *shayz long,* and meaning, in French, *long chair*) seems in great danger of becoming *chaise* (or *chase*) *lounge,* perhaps on the assumption that this piece of furniture commemorates a lounger named Chase.

chalk up   A cliché of journalism, as in *chalk up a victory, chalk up points.*

character   In general, most appropriately applied to people. Its use concerning things, in the sense of *quality, kind, sort,* and the like is a species of personification and at the same time often an exhibition of pomposity. A well-known company has for some time been advertising itself as a "maker of watches of the highest character." What is meant is *quality. Character* sometimes turns up in phrases where it merely serves to give a mushy effect to the writing: *the delicate character of the music* (*delicacy*), *activities of a public-spirited character* (*public-spirited activities*), and *concentration of an intermittent character* (*intermittent concentration*). Such expressions are characteristic, these days, of fusty prose. "The residential character of the neighborhood" might better be *nature* or *status,* but the difficulty of settling on a satisfactory substitute suggests that this may be one of those exceptions in which *character* is acceptable. "It is regrettable that an incident of this character has occurred" would be better, however, with *kind.* See also *nature.*

charge   See *in charge of; dismiss against.*

chastise   Sometimes misspelled *chastize.*

chat   *Chat* has come to be a journalese counter word. It is especially prevalent in the identifications beneath pictures, where people no longer talk, converse, palaver, gossip, speak, consult, utter, discuss, say, tell, or declare—they *chat. Chat,* at any rate, connotes casual, inconsequential talk. See also *informal.*

cheap   *Cheap* means low in value or in price, not simply *low.* Goods may be *cheap,* but prices must necessarily be *low.* See also *expensive.*

check into   A legitimate and useful expression; a variant of *check* (*up*) *on.* A critic of the expression cited as examples "He is kept busy checking into developments" and "She had asked someone to check into such rumors," saying no preposition (*into*) was necessary. But without *into* the sentences are ambiguous, for *check* alone may be understood in the sense of *retard.*

CHEESECAKE   See *Pictures.*

chief justice   The federal title is chief justice of the United States (not *of the Supreme Court*).

childish, childlike   The first connotes the disagreeable, the second the appealing, qualities of childhood.

Chinaman, Chinese   *Chinaman* is considered demeaning; the preferred form is *Chinese:* "Four *Chinese* and one American were detained in customs."

chinchy, chintzy   In the senses *cheap, unfashionable, chintzy* overwhelmingly predominates. *Chinchy* is not even listed in the *Dictionary of American Slang;* Webster gives it as a Southern and Midwestern regionalism for *miserly, stingy.*

CHINESE NAMES   The part of a Chinese name that follows the hyphen is lower-cased, not capitalized: Chou En-lai, Chiang Kai-shek.

choice   See *pick, choice.*

chord, cord   Although these words have the same ancestor and both can mean *string, chord* in its commonest use means a group of musical tones sounded together in a pattern. The folds in the throat that produce the sound of the voice are vocal *cords,* not *chords.*

chore   A chore is a routine task, especially a tedious or disagreeable one. A generation or two ago the term applied most commonly to duties assigned to the boy of the household, such as fetching water, splitting firewood, shoveling snow from the sidewalks, and whitewashing the fence.

Chore is questionably appropriate to describe what is merely an accustomed act, or what is likely to excite pleasure or interest. "One of his first chores on getting up in the morning is to read the newspaper." Reading the newspaper would not be a chore except to someone for whom it was part of his job and perhaps, the editor would hope, not even then.

Chore is often misused of what is neither routine, obligatory, nor unpleasant.

Christmas tree   A courtly bow to a Captain Donahue of the New York Police Department, who, as quoted in *The Reporter,* described a switchboard as lighting up like Luna Park, instead of like a Christmas tree. Christmas trees may get a bad name from their association with this battered simile.

circum-　Solid as a prefix: *circumnavigate, circumambient, circumlocution, circumscribe,* etc.

circumstances (under vs. in the c.)　Both versions are standard and established beyond quibble.

cite　What is cited must exist; the word is not a synoym for *charge* or *accuse* in such contexts as "The suspect's record of Communist associations was cited." This says that such a record exists; what was intended, however, was "The suspect *was said to have* [or *was accused of having*] a record of Communist associations." "The lawyer cited the victim's consent to the kidnaping" was an objectionable, if not an actionable, statement, since the victim was in fact merely being accused of collusion. See also *arrest; Attribution.*

citizen　Since the word has the meaning, among others, of one who owes allegiance to a state and is entitled to protection from it, it should be used with care to prevent the ambiguity that often arises when *inhabitant* or *resident* would be a better choice. People were citizens of cities in the days when cities were states; it may be better now to speak of them as inhabitants or residents, of their cities. "A citizen met the bus that delivers the papers." Since this was merely a resident, and not a citizen as distinguished from an alien, *resident* would have been the happier word. "The county now has 221,900 citizens, a record." This sentence, from a population report, referred to inhabitants, and could be genuinely misleading as distinguishing between citizens and aliens. Yet it is not wrong to speak of "a citizen of Chicago" or "a citizen of Utah." And *citizen* sometimes is unavoidable, as in *citizens' advisory committee.*
　　The British have their own word for it; they have not citizens but *subjects.*

civilian　A civilian is one not in military service; use of the word to differentiate those not in any kind of uniform, as for example nonpolicemen, is questionable. Next we will be offered some such distinction as *mailmen and civilians.*

claim　Not in the best odor in the sense of *say* or *assert;* journalese. Properly, *claim* carries the idea of asserting a right, or ownership, and its use for a simple declaration grates on the ear: "Some grammarians claim the construction is incorrect." *say, maintain, believe.*

clamp   Journalese in such connections as *clamp a lid of secrecy, place security clamps on.*

clarify   *Clarify* means *clear* or *clear up,* and is wrong in the sense of *answer:* "He spoke to clarify questions farmers may have about tractors." Only the asker, if a question is obscure, can clarify it; this speaker's intention was to *answer* the farmers' questions. Apart from this, *clarify* is too great a favorite in official prose, where things are always supposedly being clarified. Sad to state, they are rarely *cleared up,* either by the use of *clarify* or in fact.

classic, classical   As adjectives, the forms mean the same thing, but idiom has attached one or the other to various nouns: *a classical education, classical music, a classic example, a classic style. Classical* may often be substituted for *classic* (*a classical example*) but the reverse is not true (*a classic education*). Trust the ear.

"CLEAN COPY"   The shibboleth of many a newsroom, and no one can reasonably quibble with the general objective. Copy that has been badly messed up with strike-overs and scribbled interlineations is the bane of both the copy desk and the composing room. An absolute ban on strike-overs, as is often enforced, is a good idea. So is discouragement of breaking words at the ends of lines in typescript, which can raise unnecessary questions about hyphenation in the composing room. And finally, legibility is the least that can be expected of emendations.

The worship of clean copy, however, has been known to find expression in a reverence for unblemished typescript for its own sake. In this way, mediocre writers who never hit a wrong key, nor change their minds about choice of words or the structure of a sentence, gain a fraudulent stature.

"That guy certainly writes clean copy!" is the admiring verdict. The unspoken implication is that clean copy is, *ipso facto,* good copy. Unfortunately, it may be beautiful stuff to look at but terrible to read. Clean copy, in the sense of unamended typing, ought to be recognized for what it is—a feat of stenography, having nothing to do with the quality of either reporting or writing. The work of the clean-copy artist is likely to be below par, on the principle that any piece of writing can stand improvement, and particularly what is written under the conditions of journalism. The Heywood Brouns who can grind out

81

a couple of thousand words of hard, gemlike prose without any second thoughts are—well, Heywood Brouns.

The self-critical, conscientious writer who goes over his stuff carefully, substituting better words for worse ones and unsnarling bad constructions, ought to be encouraged in his labors. All too often the natively uncritical have been abetted, perhaps unwittingly, in the notion that there is some overriding virtue in clean copy. Clean copy should be knocked off the pedestal it occupies and in its place should go well-written copy.

Ben Jonson had something pertinent to say on this subject: "The players have often mentioned it as an honor to Shakespeare, that in his writings he never blotted out a line. My answer hath been, would he had blotted a thousand."

CLERICAL TITLES See *Rev.*

clever Not quite the compliment many assume; it does not measure up to *ingenious, inventive, creative, witty*. The word connotes skill in small matters.

CLICHÉS The dictionary definition of cliché is "a trite phrase; a hackneyed expression." This leaves wide open the question, trite or hackneyed to whom? Language is full of stock phrases, many of which are indispensable, or at least not replaceable without going the long way around. The expressions that draw scorn as clichés, however, are generally those that attempt a special effect—usually drama or humor. Whether a particular expression is regarded as a cliché depends upon the discrimination of the regarder. A good way to acquire an acute and extensive awareness of clichés is to read Frank Sullivan's reports from his cliché expert, Magnus Arbuthnot, as set down in such books as *A Pearl in Every Oyster, A Rock in Every Snowball,* and *The Night the Old Nostalgia Burned Down.*

Q—Why, Mr. Arbuthnot, what on earth are you doing here?
A—I am playing hooky from my mentor, Frank Sullivan, that witty man of letters who made me what I am today. I used to be a newspaperman myself, you know.
Q—Felt impelled to return to the scene of the crime, eh? Does Mr. Sullivan know about your background as a newsman?

A.—He considered it my finest qualification when he hired me as cliché expert.

Q—Ah, yes. Well, to work. Shall we inaugurate the interview?

A—I'd rather you didn't swipe my stuff. But let's launch it.

Q—Theft is a serious charge, Mr. Arbuthnot. And incidentally, charges, in the press, are always . . .

A—Hurled.

Q—To be sure. I would prefer *made*, but then newspaper readers can seldom be choosers. Now, would you tell me . . .

A—Sorry to interrupt, but as a newsman, I never *told*. Always *advised*.

Q—Thank you. I suppose you claimed your sources were authoritative?

A—*Claimed*, yes. Seldom *asserted*. Often *contended*, though.

Q—Indeed. How has your health been?

A—I'm in the pink of condition now, although I suffered a leg fracture in a mishap a year ago.

Q—You mean your leg was broken in an accident?

A—You heard me. I also sustained some lacerations, contusions, and abrasions, but as I said, I'm O.K. now.

Q—Glad to hear it. That you're O.K., I mean. What about the time thieves broke into your apartment?

A—The place was a shambles. The marauders made their getaway with upwards of $500.

Q—Too bad. What do you do for amusement?

A—Oh, I witness a ball game now and then. They hiked the admission charge recently, but attendance has been boosted in spite of it.

Q—Do you expect to buy a car when the new models are out?

A—I anticipate that I will secure one, yes. I am anxious to see them unveiled.

Q—I'd like to buy—I mean secure—one myself. But I wish the dealers would slash their prices.

A—You're learning. If you keep at it, you'll be able to turn plain English into journalese promptly.

Q—You mean *on time?*

A—No, I mean *promptly*. At once.

Q—About your job as a cliché expert—does it pay?

A—You mean, is it lucrative? Well, it pays well enough.

Q—What did you do before you were a newspaperman?
A—Well, prior to that time, I had no visible means of support, although I was a genial host. After I inked the pact with Mr. Sullivan, I really hit my stride. Although I am famous, I have been described as quiet and unassuming.
Q—Are you easily embarrassed?
A—Well, I am red-faced when I am beaten to the cliché.
Q—It was very good of you to take this time out for us, Mr. Arbuthnot. Clichés must be the lifeblood and, paradoxically, at the same time the *rigor mortis* of newswriting.
A—You can say *that* again.

The castigation of redundancy and clichés often seems like a hopeless exercise. Indeed, faint-hearted critics of those faults regularly conclude that attempts to dislodge them are wasted effort. In the large sense, these defeatists are probably right. There is no reason to hope that the noxiousness of clichés and redundancy can be impressed on any substantial number of people. This problem comes down to a matter of taste. Taste can be cultivated, certainly, but it seems unlikely that the capacity for discrimination can be implanted where it does not exist.

Ill-read and dull-witted writers will always be proud of having picked up expressions that the finer-grained despise. Even on the upper levels of ability, opinions will differ as to whether a particular expression is overworked. George Orwell once fiercely proposed that a writer should rigorously excise from his work every turn of phrase he did not invent himself. This may be going too far. Writing that contained nothing familiar or at least recognizable in this respect might well leave the reader intolerably ill at ease. In any event, no writing exists that does not contain clichés by one standard or another. This state of affairs was once described in verse:

> If you scorn what is trite
> I warn you, go slow,
> For one man's cliché
> Is another's *bon mot*.

Cliché is often redundantly qualified by *old, usual* ("the usual parting clichés"). Conceivably there are old and new clichés, but *old* is superfluous unless clichés are being differentiated on the basis of their age.

client Applies to the customers of lawyers, particularly, and by extension to those of other professionals who tender their services for fees. Not appropriate for doctors, who have *patients*. In other connections, where the *quid pro quo* is goods or something less specialized than professional service, *client* may sound highfalutin.

climactic, climatic *Climactic* refers to *climax*, *climatic* to *climate*. "*Climatic* conditions are ideal in California"; "That is the *climactic* scene in the play."

close (closed) corporation Both forms are correct.

close to A gaucherie for *nearly* or *almost:* "Close to 750 delegates are expected to attend the convention"; "They seek to lure close to a million people." *nearly*.

cloud no bigger . . . See *Misquotation*.

clue, clew *Clue* is predominant in the sense for which the words are interchangeable (*piece of evidence*).

co- Usually solid as a prefix: *coauthor, coequal, coeducation, corespondent,* etc.; *co-operate, co-ordinate* are sometimes hyphenated, but the tendency is to set them solid, too.

   Co in the sense of *associate* is sometimes distinguished from its other senses by being saddled with the hyphen. This leads to *coextensive, coexist,* but *co-producer, co-signer*. The distinction seems worthless, however, as long as *coproducer* and *cosigner* are understandable at sight. Some deem the hyphen necessary to distinguish *correspondent* from *corespondent*, but Webster does not.

coal oil See *paraffin; kerosene.*

coed Just as *campus* (which see) is now applied to high schools, so *coed* is applied to high-school girls.

cohort *Cohort* enjoys considerable vogue as a synonym for *colleague, associate,* or *companion,* but careful writers avoid it in this sense. In the Roman army a cohort was one of the ten divisions of a legion, and in modern usage the word means a large band of people. *A Dictionary of Contemporary American Usage* speculates that the misuse in application to a single person is based on a false analogy with *co-worker*.

collation   See *banquet.*

collective   In the sense under consideration here, what Fowler might have stigmatized as a vogue word: "The people at this haberdashery keep their collective ear tuned to what men want to wear." The users of it apparently are eager to flaunt their learning, for they are dimly aware that *collective* is a technicality of grammar, applied to words that denote a group: *jury, crowd.* From there they go on to fashion a literary trick they hope is cute. The examples to be cited should show that the use of the word in this way is unnecessary, absurd, or both.

"The New York Housing Authority is no doubt laughing up its collective sleeve." Meaningless. The members of the authority may be laughing up their several sleeves, but it is hard to imagine a sleeve that sleeves them all.

"The 389 men of the customs staff resigned themselves collectively last week to days loud with questioning." Superfluous and meaningless.

"An unprepared American public and a government almost equally bewildered rubbed their collective eyes." Superfluous and meaningless.

"Local experts merely cocked their collective eyebrow at the prediction." Preposterous.

"Then they had to defend their ideas before the committee, which seemed to have its tongue in its collective cheek." How a collective cheek without a collective tongue?

"In the auditorium we could hear the audience whistling and stamping its collective feet." The collect for today is: Abstain from such sleazy tricks as using *collective* in the ways illustrated.

COLLECTIVES   It is written, in the apocrypha of journalism, that a certain editor deemed the word *news* to be plural. This was a curse and an abomination to his staff, but being wage-earners and dependent on him, they held their peace. And it came to pass that one day he sent forth a scribe to a far city, where great tidings were awaited.

But many hours passed and there was no word, and this same editor chafed in his impatience. At length he dispatched a message saying, "Are there any news?"

And lo, the scribe was strained beyond endurance, and gnashing his teeth, he answered straightway, "Not a single new."

That editor is probably dead, if he ever lived, but his intransigent and not altogether reasonable spirit lives on in many today who insist that words like *couple, group,* and *team* are invariably singular. This leads to such sentences as "The couple is considered the best performers of Shakespeare on the New York stage"; "The group has been discussing the problem among themselves"; and "The team that wins the game will have their names engraved on the cup."

The way out of this trap is embarrassingly easy. The general principle is one that will show the way out of other quandaries: Don't adopt any rule on hearsay; make sure it has some basis in usage, grammar, and common sense. Whatever rules you do adopt, don't follow out the window. Words like *couple, group, team* and other collectives, including *crowd, committee, class, jury, herd,* and *number,* are either singlar or plural according to the way they are used. *Number,* perhaps the most frequently used, has its own rule of thumb: preceded by *a,* it is plural; preceded by *the,* it is singular.

Examples of proper usage are "The handful of faithful *were* well rewarded" (*was* would make that devoted handful seem squeezed into a fistful); "A score *were* injured in the wreck" (the singular is patently absurd here); "The crowd *was* dispersed"; "The crowd *were* waving their programs"; "The number of rooms *was* too small"; "A number of us *are* going going on a picnic."

Common sense, that uncommon attribute, will show the way. Don't strain to put on paper something you would not naturally say. This principle ought to take you blindfold through a sentence like "An ever increasing number of students spend their first two years in junior college," which sounds fine and is correct as it stands, but may lead you astray if you pick it apart.

It is well to be consistent. If you say "the team *is*" don't use *their* as a reference, at least in writing; say *its. Their* in this construction is condoned in talking, however.

The words *couple* and *pair,* without which the society pages would have to go out of business, deserve additional mention. In reference to a man and a woman, *couple* should always take a plural verb. Not even marriage should extinguish individuality to the extent of justifying reference to two people as one. Sentences like "The couple will spend *its* honeymoon in the Bahamas" are preposterous. See also *Subject-Verb Agreement.*

collide, collision   A moving object may collide with a stationary one; Webster cites as an illustration *waves colliding with the* *rocks.* If two (or more) things are said to collide, however, both or all must be in motion. A moving automobile may collide with a parked one, but two cars that collide must both be moving. *Collision* (unlike *collide*) is restricted to the impact of moving things; the term would not apply to the moving car and the parked one.

COLLOQUIALISMS If the admonitions we often hear were scrupulously and literally followed, much of what we read would sound like a cross between a mayor's proclamation and a frosty exchange of courtesies between ambassadors. The reason is the distinct and deplorable tendency favoring stuffy writing. The admonishers wouldn't want to hear it put that way, of course. They would be likely to say that they prefer a formal tone of expression, or that they want to encourage dignity.

This attitude is nothing more nor less than a facet of the pomposity that has afflicted writing since the Year One. The professorial, textbook style is repellent wherever it is encountered. Reviewers apologize for books that are pedantically written but otherwise have merit.

Stuffiness is especially repellent in news reportage. The news is all narrative, and narrative that isn't breezy is hard going. News situations, in general, are repetitious enough in their outlines. The reader should not be bored even more by starchy prose.

Now, this subject has endless ramifications, and this disquisition will be narrowed down to one aspect of it, namely, the old-maidish alarm caused by words identified as colloquialisms. To judge by the fright they create, colloquialisms may be less acceptable to some people than slang, vulgarisms, or obscenity. There is good reason to believe that most of these people simply do not know what *colloquial* means. The fine print in the front end of *Webster's New International Dictionary* (Second Edition) said on this subject:

> It is unfortunate that with some the term *colloquial* has somewhat fallen into disrepute, the impression having gained ground that a word marked "Colloquial" in a dictionary or similar work, is thereby condemned as not in the best use.

This became so well recognized that recent editions of some dictionaries avoid the term *colloquial* altogether in favor of *informal* or *familiar*. The new Third Edition of Webster does not use the label *colloquial* nor any equivalent; the editors hold that what is colloquial is standard.

Colloquial means *conversational* or *informal*. The opposite of *informal* is *formal*, and colloquialisms are sometimes said to be appropriate in informal writing, among other places, but not in formal written discourse.

Well, what is formal written discourse, anyway? Proclamations and diplomatic communications, turgid and often laughable in their choice of language, surely come under this heading. So do legal documents, about whose pomposity even lawyers are growing uneasy, to judge from indictments of legal lingo in bar-association journals. But come now, do we want communicative writing of any kind to be bracketed with dull stuff like this? Formal prose of every description is reached by the same road, one marked NO COLLOQUIALISMS.

We have no business shunning the conversational or the informal, unless we also want to drive off the reader. Even the academician turns with a sigh of relief from the mealy prose out of which he grinds his daily bread to something written with the comfort and interest of the reader in mind.

collusion Not to be confused with *cooperation, collaboration, concert,* all of which neutrally refer to joint action; *collusion* denotes a fraudulent or dishonest purpose.

COLON There is a widespread idea that what follows a colon should start with a capital letter when it comprises a complete sentence. There is no basis for this. "The box was full of weapons: knives, guns, and clubs"; "His favorite principle was: know the rules, so that you may violate them wisely."

"Members of the committee are: Jane Doe, Oscar Zilch, Perry Moore, and Lucinda Knight." Why the colon after *are,* any more than in "I am: Oscar Zilch," since the constructions are identical? It seems likely that the use of the colon in sentences like the example has grown out of the rule, often loosely understood, that a colon is used to introduce a series— but *not* if the series immediately follows the verb, as in the example. A series, to take a colon, should form an appositive: "Members of the committee are all students: Jane Doe, Oscar Zilch, Perry Moore, and Lucinda Knight." The colon balances off (a) *students,* and (b) the names.

A dash or comma would be possible in place of the colon in this last construction. One of them surely is necessary to make the sentence understandable. The colon may be removed, on the other hand, from the first example without loss. The simplest rule to cover this situation will cover many another as well: Don't put in anything you can do without.

colored   See *Negro*.

combine   A combination of persons or interests; the term, however, should be used guardedly, for it may have an unsavory connotation.

combine together   A redundancy; *combine*.

COMBINING WORDS   See *back yard*.

come of age   "He will become of age next year." The idiom is *come of age,* not *become*.

comic, comical   In general, what is comic is funny with the intention of being so; what is comical is funny whether or not that is the intention. Consequently *comical* is often derisive. The uses tend to overlap, however, and *comic* often displaces *comical* in its strict sense.

COMMA

Superfluous commas   Hostility toward the comma is rampant these days. This attitude is part of a revolt against Victorian diction that ignores all the changes in the language since 1900. But the usual bald adjuration, "Use the comma sparingly," is about as good advice by itself as "Use the letter *s* sparingly," which might lead to *succes, misive,* and *imposible*. Pick an elderly classic off the shelf, or turn the discolored pages of a fifty-year-old magazine, and you will quickly find what look like superfluous commas to today's eyes. Some of them precede *that*. Others set off adverbs, which we seem to find more assimilable than our forebears did.

Let us lift a couple of examples bodily from *The King's English* (Fowler): "Yet there, too, we find, that character has its problems to solve." Meredith.

"We know, that, in the individual man, consciousness grows." Huxley.

Many would remove all the commas from both these sentences. An examination of current writing shows that commas are more often omitted when required than used when unnecessary; the comma-haters are barking up the wrong tree.

Let us consider a couple of instances in which commas *are* used unnecessarily. One of these is in mistaking ordinary adverbs, which do not need to be set off, for parenthetical elements, which do. Here are some examples of this: "The farm laborer could not start his car but, apparently, a car thief could" and "Yesterday, he drove to the city." Writers who use such commas are probably misled by the accepted (but not invariable) practice of setting off such interruptives as *of course, therefore,* and *however.*

Commas and Adjectives Another superfluous use of commas is in separation of adjectives that apply cumulatively, rather than separately. Example: "After a hard, second look . . ." This was not a look that was second and, as a separate idea, also hard, but rather a second look that was hard. The mistaken comma after *hard* makes the word apply to *look* alone and not to *second.* The same reasoning fits *balky, old sultan* and *two, short, gloomy acts* (correct: *balky old sultan; two short, gloomy acts*).

A little thought—but not much—is required to differentiate these constructions from *a hot, dusty road* (a road that is hot and also dusty) and *a short, exciting chase* (a chase that is short and also exciting). But how can we tell for certain, especially in doubtful cases, whether to use the comma to separate adjectives? Well, the comma should be easily interchangeable with the word *and.* If not, it is out of place. Compare *hard and second look,* which is impossible, with *hot and dusty road,* which sounds acceptable, indicating that the comma was called for.

Yet the comma may be omitted from any series of adjectives preceding a noun without causing any damage, and this practice seems to be gaining: *a hot dusty road, a short exciting chase.* At any rate, commas are better left out of such constructions than used where they don't belong.

One-Legged Comma Some of us, when confronted with the question whether an element should be set off, want to have it both ways. To be set off, of course, the element must have a comma at both ends—like the parenthetical *of course* in this sentence. (Or, with one comma, the element must be at the beginning or end of the sentence, which amounts to the same thing.)

Some solve the problem by placing the comma at one end of the clause or phrase and leaving it off the other. This brings about the grammatical infirmity that might be called the one-legged comma. A pathetic offspring of indecision and ignorance, it is limping its way across more and more pages.

The simplest and most frequent example of the one-legged comma occurs with the prepositional identifying phrase: "Judge George Buck of Erskine County, signed the restraining order." This should be either "Judge George Buck, of Erskine County, signed . . ." or "Judge George Buck of Erskine County signed . . ." The use of commas in this construction is old-fashioned, and generally the no-comma version is considered preferable. The same principle applies to such phrases as "Richard R. Roe of the Foreign Affairs Committee" and "J. David Nelson of *The New York Times*." (For an exception see *Obituaries*.)

Let us look at some cases of one-leggedness where there should be two commas or none. The place where another comma belongs is indicated in each example by a pair of brackets. Either a comma should be placed there or the other one should be omitted, as the writer prefers.

"Severe storms [ ] accompanied by hailstones up to three-quarters of an inch in diameter, pounded western Texas."

"A 47-year-old man [ ] who had just been released from jail after serving a term for drunkenness, was found burned to death beside a fire."

"This, obviously [ ] was a planned diversionary movement."

"Committee members [ ] who had feared White House suppression of the report, were jubilant." This example is not as freely a matter of choice between two commas and none; the decision depends on whether the clause is restrictive or nonrestrictive. With commas (nonrestrictive), the sentence would say all the committee members had feared suppression; without (restrictive), that only those who had feared suppression were jubilant. Probably the nonrestrictive sense was meant.

Now for examples in which two commas, and no less, are necessary:

"All New Orleans schools were closed as a precaution but the storm, bringing winds of 64 miles per hour [ ] passed the city without causing much damage." A comma is necessary, of course, to mark the other end of the participial modifier. While we're at it, a comma before *but,* to separate coordinate clauses, would do no harm but is not essential.

"Dr. Manlio Brosio, Italian ambassador to Britain [ ] flew to Rome yesterday." A comma should mark the other end of the appositive phrase. The same is true of "Joseph Anderson, a carpenter [ ] of 1843 Weyburn Place."

Finally, a few examples that would be better with no comma at all:

"A corporation, which is unique in the rubber industry has been formed." Placing a comma after *corporation* suggests a nonrestrictive clause, which would mean that corporations hitherto have been unknown in the rubber industry. Consistency would require a comma after *industry*. But this writer meant that the corporation he was writing about was unique within the industry, and he would better have expressed this by leaving out *which is* as well as the comma: "A corporation unique in the rubber industry has been formed."

"A gray-haired man in a brown hunting shirt, jumped into the barricade." Presumably the comma set off, or half sets off, the phrase *in a brown hunting shirt,* but such prepositional modifiers do not take commas.

"A few lawgivers, themselves, call it the biggest boondoggle in Washington history." Commas around reflexive pronouns (those ending in *self* or *selves*) are excessive.

False Linkage The tendency to spare the comma may spoil the sentence, as we have noted. Another manifestation of this is what might be (and probably has been) called false linkage. That is, by omission of the comma, elements that should be separated are unintentionally joined.

"No rain is expected for tonight [ ] and tomorrow the high temperature is expected to be between 70 and 75 degrees." The reader must retrace his steps in the middle of the sentence because at first the prediction of no rain seems to cover tomorrow as well as tonight. The omission of the comma might be defended on the ground that a comma is unnecessary between coordinate clauses. But this principle does not hold unless the sentence is clearly understandable without it. Smoothness requires "No rain is predicted for tonight, and tomorrow . . ."

Generally, the comma should be used between coordinate clauses unless they are very short. Even then, clarity of sense should govern. "Rain will fall and wind will blow" gets along all right without one, but "He was a man of action [ ] and deeds interested him more than words" does not. Here are some commaless culls:

"The Democrats are counting on regaining rural votes that went to the Republicans last year [ ] and the committee is working to that end."

"He said military aid should not be given countries able to

provide for their own defense [ ] and economic aid in the guise of military assistance should be ruled out."

"The weather in Asia was unusually favorable for production [ ] and growing conditions in India and Pakistan were the best in many years."

False linkage and confused meaning can also result from failure to set off a clause that interrupts: "The guards and prisoners who refused to join in the break were tied and left in the fields." No, there were no guards who *consented* to join in the break. What was meant is this: "The guards, and prisoners who refused to join in the break, were tied . . ."

Here's an oddity: "He has two grown daughters and a son at West Point." Co-education has not really been adopted by the military academy. This is really another instance of co-ordinate clauses needing a comma separation, for ellipsis has squeezed out *he has* after *and. He has two grown daughters, and a son . . .*

Serial Comma Sometimes it seems as if we are running in circles. Years ago the grammars and the schoolmarms prescribed the comma before the last item in a series: "A press is a maze of gears, shafts, cams, and levers." For a long time newspapers resisted the use of the comma in this position, and finally the grammarians and pedagogues gave in.

And now that the battle is won we have a noticeable trend to restore the final comma. The point of the campaign against it, like that of many another prejudice, has always seemed dubious. It is true that usually the meaning is unaffected by the absence of the final comma, but now and then that comma is essential. What happens, of course, after its use has been discouraged is that it is left out when required as well as when it is not.

This may explain the tendency toward its restoration. Just to show that there *are* instances requiring the final comma, consider: "They had brown, green, gray and blue eyes." *Gray eyes and blue eyes* is meant, but *gray-and-blue eyes* is what may be understood without the comma.

Retention of the serial comma is recommended because this removes the necessity for deciding whether it is essential to the meaning.

The last adjective in a series should never be separated by a comma from the noun it modifies: "It was an expurgated, declassified [,] speech."

Most of the trouble with serial elements grows out of the

confusion of one series with another; or, to put it another way, the failure to recognize where one series ends and another begins.

"Voters will go to the polls Tuesday to elect four city councilmen, three school board members, to decide on eight charter amendments and three special propositions." We have here two different groupings, and they would be more readably presented "to elect four city councilmen and three school board members, and to decide on . . ."

When apparently mixed constructions like this are not unconscious, they are probably imitations of the telegraphic style affected by the news magazines, notably *Time,* in sentences like "New construction techniques added strength, durability, sharply reduced costs." Neither this nor the example preceding is either unintelligible or misleading. But a non-*Time* disciple would probably write "New construction techniques added strength and durability, and sharply reduced costs." The second version seems less rocky and easier to follow. This may be because the condensed treatment has not caught on widely, and wherever it appears it is conspicuous.

Nouns of Address   These should be set off: "Johnny says: 'I'd like to take photography Mr. Counselor.'" *photography, Mr. C.*

Comma After Conjunctions   Some of those who neglect the comma when it is needed are fond of slipping it in after conjunctions, especially *and, but, so,* and *or.* There is no reason for this. Examples: "They have found it pays, and, we have too"; "Money may not make you happy, but, it will enable you to be miserable in comfort." *and we have; but it will.*

Don't be confused by sentences in which a comma legitimately falls after the conjunction because it is setting off a parenthetical element, as in "They have found it pays, and, *I must admit,* we have too." Don't be misled, either, by sentences that start with *and, but, so,* etc. This construction is common in informal writing, and informal writing ought to be commoner than it is. But a conjunction is still a conjunction, no matter how you slice the sentence. So forget the commas in "And, I took him up on it" or "But, the cork wouldn't come out of the bottle" or "So, we took the train instead."

In speech, *and, but, so* at the beginning of a sentence are often stressed, but this stress is not indicated by the comma, which denotes a pause.

Adverbs and Commas   Adverbs usually are no longer set off by commas. When they are, the writing tends to sound old-

95

fashioned. In the examples, the bracketed commas are excessive. They slow down the modern reader, who does not expect to have his adverbs served up singly on platters.

"There [,] he ogles pretty girls, bicycling to work."

"There is [,] also [,] a bespectacled chimpanzee in the cast."

"Collectively [,] these men represented the shifting balance of power."

"Now [,] it was the turn of the United States."

"Later [,] he rode without incident through the same streets."

"Yet [,] the farmers scratched out a bare existence."

"Soon [,] U.S. jets screamed through the mountain passes."

"Here [,] they are safe from enemies."

"Finally [,] the president took action."

"Yet [,] this [,] too [,] is important."

"Sometimes [,] I rode a donkey [,] but [,] mostly [,] I was afoot."

"This [,] probably [,] is less true in other parts of the country."

"In the machine shop [,] alone, 26 windows have been shot out."

"Catholics must accept papal pronouncements in matters of faith and morals [,] only. *only in matters of* would have been a better arrangement.

Commas are sometimes needed to set off adverbial phrases (as distinguished from single-word adverbs), but here they are often perversely neglected:

"During the three months while the office was vacant [ ] policy, including new programs, lay dormant." It is easy to see that the absence of the comma indicated by the brackets may cause the reader momentarily to take *vacant* as modifying *policy*.

"In the summer of 1958, Krupp and the other great Ruhr industrialists signed an agreement." The comma is all right but not indispensable.

"At the moment, the medical goal is cure or control of heart ailments." This comma is dispensable on the ground that the sentence would read smoothly without it.

Suspensive Modifier   The comma is desirable to set off a suspensive modifier. "Ancient Ostia is near, but not on the sea." Thoroughly ambiguous, and may easily be taken to mean that Ostia is near some place previously mentioned. Two commas are called for: "Ancient Ostia is near, but not on, the sea."

Comma with "But"   Qualifying modifiers with *but* need not be set off: "notables from neighboring, but friendly provinces." *neighboring but friendly.*

Comma with Dash   The comma in conjunction with the dash is extremely old-fashioned: "They jar the ear of some,—the soul of others." In modern American practice, doubling is not done, perhaps because it is not possible to sort out the effect of each punctuation mark. The example should have used the comma alone. If a dash is used to set off one end of a phrase, a dash (not a comma) should also be used at the other end: "Hoses were played on the structure—a wooden frame building of three stories [,] from all angles, but smoke rose stubbornly." The bracketed comma should have been a dash.

Separation of Subject and Verb   The separation of subject and verb by a comma is one of the commonest errors in print:

"A barefoot, tattered boy [,] leads two pet black goats down a concrete street."

"The conductor of a Toonerville Trolley bus [,] leans out the side and helps passengers aboard."

"In a broad policy speech before the Assembly, Lord Hume [,] assailed the concept as sterile."

Even when the subject is compound no comma should separate it from the verb:

"On July 5, *she and eight other American students* [,] set sail for Southampton aboard the *Neptunia.*"

Nor should the elements of a two-part subject be separated, as by the comma after *vote:* "The closeness of the popular vote [,] and the tiny margin by which key states were carried [,] have led to revised estimates of party strength." (The comma after *carried* is also superfluous.)

"This [,] and other factors [,] were discussed." Both commas are superfluous.

Commas are called for to separate modifiers following a subject (here, *negotiations*) but not after the last one:

"For the time being, the pending negotiations on Berlin, a nuclear test ban, and disarmament [,] are stalled."

"The story which followed [,] utilized a time-tested formula." This punctuation, which is very common, probably reflects confusion whether the clause *which followed* is restrictive or nonrestrictive. If it is restrictive—a fact that context would determine—there should be commas both before and after the clause. If it is nonrestrictive: "The story that followed utilized . . ." See also *Restrictive and Nonrestrictive Clauses.*

Comma for Period or Semicolon The comma should not displace the period or the semicolon; this fault is known among schoolmasters and hapless dunces as the comma splice: "German land investments have sent values rocketing in some areas, good farms of 200 acres now cost twice as much." . . . *some areas. Good farms . . .* or . . . *some areas; good farms . . .* In technical terms, a comma should not stand between independent clauses. See also *Appositives; Ellipsis; Restrictive and Nonrestrictive Clauses.*

COMMANDMENTS, SEQUENCE OF   A towel-company ad that appeared in a number of national magazines read: "Friend of ours in the hotel business received a conscience note enclosing a five-dollar bill the other day. 'I am an old lady with a Christian upbringing . . . don't know what possessed me, but when I left your nice hotel last week I broke the Seventh Commandment. Now I can't sleep nights. Please forgive me . . .' "

A critic of this ad commented: "O.K., lady. Far be it from me to cast the first stone."

His assumption that the Seventh Commandment is the one forbidding adultery was probably shared by millions. But this lady, whose title to ladyhood was clearer than may appear at first glance, evidently was reared in a faith in which the Seventh Commandment forbids stealing. (She had made off with a towel she admired, and was sending the money in to pay for it.)

For reasons clear only to a theologian, different faiths use different numbers for some of the commandments. To Catholics and Lutherans, the Sixth prohibits adultery and the Seventh theft, while to most other denominations the Seventh deals with adultery and the Eighth with theft, corresponding to the sequence in the King James Version of the Bible. Those who essay to quote scripture for their purposes are warned that reference to a commandment by number alone may not be enough, and may indeed be the broad road to perdition.

The methods of numbering were commented on in the May, 1957, issue of *Changing Times* as follows:

There are two ways of dividing Exodus 20:2-17 (and Deuteronomy 5:6-21) into a set of ten commandments. There is no doctrinal difference between these, and both cover precisely the same material—it's a matter of practice in the arrangement of that material.

The original Jewish arrangement, also used by almost all Protestant denominations, considers the First Commandment to be verses 2 and 3, '. . . . Thou shalt have no other Gods . . .'; the Second to be verses 4 through 6, 'Thou shalt not make unto thee any graven image . . .'; and the Tenth to be verse 17 in its entirety. In Roman Catholic and Lutheran practice, the injunction against idolatry is considered part of the First Commandment. This advances the numbering of the subsequent commandments. . . . Then the number ten is preserved by dividing verse 17 into a commandment against coveting thy neighbor's wife and one against coveting his worldly goods.

commence   Where *begin* or *start* will serve, *commence* has taken on an old-fashioned sound and harks back to more leisurely, spacious days.

commentate   The designation *commentator* has given rise, by the process known as back-formation, to the verb *commentate:* "Mrs. Jones will commentate on the fashions being shown." For that matter, it might well be *commentate the fashions* (omitting *on*) ; *Webster's Third Unabridged* lists the verb as transitive, and it must be admitted that this usage is common.

Objectors may hold that a commentator *comments*, and that *commentate* is both unnecessary and illegitimate. The *Oxford Universal Dictionary*, however, lists *commentate,* and what is more surprising, traces it back to 1859 in the sense at hand— long before radio and its commentators, to say nothing of television. The word is described as rare, though it is not so rare nowadays as its critics might wish. It must be conceded that we sense a difference between *comment* in its usual sense and what a commentator does. *Commentate* has risen to this occasion.

Commie   *Commie* for *Communist* sounds ridiculously friendly, especially when used, as it often is, by people who could not be more bitterly opposed to communism. Why should *Commie* sound friendly? Perhaps because the endings *y* and *ie* are characteristic of expressions that connote affection, and also of baby talk. Compare *dog* and *doggie, Bill* and *Billy.* Oddly, it seems that the same people who use *Commie* often mispronounce *Communist* as *Commonist,* rather than *Commyoonist.*

common sense, commonsense Two words as adjective and noun (*full of common sense*); solid as a modifier (*a commonsense decision*).

communicate, communication *Communicate* is a new pomposity for *tell*, and *communication* is an old one for *letter*. A. J. Liebling commented interestingly on the spread of these terms in connection with journalism: "Communication means simply getting any idea across and has no relation to truth. It is neutral . . . *Journalism* has a reference to what happens day by day, but communication can deal just as well with what has not happened, what the communicator wants to happen." The use of *communication* to describe what schools of journalism teach has coincided revealingly with their introduction of courses in advertising and public relations.

Communist, Socialist *Communist, Socialist,* and derivative terms give rise to confusion in the matter of capitalization. Analogies with *Democratic* and *Republican* may be helpful. There is no disagreement that *Democrat*(*ic*) and *Republican* should be capitalized in reference to the parties. Nor is there any indecision about lower-casing *democratic* and *republican* in their general, nonpartisan senses (*a democratic system; the republican form of government*).

But the analogy does not carry us all the way. Although a Republican is democratic, and a Democrat is a republican, in general, there is a sharp distinction between the partisan and the philosophic senses. But a Communist (party member) and a communist (theoretical) are hard to distinguish with the naked eye, and this is equally true of a Socialist as against a socialist.

The question usually raised is this: Should *Communist* and *Socialist* be reserved for party members, and *communist* and *socialist* be applied to nonparty members who are nevertheless believers in the principles? Some think so, and it is impossible to refute their reasoning. But it is also difficult to make such a distinction in a practical way. Often it is not possible to determine party membership; as a practical matter, the descriptives are seldom called into play except in reference to those whose affiliation has been established.

One rule of thumb that is widely used calls for capitalizing the forms *Communist* and *Socialist* and for lower-casing *communism* and *socialism*, arbitrarily and consistently. *a notorious*

Communist; the Communist Party; a Fabian Socialist; a Social-ist mayor; the communism of Marx; creeping socialism.

This generally works out to preserve the distinctions we have noted as between party membership and philosophy. Exceptions may occasionally be desirable, however, as in *communist philosophy* when the reference is to general theory rather than the party line.

Communistic is an alternative form of *Communist* as an adjective, just as *Socialistic* is an alternative form of *Socialist*. The shorter forms are tending to displace the longer.

A word of warning: If you call someone a Communist, you had better be prepared to prove it, because the term is libelous when misapplied. The designations *Republican* and *Democrat* are derogatory only in such places as Atlanta, Ga., with respect to the first, or San Marino, Calif., and Scarsdale, N.Y., with respect to the second.

a comparatively few   Not standard; *a comparative few* or *comparatively few*.

COMPARATIVES   See *Ad Lingo; Comparison of Adjectives.*

compare to, with; contrast   *Compare to* means *liken to* or *place in the same class*: "He *compared* me *to* a thief" means "He *likened* me *to* a thief." *Compare with* means *examine in relation to*: "He *compared* me *with* a thief" means "He set my qualities beside those of a thief, to show either similarities or differences." This distinction is even more useless than some others that are fancied by purists, however, because the senses overlap. As Perrin notes, in the common construction with the past tense, *with* and *to* are used indiscriminately, and it may as well be recognized that *compare with* and *compare to* no longer convey reliably distinctive meanings. For practical purposes, it may be assumed that both *compare with* and *compare to* will be taken to mean *note differences or similarities or both*. When unlikeness is pointed out, *contrast* is generally used: "The paintings were contrasted with those of an amateur."

COMPARISON OF ADJECTIVES   Strictly, forms like *better, richer, smarter* (comparative adjectives) are used for comparing two things, and *best, richest, smartest* (the superlative forms) are used for comparing three or more. This nicety tends to be disregarded, however, and the superlatives are used indifferently in both circumstances: *The best* (*richest, smartest*) of the two. This gives the purist apoplexy; he insists it should be *The better* (*richer, smarter*). *Of the two* is then unnecessary, he reasons, because the comparative forms themselves imply two.

The distinguished authority C. C. Fries says, in *American English Grammar*, "The use of the superlative rather than the comparative for two, thus ignoring a dual as distinct from a plural, is a fact of standard English usage and not a characteristic of vulgar English."

Fowler permitted himself to say (of *dinghy* vs. *dinghey*), "The first is best"—not *the better*, as Fowler's self-appointed betters would insist. See also *Ad Lingo* for comparatives used in an absolute sense.

compatible, -ibility   Sometimes misspelled *compata-*.

compendium   Sounds all-embracing and is often used as if it were, but it is not; a compendium is a brief compilation, abridgment, or abstract.

competence, -cy   Interchangeable in the sense of *ability* though *competence* predominates.

compile   Not the equivalent of *write* or *compose*. To compile is simply to gather together or assemble; compiling is what the anthologist does. To say of a man who has written a book that he compiled it is to insult him.

complacent, complaisant   The first means *self-satisfied*, the second *eager to please*.

complected   Not good usage for *complexioned*: "A dark-*complexioned* [not *complected*] man."

complement, compliment   To complement is to complete or fill out; to compliment is to praise. "The jacket complements her ensemble"; "She was often complimented on her taste in clothes."

completely destroyed   See *totally destroyed*.

compose, comprise, consist of   The choice among these expressions causes hesitation. In the sense at hand, namely, *be made* *up of*, there is nothing much to choose from. *Comprised of* is a mistake by analogy with *composed of*. *Comprise* means include or embrace, and does not take *of*. *Webster's Dictionary of Synonyms* offers as an example of correct use "The district *comprises* three counties and part of a fourth." The temptation to write "The district is comprised of. . ." should be resisted, for the whole comprises the parts, and not the reverse. Many will consider "The district *is made up of, consists of,* or *is formed by*" plainer language, and thus more desirable, than *comprises*.

COMPOUND MODIFIERS See *Hyphens*.

COMPOUND NOUNS See *Hyphens; Plurals*.

COMPOUND VERBS (DIVIDED) See *Division of Compound Verbs* under *Verbs*.

concede See *Attribution*.

concert, recital *Concert,* by derivation, implies a performance by a group, whereas a recital is a performance by a soloist. The distinction is generally observed, although *concert* is sometimes applied to what are technically recitals without arousing public indignation. A performance by an orchestra, however, is never referred to as a recital.

concertize Sometimes aspersed, but in good standing; there is no concise substitute. See also *-ise, -ize*.

conclave Usually a journalese variant for *convention*. It is superstition, however, that the word necessarily denotes a secret or private gathering, and that it is not equivalent to *convention* or *conference*.

conclude Unidiomatic followed by an infinitive: "The citizens' committee concluded to file a separate report." *decided to;* or *concluded that it would*.

concrete See *cement, concrete*.

concretize Standard, although like *finalize* it has the sound of gobbledygook, where it may have originated.

condemn   Strong meat; it is close enough to *damn* that the linkage should be kept firmly in mind. The usual error is to use it as a synonym for *criticize* or *blame*. The writer of a letter of recommendation said, for example, that he did not feel the subject should be condemned for having changed jobs, and made his beneficiary cringe.

condition   *Condition* in *heart condition, lung condition* is a faceless euphemism for *disease* or *ailment*. Every heart has some condition, healthy or otherwise.

condom   Almost universally mispronounced cundrum, and consequently often thus spelled. The device, incidentally, takes its name from its reputed inventor, an 18th-century English physician.

confess to   Too often people confess *to* their misdeeds, instead of simply confessing them. The use of *confess to* produces some striking gaucheries: "Joan Crawford and Phil Terry also confessed failure to their marriage." From some backwoods weekly? Not at all; this appeared in a leading newsmagazine— a frontwoods weekly, one might say. *Confess to* appears to have encouraged, by analogy, *admit to*: "Greene frankly admits to a youthful membership in the party"; "She admits to having been a brat as a child"; "He admits to a gourmet's interest in food." Fowler said *confess to* is idiomatic and *admit to* is not. Nevertheless, *to* is unnecessary with either *confess* or *admit,* and these constructions are usually found in diseased contexts.

conform   Takes either *to* or *with.*

congratulate   So widely mispronounced *congradulate* that the bastard version may be expected to creep into print, as indeed it does.

(the) Congress   See *the.*

Congressional Medal of Honor   A misnomer oftener applied than the correct designation (*Medal of Honor*) to the nation's highest military award. It is indeed, however, conferred by congressional action, which accounts for the error.

congressman   There is every reason why *congressman* should mean either *senator* or *representative,* and some insist that it does. A senator is so rarely referred to in this manner, however, that it may as well be conceded that usage has attached *congressman* irrevocably to representatives.

CONJUNCTIONS See *as, like; while; Comma and Conjunctions* (*and, but, so*) under *Comma.*

connexion British spelling, but it would be sensible if such forms were adopted in America.

consensus of opinion *Of opinion* is redundant with *consensus,* which, incidentally, is often misspelled *concensus.*

conservative It may be misleading to capitalize this term as a political descriptive in the United States, since it suggests a nonexistent national Conservative Party. Such parties have been organized within states, and when reference is made to a member of these, it should be explicit: *a member of New York's Conservative Party,* not *a Conservative.* See also *liberal.*

consider Let us consider *consider,* the breeder of a whole nest of peccadilloes. First, *as* after *consider* is not idiomatic. "He was considered as a coward" should be "He was *considered* a coward." This also applies to *termed.* The error probably comes from a mistaken analogy with *regard,* which properly takes *as:* "He was regarded as a bum."
"Unfortunately, too many editors and reporters nowadays consider official handouts *as* news" is ambiguous in a wry way. The complainant meant that what is not news is being treated as if it were, instead of being rejected. But he may be understood as regretting merely that handouts are getting consideration. *For* may be more explicit than *as* when *consider as* is used in the sense of *give consideration to;* "Steam was considered as the source of power" (but electricity was used).
Consider is often sloppily used in place of *deem, believe, think, feel, decide,* and the like, and it sometimes usurps the place of *regard as.* "The official imposed the ban because he considers the art work is obscure" and "The general considers the Russians will not provoke a showdown" really call for *believes* or *thinks.* (But *considers the art work obscure,* omitting *is,* is another cure.) "The office of public information does not consider that bias or distortion has been shown." *believe, feel, agree.*

"My mother's family was opposed to her marriage with my father, considering that he was not good enough for her." *Considering that* may easily be read in the sense of *because*, but the writer meant ". . . regarding him as not good enough for her." See *regard*.

"Naturally, if they can get it at that price, the Soviets will consider they have a bargain." Unidiomatic for *decide, conclude*, or *consider it a bargain*.

considerable, considerably The adjective (*considerable*) for the adverb (*considerably*) is not good usage: "He was considerable put out by the criticism." *considerably*.

consist in, of To *consist in* is to inhere or reside in: "The value of the advice *consists in* its honesty"; to consist *of* is to be made up, or composed, of: "The cake *consists of* flour, milk, eggs, and other ingredients." See also *compose, comprise*.

consistency is the hobgoblin . . . See *Misquotation*.

consistent, -ly Often misspelled *consistant, -ly*.

consummate Often misused as an adjective by music critics and as a verb by society writers. The more ecstatic kind of critic links *consummate* with *artistry*. *Consummate* in this sense means *perfect;* it is the kind of praise that should be too seldom bestowed to create the cliché that *consummate artistry* unquestionably is.

Since Nice Nellyness is the ruling spirit of the society page, it comes as a thunderbolt to read there, in an otherwise prim account of a wedding, that *the marriage was consummated*. Disaster perhaps justly lies in wait for the writer who picks up a phrase that sounds impressive and takes it for her own without making certain what it means. *Consummate* in this connection has to do with sexual intercourse; the consummation of a marriage is a legal consideration, not a subject for public comment.

Sometimes these felonies are compounded by spelling *consummate* with one *m*.

contact The fight against *contact* as both verb (I'll *contact* him") and noun ("George has some good *contacts* in that town") is unquestionably a losing one. Some years ago, *contact* as a verb was complained of as abominably overworked. It is a nice question whether this use has now subsided, or whether we are so used to seeing it we no longer particularly notice. *Contact,* strictly speaking, means *touch,* and in the sense at hand it is used to mean *get in touch with.* As the shortest distance between two points, *contact* in this sense will hardly be pushed aside. It has an inclusive meaning that none of the substitutes sometimes proposed can offer.

"In this event, the family physician is *contacted.*" *Called?* This is ambiguous for *telephoned* or *summoned,* and neither may fit. *Consulted* is possible, but not likely.

"Eleanor said her mother has not tried to *contact* her since her arrest." *Call?* This does not include *visit,* which *contact* does. *See* does not include *call. Reach* does not include *visit. Get in touch with* is always possible as a substitute. *Contact* as a verb can be avoided, and it is up to the writer to decide whether it is worthwhile. In deciding, he may as well keep in mind that *contact* as a verb has not fully emerged into the sunshine of complete acceptance, and is still partly in the shadow of its commercial origin. *Contact* as a noun ("He made a number of useful *contacts* on the trip") is hardly open to aspersion any longer.

contagious Sometimes misspelled *contageous.*

contemptible, contemptuous These deserve to be told apart, as much as *infer* and *imply.* What is contemptible is deserving of contempt (*a contemptible evasion*); *contemptuous* applies to the person or act expressing contempt (*a contemptuous smile*).

contend An unexplainable variant for *say, assert,* and the like, when used, as it often is, of statements with which no disagreement is indicated. "When the average man takes his daily shave, he removes almost as much skin as hair, a dermatologist contends." *reports, explains, says.*

"Mrs. Jessie Cartwright contends housewives have forgotten how to wash these items." *says, believes, concludes.*

contiguous Although *contiguous* is sometimes admitted in a looser sense, it might be restricted to what touches: "California and Nevada are *contiguous.*" *Adjacent* and *adjoining* are suitable in the senses *near to one another* or *side by side.*

continual, continuous Let us shed a tear for the erstwhile distinction between these words, which has faded into nothing, despite agonized efforts to keep it alive. Generally speaking, distinctions are a good thing, because they make for exactness. But first, the writer must intend the distinction, and next, the great body of readers must be aware of it.

Some distinctions have been lost because the words that once made them are so similar people have trouble telling them apart. There was a time when *continuous* was regarded as meaning *uninterrupted,* and *continual* as meaning what we now usually express by *intermittent. Continuous* and *continual* now are used interchangeably in the sense of "going on indefinitely, with or without interruption." Webster now cites each as the synonym of the other.

To convey the precise original sense of *continuous,* we are now safer to write *incessant;* and to convey the original sense of *continual,* as noted, we are likely to write *intermittent.* These substitutes are unmistakably recognizable for what they are intended to mean, which is more than can be said of *continual* and *continuous,* even if the writer has made his selection knowingly.

To help those intent on preserving the distinction, Theodore M. Bernstein of *The New York Times* has invented a mnemonic device: the *ous* of *continuous* may be regarded as standing for *one uninterrupted sequence.* But perhaps the mere need for such a device constitutes a final damnation. Curiously, instinct leads us to the right choice in tangible connections: we naturally say *a continuous rope, a continuous electrical conductor.* This may help in making the choice for what is intangible.

If any more need be said, let it be this: Margaret M. Bryant of Brooklyn College, writing in *Word Study,* cited statistics leading to the conclusion that *"continual* and *continuous* are now being employed interchangeably by even the literary writers."

continue on　A common redundancy; *continue* alone suffices.

CONTRACTIONS　The avoidance of contractions is an aspect of the fear of informality. The attitude toward them ranges, when it is hostile, from outright prohibition to discouragement "except when appropriate." Qualified discouragement would be all right except that experience shows it is usually interpreted as a general ban. Many of us lack confidence in our ability to decide when contractions *are* appropriate.

The objectionable use of contractions is actually all but nil.

Thus the bad breath blown upon them might as well be saved. Rudolf Flesch, in *The Art of Readable Writing*, came to this conclusion: "If you want to write informal English, the use of contractions is certainly essential."

A little girl who had to walk through a graveyard on her way home was asked, "Aren't you afraid?" After this question had gone through the hands of an editor whose mother had been frightened by a stylebook, however, it came out "Are you not afraid?" The headline on a feature story read: "It Is Official! June Was Hot!" Well, "It Is Official" is simply not idiomatic; many a reader will wonder what reason could be given for sidestepping "It's Official."

One can imagine the editor responsible for "Are you not afraid?" and "It Is Official" staidly announcing to his friends, upon being presented with an heir, "It is a boy!" This might prompt "Here is to you" as a toast in reply. But here is, or here's, hoping that all such follies will be forestalled by judicious acceptance of contractions.

The hook on the apostrophe indicating a contraction points to the left: *Forget 'em.* This is an academic matter on the typewriter and in some printing type faces in which the apostrophe points straight down.

contractual Often misspelled *contractural.*

contradict See *refute.*

contrast See *compare to, with; contrast.*

controversial ". . . we have changed the meaning of the word *controversial.* It now means something (or someone) about which we cannot afford to engage in controversy—virtually the opposite of the former meaning. Even for lawyers, controversy is made to sound like a disreputable thing, as this description suggests: 'His background has not prevented him from building a lucrative practice, mainly with respectable trade unions but with some controversial ones as clients.' "—Jacques Barzun, *House of Intellect.* See also *noncontroversial issue.*

contusions See *Technical Terms.*

converse See *reverse,* etc.

convert Not standard when used intransitively concerning religious conversion: "The actress was reared a Christian Scientist but converted to Judaism after she was an adult." *was converted.* See also *reconvert.*

convince   See *persuade, convince.*

cool, cooly, coolly   As an adjective applied to large sums of money (*a cool million*), *cool* has been under fire as hackneyed for at least 40 years. *Coolly* is predominant and preferable to *cooly.*

cooperate, co-operate, coöperate   The second and third forms are being discarded as nuisances. It used to be objected that the spelling *cooperate* would force the talker to pronounce the first two syllables as one, but in fact no one feels any such compulsion. See also *Diacritical Marks.*

coordinate, co-ordinate, coördinate   See *cooperate,* etc.

cop   Many anguished campaigns have been kept in motion against the use of *cop.* The idea is that more respect than is conveyed by the word should be shown to officers of the law. Newspapers, especially, have been enjoined to eschew the expression. Some do so, but even the rest are aware, certainly, that the term is not a reverential one. But as far as most newspapers are concerned, *cop* is just too handy a headline word to be resisted.

Many people are likely to boggle at the idea of paying any special respect to police officers, to the extent of banning a useful and generally accepted word. Language, in any event, can only reflect respect; it cannot create it. Though *cop* may be objected to as not showing respect, it does not show any particular disrespect, either. It does show familiarity, perhaps of a kind that many policemen like to think of as existing between themselves and the public. *Cop,* which is generally still regarded as slang, is prevalent enough so that it is well on the way to becoming standard. The term is traced by Simeon Potter in *Our Language* to "copper, one who *cops* or *caps* (Latin *capere,* 'to take')."

The late John Lardner, writing in the *New Yorker,* drew a distinction between *cop* and *copper.* The latter, he said, is invariably disparaging, and he speculated that objectors to *cop* are confusing it with *copper. Copper,* it is true, is favored by fugitives from justice. Some critics of *cop* hold that the term is the equivalent of *shyster* as applied to a lawyer, or of *quack* as applied to a doctor. This view has no real basis, however, for no question of competence or integrity is implied by its use.

Commenting on this subject, Hal Boyle of the Associated Press wrote in part:

"Cops don't like the average citizen to call them cops. But what do they call themselves when talking to other members of their profession? Cops! . . . What man in the long blue line doesn't take pride in being called 'a good cop'? What policeman can resent a big-eyed kid who looks up at him and says, 'When I grow up I want to be a cop just like you'? Any word can be good or bad, depending on the way it is said. People can be policed, but nobody can police a language."

The *Police Review,* a police force magazine in London, reported the British bobby prefers to be called a cop these days. *Bobby* was described as sounding a bit prissy. See also *officer*.

cope "Every company sent one girl representative. They all managed to cope without blushing." *Cope* without *with* and an object is correct, but so infrequent in modern usage it is likely to seem an error. The usual form is illustrated by "cope with the exhibit of pornography in the courtroom." This brings to mind the man who was asked whether he liked Kipling. "I don't know," he replied. "How do you kipple?"

copyreader See *Newspaper Terms*.

cord See *chord, cord*.

corespondent, correspondent A corespondent is one charged with adultery in a divorce case; the respondent is the one sued for divorce, and so the corespondent is the outer point of the triangle. A correspondent is one who sends information in writing—letters, dispatches, whatever. Hyphenating *co-respondent* is now old-fashioned.

corn The difference between American and British usage sometimes causes confusion. In America, corn is Indian corn (or maize); in Britain it is wheat or oats.

coronary See *heart attack*.

corps, corp *Corps* (pronounced *core*) as in *Corps of Army Engineers, corps of cadets* is often illiterately rendered *corp*, an expression that does not exist, except with a period as an abbreviation for *corporation.*

corpus delicti Often used in reference to the body of a victim of murder, but it does not really mean that at all. It is the evidence necessary to establish that a crime—not necessarily murder—has been committed.

couldn't care less The expression is exhausted from overwork.

council, counsel A council is a governing or consultative body (*city council; council of elders*). *Counsel* is advice (*good counsel is often ignored*) ; the designation of one who advises (*the defendant was represented by counsel*—in this case, a lawyer) ; or a verb meaning *to advise* (*we were counseled to change our plans*). "He preached a council of moderation." *counsel.*

councilor, counselor First, both words may be spelled with two *l*'s. A councilor is a member of a council, although sometimes the term is used as the title of an office without reference to a council. A counselor is one who counsels, or gives advice ; there are, among other common varieties, investment counselors, camp counselors, and student counselors. *Counselor* is also a term of address applied, usually by judges in a courtroom, to lawyers serving as counsel. Applied to a lawyer in other circumstances, it usually has a jocular tone. A *county council* is a governing body ; a *county counsel* is a legal adviser.

count noses As a means of ascertaining or reporting attendance, this method has its limitations, for it does not allow for the two-headed. Anyway, for a change it might be more interesting to count ears and divide by two. For unnecessary counting, see *Numbers.*

counter- Solid as a prefix : *counteraction, counterattack, counterproposal, counterrevolution,* etc.

counting See *Numbers; firstly.*

couple, couple of *Couple* is either singular or plural as the context demands. See *Collectives.* The omission of *of* after *couple* is slovenly : "Regan gave up a couple walks in the seventh inning," "a couple halfbacks," "a couple rounds." By way of analogy, no one writes "a pair aces" or "a team horses."

court litigation   Redundant. Litigation is inevitably associated with a court.

coveted   In writing of the Pulitzer prizes or any other award, writers should be enjoined, "Thou shalt not *covet*."

crack   Overdone as an adjective applied to a train, regiment, division, or whatever. As a clipped form of *wisecrack*, see *quip*.

crack down on   The frequency with which this expression is used in connection with enforcement of laws or rules is enough to make the thin-skinned crack up.

crackling   A favorite adjective when press associations are patting themselves on the back for a piece of reportage considered sparkling. This use is legitimate enough, though it might be kept in mind in this connection that sometimes what crackles is stiff.

craft   Both singular and plural in reference to vehicles and vessels. It is not standard to say "Both crafts were damaged 35 to 40 feet above the waterline." *craft*. Several *aircraft;* not *aircrafts*. But *arts and crafts*.

credulous, credible, creditable   Both *credulous* and *credible* have to do with belief; *credulous* applies always to people, and means *willing to believe*. It generally suggests simplemindedness. *Credible* means *believable, worthy of belief,* and applies usually to statements and the like, though it may apply to people: *The explanation was credible; a credible witness.*
 Creditable may be synonymous with *credible*, but it also has the sense of *worthy of credit, suitable, acceptable:* "The orchestra gave a creditable performance." In such contexts, *creditable* is the faint praise, like *adequate*, that damns.

criminally assaulted   A newspaper euphemism (like *attacked,* which see) for *sexually attacked* or *raped*. Any physical assault is criminal.

criterion, criterions, criteria   *Criterions* is acceptable as the plural; so is *criteria*, the pristine Latin form, but *criteria* should not be used in the singular: "This is the criteria that has been set up." *criterion*.

critical　As used of those who are laid up ("The patient is in critical condition") *critical* should be handled with care. It does not mean simply seriously ill, but in a state of crisis, or hovering between life and death. Criticisms of the word as often used in headlines ("'Auto Victim Critical'—and he has a right to be") are captious.

criticize, criticism　The terms have taken on a generally adverse coloration, and it is no use to argue, as some do, that they are properly used only in the neutral senses of *appraise* or *assess.* The context shows what is intended; music criticism, for example, may be favorable, faultfinding, or, in the usual case, both at once. Although this is generally understood, it does not prevent *criticism* from having a connotation of disfavor. At best, it produces an image of the critic as one who is hard to please. *Criticise* follows the British idiosyncrasy in spelling and may be considered affected in the U.S.

crotchety　That is, cranky; often misspelled *crochety.* It may help to remember that the word comes from *crotch,* not *crochet* (needlework), though the terms have a common origin in the idea of *hook.*

crumby, crummy　The preferable spelling of the slang term meaning *shoddy* is *crummy.* Inconsistently, a fellow held in low esteem is a *crumb* (not *crum*).

crystal　Sometimes misspelled *chrystal.*

cultivated　See *culture, cultured.*

culture, cultured　Everyone knows what is meant by culture in the general sense under consideration here—appreciation and cultivation of the arts. But the word has fallen under a certain amount of suspicion as implying a self-conscious and perhaps ostentatious effort. This connotation may have been encouraged by the heavy-handed dedication to culture that has characterized many Communist countries. Their idea of culture corresponds roughly with ours, but it has as a central feature the prescription by the upper levels of bureaucracy of what is acceptable culture, and the repression of artists whose productions do not fit the state's mold. We reject and even scorn the management of artistic expression in any field, knowing that what is worthwhile springs from inspiration, and that the surest way to mediocrity is by laying down mandatory guidelines for the artist.

Cultured as applied to a person has acquired an unfavorable connotation that reflects not so much on the described as on the describer, for the term is never used except with the intention of paying a compliment. *Refined* was once commonly used to convey the idea of education and breeding, but it is now quasi-humorous. *Cultured* may also suggest an essential crudity overlaid by a veneer of interest in artistic and intellectual matters—an interest maintained, that is, mainly for effect.

What then? It is observable that to put across the idea that would once have been given by *cultured*, people who choose their words carefully now tend to use *cultivated*, to which no shadow clings.

cum   The persistence of this Latin preposition, which means *with*, in phrases like "the vagaries of want-cum-debt creation" and "education-cum-football" is intellectual ostentation; indeed, such phrases have taken on a facetious overtone. Those who know no Latin may be confused by *cum*, and the rest enjoy no advantage from its use. Even by those who know what *cum* means, "the vagaries of want *accompanied by* debt creation" and "education *with* football" are worth consideration. The use of such foreign snippets in writing aimed at a wide audience is dubiously justifiable when they have exact English equivalents.

cumulative   See *accumulative, cumulative.*

currently   Like *presently* (which see), *at present,* and *now, currently* is unnecessary except to contrast the present with some other time.

custom, custom-built   The debasement of *custom* and *custom-built* can be blamed on the advertising gentry. It once meant "built to the specifications of the buyer" and still does, unless it appears in an ad, where everyone now realizes it dishonestly means "mass-produced, but having some pretensions, not necessarily justified, to quality." *Custom-built* and *custom* are generally misapplied in this way to automobiles and houses. See also *estate.*

cut, halftone   There is nothing wrong with using the terms within the publishing fields for *engraving*, but there is small excuse for their appearance in print aimed at a general audience, displacing *illustration, picture, photograph, drawing*, etc., as suits the occasion.

cut in half There have been bitter protests against *cut in half* (and its analogues, *saw, break*, etc., *in half*). The objectors argue that *cut in half* is illogical; make it *cut in halves*, they say, or state it otherwise, as *cut in two*. Logic, unfortunately, will not unsnarl tangled language, especially where idiom is entrenched. (Idiom, in a nutshell, is established, natural expression that defies logical or grammatical analysis.) *Half* lends itself to a number of other forms where any other fraction will not do: *half an apple* (but never *quarter an apple*). He who can swallow *half an apple* but chokes on *cut in half* is inconsistent; both are idioms. *Cut in half* is one of those cases in which the writer is free to avoid the expression if it offends him, but is on uncertain ground in criticizing its use by others.

cutlines See *Pictures*.

czar, tsar *Czar* now predominates.

—D—

dame The title is analogous to *sir* (which see) and thus may not properly be used with the last name alone (*Dame Sybil Reagan* or *Dame Sybil;* never *Dame Reagan*).

DANGLING PARTICIPLES
"Dear Sir:

We enclose herewith a statement of your account. Desiring to clear our books, will you kindly send us a check in settlement?"

The reply ran:
"Sirs:

You have been misinformed. I have no wish to clear your books."

This little exchange, adapted from an example in Fowler, neatly illustrates the answer to the question, When is a dangling participle? Or, more properly, When is a participle dangling?

To start at the very beginning, let us first settle another question: what is a participle? Elementary. A participle is a verb form usually ending in *ing* or *ed*, like *desiring* or *settled*, and used, as far as this discussion is concerned, as a modifier. The past participle, of which *settled* is an example, is sometimes formed irregularly, as in *born, seen,* and the like. Participles may also take auxiliaries: *having settled, being seen, having been born.* This does not exhaust the technical distinctions, by any means, but should be enough to give the idea.

Phrases containing participles and occurring at the beginnings of sentences usually modify the subject of the clause that follows. The trick in handling them correctly is to be sure that this subject *is* the element intended to be modified.

The fellow being dunned in Fowler's example, who was probably only a grammatical deadbeat, took his creditors literally and applied the force of *Desiring to clear our books* to *you.* Now, you may say, the scoundrel really knew better than that.

So he undoubtedly did. Dangling participles rarely confuse meaning. At the least, they cause the reader a moment of hesitation while he pairs up the modifier with the modified. At the worst, they create an absurd effect, making the writer sound like an ass and perhaps creating an opportunity like the one our deadbeat seized.

"In applying the brakes, the car skidded off the road." Power brakes are with us indeed, but even cars equipped with them do not apply their own.

"Born of a poor but proud Catholic family, few would have predicted greatness for young Konrad." But it was Konrad who was born, not *few,* as this sentence reads.

"Internationally known for its Tournament of Roses, selection of Pasadena as headquarters for the company was a natural choice." ". . . *Roses, Pasadena was a natural choice as headquarters for the company.*"

What is the cure for dangling? There is none, perhaps, except close attentiveness to what one is writing, which of course is more of a panacea than a specific. Like Indian Snake Oil, it will cure whatever ails you, including hyphenitis, comma coma, and disorders of the colon, as well as the dangles.

Bob Considine once quoted D. C. Claypoole, the newspaperman to whom George Washington confided his plans not to run again, as having written: "He received me kindly and after paying my respects to him desired me to take a seat near him."

Did George pay Claypoole's respects to himself, and if so, how was it managed? Well, that's what the man said, if not

117

what he meant, showing that the crazy, mixed-up participial phrase is not new to American prose.

Danglers that rest on an indefinite subject are not so objectionable, perhaps ("Reading recent speeches of Albanian officials, it is clear they embrace the full Communist line") but such constructions indicate lack of care or of sensitivity to structure by the writer. It is as easy and more exact to say "From speeches of Albanian officials, it is clear . . ." See also *Appositives.*

DASH   When dashes are used to set off a phrase for emphasis, care should be taken to put them in the right place. "The minister is giving too big—and too profitable a role—to private industry." The second dash belongs after *profitable,* not after *role; too big* and *too profitable* both modify *role: "The minister is giving too big—and too profitable—a role to private industry."*

The dash sometimes displaces the comma: "Although Scranton is still a depressed area because of the continuing decline in anthracite coal mining—such projects have provided more than 10,000 new jobs." *coal mining, such projects . . .* The dash creates too sharp a break here.

"Final election returns indicate that four incumbent city councilmen will return to office—three face runoffs and one was defeated." All tangled up; the four are not the three plus the one, as the dash suggests, but four others. Correct: ". . . *will return to office, three face runoffs, and one was defeated."*

Either the dash or the comma should be used at both ends of an element that is set off, not a dash at one end and a comma at the other: "Then—with his appeal matured by further experience, he will be ready for the national prize." Either *Then, with . . . experience, he . . .* or *Then—with . . . experience—he . . .*

dash to safety   A cliché.

data, datum   *Data* is technically the plural of *datum,* but this remains of interest only to Latinists. *Data* is almost invariably used as a collective with a singular verb: "The data is interesting but unreliable." Its use with a plural verb is still correct, of course, but unusual: "The data are mostly in the form of *percentages." Datum* is all but extinct.

DATELINES   See *Datelines* under *Time Elements.*

DAY OF THE WEEK See *Time Elements*.

de- Solid as a prefix: *decentralize, defoliate, deoxidize, desegregate, desalt,* etc. Sometimes hyphenated to prevent a doubled *e* (de-*emphasize,* de-*energize*) but the tendency is away from this.

de, du, la, le, van, von, zu, etc. It is common practice to lower-case such particles when they occur within a name (*Charles de Gaulle*) but to capitalize them when they stand first (*De Gaulle, Von Hohenzollern*). This is a matter of mechanical style, however, in which consistency is what counts; sometimes they are uniformly capitalized, sometimes uniformly lower-cased.

deadline See *Newspaper Terms*.

dear Campaigns have been mounted against the use of *dear* in the salutations of letters, especially those addressed to people with whom the writer is not on familiar terms or may even dislike. The objectors cannot reconcile the use of what they regard as a term of endearment for anyone not actually regarded with affection.

This is a case of wild misinterpretation; the *dear* in a salutation is a formality that lost all its warmth long ago. This is shown by the fact that when people want to convey affection they do not rely on the dried-out *dear* but instead say *dearest* or something else. The objections to *dear* have not caused any noticeable number of people to abandon the form, but they have caused some uncertainty among the ignorant and impressionable.

Dear (with a name, of course) is the casual, impersonal salutation; what is not understood by many is that *My Dear* is more formal, rather than more intimate or affectionate.

debut As a verb has a slangy sound. "The automobile industry debuts its new models in the fall." *introduces.* "Prohibition debuted last week south of the border." *began; made its debut.*

DECIMALS The form *.24 of an inch* (of rain, for example) is preferable to *.24 inches* as less liable to both misinterpretation and typographical error. The form *24 hundredths of an inch* is even less so. See also *Fractions*.

decimate The primary meaning is comparatively weak; the Latinist knows that it means to strike down one in ten (men), and he is shocked to see it used in the sense *destroy a large part of. Decimate*, like *mediocre* (which see), however, has grown muscles, and the stronger sense is recognized. The restricted, original meaning is so specialized that it is nearly useless today. Allowing the extended meaning, *decimate* is often used absurdly, as in "Some classrooms were nearly decimated by the student strike." *emptied.*

declare Often used as a random variant for *said*, but it has more force. See *Attribution.*

decline (comment, etc.) Journalese shorthand for *decline to comment:* "The student was courteous but he declined comment." *Decline* suggests *reject*, or refusal to accept something that has been offered, and the sense of the example is that comment was offered to him which he refused to accept. "Secretary Rusk refused comment on the conference." Refused to accept comment? No, refused to make it, i.e., *refused to comment.* "The Negro declined use of his name." *refused to allow his name to be used.*

defense, defence Some variants in spelling are conspicuously associated with geography, and this pair is an example. The first is American practice, the second British.

defend to the death See *Misquotation.*

defi What ever happened to *defi?* No front page used to be complete unless it had one being hurled. It looks as if there are fashions in headlinese, and as if some bromides wear out, only to be replaced by others. Or is it defiance itself that has gone out of style in an age of conformity?

DEFINING, NONDEFINING CLAUSES See *Restrictive and Nonrestrictive Clauses.*

definitely In the sense *certainly, indeed* ("The program has definitely been canceled") as opposed to its precise sense of *in a well-defined way* ("The boundary was definitely established on the final map") the word has a slangy tone. *Definitely* and *but definitely* for *yes* or *of course*, in reply to a question, are fads. *Definite, definitely* are sometimes misspelled *definate, definately.*

DEFINITIONS   See *Dictionaries*.

defy   Creates a ludicrous effect when inadvertently used in an infinitive construction. "Negroes defied National Guard troops to stage a demonstration that prompted 14 arrests." It was not the National Guard, but the Negroes, who staged the demonstration: *defied National Guard troops by staging*. See also *Infinitives of Purpose* under *Infinitives*.

degrees, honorary   See *Dr.*

Democrat, -ic   In recent years leaders of the Republican Party have drummed up a crusade to encourage the use of *Democrat* as an adjective, rather than *Democratic;* for example, *Democrat senators*. The object is primarily political, rather than linguistic. The sponsors of the crusade have explained that they fear *Democratic* suggests Democrats have a monopoly on the concept of democracy. The usage was first noticeably employed by a senator whose handling of language exhibited other peculiarities.

   This foible was delicately pinpointed in a *New Yorker* piece by Richard H. Rovere, who described how the writer of a letter being read before a congressional committee, "employing a well-known mannerism, had written of *Democrat senators*." The man reading the letter, Mr. Rovere recorded, "paused after *Democrat*, coughed a polite little cough, and said 'ick senators.'"

   Nobody should read any political pleading into this little lecture, because literateness ought to be as bipartisan as foreign policy. *Democrat senators* is no better English than *Republic senators* would be, and it is likely to leave the reader feeling a mixture of distaste and puzzlement.

   As for general acceptance, even by Republicans, this crusade has gone about as far as a snowball in hell. The reason has nothing to do with political implications but is based rather on the rocklike public resistance that always meets deliberate attempts to tamper with established forms, regardless of motive. An instinct of courtesy toward one's political opponents may figure here, however.

   Now, on top of all his other woes, the poor editor must decide whether quoted matter full of expressions like *Democrat Party*, planted there by Republicans, should be allowed to stand. If he does let them stand, he may incur the disdain of linguistically sensitive readers who have not heard of the crusade and will set them down to sloppy editing. But if he changes *Democrat* to *Democratic*, he may run the risk of meddling in editorial policy.

The capitalized forms (*Democrat, -ic*) should be reserved for references to the political party, the lower-case forms for references to democracy, the political system. Otherwise there is confusion.

demolished   See *totally destroyed.*

denier   Some terms that are freely used by advertisers are understood by hardly anyone. Take *denier,* for example, as applied to women's stockings. The average woman has a fuzzy idea *denier* has something to do with fineness, but only the rare one can say even approximately what *denier* is. Webster defines *denier* as "a unit expressing the fineness of silk, rayon, or nylon yarns in terms of weights in grams per 9,000 meters of length." The smaller the denier number, the greater the fineness.

dependant, dependent   Both forms are acceptable as the noun: "There is a tax deduction for dependents [dependants]." As an adjective, however, only *dependent* is acceptable: "Our plans are *dependent* on the weather."

deprecate, depreciate   To deprecate is to disapprove of; to depreciate is to belittle or devalue. A remark, for example, may be either deprecatory or depreciatory. The line is not always easy to draw, but the writer at least should be aware of the difference and have a clear idea what he aims to convey.

desalinate, desalt   As usual, the onward bounds of science are leaving some of us behind, at least in the use of terminology. *Desalting* is the simple word for the work aimed at taking the salt out of sea water, and the one everyone would understand instantly. But usually *desalination* or *desalinization* is used. Even this was not good enough for a press association, however, which came out with its own invention, *desalinification.* It shows originality but no regard for either the reader or existing terms, which seem sufficient. *Desalinification* was just a wild jump off the end of the dock, deep into the undesalinified briny.

desegregation, integration   A useful distinction between *inte-*

gration and *desegregation,* which has attracted wide attention and gained considerable approval, has been proposed by the Southern Education Reporting Service. It applies *desegregation* to the abandonment of racial separation, for example in schools and the use of other public facilities. *Integration* is applied to the disappearance of all distinctions based on race. Dr. Kenneth B. Clark of the City College of New York holds that *desegregation* consists of "social, political, legal, judicial, administrative, or community processes" for removal of racial barriers. He adds that it "can be and usually is brought about by laws and governmental authority." Dr. Clark confused matters when he used the word *social.* The distinction could be clearer if *desegregation* were restricted to fields where legal rights are asserted, as in education, voting, and use of public facilities. None of these necessarily involve social commingling, which is not a legal consideration but a matter of choice of association, and it is here that *integration* is properly applied in terms of the distinction being encouraged.

Webster's Third New International gives both the limited and the broad senses of *integrate,* which does not help, although it fairly reflects general usage. By and large, *integration* and *desegregation* are used interchangeably; *integration* and *integrate* are somewhat shorter and thus easier to use in headlines. As adjectives, *biracial* and *mixed* are shorter than *integrated* and preferable to it in the sense of *desegregated.*

Logic and precision, as well as derivation, support the distinctive use of *desegregation* and *integration* in racial connections. Yet *integration,* in its strict sense, is little needed, and even when used distinctively must be qualified in some unmistakable way because it is so often interchanged with *desegregation.*

desert, dessert People who probably know better confuse these terms, quite likely out of inattention. Desert is wasteland, or at least dry, relatively barren country; dessert is the sweet that ends the meal. *Desert,* however, is also what one deserves; the phrase *just deserts* is often misrendered *just desserts.* For that matter, *just* is redundant here.

-designate Hyphenated as a suffix: *chairman-designate, secretary-designate,* etc.

designed Overworked in the sense *intended* or *planned;* journalese. "The rose bushes are designed to act as a net to catch cars hurtling off the road." *intended.* "The new fire engine is designed for protection of the entire county." *intended.* "The demonstration is designed for a lay audience." *intended* or *planned.* Sometimes, before an infinitive, the word could be omitted altogether: "Theater officials announced a new program [designed] to appeal to service clubs"; "Permission has been granted for filing of a complaint [designed] to block the payment."

desirable, etc. This word and its related forms are sometimes misspelled *desireable, desireability,* etc.

(be) desirous of Stilted, mushmouthed, or perhaps both, for *want to.*

despite the fact that The long way for *although.*

despoliation, despoilment Synonyms; *despoilation* is a misspelling.

destroyed See *totally destroyed.*

device, devise A device is a contrivance, to put it briefly, and to devise is to contrive. In nontechnical usage, *device* is always a noun, *devise* always a verb. *An ingenious device; devise a solution.*

DIACRITICAL MARKS Marks such as the umlaut (as in *schön,* German for *beautiful*) and French accents (as in *fiancé, cliché*) sometimes create a problem for the writer who wants to preserve them, because the typesetting equipment of many publications, particularly newspapers, does not contain accented letters. (For their formation on the typewriter, see *Typewriter Tricks.*) Words that have been taken over from French into English, such as fiancé, protégé, and cliché, are tending to lose their accents. Diacritical marks occur rarely in English words, and many users of adopted words either are unaware that they require accents in strict usage or are willing to dispense with accents. A handful of newspapers, however, and most books and magazines carefully retain accents; there is no question of the favorable impression this makes on the critical reader, together with the discriminating use of italics and of capitals and small capitals. Some words that possess accents in French have come into good English usage unaccented; one of them is *employee,* now sometimes spelled *employe.* It was once possible to distinguish between male and female by *employé* and *employée,* but now both spellings, unaccented, refer indiscriminately to workers of both sexes. The careful writer can only be referred to the dictionary for the decision on the use of accent marks in particular cases (Webster retains them on *fiancée, fiancé, cliché, protégé,* and *protégée,* for example.) Oddly, even when the accents are ignored, standard usage maintains the sex distinction in the spellings *fiance* and *fiancee,* in distinction to what has happened to *employe* and *employee.*

The German umlaut usually creates problems only with foreign titles and names, such as *Götterdämmerung* and *Lübeck.* The accepted convention is to render the umlauted *a, o,* or *u* as *ae, oe, ue: Goetterdaemmerung, Luebeck.* Often, however, the problem will be ignored, as in *Gotterdammerung.*

The dieresis (as in coöperate) is about the only native diacritical mark. It indicates, of course, that the *o* beneath is given the short sound. But coöperate is nearly always rendered *co-operate* or *cooperate;* the dieresis is being dropped, like French accents in Anglicized words.

DICTIONARIES   A lack of esteem for dictionaries prevails in some quarters on the ground that they are not infallible. They are indeed fallible, like all human endeavors. Disesteem for dictionaries was encouraged by testy Ambrose Bierce, who acidly wrote them off as bloated, absurd, and misleading. In their place, presumably, or perhaps to counteract their evil influence, he offered his own revelation, *Write It Right* (1909). This little book, now a curiosity, contains considerable patches that no longer make much sense.

If you turn from the dictionary in haughty superiority, what are you going to turn *to?* Unaided notions of usage, meanings, and mechanical practices are likely to be only prejudices. Reputable dictionaries, with all their faults, are the work of boards of lexicographers who assiduously study words, consult experts in special fields, and analyze writing and speech at all levels to determine what accepted practice really is.

About the worst thing that can be said and substantiated about dictionaries is that they are likely to be behind the times. This is hardly avoidable, because a major revision takes many years. Sometimes a new word may be born, live gloriously, and die in the interim between editions. Scientific terms, especially in these times, are invented and come into wide use between editions too.

Rapid changes are comparatively rare. The great body of the language shifts and takes new directions, but hardly faster than a glacier. Divergence from the fiats of the dictionary might most constructively take the form of a more liberal attitude toward slang and toward old words that are swimming into new orbits.

The appearance in 1961 of *Webster's Third New International,* its first revision in 27 years, stirred up a flurry of adverse commentary. Pained complaints were prompted by the fact that it presents, without deprecation or discouragement, a large number of terms defined in senses that were not associated with those terms 50 years ago. For example, *shambles* as *a scene of wreckage, contact* as a verb ("I'll contact him") and *transpire* as *happen.*

The new dictionary has been described as guilty of "permissiveness," reflecting the wrongheaded though widely held —especially among journalists and high-school teachers of English—conviction that the business of a dictionary is to lay down the law.

But in following the principles that usage determines correctness, and that there is no such thing as external authority in language, the Webster editors conformed with scholarly conclusions that have developed over the last half-century and are now so firmly established as to be beyond question.

The business of a dictionary is to report how words are used, and not to prescribe or proscribe meanings. When diverging usages are still new enough to be recognizable, such as *like* as a conjunction ("Winston tastes good" and all that), they tend to offend the discriminating.

Yet there is no resisting new usages if they gain acceptance, nor is there any evidence that discouragement has had any appreciable effect. Let us remember that *blizzard* was once slang. There is no agreement even among the educated and highly literate on the propriety of divergent uses at various stages of acceptance. Nor is it true that lexicographers agree that once a misuse has occurred, it must be accepted. On the contrary, their conclusions represent a consensus based on millions of examples culled from a tremendous variety of sources.

The greatest recent advances in lexicography, until the appearance of the Third Edition, were in desk dictionaries, such as Merriam-Webster's own *New Collegiate, The American*

College Dictionary (Random House) and *Webster's New World Dictionary* (World). All are excellent. And all agree on what governs "correctness." This leaves the complainants insisting that everyone, including the experts, is out of step but them.

There is a place for judgments on usage. That is the business of this book. But this is such a shifting field that the critic does well to confine his exhortations to instances where precision is at stake. Sad to say, precise significations are also often damaged by changes in usage. The thing to do then is recognize the fact and allow for it. What sense is there in imitating King Canute and pretending, for instance, that *continuous* and *continual* are still distinctive? Unless, of course, the writer is content to ride off in all directions on his steed of purism and leave the reader behind.

Finalize, implement as a verb, for example, and other expressions are associated with gobbledygook. But it is clear that they have wide and growing use in good prose.

It is worth noticing in this connection that the designation *colloquial*, misunderstood by many as the equivalent of *substandard* or *loose*, was dropped from the new edition. What it really means is "characteristic of conversation," and this is no taint. Status labels like "slang" (*cornball*), "substandard" (*hisself*) and "nonstandard" (*irregardless*) have been retained but narrowed in application.

Without affecting their realistic approach to language, however, the Webster editors could have spared themselves much obloquy simply by designating certain usages as "sometimes [or *often*] criticized." Perhaps they now wish they had.

It is a widespread delusion, incidentally, that preferred usage is indicated by the order in which the senses of a word are listed (spellings, however, are listed in order of preference). This was not even true of the Second Edition. All senses, unless explicitly qualified, are of equal standing. The Merriam-Webster dictionaries list meanings of a word in the historical order of their development. This is a scholar's device that places noncurrent, archaic, and even obsolete significations ahead of current ones. It is the rare user who is interested in the development of meanings. *The American College Dictionary,* on the other hand, follows a more practical plan in placing central or common meanings first, and obsolete, archaic, and rare ones afterward. The *Oxford Universal Dictionary,* the abridgment of the great *Oxford English Dictionary,* uses the same plan as Webster but redeems it with a system for indicating current status, although this system is not apparent to the casual user.

In general, it may be said that the Third Edition aims at representing English as it is used by the literate majority in this country. That means it recognizes as standard the informal style that is now everywhere current—in books, newspapers, the casual conversation of the educated, speeches, and what have you. By contrast, the earlier Webster, like its contemporary grammars and works on usage, took its cue from something called the "formal" style, which has now passed out of existence except perhaps in mayors' proclamations and legal documents, and even a generation ago did not represent a cultivated consensus.

died from, of People used to die *of* things, rather than *from* them, and in spite of the widespread use of *from* in this connection it is still not regarded as acceptable.

diesel Although the name of a man, this descriptive, as applied to the engine he invented, has passed into general use and is seldom capitalized.

diet on Rare, though legitimate, in the sense *eat* or *subsist on*, and likely to be misunderstood: "This pet owl diets on mice and chicken." What one *diets on* is likely to be thought of as restricted diet: "On my doctor's orders, I am dieting on nonfat foods."

differ from, with; different than; different, various Generally *differ from* is used to indicate dissimilarity (*the petunia differs from the camellia*) and *differ with* to indicate disagreement (*the defense counsel differs with the prosecutor*). But *differ from* may also be used for disagreement.

The idea that there is anything wrong with *different than* is a superstition; the phrase is idiomatic when it introduces a clause. The usual forms are illustrated by "The rich are different *from* you and me" and "The weather is no different *than* it was yesterday." *Different to* is excoriated by British critics, but this form is unknown in the United States. *Different* is often used unnecessarily: "We called on twelve different people." The word is excess baggage unless there is some occasion to stress differences; if *unlike* cannot be substituted for *different*, it is better left out. *Various* is preferable to *different* merely to indicate diversity without emphasizing unlikeness: *"Various* [not *different*] actors have performed the role."

dilapidated   It is a delusion that the term applies only to what is made of stone; like many another, it has respectably parted from its Latin derivation. Furniture, for example, though seldom made of stone, may properly be referred to as dilapidated. Sometimes misspelled *de-*.

dilemma   A dilemma, strictly speaking, is not merely a problem, challenge, predicament, but one that presents a choice between *evils;* this is made evident by the phrase *horns of a dilemma*. The problem of a choice between the love of two beautiful women is not a true dilemma, for neither alternative is distasteful; nor is a choice between what is desirable and what is undesirable. But modern usage allows the simpler sense of *difficult problem*.

diminution   Often misspelled *dimunition*. It may help to remember than *diminution* comes from *diminish*.

diphtheria, diphthong   Often misspelled *diptheria, dipthong*.

dis-   Solid as a prefix: *disassociate, disadvantageous, disembowel, disfranchise, dissymetry*, etc.

disapprove of what you say   See *Misquotation*.

disassociate   See *dissociate*.

disastrous   Sometimes misspelled *disasterous*.

disclose   See *Attribution*.

discomfit, -ure   Observable usage, for better or worse, has toned these words down from their precise and original meanings. Perhaps because of their resemblance to *discomfort*, they are commonly used in much the same sense. *The American College Dictionary*, recognizing this trend, admits *disconcert* as one meaning. Fowler noted a tendency to use *discomfit* in too weak or indefinite a sense, and it may be said that the tendency has gone full speed downhill since. He who wants to preserve *discomfit* and *discomfiture* in their pristine senses (*overwhelm* or *utterly defeat*) is free to do so, if he

129

is willing to chance being misapprehended. "The guest was discomfited by the lack of a salad fork" is a typical example of how tamely *discomfit* is called into play these days.

discover, invent   Often confused. To discover is to find what already exists, as for example a new element. To invent is to devise or create. Machines are invented. It is possible, however, to create new elements. See also *engineer, scientist.*

discreet, discrete   The difficulty here generally arises out of intention to use *discreet,* coupled with ignorance of how it should be spelled. *Discrete,* though uncommon, is a word of another meaning, namely, *separate. Discreet* means *circumspect* or *prudent.* "The information was discretely distributed to more than 1,000 publishers." One by one? Unlikely. More likely : *circumspectly;* that is, *discreetly.*

disinterest, uninterest   *Disinterest* is impartiality; *uninterest* is lack of interest. An umpire, ideally, is disinterested; one who does not care about the game is uninterested. *Disinterested* is loosely used in the sense of *uninterested.*

dismiss against   When the defendant is in luck, it is often written that "the charge was dismissed against Jones." This is a poor arrangement of words, since it tends to link *dismissed* with *against,* and thus to suggest nonsense. It would be preferable to say, "The charge against Jones was dismissed." Sometimes suspects are exonerated *from* a charge, but here the right preposition is *of.* Likewise, they plead (guilty, not guilty) *to,* not *of,* charges.

dispel   Sometimes misspelled *dispell.*

dispensable, indispensable   Sometimes misspelled *dispensible, indispensible.*

dissatisfied   Sometimes misspelled *disatisfied.*

dissension   Often misspelled *dissention,* perhaps under the influence of *dissent.*

dissociate, disassociate   Both are correct, but *dissociate* is to be encouraged on the principle that what is simpler is preferable.

130

distaff Everyone knows that *distaff*, dearly beloved of journalists, is used to mean *pertaining to women*, but who knows exactly what a distaff *is*, anyway? Well, a distaff is a gadget used in hand spinning, an operation few can now remember. When a figure of speech grows so old that its basis is no longer common knowledge, it may be time to drop it, especially when it is as overworked as this one.

divide, etc. A common and unhappy redundancy occurs in constructions like *divide into divisions*.

divorce *Divorce* as a verb, for better or worse, is transitive. "They divorced after two years" is therefore impossible; correctly, "They were divorced after two years."

divulge Appropriately used of what has been secret or concealed; not a simple synonym for *say, tell, announce*, etc. See also *disclose* and *reveal*.

dock, pier, wharf The restriction of *dock* to the waterway beside or between piers or wharves is nautical cant, not general usage. *Dock* is properly interchangeable with *pier* or *wharf;* Webster equates the terms. *Dock workers* exemplifies the relation, for the reference is almost invariably to longshoremen, and not to workers in drydocks.

doctor (title) See *Dr*.

dogs Some routines are, to be sure, more tiresome than others. But certainly none is more so than the invariable habit, in pieces having to do with dogs, of falling back on such expressions as "a dog's life," "going to the dogs" or "doggoned." This practice in itself is bad enough, but it is saddening to discern in addition the smug assumption that cleverness has been called into play and that the reader will be amused.

dollars Often used redundantly in such forms as *$780 million dollars; dollars* has already been specified by the dollar-sign.

dollar-value The term has jumped the chasm (or is it just a crevice?) from the ads to the text ("The dollar-value was quoted as $6,000"). *value*.

Dolley (Madison) The usual form is *Dolly*, and this is how it is to be found in many reference works. *Dolley,* however, is the form Mrs. Madison used herself; the fact is amply documented.

donate Criticisms of the word as a back-formation are accurate but meaningless; the word has been well established for a long time and serves a need. It should not be used indiscriminately in place of *give,* however; it connotes charity or philanthropy.

don't let's Not good usage ("Don't let's count on it"). Suitable for a folksy or jocular effect; common in conversation. Otherwise, "Let's not count on it."

donut This breezy spelling of *doughnut* has not caught on except in signs where, perhaps, *doughnut* will not fit. One thing against it is that it looks as if it should be pronounced *doonut.*

double in brass Probably open to criticism as a cliché when used as a figure of speech, but apart from this its point is often blunted. A photographer for a newspaper, for example, was described as doubling in brass because he also took pictures for a magazine. *Double in brass* is applied in the world of music to a player whose primary instrument is a string or one of the woodwinds, but who is capable of playing a brass, such as a trumpet or trombone, when necessary. The term has also been used in vaudeville and circuses concerning performers who doubled as musicians. A reporter who was also a photographer might be described figuratively as *doubling in brass,* but the expression is no more suitably applicable to one who does the same thing in different places than to a musician who plays the violin in two orchestras.

DOUBLE NEGATIVE The ordinary double negative ("It didn't do me no good") is conspicuous and avoided by all except the uneducated. Other words besides *no* and *not* are negative, however, and some doubling slips by unnoticed: "Few will deny the high temperatures of the last few days weren't pretty uncomfortable." The negatives are *deny* and *weren't.* Correctly, *were pretty uncomfortable.* See also *hardly, scarcely; minimize; Reversal of Sense; underestimate; reverse,* etc.; *undue; not . . . not.*

Double Possessives See *Possessives.*

Double Punctuation No longer considered meaningful, as in

132

"Here, indeed, may be the real purpose of the bill,—to dull our awareness of taxation." Either the comma or the dash alone should be used in such circumstances. Here the dash is called for.

doubtlessly   Cumbrous and unnecessary; *doubtless*.

dove   As the past tense of *dive,* a particular target of scorn in stylebooks. Why this should be is a mystery, for not only is *dove* standard, but it is also in commoner use than *dived,* which is becoming literary.

down-, -down   Solid as a prefix: *downgrade, downhaul, downstream, downtrend,* etc. Solid as a suffix: *breakdown, comedown, countdown, rundown,* etc.

DOWN STYLE   See *Capitalization.*

downplay   Idiom calls for *play down.* "Exports of food from Communist China are downplayed or not mentioned." Journalese; *played down.*

downward revision   See *Euphemisms.*

Dr.   We all love the distinction that comes with a title, and some love it so much they are willing to enjoy the title without possessing the distinction. That goes especially for those who use honorary degrees. It is well understood that institutions of learning really honor themselves in conferring such degrees. If the recipient has not distinguished himself enough to make this so, the affair is even hollower than usual.

No question ordinarily arises concerning the use of the title *Dr.* by doctors of medicine and dentists. Although osteopaths and chiropractors also have a right to it, generally speaking people expect them to be identified specifically. A number of states have laws, possibly inspired by M.D.'s, requiring anyone who uses the title *Dr.* professionally on signs, cards, and the like to specify the branch of healing he professes. In England, physicians use the title *Dr.,* but a surgeon or other specialist, particularly one who has made a reputation, is called *Mr.*

Practice is divided among optometrists on styling themselves *Dr.,* and there is resistance by the public, including newspapers, to so designating them. Optometrists hold a degree, however, that gives them the title. State laws often also apply here.

The reader is likely to assume that a medical man whose name is preceded by *Dr.* is an M.D. If he is something else—a dentist, chiropractor, or veterinarian—it is a good idea to say so, and certainly when the context has something to do with his profession.

Now for the Ph.D.'s and other academic doctors. Whether one of this ilk uses the title *Dr.* appears to depend on his modesty. Around great universities, where doctors of philosophy abound, it is generally considered sophomoric to affect the title *Dr.*, although it is often applied by others as an honorific to the heads of departments and the like. Its use otherwise is commoner in small colleges, just as title-happiness generally is endemic in small towns.

But let the Ph.D.'s have their *Dr.'s.* After all, they worked seven or eight years for them, and the title goes naturally with the flaunting of Phi Beta Kappa keys in the world of education. Let us save our purplest scorn for those who adopt the title on the strength of honorary degrees. Clergymen (usually D.D.'s) are the chief offenders in this respect.

One worthy was appointed president of a small football college for his promotional zeal, although he had no scholarly background. The trustees were concerned, however, at his lack of a Ph.D., for they considered the title *Dr.* a highly desirable ornament to the office. Arrangements were quickly made to have another small college confer a Litt.D. on the new president, who thereafter dubbed himself *Dr.* and made it stick with the obsequious cooperation of the local press.

The commonest honorary degrees are D.C.L. (civil law), D.D. (divinity), D.Sc. (science), D.Litt., D.Lit., Lit.D. (literature) L.H.D. (humanities), LL.D. (laws). The commonest earned doctorates outside the medical fields are Ph.D. (technically philosophy, though awarded in many fields), S.T.D. and Th.D. (theology), and Ed.D. (education). On the lower rungs of the scholastic ladder, it has been common in England for the holders of masters' and even bachelors' degrees to so identify themselves, especially on the title pages of their books ("William J. Periwinkle, M.A. Cantab."). But the practice seems to be dying out, and in the United States is possibly even disdained.

Indications of the title *Dr.* should not be repeated: *Dr. George Anderson, M.D.* Either *Dr. George Anderson* or *George Anderson, M.D.* This applies also to other doctorates, such as Ph.D., D.D.S., D.D.

dramatic, -ics   See *-ic, -ics*.

drouth, drought   Equally correct although *drouth* seems in greater favor, perhaps for the same reason that *draft* has supplanted *draught* in most senses.

drowned, was drowned   *Drowned* is preferable to describe an accident: "He drowned last year in the channel." "He *was drowned*" suggests murder, although this form is often carelessly used when no such suggestion is intended.

drug   The shunning of this word as a noun in the sense of *narcotic*, as is sometimes done for fear of offending druggists, is a silly concession to commercial influence. It is akin to refusing to print requests that no flowers be sent to a funeral, lest it hurt the business of florists. *Drug* covers medicines that are not narcotics, however, and thus is not as specific.

drunk, drunken   *Drunken* is the preferred form of the adjective for attributive use; that is, in front of the noun modified: *a drunken driver. Drunk* is preferable as a predicate adjective: "The policeman himself was drunk." Nevertheless it may be that *drunk* as an attributive (*drunk driver*) is verging into acceptance.

drunkenness   Often misspelled *drunkeness*.

ducat   Journalese for *ticket*.

due to   Falls into the category of expressions that are much used but faintly suspect. Anyone who is at all attentive to usage has an idea, at least, that *due to* is wrong in certain constructions. Usage has established it, however, and it may now be freely used as one chooses.

A review of the grounds on which *due to* was once aspersed may be of interest. The old idea, as set forth by Fowler, was that *due to* could not stand in the place of *owing to* or *because of*. In other words, *due to* could not be used as a preposition introducing an adverbial modifier. This discussion is getting loathsomely technical, so let us try to illuminate it with some examples. The old idea was that "Asian flu is *due to* an imported virus" is acceptable, because here *due* serves as an adjective modifying *flu,* but that "*Due to* Asian flu, he missed three days of school" is no good, because here *due to,* as a preposition, introduces a phrase that modifies the verb *missed.*

All this is hair-splitting, as our age views these matters. Either *owing to* or *due to* will sound acceptable in these constructions. Anyway, it has been demonstrated that *owing to* and *due to* are identical in origin, and if *owing to* can grow up and become a preposition, why arbitrarily bar the path of opportunity to *due to?*

For the benefit of those who insist on hewing to the old prejudice, there is an easy way to tell whether a doubtful *due to* conforms. The idiomatic line between *owing to* or *due to* is pretty blurry, but not the one between *due to* and *because of*. If *because of* can be substituted for *due to*, then *due to* is wrong—according to the old rule. "Asian flu is because of an imported virus" is clearly impossible, and thus *due to* is acceptable. But "Because of Asian flu, he missed three days of school" is fine, and so *due to* is not. All this is balderdash in the view of modern authorities.

Due to the fact that, a popular locution, is objectionable not because it uses *due to* as a preposition, but because it is the long way around for *because.*

dumbfound, dumfound   Both are correct, and the forms are about equally prevalent.

dump   Journalese in reference to the falling of rain or snow ("The storm dumped two inches of snow on the city").

duo   See *Useless Counting* under *Numbers; Pronouns.*

during the course of   Redundant for *during.*

during the time that   Redundant for *while.*

dyeing, dying   The confusion is in using *dying* for *dyeing;* it may help to remember that the *e* of the present tense, *dye,* is kept in the participle of the word for changing color.

—E—

each   If *each* stands as subject, it takes a singular verb: "Each of the prisoners *takes* his ration and *moves* along." (Not *move, take.*) Yet often this would be written *take their ration(s) and move;* that is, *each* is treated as a collective, a usage that is verging into full acceptance.

each and every one A pomposity; *each, each one,* or *every one. Each and everyone* is an error.

each other's A proper form though sometimes questioned (*each other's hats*). *Each others'* is wrong. But as in the example, the expression is plural in sense (not *each other's hat*).

earth, moon, sun Our age's preoccupation with space and the frequent references to planets and stars (Jupiter, Saturn, Mars, Venus, Betelgeuse, Arcturus) seem to have given rise to an uneasy feeling that we're not giving the most important planet of all (to us) its due, and as a result efforts are made to right matters by writing Earth, and, less often, *Moon* and *Sun.* The lower-case usages are so well established, however, that the capitalized versions look stilted. Dropping the article in these instances is unidiomatic and may be ambiguous: *earth* without *the* means *soil.* "A report on the discovery of a new planet 500 times as large as earth was made . . ." *the earth.*

East As a part of the United States, by common consent (like *North, South, West*) usually capitalized. Often capitalized in reference to the orient (which term, however, is lower-case).

Easter Sunday Technically redundant, but so well established that criticism of it is quibbling.

economic, -al Although *economic* may mean either *pertaining to the science of economics* or *money-saving,* usage generally favors *economical* in the sense of *money-saving:* "Economic, as well as social, factors were considered"; "The use of dried milk is *economical.*" "The present system is an economical waste." An absurd contradiction; *economic.*

economics, economies Economics is the science; dismal, they once called it. *Economies* is the plural of *economy,* in one ordinary sense a business and industrial system; in another, a saving. "The Common Market has boosted to unprecedented heights the economics of its members." *economies.*

ecstasy Often misspelled *ecstacy.*

editor, editorial See *Newspaper Terms.*

EDITORIAL (AND ROYAL) WE The editorial *we* is falling rapidly into disrepute as stuffy. It is probably justifiable in editorials, at least when the ideas being presented are actually those of more than one person. But under a by-line, the use of *we* suggests a split personality in the writer. Few things sound more absurd than *we ourself,* a fixture of the *New Yorker's* Talk of the Town department.

The use of *I* has been denounced, of course, as immodest. Consequently some of us, when we have occasion to bring ourselves into the act, coyly masquerade as *this writer, this correspondent, the present writer, the present reporter,* etc. *The present writer* may indeed be present, but one may be left with the suspicion he's not all there. The fact is that *this writer, the present writer,* and the like are more obtrusive than *I* and thus falsely modest. "Many letters received by this correspondent" could be neatly trimmed down to "Many letters to me." Rudolf Flesch, among others, has shown how the creation of a personal link between the writer and his audience promotes readability. So when the writer under a by-line speaks for himself, let him have the honesty to come out with *I* and not don a false face or pretend he's two other people.

I has been forthrightly used by such essayists as G. K. Chesterton, Charles Lamb, Robert Louis Stevenson, William Lyon Phelps, Joseph Addison, and Thomas Huxley, if examples are needed.

The editorial *we* is likely to be associated by many with the royal *we,* the style affected by royalty and the princes of various churches in official pronouncements. Readers are thus likely to associate *we* less with modesty than with hauteur, and with presumptions to power and status.

The editorial *we* had a counterpart in classical Latin. The royal *we* goes back to the time in Roman history when it was used in joint decrees of two or three men. Thus it may be said to have had an honest origin, unlike the editorial *we,* which often creates a misleading impression of multiple authorship.

A columnist addicted to the editorial *we,* which sounds absurd under a by-line, continually refers to *our wife.* This amazingly suggests polyandry. Care is necessary in use of the editorial *we* even in its natural habitat, the editorial column. Editorialists do not always make it clear whether they mean by *we* (a) the newspaper (b) the United States as a government or (c) the people of this country. Naming the newspaper (*The* Bladder *believes* . . .) is more explicit and less pompous. "Since this reviewer took the time to listen to both versions we feel duty-bound to add our two cents' worth." Illogical; the third-person *this reviewer* calls for *he* and *his* instead of *we* and *our*. Translation: "Since I took the time . . . I feel bound to add my . . ." "Folk-singing has changed since we were a boy." Absurd. See also *one*.

educator A term regarded with some suspicion among those to whom it is applied. The most telling criticism, perhaps, is that it is inexact and pompous. *Teacher*, when it fits, is better. *Educationist* is often derisory.

-ee It has been useless for some time to insist that this termination denotes the person (or thing) to which something is done, rather than the doer. True, the *lessor* is the one who grants the lease, and the *lessee* is the one to whom it is granted. The *draftee* is the one who is drafted. The *addressee* is the one to whom something is addressed. The *appointee* is the one who is appointed. The *employee* is the one who is employed.

But this pattern is far from invariable. The *refugee* is not the one who is given refuge, necessarily, but the one who seeks it. The *standee* is not the one who is stood (up?), but the one who stands. Similarly, *escapee* has Webster's recognition as one who escapes.

It is usual for *-ee* to denote the doee, rather than the doer. There is a tendency to coin words, often with the intention of humorous effect, by adding *-ee: handshakee, nicknamee*. A surprising number of such expressions have found their way into Webster, among others *civilizee, counselee, interviewee, permittee, quizzee*.

effect See *affect, effect*.

efficacy, efficiency *Efficacy* means *effectiveness; efficiency* has to do with economy of effort and productiveness. "The panel disagreed on the efficacy of alcoholics and reformed alcoholics." *Efficiency;* the reference was to the way they performed their jobs.

e.g., i.e. Often carelessly interchanged. *E.g.* stands for *exempli gratia: for example. I.e.* stands for *id est: that is*.

egghead At worst, a disparaging, and, at best, a patronizing, term for *intellectual*, though why intellectuals should be either disparaged or patronized is a sad question. *Egghead* was said to have been first applied to the followers of Adlai Stevenson by a Connecticut Republican, John Alsop, whose brother, Stewart, used it in a nationally syndicated newspaper column on Sept. 26, 1952, *Newsweek* reported. Warwick Deeping, however, wrote of "a little eggheaded pedant" in *Second Youth* in 1920. Those who enjoy demeaning intellectuals as eggheads might ponder these words of Ken Purdy as they appeared in the *Democratic Digest:*

> Whatever illusions to the contrary they are currently entertaining in Washington, the fact of the matter is that the world, when it is a place worth living in, is run by eggheads. It was an egghead, not a practical man, who found fire, an egghead cut the first wheel and wrote the first law. The bow and arrow was invented by an egghead, and the atomic bomb was made possible by an egghead— a long-haired egghead at that—who sat for a long time staring at some funny symbols on a blackboard. The practical men—characters with the talents of bricklayers who wear signs on their chests saying "I am a Production Genius"—are apt to forget that they owe their very reasons for existence, always and in every case, to an intellectual.

egoist, egotist The egoist places his own interest first as a principle of conduct; the egotist is a braggart. The distinction, however, is being blurred by careless interchange, and in any event seems to be of little value, since the one is likely to be the other.

either Sentences along these lines have become something of a fad: " 'I don't, either, water the beer,' he protested." If there is a reason for the commas around *either*, it would be interesting to learn what it is.

Either as a pronoun is generally singular, but the once hard and fast rule to this effect is repeatedly breached when *each* is followed by a phrase containing a plural. Webster now cites "either of them is satisfactory" and "either of them are satisfactory" as acceptable alternatives.

Either, like *both* (which see), often precedes prepositions it should follow. "No date has been set either for the election or independence." *for either the election or independence.*

eke out The expression does not mean simply to *add to*, as is sometimes earnestly argued by appeals to etymology (a most unreliable basis for decisions on usage, whose great principle is change; strict observance of derivation would never allow change). It also means *squeeze out*. The classical example here appears to be *eke out a living,* which most dictionaries cite.

elderly   Means getting on in years, and efforts, especially by editors, to fix a starting point, say at sixty or seventy years of age, for the application of the term constitute one of their more harmless follies. It is noticeable that, as they themselves grow older, their starting points tend to rise. Elderliness, like many other qualities, often resides in the eye of the beholder. To a teen-ager, her parents of forty are likely to qualify for this descriptive. To a more lenient judge, elderliness is beyond the middle age. *Elderly,* unless applied conspicuously too soon, is a gentler term than *aged* or *old,* and as such has its uses. See also *youth, senior citizen.*

-elect   Hyphenated as a suffix: *president-elect, secretary-elect,* etc.

electro-   Solid as a prefix: *electrodynamics, electroplate, electromagnet,* etc.

electronic, -ics   See *-ic, -ics.*

ELEGANT VARIATION   See *Pronouns; Variation.*

elevated   Pretentious as a substitute for *high* ("Elevated temperatures are a symptom of disease"). This is true also to some extent of its use in place of *promoted:* "He was *elevated* to his present position last January."

eliminate   Often misused for *prevent;* what can be eliminated must already be present. "Use of this material will eliminate possible failure caused by brittleness." *prevent.* "The insulation eliminates rings caused by dishes." *prevents.* See also *avoid.*

ELLIPSIS   Ellipsis is the grammarian's word for omission of what is readily understood. It is a useful device that should be encouraged, short of ambiguity or conveying a misleading idea. Let us consider instances in which ellipsis is and is not desirable.

An element may usually be profitably omitted from the second of parallel constructions in which it would be repeated in the same position. Often such constructions involve numerical comparisons. In the examples cited, the words in parentheses would be better left out:

"McDonald said 189,344 members are on leave and 257,026 (members are) on part-time schedules."

"In 1958 there were twenty-one days of 100-plus readings and in 1953 there were twenty (days of 100-degree or higher weather)." Here, afraid to repeat *100-plus readings,* the writer strained to invent a variation; he might better have saved his effort and ended on *twenty.* More of the same:

"The plant is capable of handling 650 tons per hour, but is handling only 500 (tons per sixty minutes)." The substitution of *sixty minutes* as a variant for *hour* may strike some readers as ingenious, but it will strike many others, alas, as stupid. See also *Variation.*

"Jones was cited for driving without due caution, and Smith (was cited) for driving without a license."

"Turnover totaled 420,000 shares, well below Monday's 570,000 (-share figure)."

"The college has enrolled 10 per cent more full-time students this year than (were registered for classes) at the end of the first week of school last year."

The words that may be omitted may involve a comparison, rather than a repetition:

"Mohammed Reza is now more firmly on his throne than (he ever had been) since he became Shah."

Sometimes, however, it will not do to fail to repeat verb forms:

"On his arrival, he was told the job was filled and offered $100 as expense money." This should read *was offered* to complete the construction paralleling *was filled.* As it stands, *offered* may be taken as active instead of passive.

"The spokesman said another firm has or is about to file for a franchise." This should be *firm has filed,* for the missing word is not smoothly supplied by the reader. Careless ellipsis may be confusing in other constructions: "The men forced the singer to take sleeping pills after they stripped and photographed her in the nude." *stripped her.* When the forms of the parallel verbs differ, they should be given in full: "A little thing like an advance in short-term interest rates could have gotten lost in the shuffle, or taken in stride." *or have been taken in stride.*

Another form of ellipsis is recommended in relative clauses, usually those starting with *which, who,* or *that.* The idea has sometimes been stated in this way: Cancel the pronoun (*which, who, that*) plus companion forms of *to be* (*is, are, was, were*). This is how it works:

"There is a difference between what they announce as crop yields and the amount (that is) available to the people." In this example and others the words in parentheses are dispensable.

"Work is under way on an ice rink (that is) scheduled to open next month."

"The bridge would give access to the island, (which is) now served by a ferry."

"Members of the Pioneer Methodist Church, (which was) built in 1858, will celebrate next week."

"Elman, (who was) an amateur musician before he escaped, now performs professionally."

That or *which* may also be omitted when they are the subjects of other verbs: "Sibelius was stricken with a brain hemorrhage at the villa (which) he built near Helsinki fifty-three years before."

"Local issues were responsible for the clobbering (which) the Republicans took in the Maine election." Technically, those two *whiches* should have been *thats*, anyway. For this aspect of the problem, see *that, which* under *Restrictive and Non-restrictive Clauses.*

Ellipsis of a different kind is employed to shorten quotations for the writer's purpose, and in these instances the reader must be placed on notice that he is getting a curtailed version: "The speaker said the book was 'ill-conceived, hastily written . . . and obviously the work of an ignoramus.'" The use of three or four spaced periods for this purpose has become such a standardized and well-accepted convention there is no point in using *x*'s or asterisks. Four spaced periods are commonly used when the portion omitted follows a completed sentence.

In such constructions as "Adjectives become nouns and nouns verbs" the comma may be used but is not necessary between *nouns* and *verbs*, where *become* is understood. The comma is likewise unnecessary to mark the point at which a phrase is to be understood as repeated: "A sentence should contain no unnecessary words, a paragraph [,] no unnecessary sentences." The bracketed comma is superfluous.

Ellipsis is improper when the word to be supplied is not identical with the one that has been expressed (like *become* in the preceding example). "One person was killed and seven injured in the accident." *were injured*. "The county is now or will develop a nature-study center on the tract." Properly, "The county is now developing, or will develop . . ." In any event, only the *second* of two identical words may be omitted; the reader cannot be expected to supply from his mind what has not been placed there. See also *Verbs; False Comparison*.

else's Forms like *everyone's else* and *nobody's else* are technically correct and were once in common use, but now they sound like gaucheries. The accepted forms are *everyone else's* and *nobody else's*. "His fan mail outruns everyone's else" should be "His fan mail outruns *everyone else's*." The principle applies generally to pronouns with *one* and *body; no one, somebody, everybody, everyone*.

elusive See *allusive, elusive, illusive*.

emigrate, immigrate The choice is a matter of viewpoint. One who leaves a country *emigrates* from it; one who comes in *immigrates*. Thus someone in the United States may speak of a person emigrating from another country, or immigrating into this one. The same principle holds for *emigrant* and *immigrant*.
   Out-migration and *in-migration* were born, apparently of inability to distinguish between *emigration* and *immigration*.

eminently, imminently *Eminently* means *notably* or *conspicuously:* "The settlement was considered *eminently* fair." *Imminently* means *in a short time* or *very soon,* and is usually said of something that threatens: "The attack was expected *imminently*." Then there's *immanent,* which means *existing within:* "The god was regarded as being *immanent* in the stone image." *Immanently,* a rarity in its proper sense, sometimes turns up in the place of *imminently*.

emissary Once had a predominantly unfavorable sense, suggesting spying or similarly underhanded activity. Efforts to restrict it to that meaning are misspent, for it is widely used to mean an agent or representative, with no derogatory connotation. Webster gives both senses. Once a distinction has been hopelessly lost, as in this instance, it is foolish to insist that it be observed. What matters is not what the writer has in his mind, but what he can reasonably count on putting into the reader's. The writer who now relies on *emissary* to imply dirty work is trusting his weight to a broken plank.

144

emote Many will scorn it (as they will *enthuse*) as a back-formation from *emotion*. This is a puristic approach. Yet the fact remains that *emote* is strongly associated with meretricious acting, and for that reason connotes a jocularity of which the writer should be aware. "People like to read things which make them emote." Did the writer of this seriously mean "experience emotion"? If so, that is what he should have said, for *emote* suggests an insincere or superficial sensation.

employ Pretentious where *use* will do.

enamored Takes *of; with* is an interloper avoided by the discriminating.

end result Redundant unless there is reason to differentiate between final and intermediate results.

endeavor Often pretentious for *attempt, try:* "We will endeavor to get your statement to you by the first of the month hereafter." *try*.

ended, ending *Ended* is preferably used of what is past, *ending* of what is to come. "The report covers the decade *ended* [not *ending*] in 1950." "He is enrolled in a course ending next year." *Ended* never displaces *ending*, though the reverse often incorrectly happens. See also *Participles and Time Sequence* under *Time Elements*.

endemic, epidemic What is endemic is always present; an epidemic breaks out and then subsides. Hookworm, for example, is endemic in rural areas of the South.

endorse, indorse *Endorse*, it was once held, meant to write one's name upon, and *indorse* to approve or vouch for. Thus, strictly, one would *endorse* a check and *indorse* a product. But this distinction has gone the way of *continuous* vs. *continual*. *Indorse* and *endorse* are cited by Webster as synonyms. Both words are now freely used in both senses, except that *endorse* seems to be putting *indorse* out of business altogether. There is no loss here, really, for the context always shows what is meant.

engine, motor The occasional efforts to pretend there is a distinction that can be consistently applied are wasted. Idiom holds sway here. Machines run by steam are always *engines;* those run by gasoline are indifferently *engines* or *motors*; those run by electricity are nearly always *motors*. Derivation is no help; a *motor* is that which imparts motion, and an *engine* is that which has been produced by ingenuity. *Engine* is sometimes applied to machines run by electricity but having a reciprocal action. In rocketry, *engine* is applied to rockets that use liquid fuels, and *motor* to those that use solid fuels.

engineer, scientist Scientists have expressed annoyance at the use of their designation for others. The general distinction is that a scientist is concerned with the creation of knowledge, and an engineer with its application. Others who apply technical knowledge but do not originate it may be properly referred to as *technicians,* in the absence of some more explicit term. *Scientist* is so general, even if properly used, that it is hardly satisfactory these days. Some more explicit designation, such as *biologist, astronomer,* or *physicist,* is desirable.

England See *Great Britain.*

enigmatic Means *puzzling* or *mysterious,* but is often misused in the sense of *dubious* or *questionable.* "The success of the new system is enigmatic" was intended to mean, not that the success was inscrutable, but that it was in doubt.

enormity, enormousness The fight against *enormity* (which once strictly meant wickedness on a large scale) in the sense of *enormousness* is probably lost. Webster defines *enormity* as *outrage* but also gives *hugeness, immensity. Enormity* is used far oftener in this sense than otherwise, and no one misunderstands. The difficulty seems to be that a noun derived from *enormous* is needed, and *enormousness* is clumsy. The *Oxford English Dictionary* defines *enormity* in the sense of "excess in magnitude" as an incorrect use, but it also notes that this error dates from 1846.

enquire, enquiry *Inquire, inquiry* are more prevalent; the other forms are somewhat old-fashioned in the U.S. but current in Britain.

en route Correctly, two words; not *enroute.*

ensure, insure *Ensure* and *insure* are interchangeable in the sense *make certain:* "Hard work will not *ensure* success";

"Careful workmanship *insures* quality," but *ensure* has a noticeable edge. *Insure* is predominant in the sense *guarantee against loss*.

entangling alliances   George Washington is generally misquoted as having warned against them in his Farewell Address. The phrase, however, comes from Jefferson's First Inaugural Address: "Peace, commerce, and honest friendship with all nations—entangling alliances with none."

Washington did say, toward the end of his Farewell Address: "Taking care always to keep ourselves . . . on a respectable defensive posture, we may safely trust to temporary alliances for extraordinary emergencies." He also said: "The great rule of conduct for us in regard to foreign nations is, in extending our commercial relations, to have with them as little political connection as possible."

enthuse   Scorned by many as a back-formation from *enthusiasm*. "He was enthused over the implications of the test" will sound better to many with *enthusiastic*.

entitled, named, called   A name or title following any of these (and other words conveying the same thing) is not set off by a comma: *a book entitled* "The Naked and the Dead"; "A Streetcar Named Desire"; *a man named Peter*. (Not *entitled* [,], *Named* [,], called [,].)

entomologist, etymologist   These sesquipedalianisms are seldom called into play except by those who know what they are talking about. But now and then smaller fish confuse them. An entomologist is a scientist who specializes in insects; an etymologist is a scholar who studies the derivations of words. The nouns are *entomology, etymology*.

envelop, envelope   The verb for *cover* or *wrap up* is usually *envelop*, though *envelope* is a variant; the noun for what carries a letter is either *envelop* or *envelope*, though the latter is the usual form.

epithet   To most people the connotation is basically derogatory; an epithet is a bad name. This is one sense of the word. In another sense, *epithet* is neutral, and means simply a descriptive term; this use is generally found in technical and literary contexts. Both senses are standard; the writer should be aware

147

that the one is more familiar than the other, lest he commit ambiguity.

epitome An epitome is a summary, condensation, abstract, or an ideal representation; not an acme, apex, high point or climax. "His attire was the *epitome* [ideal representation] of fashion" is correct, but "That triumph was the epitome of his career" is not; *high point, climax.*

equally *As* is superfluous with *equally:* "He remained equally as uncompromising on the other issues." *equally uncompromising.*

equine The journalese variant for *horse.* See also *Variation.*

equivalent As a noun, takes *of:* "the equivalent *of* [not *to*] Boston's Massachusetts Institute of Technology." The adjective takes *to:* "It was equivalent *to* Boston's . . .

-er, -est Whether to use *more* and *most* in forming comparatives and superlatives, or the terminations *-er* and *-est,* is a matter of having an ear for language. Sometimes either variation is equally acceptable. But not here: "His most keen perceptions are in the realm of French music." *keenest.* See also *Comparison of Adjectives.*

ere See *Poesy.*

errant, arrant Sometimes confused. *Errant* means *wandering* or *straying; arrant* means *thoroughgoing* or *outstandingly bad.* "This is errant nonsense." *arrant.*

espresso The coffee is *espresso,* not *expresso.*

-esque Solid as a suffix: *Kiplingesque, Junoesque.*

essay See *assay, essay.*

estate The term has had a damaging comedown, at least in real-estate promotion. No one is surprised or even amused any more to find ordinary subdivisions ballyhooed as "estates"; the term has even been applied to trailer parks. It's almost enough to make a man wish he weren't rich.

etc. Stands for *et cetera* and means *and so forth*. Often carelessly given *ect.* A comma before *etc.* is unnecessary ("They form their own opinions about economics[,] etc.") even though it is oftener there than not. *Etc.* is often lazily used as a bushel basket; the quoted sentence is probably an example. The reader should easily be able to see what *etc.* is intended to suggest. *And etc.* is redundant.

-eth The unavoidable demand on the writer who gets cute is that he know what he is doing. He makes an ass of himself, for example, by using foreign words or phrases in the wrong sense, or by misspelling them. After having gone out of his way to exhibit his erudition, he is surely in a ridiculous position when he shows that his grip on it is shaky. By the same token, if he finds it desirable to revert to Middle English for special effect, he ought to keep in mind that the termination *-eth* goes only with the third person singular (*he, she, it*): *He thinketh, she smileth, "The Iceman Cometh."* Most of us pick this principle up by osmosis, from the Bible and other ancient readings: "I will lift up mine eyes unto the hills, from whence *cometh* my help." It invites derision to write things like *I cometh, you smileth*. The second-person ending is *-st*, and it calls for *thou* as a subject. (Quaker usage is specialized, and invariably calls for *thee*.) See also *thee, thou*.

eulogy Takes *a*, not *an*.

EUPHEMISMS Life is a hard business, as someone has said, and we often seek to soften its blows by giving them agreeable names. This device—for example, saying *passed away* instead of *died*—is known technically as euphemism, or pleasing talk. Euphemism is not something that can or should be done away with. In many instances, the bluntest names for things are intolerable in polite society and censorable in print. The so-called four-letter words fall in this category. On the rare occasions when they appear in print—in novels, for example—the effect on the reader may be one of shock, refreshment, amusement, or a mixture of all three.

But we should at least be aware when we are using terms that are at one or more removes from the most explicit versions. Euphemisms are distasteful when they indicate unnecessary squeamishness. The trend of our ordinary expression for many years has been away from the complex, the pretentious,

149

the coy, and the flowery, and toward the simple, the unassuming, the frank, and the unadorned.

It is not so long ago that *social disease* was as close as anyone but a doctor would come to saying *syphilis* or *gonorrhea*—and even the euphemism was used with reluctance. In fact, the medical campaign to curb syphilis was seriously impeded by the refusal, at first, of mass publications even to name the disease.

Let's skip around among some typical euphemisms. A cut or increase in wages or prices is often glossed over as a *downward revision* or an *upward revision* (or *adjustment*). In the jargon of business, especially, prices are never raised, but delicately *revised upward*. This may be all right for the public relations man, whose vocation is to gloss, but certainly such genteelisms should not be adopted by others with the idea that they possess some desirable elegance.

Heart condition is popular for *heart ailment. Heart condition,* more than one critic has said, is meaningless, since every heart has a condition, better or worse. *Heart attack* (which see), while we are on this subject, is a useful workaday term that has been unaccountably denounced as denoting an attack by the heart. The publicity attending heart ailments in high places has led to widespread lay use of *coronary* as noun for what was once *heart attack. Cardiac,* too, has been enthusiastically taken up by the laity.

Realistic is a key euphemism in collective and other kinds of bargaining. *Realistic,* in this connection, is what its user's proposals are, in contrast to those of the other side, which are invariably *unrealistic.*

During the war we became familiar with *planned withdrawal*, the military's euphemism for *a retreat.* General Jonathan Wainwright was so outraged by this kind of mush that he described one reverse in these unequivocal terms: "We took a hell of a beating."

The name *Woman's Christian Temperance Union,* as nearly everyone must be aware, is a misnomer, for its members advocate abstinence, not temperance. *Abstinence* has an unyielding sound, however, and it may be that the temperance ladies can no more stand the shock of solid words than they can stand the fumes of hard drink. *Belly,* to follow the liquor down, is all but indecent; genteel people speak only of the *abdomen.* When will the Nice Nellys succeed in cleaning up the Bible to "Thy abdomen is like an heap of wheat set about with lilies"? See also *Profanity.*

evacuate   In the sense *remove people from a place, evacuate* is standard, superstition to the contrary.

ever   Often unnecessarily joined to an adjective with a hyphen: *ever* [-] *increasing size.*

ever so often, every so often   The second is the form of the idiom for *now and then; ever so often* is an intensive of *often*, and means *very often.*

everybody, everyone   These are singular, and so are nouns qualified by *every;* consequently pronouns relating to them should be singular. "Everybody shouldered *his* pack and moved on"; "Everyone talks and eats *his* popcorn during the intermission." In conversation, however, the terms are often treated as plural collectives: "Everybody shouldered their pack . . ."; "Everyone talks and eats their popcorn . . ." Plural pronouns relating to *every* compounds are conspicuous because the compounds never take plural verbs even colloquially.

There is no preference in acceptability between *everyone* and *everybody*. This applies also to *someone, somebody; no one, nobody.*

The pronoun *everyone* should be distinguished from the adjective-pronoun phrase *every one:* "He had something cheerful to say to everyone of his admirers." *every one.*

everybody talks about the weather. . . .   See *Misquotations.*

everyday, every day   The adjective *everyday* (*an everyday occurrence*) and the adverbial phrase *every day* (*It happens every day*) should be distinguished. "Everyday the papers are full of his exploits." *Every day.*

every time   Preferably two words, not *everytime;* unlike *everywhere, everyone, everything.*

evidence   As a verb, often pretentiously displaces *show:* "The basket evidences careful workmanship." *shows.*

evidently, evidentally, evidentially   *Evidently* means *perceptibly, obviously. Evidentially*, often misused for it (probably as a misspelling) means *related to evidence. Evidentally* is a misspelling and nothing more.

151

evince Though good English, the word has tended to become a newspaper variant for *show*.

ex- May *ex-* properly be attached only to its noun, and not to the noun's modifier? For example, should it be *Waldorf ex-headwaiter* rather than *ex-Waldorf headwaiter?* The answer is *ex-Waldorf headwaiter*. The fellow was, of course, a former headwaiter at the Waldorf, and the only way to express this smoothly is to put the *ex-* in front of *Waldorf*.

It is not possible, anyway, to keep *ex-* attached only to nouns and not to their modifiers; witness *bathing ex-beauty*. It has been argued that ambiguity may arise from the likes of *ex-Democratic attorney general* (that is, *ex-Democrat, ex-attorney general*, or both?), but only the determinedly wrongheaded will see a problem here, for *ex-* obviously modifies all three words as a unit. At any rate, the problem of the placement of *ex-* is pretty much limited to headlines, because otherwise it can be sidestepped by using *former*.

Nevertheless, like every other rule, this one must have its exceptions. A headline read "Ex-Negro Student Fined in Mississippi." The subject was an ex-student but not, as the headline seemed to say, an ex-Negro. Perhaps the suggestion of ex-Negro is so remote that there is really no problem. But in this case *Negro ex-student* may have been preferable; it surely would have been unambiguous.

Before exiting on *ex-*, let's have a look at *ex-felon*, a puzzling creation that pops up now and then. It evolved, probably, on the model of *ex-convict*, and in a strict sense both expressions may be open to the same objection. *Convict*, however, has come to mean almost exclusively *one serving a sentence*, and thus *ex-convict* fills a distinct need. But *felon* is not associated with imprisonment; it means simply *one who has committed a felony*. *Ex-felon*, then, may well be meaningless, and he who commits a grievous offense against the law may proudly take his stand with the Englishman and declare, "Once a felon, always a felon."

Ex- is hyphenated as a prefix meaning *former: ex-convict, ex-president, ex-queen*, etc. Otherwise, in the sense *out of*, solid: *excommunicate, expropriate, exterritorial*, etc.

exact, exactly *Exact* cannot be used as an adverb: "The exact same policy," "The exact same pressure." *exactly the same.* See also *Figure at Beginning of Sentence* under *Numbers*.

except, excepting   *Excepting* where *except* will serve is not only exceptionable but disagreeable. It may reflect the justly scorned love of the long word. At any rate, no one who knows *excepting* can be unaware of *except. Excepting* has its own uses, and ringing a change on *except* is not among them. An example: "Everything about the new cars is easier to handle excepting the payments." *except. Excepting* as a preposition is acceptable only if it follows *not* (*not excepting the payments*).

excess verbiage   A redundancy; *verbiage* denotes excess.

EXCLAMATION POINT   Overuse of this mark is no longer the vice it once was, to judge from the criticisms that appeared in style manuals of a generation or two ago. Columnists (and others writing in a colloquial tone) often use the exclamation mark to call attention to a japery; perhaps they would be better advised to append (joke); at any rate, this punctuation adds no humor, and may, by reason of its obtrusive effect, subtract some.

One-word interjections (Ouch! Indeed!) generally take the exclamation mark. Fowler complained that it was often needlessly used with such statements as *You surprise me, How dare you?,* and *Don't tell such lies,* which he described as mere statement, question, and command. He seemed in this, however, to overlook the fact that emphasis is conveyed by the exclamation mark. *You surprise me,* period, is cool and tame; *You surprise me!* conveys excitement. *How dare you?* is much less indignant than *How dare you! Don't tell such lies,* period, is contemptuous; *Don't tell such lies!* is outraged. Whether such statements should be followed by the exclamation point must be left to the intention and judgment of the writer; he is not open to critical quibbling over the suitability of his punctuation if he conveys what he intends to, and does not falsify or misrepresent the tone.

Exclamation points used after ordinary statements with the hope of giving them a transfusion are gushy; fortunately, this kind of thing is seldom found in print except for letters to the editor; more often it occurs in schoolgirls' letters. Some women, however, do not outgrow this idiosyncrasy, and men who possess it sound girlish. All this goes double for doubled exclamation points. ("I appeal to you for advice!!") ("Some of us are in a minority all the time!! Must we be content with perpetual inconsideration? I think not!!")

153

F. Scott Fitzgerald, confronted with an example of this over-excited style, advised: "Cut out all those exclamation points. An exclamation point is like laughing at your own joke." (*Beloved Infidel.*)

"That means that each year there were 20,000 applications for operatic jobs in New York City alone!" Without the exclamation point, this would be a quiet statement; with it, the writer draws our attention to a disparity.

See also *Typewriter Tricks*.

ex-felon   See *ex-*.

exhaust   As applied to people, a transitive verb, which means it must take an object. "She exhausted easily" should have been "She *became exhausted* easily."

exhilarate   Sometimes misspelled *exhilirate*.

exist, existence, existing   The notion that only what is alive exists is a superstition. *Exist* means *be* as well as *live*, and is properly applied to inanimate things and even insubstantial ones, such as ideas. *Existence* is often misspelled *existance*. See also *presently*.

exonerate   Sometimes misspelled *exhonerate*.

exonerate from   See *dismiss against*.

exotic   It has long been held by nigglers that the word means only *foreign, from another country*. And they were right, up until 1925 or so. Now, as anyone with an eye for usage is aware, it also means *strikingly out of the ordinary, unusual, excitingly strange*. These senses are now commoner than *foreign*.

expect   An affectation or a localism for *suppose, suspect, imagine, assume:* "I expect you are the new parson." *assume.* See also *anticipate*.

expel   Sometimes misspelled *expell*.

expensive   Means *high-priced*. "The average man found the prices pretty expensive" is an absurdity. *Goods* may be expensive, *prices* must be high. See also *cheap*.

expertise, expertize *Expertise* is a noun meaning *expertness* that Fowler might have criticized as a vogue-word. At any rate, it is in high fashion with pundits and those who aspire to being thought wise. *Expertize,* a comparatively odd fish, is a verb meaning *give expert judgment on.* They are unlikely to be confused in talking, for *expertise* ends in *eez.* But writing is another matter: "He named a committee of conservative businessmen to expertise the foreign aid program." *expertize.*

explain See *Attribution.*

expose Often used in a mushmouthed way: "Entering freshmen are now so deficient they must be exposed to a remedial reading course before they can proceed." This would better be expressed exactly: *must take a remedial reading course. Exposure* suggests what is undesirable, ephemeral, or both; neither sense is appropriate to this situation. "Children are being exposed to new exhibits in art, music, and science at the preschool level." *are being shown, are seeing.*

extended Unnecessary, inexact, and pretentious as a variant of *long,* as in *an extended illness.* What is extended is that which has been given greater extent, and thus an extended illness is not simply a long one, but one that has gained a new grip on its victim after signs of remitting.

extension Sometimes, oddly enough, misspelled *extention,* perhaps by mistaken extension from *extent.*

extol Often misspelled *extoll,* perhaps because the *l* doubles in the past and participial forms (*extolled, extolling*).

extra The indiscriminate use of *extra* as an adverb is adese, and it has percolated alarmingly into other prose (*extra good, extra strong*). *Extra* for *unusually, uncommonly, extremely* has a slangy or dialectal tone.

extra- Solid as a prefix: *extracurricular, extralegal, extramarital, extramural,* etc. But *extra-alimentary* (followed by *a*).

—F—

fact, facts Good, solid words, but you would never know this from the mealymouthed way they are often used. Webster now recognizes a broad (its word) application of *fact* to "something presented rightly or wrongly as having objective application (his *facts* are open to question)." This is not quite so clear-cut a contradiction of the generally accepted sense as "He has his facts wrong." But contradictory senses of the same word are hardly to be encouraged. For example, "The *true facts,* on the other hand, are . . ." A fact is either true or not a fact. The frequent remark, "He has his facts wrong," is nonsense. If what he has are wrong, they are not facts. *Actual facts, real facts* are redundant.

The expression *the fact that* is often used of what is not fact: "This could be just an expression of the fact that the Russians are unconcerned and content to play a waiting game." But the context made clear that this was speculation, and alternative explanations were given. The statement might better have been "This could be just an indication that . . ." The phrase is often excess baggage: "We admit the fact that an injustice has been done." *We admit that . . .*

fail Carries a strong implication of falling short in an attempt, but it is often used where there is no question of an attempt: "Buckingham Palace *failed* to confirm the story"; "The burning bed *failed* to disturb the sleeper"; "The weekend of rain *failed* to affect the river level." If there is any virtue in direct statement, *did not confirm, did not disturb,* and *did not affect* are preferable.

fail to dampen (enthusiasm) A cliché of journalism with respect to rain or some other untoward circumstance.

fair-trade laws A political euphemism. Fair-trade laws have nothing to do with fair trade from the consumer's viewpoint; their purpose is to force retailers to maintain a price structure fixed by the manufacturer, a stratagem that the bargain-hunter, at least, considers highly unfair, as does the cut-rate merchant. But it is called free enterprise. Many publications, unwilling to fall into the trap of misrepresentation that is set by this term, preface it by *so-called*. See also *right-to-work laws*.

fallout If we must have it at all, let us make it one word; fallout, not *fall out* (a verbal), nor *fall-out*.

FALSE COMPARISON Careless writers, apparently by carrying ellipsis too far, often stumble into false comparison. They write: "Older houses are still selling here, unlike many cities" or "Like many patient folk, Russian violence can be brutal." Alertness would show the need for "unlike *those in* many cities" and "like *that of* many patient folk." The difficulty in such instances is that a relative pronoun (usually *that*) and a preposition have been inadvisedly squeezed out. In the examples, as a result, *older houses* are compared with *many cities*, and *patient folk* with *Russian violence*.

Here are other examples, in which the originally omitted but necessary words have been italicized:

"Addiction in California appears to differ from *that in* other states."

"Robert Sarnoff, president, admitted that NBC's situation was in some ways tougher than *that of* the other networks."

"Five bids were lower than *that of* the American Seating Company."

Sometimes the error is caused by omitting the preposition alone, as in "Receipts from livestock sales were 7 per cent less than the corresponding period last year." The receipts were not less than the corresponding period, as reported, but less than *in* the corresponding period.

"An illusion of reality can be more completely brought to an audience on the screen than *by* any other medium." *by* is necessary.

"Personal income was up 8 per cent last year, higher than any other state." Ambiguous; was the increase or the income higher? *than in*.

"Yet, like his friend, the late Dag Hammarskjöld, Hallstein's dedication has overcome his lack of bonhomie." *Dedication* is set beside *friend*. *Yet Hallstein's dedication, like that of his friend* . . .

false illusions A common redundancy; falsity (i.e., nonreality) is the essence of illusion.

FALSE LINKAGE See *Commas*.

FALSE POSSESSIVE   See *Possessives*.

FALSE TITLES   *"Griffelkin* is an opera for children by distinguished young California composer Lukas Foss." Piling up descriptives is an idiosyncrasy of journalism, brought on by the urge to compress. The result, however, is hard to digest. *by the distinguished* . . . See also *Occupational Titles* under *Titles*.

falsies   See *bosom, breast*.

famed   Journalese for *famous* (or even *well-known*).

fantasy, phantasy   Generally interchangeable, though *fantasy* predominates except in the sense of mental images produced by dreams, drugs, or illness, which are usually *phantasy*.

far from the maddening (madding) . . .   See *Misquotation*.

farcical   Sometimes misrendered *farcial;* there is no such word.

farther, further   The purist holds that *farther* applies to distance and *further* to anything else, e.g., *a farther journey, a further consideration*. Few others appear to be aware of this distinction, however, and some who are ignore it. This may be the kind of choice best governed by ear. Fowler hazarded that *further* would drive out *farther*, since *further* may be used both to indicate distance and in the figurative sense (*a further* [*farther*] *journey*), whereas *farther* will not do in the figurative sense: a *further* (never *farther*) *consideration. Further* and *farther* are both still actively in use, however. The use of *farther*, as we have seen, is restricted by idiom; attempts to place limits on *further* serve no purpose.

fartherest, furtherest   Illiteracies; *farthest, furthest*.

faze, phase   *Faze* means *disconcert* or *daunt*, and is usually used with a negative: "We were not *fazed* by the setback." *Phase*, often wrongly used in that sense, is a noun meaning *aspect:* "The lecturer described the *phases* of the moon." With *in* or *out phase* is a verb, usually found in military contexts, meaning *place in* (or *take out of*) operation by stages: "This program will be *phased in* by Christmas."

feature As a verb meaning *exhibit as a prominent aspect,* in good standing but often overworked: "Yankee Stadium usually features bases 90 feet apart"; "The new church will feature a large sanctuary." In such instances it would be better to use simply *has* and *will have,* or to give a more unmistakable emphasis to what is being pointed out as a feature.

feel Alice Hamilton, M.D., found amusing "the increasing rejection of *believe* and *think* in favor of *feel*" (*Atlantic,* September, 1954). The prejudice against *feel* in this sense has long seemed to be a superstition, especially in its rabid form, to the effect that nothing is felt that is not apprehended by the sense of touch. True, the good doctor did not go to that extreme. But then all cats are gray at night, and disapprovers of *feel* in any other than the tactile sense will quote such diagnoses as hers to their purpose.

To the extent that no word is the exact equivalent of another, *feel* is not the exact equivalent of *think* or *believe.* Its use, however, does not necessarily imply reliance on the feelings or motions. In the general meaning of *have a notion, be more or less convinced,* or *sense,* it is well enough established to be beyond cavil. Shakespeare used the word in that way: "Garlands, Griffith, which I feel I am not worthy yet to wear" (*Henry VIII*); so did Trollope—"She felt that she might yet recover her lost ground" (*Barchester Towers*); Thomas Hardy —". . . we feel our rout is imminent . . ." (*An Ancient to Ancients*); and Abraham Lincoln—"It is difficult to make a man miserable while he feels he is worthy of himself."

Feel has numerous extensions, and some lexicographers, it is true, do not divorce it from emotion. Webster gives *believe, think, hold,* and cites: "I am a reader, so I feel I have a right to criticize authors," by Alice Hamilton. Not the same Alice? The *Oxford English Dictionary* gives one sense as "to apprehend or recognize the truth of something on grounds not distinctly perceived." It is not easy to perceive distinctly what the learned dons are driving at here, but look at an example they cite: "The proposed legislation was felt to be expedient." Substitute *believed* or *thought* for *felt,* and if the result makes you queasy, call Dr. Hamilton.

Oddly, a sense the *Oxford English Dictionary* specifies as "to believe, think, hold as an opinion" is designated obsolete. Examples are cited from writings going back as far as 1382, however, which indicates at least the modern and apparently growing use springs from an ancient and possibly noble line. We may ignore the fact that many such lines have produced bastards, because people who make their way in the world establish their own reputability. So do words.

A revival seems afoot, however, because *The American College Dictionary* defines *feel* as "to have a general or thorough conviction of"; the *General Basic English Dictionary* as "have idea that"; and *Webster's New World Dictionary of the American Language* as "to think; believe; consider." The *Standard College Dictionary* gives "to have intellectual convictions or opinions." *Laird's Promptory* gives *to believe* as one sense of *feel*, and offers as equivalents "consider, hold, sense; SEE, THINK, BELIEVE." Allen's *Synonyms and Antonyms* gives *believe* as a synonym of *feel*.

Feel, then, does not appear to be such bad medicine after all. If they are not too bitter a pill, these lines, spoken by the Prince of Wales in *Henry IV, Part II,* may be prescribed for all who would impugn useful words on shaky grounds:

> I feel me much to blame,
> So idly to profane the precious time.

feel bad, badly Authorities ranging from the permissive to the severely conservative can be cited to the effect that the forms are now standard and interchangeable. It is sometimes argued that a predicate adjective (*bad,* to modify the subject, *I,* as in *I feel bad*) is required, rather than an adverb (*badly*). This reasoning is done in, however, by the unanimous recognition of *badly* in the new dictionaries as an adjective in this construction. This holds true whether such expressions as *I feel badly* are used to express regret or physical discomfort.

feline The journalese variant for *cat.* See also *Variation.*

female Unsuitable or forcedly facetious in place of *girl, woman, lady.*

feminine Most appropriately used of womanly qualities. "The accused said the suspect sometimes bought feminine clothes in London's West End." This seems slightly off key; why not *women's clothes?* If a woman were spoken of as partial to masculine clothes, the sense conveyed would be women's clothing of masculine cut.

FEMININE FORMS Many of these, such as *ancestress, aviatrix, authoress, poetess, postmistress*, have fallen into disuse, perhaps proving that equality of the sexes is truly here. *Postmistress* is not recognized by the federal government, which designates all postmasters *postmasters*.

Fowler urged not only the retention but the multiplication of feminine designations as "a special need of the future," proposing *doctress, teacheress, singeress*, and *danceress*. The trend, as noted, has gone in the opposite direction. The confusion Fowler feared is often avoided by the use of given names, clearly indicating sex (*Dr. Alice Warren*). Some women in professions use their initials only. This, without any other indication such as *Miss, Mrs.*, is a discourtesy in signing letters, for it may leave the recipient at a loss in replying.

fewer, less The rule is that *fewer* applies to individually distinguishable units (*fewer people, ships, houses*), and *less* otherwise (*less sugar, less time*). It is conspicuously apparent, however, as Perrin notes, that "*Fewer* seems to be declining in use and *less* commonly takes its place." *Less people* is so common as not to attract attention. Perrin cites *less hands* and *three less seats*.

Fiberglas, fiber glass The first is a trademark, and in deference to its owners should be capitalized, although there is no way such deference can be enforced. The generic term, which is preferable for general use, is *fiber glass* (sometimes *fibrous glass* or *spun glass*). See also *Trade Names*.

fictitious Often misspelled *ficticious*. The word has a favorite application to checks written with intent to defraud. *Fraudulent* seems a better choice here, for, as Webster points out, "*fictitious* implies fabrication and, so, more often suggests artificiality or contrivance than intent to deceive or deliberate falsification."

fiddle Except as applied to what country performers play, the term is considered derogatory by the layman, who respectfully says *violin*. Yet it is the common expression among musicians themselves. Nevertheless, *fiddle* as a neutral term is proprietary; the musician knows he means no offense by it, but he may resent its use by others.

161

fight with, against   *Fight with* is ambiguous: "He fought with the Spaniards" fairly prompts the question: "Which side was he on?" The context usually explains. Nevertheless, *fight against* or recasting is worth consideration.

figuratively   Often displaced by *literally* (which see).

figurehead   Often misapplied to people. "The teacher is one of the figureheads if not the most important member of our community." A figurehead is a symbol, one with no real authority or responsibility, a leader in name only. Calling a person a figurehead is thus derogatory; the meaning intended in the example was leading citizen. "Bach is now recognized as the figurehead to whom all musical innovators have turned for inspiration in the 20th century." Unintentionally demeaning; *lodestar, bellwether,* or something equivalent.

FIGURES   See *Numbers*.

final culmination   "This club is the final culmination of the kind of intimate feeling we have been searching for." Redundant; *culmination*.

finalize   *Finalize*, like *implement* as a verb, is hopelessly associated with gobbledygook, and its user may bring scorn on himself.

fine   The idea that *fine* may not be used to denote superior quality, as in *a fine man, a fine day,* but must be reserved for the idea of physical fineness (*fine-grained*) is a superstition. It is true, however, that *fine* is not in good standing for *well*, as in "He is doing fine."

finishing touch   Sentences employing this and similar phrases including *touch* are often subjected to some painful twists. A finishing touch sounds like something that would be *given* a building, plan, or whatever. But frequently we see that finishing touches are being *made to, made on,* or *put to*. "He put a personal touch to his story"—surely a gaucherie for "He gave his story a personal touch." There does exist, of course, the touch that is *put on*, the touch for five dollars before pay day, which is just as painful but in a different way.

firm   As a noun, has a technical meaning (a partnership of two or more persons not recognized as a legal person distinct from the members composing it) but this sense is hardly to be imposed exclusively in nonlegal connections. In general usage, *firm* is a synonym for *business enterprise* or *organization*.

first and foremost   May be left to political orators, together with *point with pride* and *view with alarm*. The bombast of political oratory.

firstly, etc.   The adverbial endings on ordinals are unnecessary: *first, second*, etc.

fix   Now standard in the sense *repair: fix the washing machine*.

flag   See *Newspaper Terms*.

flagship   "The *President Jackson* was the first American flagship to enter the canal." Unhappy compression is at the root of the trouble. The writer meant "the first ship flying an American flag," but by condensing it, presumably to "the first American-flag ship," set the stage for "the first American flagship." This is confusing and erroneous, for a flagship, as every old salt knows, is a naval vessel carrying the commander of a force, or, occasionally, a merchantman designated as foremost in a fleet.

flair, flare   In the sense of *bent, talent, ability*, it's always *flair*: "He has a flair for commerce." *Flare* has a number of senses, but it is not interchangeable with *flair* in this one. *Flair* and *flare* are both acceptable in certain circumstances to mean a widening, however.

flaming inferno   Redundant. An inferno is a hell, and the use of the word for something that is burning permits no doubt as to the variety of hell.

flammable, inflammable   Fire underwriters and others interested in safety have promoted the use of *flammable* in preference to *inflammable* on the assumption that *inflammable* may be misunderstood to mean *noncombustible*. This reasoning may have some merit, and there is a noticeable increase in the use of *flammable*, especially in labels on trucks and other containers, though *inflammable* has by no means been driven to the wall. The words are synonyms and equally reputable.

flaunt, flout Often confused. *Flaunt* means to display in an ostentatious or boastful manner: "The faction *flaunted* its superior strength." *Flout* means *mock:* "A speeding motorist *flouts* the law."

flautist, flutist The first may be considered affected. It looks like a charming antique, but Fowler said the second is in fact the older form.

flier, flyer · *Flier* is predominant in the sense of *aviator, flyer* in reference to trains and handbills.

flotsam, jetsam Since these words are often paired, they are assumed to be the same or similar things. Flotsam is goods lost by shipwreck and found floating in the sea; jetsam is goods thrown overboard during a storm to lighten a vessel. The difference can be remembered by their relation to *float* and *jettison.* An account that applied flotsam and jetsam to debris from a sunken submarine was erroneous; it could only have been flotsam.

flounder, founder Sometimes confused as verbs. To flounder is to struggle or thrash about; a fish out of water flounders. To founder is to go down, in the case of a ship to fill with water and sink. Ships are sometimes described as floundering, as well they may in a stormy sea, but the intended meaning generally is *founder.* "This attitude misses the whole point on which the policy of the United States has floundered." Conceivably; but more likely *foundered* (failed). "In public favor, the governor is foundering even worse." *floundering.*

flu Now standard for *influenza,* though the longer form is still seen. There is no occasion for *'flu;* if one must go this far, he had better make it *'flu.'* The clipped form is both convenient and unmistakable, which are unbeatable recommendations for any innovation.

flush, flushed *Flush* is the term for *fully supplied, well filled;* a man who had just received his pay check might describe himself as flush. *Flushed* is the term for *excited, thrilled,* as in *flushed with victory* (alas, a cliché).

-fold Solid as a suffix: *twofold, fourfold,* etc.

folks Folksy for *people:* "Folks who live in this city."

following In the sense of *after* ("*Following* the movie, they had some ice cream"), *following* is sometimes damned, but the worst that can fairly be said of it is that *after* is shorter, plainer, and more natural.

for, thus Starting sentences with *for* and *thus* is an affectation by some writers, particularly columnists. This is warranted only when the sentence draws a conclusion based on what has gone before; the words are the equivalent of *consequently*. "But will the prisoners again read into the President's words a promise such as they thought they had in April 1961? For they risked their lives then." The second sentence does not draw a conclusion from the first; it merely carries the argument forward: "They risked their lives then." See also *Attribution*.

force, -d Often used inappropriately, conveying a stronger sense of compulsion than is warranted. "Pupils through the third grade at the Roosevelt School will be forced to attend half-day sessions this term." This conjures up an image of the wretched kids manacled together and marching to their half-day sessions in lock step. It would be more in key with the circumstances to say "Half-day sessions *will be necessary*" or that the pupils *will have to attend* half-day sessions. "If the county cannot make up its mind, the city will be forced to make other plans." *will have to.* "Some of the sixteen squad cars were forced to go bouncing over bumpy roads to catch the elusive hot rods." *had to go.*

fore- Solid as a prefix: *forebrain, foredeck, foredoom, foregoing,* etc.

forecast, forecasted Both forms are acceptable as the past tense ("He forecast a blizzard today") but those who value economy will prefer the first.

foreseeable future Often criticized as foolish, since none of the future, not even the next second, is foreseeable.

foreword Often misspelled *foreward*, under the influence, perhaps, of *forward*. It may help to remember that a *foreword* is a *word* at the *fore;* that is to say, an introduction. While an *introduction* or *foreword* to a book may be written by either the author or someone else, a *preface* is a statement by the author.

165

Fowler denounced *foreword* as an interloper that had displaced *preface*, and wistfully expressed the hope that *foreword* would be unhorsed. The words have survived, however, side by side, a monument among many others to the feebleness of the influence of those who would influence the course of the language, however slightly, in accordance with their own preferences. The distinct sense of *preface* guarantees its continued existence.

former, latter Strictly correct usage requires that *former*, even when used without *latter*, may refer only to the first of two. In the light of this rule, a mistake is made in writing "He spotted a man and a woman and two children, all obviously hurt, the *former* most seriously." The right words here would be *the first* or *the man*. Although *former* and *latter* are correctly used in denoting each of two, this device often becomes a puzzle that makes the hapless reader look back and figure out which is which.

Samuel Johnson, if we can trust Boswell, belonged to this school:

> He disapproved of parentheses; and I believe in all his voluminous writings, not half a dozen of them will be found. He never used the phrases *the former* and *the latter*, having observed, that they often occasioned obscurity; he therefore contrived to construct his sentences so as not to have occasion for them, and would even rather repeat the same words, in order to avoid them.

See also *was a former*.

for the purpose of Verbiage in place of an infinitive construction. *For the purpose of circumventing* equals *to circumvent*. "The lawsuit was filed *for the purpose of intimidating* the mayor." *filed to intimidate*. See also *so as to, in order to*.

for the (simple) reason that Excessive for *because*. Beyond this, *simple* insults the reader's intelligence.

fortuitous, fortunate *Fortuitous* means simply *chance* or *accidental*, as in *a fortuitous encounter*. It is incorrectly used in the sense of *fortunate*, as in *a fortuitous deal*. "A time of transition may be fortuitous after all, went the argument." *favorable, advantageous*.

for whom the bell . . . See *Misquotation*.

fouled up This slang expression seems to have come into general use via the Navy. *Fouled*, in a legitimate nautical sense, means tangled; it is generally said of anchors whose chains are wound around them, and two crossed, fouled anchors form the insigne on a Navy officer's hat. Let those who may see a touch of poetic justice in this. Nothing is more natural than the conversion of *fouled* into *fouled up*, meaning *hopelessly confused*. This gave rise in turn to *snafu* (situation normal; all fouled up), now being forgotten. *Fouled up* may be distasteful, not because it is slang, but because of the repulsive suggestion of *fouled* in its most general sense.

founder See *flounder, founder*.

FRACTIONS It is well to defer to consistency by shunning such mixtures as *one and ½ feet, two and ¼ miles*, in favor of 1½ *feet, 2¼ miles*, or *one and one-half feet, two and one-quarter miles*. And *.13 of an acre is* preferable to *.13 acres*, as less likely to lend itself to error. Technical publications often place a zero in front of a decimal point: *0.13 of an acre*.

When fractions must be constructed, it is better to separate the numerator and the denominator with the virgule than with the hyphen: 6⅞ (not *6 7-8*). See also *Decimals*.

Frankenstein Often as not applied to a monster. Frankenstein was not the monster, however, but the scientist who created it, as set forth in the novel of that name by Mary Shelley. The misapplication is so prevalent it is recognized by most dictionaries. In much the same way, Horatio Alger is often referred to as the hero instead of the author of his rags-to-riches stories.

frankness See *candor and frankness*.

fraternal Sometimes confused with *paternal*, as in birth announcements speaking of a child's maternal and fraternal grandparents.

free pass, free gift Redundant; a pass by definition is free, as is a gift.

freely, free *Freely* means *liberally, without stint*, not necessarily *free of charge*. The person who wrote of *a freely-distributed paper* did not mean it was distributed widely or

167

without restraint, but rather that it was a throwaway. (In the trade, periodicals that are left at doorsteps or otherwise disseminated at no cost to the recipient are genteelly referred to as "controlled circulation" publications. After all, *throwaway* is hardly an edifying term, at least from the viewpoint of the publisher, and it may put ideas in the mind of the householder.) The example should have said *a paper distributed free of charge.* Besides, the hyphen, as in all instances when an adverb ending in *-ly* is joined to another modifier, is wrong. "They charge for the groceries, but Della dispenses freely her cures for what ails you." *without charge; free of charge;* or even just plain *free.*

freezing, subfreezing   Freezing weather requires subfreezing temperatures; consequently *subfreezing* is unnecessary.

frenetic, phrenetic   The word means frantic, and the two versions are equally acceptable, though the first predominates.

friendlily, friendly   *Friendlily* is standard, but seldom used because of its awkward sound. *Friendly,* however, cannot be used as an adverb: "A few were not very friendly disposed toward him." *friendlily.*

from   Redundant in sentences like "The only other source of money is from the general fund." *source is the general fund.*

from here on in   A redundant pomposity.

from ... to   A redundant construction in such contexts as "The Chinese still hold from 12,000 to 14,000 square miles of Indian territory." *hold 12,000 to 14,000.*

from where, whence   "This was their last meeting place, from where they were sent on individual missions." This construction is sometimes criticized on the ground that *where* is an adverb and cannot be the object of a preposition. *Where,* however, may also be a pronoun. Even so, *from where,* though fairly common, cannot be said to have any real pretensions to good usage. The prejudice against it has some inconsistencies. Invert the word order, and it is acceptable: "*Where* did the cake come *from?*" equals "From where did the cake come?" but the latter is clearly less acceptable. *Here* has established itself in similar constructions (*From Here to Eternity*), and no one objects. So has *there*: "*From there* the trail winds through a meadow." And so, someday, may *where*, but the day is not yet here. *Whence* will grammatically take the place of *from where* (and *from which*), but it is bookish. Nevertheless, *whence* (like *thence, from that place*) might usefully be placed in common service. *From whence* is technically redundant (*the port from whence he will sail*) but some critics regard this as a quibble. In summary, prepositions before *where* (*to where, from where*) are noticeably avoided.

front runner   Originally meant a fast starter that soon falls behind. Now often used to mean simply the leader.

front yard   See *back yard.*

-ful   Plurals of words ending in *-ful* are normally formed by adding *s*: *handfuls, teaspoonfuls, cupfuls.* Not *handsful, teaspoonsful, cupsful.*

full-fashioned   In reference to hosiery, and meaning knit to fit the leg, this is the correct form; not *fully fashioned.*

fulsome   Means *excessive* or *disgusting*, not *ample* or *abundant.* Fulsome praise is objectionable, not lavish, praise; the word connotes insincerity and baseness of motive.

funny   It is naive to label what one is setting down as funny; if the reader does not perceive the fun unassisted, no amount of labeling will convice him it is there. See also *interesting.*

furlough, leave   *Furlough* is no longer in use; all branches of the military now say *leave.*

furnish   You say you're not superstitious? All right, put your little hand in mine and we'll walk under a ladder. Superstition holds that *furnish* is not properly used in the sense of *supply;* you can furnish a home, the argument runs (i.e., equip it with furniture), but you cannot furnish the beer for a picnic (linguistically, that is). If this is one of your pet notions, Webster has a surprise for you. He says the word means "provide . . . equip." A corollary, as a superstition, is that *furniture* is what you put in a house, and *furnishings* what a men's store, for example, sells. *Furnishings* is correct in both senses.

further   See *farther*.

fuse, fuze   The common term is *fuse* for the device used to ignite explosives and also for the electrical circuit-breaker. Generally it is *fuze* in connection with ordnance, especially in technical contexts.

FUSED PARTICIPLE   This is the name Fowler invented for a subject of a gerund that is in the objective, rather than the possessive, case. "I object to *him* being appointed," is an example of the fused participle; "I object to *his* being appointed" is supposedly the correct form. The principle applies to nouns as well as to pronouns: "She resented *John's* ringing the doorbell."

The possessive is far from invariable in this construction, however. Curme, who went into the subject more exhaustively than Fowler, cites numerous examples from good writers to show that the possessive is often impossible or undesirable, and that the tendency is to use the objective ("I object to *him* being appointed") even when the possessive *is* possible. The possessive is most likely to be used when the subject of the gerund is a pronoun. But Curme writes: "We regularly use the accusative [that is, objective] when the subject is emphatic: 'She was proud of *him* doing it.' The emphasis often comes from contrasting the subjects: 'We seem to think nothing of *a boy smoking*, but resent *a girl smoking*.' "

Fowler expressed the pious hope that his discussion would leave readers sick to death of the fused participle, but the sad truth is that most of the examples he cited to bring on this mortal illness do not even make us queasy today.

futilely   Often misspelled *futiley*, but the basic word (*futile*) must be given before the adverbial ending (*ly*) is added.

future   See *Redundancy*.

future plans   Redundant, as is *advance plans*, since plans, unless otherwise qualified, are inevitably for the future. See also *Redundancy*.

—G—

gabardine, gaberdine Technically interchangeable, but the first version is so predominant in reference to the fabric that *gaberdine* is likely to be taken for an error. *Gaberdine,* furthermore, has a distinct sense as the name of a medieval garment or, by extension, any cloak. The distinction may be worth preserving.

gag, gagged See *quip, quipped.*

gag it up A tiresome descriptive, because of overuse, in the legends beneath pictures showing people, usually from show business, engaged in horseplay.

gaping hole A cliché.

gauge, gage The first gives so much trouble, often being misspelled *guage,* that it's a wonder the simpler variant *gage* has not displaced it. *Gage* is generally preferred in technical writing, perhaps because of this difficulty.

geared to Journalese, as in "The product is geared to mass acceptance."

gendarme A gendarme is not the counterpart of an American policeman, but rather of a sheriff's officer or state policeman. French cities have policemen; villages and other small communities have what we would call constables. The use of *gendarme,* then, in indiscriminate reference to any French police officer is inaccurate, and in reference to an American policeman is heavy, worn-out humor.

gender *Gender* for *sex* is felt as a facetious extension; the term strictly applies to grammatical classifications, which often do not consistently correspond with sex. "Two performers of the feminine gender" would better be "Two women performers."

general consensus Redundant; *consensus* implies generality.

general public Says nothing that *public* alone does not, when there is no contrast with some segment of the public.

GEOGRAPHICAL DESCRIPTIVES See *National Descriptives.*

geometrical See *arithmetical, geometrical.*

GERUND CONSTRUCTION A maladroit construction comes of putting a gerund between *the* and *of,* on the model of *The Taming of the Shrew* and *The Shooting of Dan McGrew.* In these instances, of course, it accomplishes what is desired; namely, setting the gerunds (*taming* and *shooting*) in the forefront.

"Stevens repeated that the responsibility for (the) filing (of) the charges was his." In this example and others that will be held up for criticism, it is recommended that *the* and *of* be left out, making the succeeding element the object of the gerund: *the responsibility for filing the charges.* As Perrin notes in *Writer's Guide and Index to English,* "This emphasizes the verbal phase of the word and makes for economy and force."

"Officials plan to save considerable time in (the) conducting (of) the charity drive." *in conducting.*

"The contract calls for (the) spending (of) $100,000." *for spending.*

"He proposed psychological tests for (the) screening (of) candidates for the priesthood." Some examples of this practice are more objectionable than others, and this is one. Even after making it *for screening,* we would have two *for* phrases in succession. *tests to screen candidates* is smoother.

"Improvement in (the) gathering (of) and reporting on such data is needed." *improvement in gathering.*

"The proposal calls for (the) setting up (of) a joint staff." *Up* and *of* are hideous side by side; *setting up.*

The worst has been saved for the last: "The kids made their own caps out of box-tops, and cheesecloth served for (the) holding on (of) the hats." *and cheesecloth held them on;* or *and used cheesecloth to hold them on.* See also *Fused Participle.*

get See *got; secure, obtain.*

Ghanaian The correct form; not *Ghanan, Ghanian.*

GI As applied to people, the term is used only for enlisted Army personnel, not for officers.

gibe, jibe *Gibe* means *jeer at:* "The hazing went no farther than

172

gibing at the freshmen." *Jibe* means *match* or *correspond with*: "His performance did not *jibe* with his campaign promises." It is true that *gibe* is recognized as a variant of *jibe*, but careful usage observes the distinction. Confusion is encouraged by the fact that the words are pronounced identically.

gift As a verb for *give* or *make a gift of*, recognized but avoided by the fastidious.

gild the lily See *Misquotation*.

give way This is the idiom (not *give away*) for *yield to* or *be displaced by*. "Radio gave way [not *away*] to network television."

given See *was given*.

glamor, glamour, glamorous, glamourous *Glamour* is the preferred spelling in America as well as Britain, although generally *o* is used in America where the British use *ou: labor* (*labour*), *honor* (*honour*). But *glamorous* is the preferred spelling for the adjective (not *glamourous*).

glittering A journalese counterword, often grotesquely misapplied to anything that is new, elegant, or impressive in any way: "a glittering new shopping center"; "John Steinbeck accepted the Nobel Prize for Literature at glittering ceremonies"; "the appointee has a glittering name." That which glitters shines or sparkles, and if figurative use justified the descriptive in many of the connections where it is invoked, overwork has made it tiresome.

gobbledygook The use of the term in its present sense (the turgid language characteristic of bureaucracy) was established by Maury Maverick in an article that appeared May 21, 1944, in *The New York Times Magazine*, *Governmentese*, *federalese*, *officialese*, and, in England, *pudder*, are sometimes used in this sense, but *gobbledygook* predominates, at least in the United States. Curiously, the word is sometimes spelled gobbledegook; this is the way it appears, for instance, in *The American College Dictionary*, and Webster now also recognizes it. The *y*-version is commoner, however, and in any event is the one Maverick used. Such versions as *gobble-de-gook* and *gobbledygock* must be regarded as errors. A good illustration of gobbledygook and its cure developed in a wartime press conference at which President Franklin D. Roosevelt read an order concerning blackouts that had been prepared by the director of civilian defense:

"Such preparations shall be made as will completely obscure all federal buildings and nonfederal buildings occupied by the federal government during an air raid for any period of time from visibility by reason of internal or external illumination. Such obscuration may be obtained either by blackout construction or by terminating the illumination. This will of course require that in building areas in which production must continue during a blackout, construction must be provided that internal illumination may continue. Other areas, whether or not occupied by personnel, may be obscured by terminating the illumination."

After the reading of this order had been interrupted several times by laughter, Roosevelt directed that it be reworded:

"Tell them that in buildings that will have to keep their work going, put something across the windows. In buildings that can afford it, so that work can be stopped for a while, turn out the lights."

The difference between gobbledygook and plain English is the difference between *terminate the illumination* and *turn out the lights*.

God rest ye merry . . . See *Misquotation*.

-goer Solid as a suffix: *concertgoer, playgoer, moviegoer, theatergoer*, etc.

good and sufficient reason An overblown phrase; is not a sufficient reason good, and vice versa?

goodwill One word as both noun and adjective: *a source of goodwill; a goodwill ambassador*.

go on a rampage Journalese, as applied to rivers that overflow.

got, gotten An uneasy idea persists that *gotten* is improper. This may grow out of the fact that the form has passed out of use in England. Where Americans say *have gotten*, the English say *have got. Have gotten* (meaning *have obtained*, as in "We have gotten the provisions") is correct and idiomatic in the United States. "We have got the provisions," the English version, sounds uncomfortable here, although it might be used as an intensive of *have*. Efforts to avoid *got* by substituting *obtained* or any other word the writer must strain after are misspent. When *got* comes naturally, it should be used. See also *secure, obtain*.

gourmand, gourmet　It might be said that the first lives to eat, the second eats to live. At any rate, *gourmand* generally implies glutton; *gourmet*, a connoisseur of food.

graduate, be graduated, etc.　Some still insist one cannot say a student graduates from college, but must say he is graduated. The passive form has been abandoned by all but pedants. *Will be graduated* (for *will graduate*) is now so uncommon as to be an affectation.

grammar　Often misspelled *grammer*, especially when advice on the subject is being given. This may only illustrate the natural perversity man must contend with, like the probability that a slice of bread will fall buttered side down.

gratuitous　Has nothing to do with gratitude, though the words are related in origin. *Gratuitous* means *granted freely, uncalled for, unwarranted*.

gray, grey　*Gray* is the preferred spelling in America, *grey* in Britain.

Great Britain, British, English　Great Britain is an island comprising England, Scotland, and Wales. The United Kingdom is Great Britain plus Northern Ireland. *The British Isles* properly applies to the United Kingdom and the islands around it —the islands of Scilly to the southwest, the Isle of Man to the west, the Channel Islands to the east, and the Orkneys and the Shetlands to the north of Scotland. For all this, *Britain, United Kingdom,* and *England* (as well as *British* and *English*) are often used interchangeably with no damage. It is well to bear the distinctions in mind, however, for those occasions when they are meaningful.

grievous, -ly　Often misspelled (as a result, perhaps, of mispronunciation) *grievious, -ly*.

grill, grille　The cooking grate is *grill;* other gratings are *grill* or *grille*, though *grille* is somewhat flossy. The verb for *interrogate* is always *grill*.

grind to a halt   A cliché.

grisly   Subject to some strange misapprehensions about spelling —sometimes resulting in *grisley*, sometimes even *grizzly*.

groom   No usage has been more castigated in stylebooks, perhaps, than *groom* for *bridegroom*; not that this has discouraged it. Its critics scornfully hold that a groom is a man who tends a horse, which is true, but it shows also the age to which their thinking tends. Outside the horsy set, the term is uncommon, and it may even be strange to the generations that have grown up since Henry Ford's great triumph. At any rate, *groom* for *bridegroom* is standard.

ground, grounds   Interchangeable in the sense of *basis: ground for objection. Grounds* is usual in legal connections: *grounds for divorce.*

GROUP WORDS   See *Collectives.*

guarantee, guaranty   Both are correct as noun and verb in the sense of *ensure, warrant,* but *guarantee* is by far the most commonly used.

guerrilla   Fowler found the spelling *guerilla*, though incorrect on the basis of derivation (from the Spanish *guerrillero*) four times as common as *guerrilla*, and concluded it might as well be accepted. Both forms are recognized, but the *rr* version is now so predominant that the other is likely to seem an erila.

guest   Vain efforts have been made to restrict this term to recipients of hospitality, as distinguished from those who pay for their food, lodging, etc. It applies equally now to the paying and the nonpaying, although one often sees the qualified *paying guests.* That expression is generally used when it is necessary to distinguish the two varieties. An editor once forbade his reporters to write of people staying at hotels as guests, and was paid off when one of them referred to such people as inmates. Fowler called *paying guest* a genteelism for *boarder,* but obviously that criticism is not and may never have been applicable in America.

guest speaker   Usually a redundancy for *speaker*.

guilt (feelings, etc.)   Although nouns steadily become adjectives, this is a matter of general acceptance and the consensus of usage. Webster does not yet recognize *guilt* as anything but a noun, and consequently such expressions as *his guilt feelings*, which offend the fastidious ear, must be considered unacceptable in careful writing. Preferable: *his guilty feelings; his feelings of guilt.*

—H—

habitual   Takes *a*, not *an*.

had   It is pedantically and, as usually follows, erroneously argued that such wording as "The man had his driver's license revoked" is objectionable. It suggests, the critics say, that the man deliberately instigated the revocation. This is wrong-headed. Such constructions are unexceptionable and their meaning is clear. One of the definitions of *have* in Webster is "to experience, esp. by submitting to, undergoing, being affected by, enjoying, or suffering." An earlier edition cited as an example "he had his back broken." A related idiom is illustrated by "The woman broke her back in a bobsled accident." This is sometimes criticized on the same grounds as the foregoing. But anyone who objects to it would also have to object to *I broke my leg* or *He stubbed his toe* or *She cut her finger.* See also *break, broke; suffer, sustain, receive.*

had (have) reference to   Wordy for *meant* or *mean:* "That was the property I had reference to." *meant.*

hail, hale   *Hale*, in the sense that concerns us here, means *haul;* people are *haled* (not *hailed*) into court. *Hail* means *call, shout a greeting*, or *acclaim:* "We hailed a taxi"; "The new king was hailed by the crowd."

half   See *cut in half.*

handle in routine fashion   Overelaboration of *handle routinely.*

handsome   See *attractive.*

hang, hanged See *hung*.

harass, etc. Often misspelled *harrass*.

hardly, scarcely Negatives, although the fact is not always sensed, resulting in such constructions as *could not hardly, scarcely nothing,* which are double negatives. *could hardly, scarcely anything.* See also *Double Negative.*

hardly . . . than (when) *Hardly* should be followed by *when,* not *than:* "*Hardly* had the words been uttered than the crowd melted away." *when.*

harebrained Sometimes mistakenly *hairbrained;* the reference is to the brain of the hare.

he, she; his, her Sex rears its head, though not very interestingly, in references that apply to both men and women: "The employee can appeal to the state if he or she feels that he or she is being exploited." *He or she* is not only clumsy but unnecessary. It is a well-established convention that in such instances that the masculine pronoun (*he*) is taken as applying to both sexes. The plural pronoun is commonly used and considered acceptable in speech, but is questionable in writing: "Every boy and girl had their own cup." *His* is preferable here. A deep thinker once invented a bisexual pronoun, *hir,* for use in such constructions, but it went over like the legendary lead balloon.

he, she (———) "The county manager noted that the assessor's requests would add up to $2 million more than he (the manager) was willing to recommend." The writer has decided that *he* alone may be ambiguous, so he (the writer? yes) has placed *the manager* in parentheses beside it. Constructions like this constitute editing that has been obtruded on the reader. There is no more reason to write *he* (*the manager*) than to let any other lapse, together with its correction, stand in print. One might as justifiably write *servise* (no, *service*). The example should have read *more than the manager was willing to recommend* (striking out *he*).

Often the *he* (———) construction is so much the worse because there is no ambiguity to begin with. "The governor decided to resign in favor of the secretary of state, so that he (the governor) could be appointed to the Senate." *He* can refer only to the governor; but if the writer was doubtful he should simply have repeated *the governor*. "Lundberg asked which of his colleagues had told the mayor that he (Lundberg) had made the criticism." Persnickety; *he* can reasonably refer only to Lundberg, but if there is doubt, *Lundberg* alone will resolve it. "It is the sort of history Parson Weems might have written about the age of George Washington had he (Weems) been a Harvard professor." *He* alone is unambiguous.

The *he* (--------) construction is called for only in a direct quotation when it is necessary to prevent ambiguity and at the same time preserve the exact form of the words quoted: "The observer reported, 'Some believe that he (Alexander) is only waiting for the right moment.'" Technically, the parentheses here should be brackets, indicating an editorial insertion.

his, her The pronouns should not be used if the antecedent is not exact: "It was the second time that tragedy struck the John Doe family. His two-year-old son suffocated two years ago." Whose son? Doe's, apparently, but the antecedent is *the John Doe family. Doe's two-year-old son* is preferable to the vague *his*. The society columns often refer to a couple (Mr. and Mrs. Richard Roe) and then proceed with something like "He is a sanitary engineer. She first met him on a European trip." This irks the fastidious, who would prefer "Mr. Doe is a sanitary engineer; his wife (or Mrs. Doe) first met him ..." "Things looked good at first for the Jones family. The Travelers Aid Society placed them in a hotel suite for the weekend, and he promptly got a job." *Jones*, not *he*.

head up Journalese for *head, lead, direct:* "The doctor was chosen to head up the study."

head over heels Often criticized by the literal-minded as illogical since over the heels is the usual place for the head. Webster gives one sense as suggesting the motion of a somersault. Alfred H. Holt, in *Phrase and Word Origins,* concedes to the critics that when one stops to think, it should be *heels over head,* and goes on to speculate that it may originally have been *over head and heels,* a translation of *per caputque pedesque* (Catullus). But it is no good trying to force language into the straitjacket of logic, least of all a sprightly idiom like this. Or is it now a cliché?

healthful, healthy The difference between *healthful* as meaning *conducive to health* ("Eating apples is *healthful*") and *healthy* as meaning *possessing health* ("The children are all *healthy*") is fading. *Healthy* is well accepted in both senses ("This climate is *healthy*"). *Healthful* may disappear, since it never does duty for *healthy*.

heart attack   The idea that *heart attack* conveys an attack upon, or by, the heart, and thus cannot be used to describe a seizure, is absurd. The expression is standard, and is preferable to the newly prevalent *coronary* and *cardiac* in reference to heart attacks. Technical language is best left to those equipped to use it exactly. *Coronary* properly is an adjective, but it is metamorphosing into a noun ("He had a coronary [i.e., *heart attack*] last November").

heart condition   See *Euphemisms*.

heartrending   The correct term; not *heartrendering*.

Hebrew   The name of a language; not properly applicable to modern peoples though sometimes resorted to as a genteelism in mistaken avoidance of *Jew, Jewish* (which see).

height, heighth   Heighth is an occasional misspelling of *height* that probably grows out of a mispronunciation. But height is pronounced *hite,* not *highth.*

heir apparent, presumptive   Technically, the heir apparent will inherit if he survives; the heir presumptive will inherit unless someone else is born whose right takes precedence. For example, in the latter instance, a younger son will often displace a daughter. Both forms are used figuratively (*heir apparent to the presidency of the company*) but *heir apparent* is commoner.

heist   This slang term for *rob* or *hold up* is not current enough outside the underworld for casual use, and well-edited publications avoid it.

helicopter   Mispronunciation as *heeliocopter* may lead to a written error, *heliocopter. Helio* is the prefix used to indicate some connection with the sun, as in *heliograph,* a device that transmits messages by using the sun's rays, and *heliotrope,* a flower that turns toward the sun. It all goes back to Helios, a Greek name for the sun god. But *helicopter* (correctly pronounced *hellicopter*) comes from *helix,* meaning *spiral,* and *pteron,* meaning *wing.*

hemorrhage Pretentious in nontechnical contexts for *bleed.* "The victims were hemorrhaging profusely." *bleeding.*

hence Fusty for *thus, therefore, consequently.*

her See *he, she.*

here at, we at *Here at* and *we at,* as in "We at Nutzan Boltz, Inc.," "Here at Lefthand Monkeywrench," have come to be standard, slightly patronizing pomposities of the public relations operators. Highly skilled practitioners sometimes manage to combine them: "We here at Lefthand Monkeywrench."

heroic Takes *a,* not *an:* "An heroic deed." *a.*

her's Not a correct form in any circumstance; the possessive of *she* is *hers; the flowers are hers.*

hierarchy Sometimes misspelled *heirarchy,* perhaps by mistaken association with *heir.*

high, highly Although *high* may be an adverb ("The plane circled *high* above the city"), the choice between *high* and *highly* appears to be governed by idiom. As an attributive modifier (before what it modifies), *highly* seems preferable; as a predicate modifier (after what it modifies), *high* is required. *Highly paid executive* is preferable to *high-paid executive.* Yet *highly priced* is intolerable for *high-priced.* (*High-price,* as in *high-price advice,* is deplorable.) *High-strung* and *high-toned* are also established both before and after what they modify.

high gear As a figure of speech ("the campaign is going into high gear") a cliché that painfully shows its age, like "going like 60."

highlight Although some dictionaries make two words of *highlight* as a noun ("The song was the *high light* of the concert"), the fact that there is general agreement on one word as a verb ("The speech will *highlight* education"), and the consensus of usage of both forms, in addition to the way it is spoken, indicate that *highlight* is to be preferred.

high-price, -d   As a modifier, the participial form is preferable: "A *high-price* call-girl racket." *high-priced.*

high, wide, and handsome   "The new satellite rode high, wide, and handsomely around the earth this week." The form of the idiom is as given; *handsomely* results from an undiscriminating overcorrectness.

hilarious   The word connotes not merely amusement, but intense mirth. It is often used in a way that hopelessly exaggerates, especially in advertisements of plays and movies. *Hilarious* takes *a*, not *an*.

hindrance   Sometimes misspelled *hinderance.*

hippopotamus   The plural is either *hippopotamuses* or *hippopotami.* The Latin form, however, may sound affected.

hiral   Federalese as a noun for the act or date of hiring: "The department had 12 hirals last week." Not in Webster.

his   See *he, she.*

historic, -al   The difference between these words is subtle, but their incorrect use is nonetheless jarring. *Historical* means *pertaining to history: A historical account. Historic* means *contributing to,* or *making, history: a historic expedition.* A historical novel is one based on, or dealing with, history; a historic novel is a literary landmark, one that makes history. "The historical ranch changed hands recently" contains a palpable error; *historic.*
    Historic (*al*), *history, historian* take *a*, not *an*, unless they are pronounced *'istoric, 'istorical,* etc.: *a* (not *an*) *historic occasion.*

hold steady   An idiom; *hold steadily* is unnatural.

holdup   See *burglary.*

home, house   Objections are sometimes raised that an unoccupied dwelling cannot properly be referred to as a *home;* such a place, the objectors insist, is a *house*. This is sentimental; no dictionary specifies occupancy as a requisite for applying the term *home*. No doubt Edgar Guest's well-known dictum that "It takes a heap o' livin' in a house t' make it home" figures in the prejudice against using *home* for an empty house. Real-estate agents knowingly choose *home* to describe their wares, as having more warmth and thus more appeal for the prospective buyer than *house*. Polly Adler, the ineffable madam, held that "a house is not a home," but then she was talking about a special kind of house, one that nobody would equate with a home. Robert Frost defined *home* as "the place where, when you have to go there, They have to take you in." *Home*, to be sure, has its own connotations, but *home* and *house* are so often used interchangeably in reference to dwellings as such, occupied or not, that any hard and fast distinctiveness has been lost.

home town, hometown   See *back yard*.

honeymoon   Another of the words sometimes forbidden by style-books; in its stead they prescribe *wedding trip*. But *honeymoon* also has a larger meaning, as in figurative application of "The *honeymoon* is over." Even so, *honeymoon* is apparently out of fashion in those fashion-ridden precincts, the society pages.

honor, honorable   To honor is to pay tribute to; the word is un-suitable in the sense of *mark* or *observe*, as in "The community will honor Public Schools Week." *observe*.

Honor is noun and verb, not an adjective, therefore not *honor guests* but *honored guests* or *guests of honor*.

Honorable is somewhat fusty as a descriptive of respect; it has no official standing: *the Honorable* (often abbreviated to *Hon.*) *James Jones*. The designation is never used with the last name alone unless followed by *Mr.: the Hon. Mr. Jones.* The usage of this term is comparable to that of *Reverend* (which see). *Honour* is conspicuously British spelling, used in America mainly on invitations ("request the honour of your presence"), where, as elsewhere in the U. S., it is an affectation.

Honorary Degrees   See *Dr.*

Horatio Alger   See *Frankenstein.*

honored in the breach   The quotation from *Hamlet* is almost always misapplied, as Fowler pointed out. The original refers to a custom that is better disregarded than observed, but common usage has assumed the sense of unwarranted disregard. This, however, is beyond repair. Perhaps even Hamlet is now being misunderstood.

hooky The preferred spelling; not *hookey* (*Play hooky from school*).

hopefully The word is staking out a claim on territory that has been preempted. It means—or once meant—*in a hopeful way,* but often it turns up with the intended sense *it is hoped.* The reader usually can make the leap from the customary sense to what the user has in mind. Sometimes, however, either sense may fit, and then there is ambiguity.

"The Baptist State Convention has put off until fall any action on the subject. Hopefully, a forthright statement will be adopted then." This literally means that the adoption will come about in a hopeful spirit. But the intended meaning was *it is hoped.*

"A new session will meet late in the spring to vote new credits to the Congo, hopefully at a reduced figure." With a feeling of hope? Nay; *at, it is hoped, a reduced figure.*

"Hopefully, said *Pravda,* the system would make every worker in every job a watchdog against waste." Which feels hope here—*Pravda* or the system? Neither, really; Pravda *said it was hoped the system . . .*

"The report will serve, hopefully, to keep Congress to the $4 billion mark." Absurd: a report cannot experience hope. *it is hoped.*

"Viewed *hopefully,* this is a period of transition." A correct use, cited just to show how well it sounds.

Obviously we have here a new use born of the irresistible urge to telescope (*it is hoped* into *hopefully*). The *Standard College Dictionary,* the newest of the desk dictionaries, is the only one that recognizes this sense.

horn As strictly used among musicians, the term refers to the French horn. Loosely, however, among both musicians and laymen, it may be applied to any brass instrument (especially trumpets and trombones), and sometimes even to any wind instrument, including such woodwinds as the clarinet. This is especially true among jazzmen and jazz aficionados.

host   As a verb, *host* is questionable ("The East Side Club hosted the convention") although society writers love it. *Host* (and *hostess* as a verb) may well be left to them, together with *chair* as a verb, *benedict, justweds,* and *nuptials.*

hotel   Takes *a,* not *an.*

hot-water heater   Surely a redundancy, but the term may be solidly enough established to have passed beyond criticism.

however, how ever   *However,* as both an adverb meaning *in whatever manner* and as a connective meaning *nevertheless,* must be distinguished from the adverbial phrase *how ever,* an emphatic form of *how:* "It was a mystery, *however* he carried it off" (*in whatever manner*) ; "We noticed, *however,* that the money was not refunded" (*nevertheless*) ; "The neighbors wondered *how* they *ever* managed to pay off the mortgage" (*how*). In this sense, *how* and *ever* are two words.

The main question about *however* as a connective is where to put it. Its function is to indicate a contrast, and it should not break a sentence except for that purpose. In "We noticed, however, . . ." the stress of contrast is laid against *we noticed.* If the arrangement were *We, however,* the stress would be against *we,* contrasted with others. If *however* comes first, the stress is against all that follows. It also modifies the whole sentence when placed at the end. The user must decide what element of his sentence is to be contrasted and place *however* accordingly. When *however* begins a second clause, it is preceded by a semicolon: "Several topics of interest will be discussed; however, election of officers will be the main business of the evening." The semicolon is necessary to relate *however* to the second clause. *However* as a connective is always set off by commas or otherwise. *But however,* as Fowler noted, is a redundancy; one word or the other should be excised.

huddle   As a figure of speech adapted from football, overworked and generally inappropriate: "Government officials and labor leaders huddled this morning." *met, conferred.* See also *kick off.*

huge throng   Redundant; a throng, by definition, is huge.

huh-uh   See *ah, aw.*

human, humans *Human* as a noun ("Humans are sentient beings") is not wrong, but is likely to sound either technical or quaint. *Person* and *people* are the natural words to distinguish, for instance, between the human and the nonhuman. "The cast consists of nineteen humans and one goat." *people.*

humanist, humanitarian A humanist is a variety of scholar; a humanitarian is one concerned about human welfare. *Humanist* is acceptable in the latter sense, but since this may give rise to ambiguity, it is desirable to keep the uses distinct.

humble Takes *a*, not *an*.

humble opinion The truly humble do not have opinions, but humbly adopt the views of their betters.

hung Generally decried for execution on the ground that only *hanged* is proper in this sense. The distinction between *hung* and *hanged* is generally illustrated by the dictum that pictures are hung, people are hanged. Nevertheless, *hung* is prevalent and standard usage in both senses.

hurl Often an excited variant of *make* or *throw*, especially in *hurl a charge*, a conspicuous concretion of the news columns. Epithets, too, are invariably hurled, together with insults and imprecations. The great advances in rocketry have given *hurl* another leg to stand on; satellites, it seems, must invariably be hurled into orbit. *Hurl* connotes great force. This makes "The people were hurling flowers and confetti at the distinguished visitor" absurdly overwrought.

hurricane, typhoon See *typhoon, hurricane.*

hydro- Solid as a prefix: *hydrocarbon, hydroelectric, hydrophobia,* etc.

hyper- Solid as a prefix: *hyperacidity, hypercritical, hyperthyroid,* etc.

HYPHENS
Hyphens in Compound Modifiers To begin with, let us bow our heads and meditate on the text for the day. It comes from the gospel according to John Benbow, in *Manuscript and Proof,*

the stylebook of the Oxford University Press, and runs: "If you take the hyphen seriously you will surely go mad."

Yet big, strong journals that do not hesitate to beard a vested interest in its den every week are so terrified of this all but imperceptible mark that they have banished it from their pages. Somehow, it makes one think of the elephant and the mouse—or perhaps the elephant and the flea.

On the other hand, there are publications that cannot abase themselves enough before what they conceive to be a minuscule deity, and in their stylebooks devote page after page of homage to it in the form of ritualistic dogma setting forth in minute detail when it shall be invoked and when not. How the hyphen got such a reputation for merciless power is a mystery, for actually he is a self-effacing little fellow, always ready to perform a needed task but just as ready to stay on the shelf when people feel they can get along without him, as they often can.

The first thing to remember about the hyphen is that it is a joiner—not like George Babbitt, the super-Rotarian, but like a Gretna Green parson. Let us pass over both the more obvious and the rarer kinds of jobs done by the hyphen to consider the two uses that seem to give the most trouble. One of the hyphen's jobs is linking compound modifiers before a noun. In this instance, the hyphen weds two ordinarily separate words used in such a way that they form a single idea. There is some leeway here, for many such combinations are perfectly understandable in the intended sense without the hyphen, though the purist would insist on it. In spite of the purist, however, the tendency is to drop the hyphen.

Strictly, the correct forms would be *snow-covered hills, an odd-looking man, dark-brown cloth,* and *a power-driven saw;* but who would be likely to misconstrue *snow covered hills, an odd looking man,* or *a power driven saw?* You will often see such expressions written without the hyphen, and it seems stupid to quibble when the sense is clear.

But *strong navy agitation,* which conveys "strong agitation by (or concerning) the navy" is a horse of another color from *strong-navy agitation,* or "agitation for a strong navy." Contrast also *an old time clock* (an old-time clock or an old time-clock?); *a single tax organization* (a single organization concerned with taxes or one concerned with the single tax?); *a small animal hospital* (a small hospital for animals or a hospital for small animals?).

Compound modifiers formed by several paired expressions are tricky propositions, and probably best avoided. The difficulty here is that it is not immediately evident just what the hyphen is joining. Take, for example, "a coalition of Southern white-big city-big labor-ethnic minority votes." This can be confusing, if the reader sees the hyphens as connecting *white-big, city-big, labor-ethnic*. Give the reader credit for some intelligence, you say? All right, but even so, chances are that this is the kind of construction he will have to go back over, sorting out the elements and deciding on the pattern the writer meant them to fall into. When this task is imposed on the reader, too much is being demanded of him. The idea would be more smoothly conveyed by "a coalition of votes representing Southern white, big-city, big-labor, and ethic-minority elements."

"He was not accepted by the New Deal-Fair Deal Kennedy Democrats of Texas" is easier to assimilate, perhaps because the capitalization helps the reader to see the pattern. Such constructions should be used with care, if at all.

Hyphens with Numbers The hyphen is often carelessly omitted part way through compound modifiers, especially those containing numbers: *a 25-mile an hour speed* is properly *a 25-mile-an-hour speed*. Likewise, a *500-foot long relief map* should be *500-foot-long*, and a *12-foot thick concrete wall* should be *12-foot-thick*. On the other hand, numbers preceding nouns as simple modifiers are sometimes mistakenly followed by hyphens: "sentenced to *180-days* in jail" should be *180 days*. Similarly, "*400 million dollars worth* of business" should not be *400-million-dollars' worth*.

Sometimes hyphens are wrongly used with the figures denoting a measurement: *a flight of 7 hours-28 minutes-25 seconds; a man 5-feet 6-inches tall*. Preferred practice inclines toward commas (*7 hours, 28 minutes, 25 seconds*) or nothing (*5 feet 6 inches tall*). The hyphens are correct when the measurement is a preceding modifier: *a 7-hour, 28-minute, 25-second flight; a 5-foot, 6-inch man*. Compound modifiers other than those containing numbers may have more than two parts, all of which should be linked. "Contributors of the most sought-after items" was intended to be "contributors of the *most-sought-after* items." The senses differ.

The hyphen, when it joins two figures, means *through*, and it is generally used in this way with dates: July 15-19. It is undesirable because possibly misleading, then, to use the hyphen in place of *to* in indicating a span: "We have been paying about 40-50 per cent of the cost." The example illustrates another common fault: since *40 to 50 per cent* is an approximation, *about* is redundant. Better: "We have been paying 40 to 50 per cent of the cost."

Although, in the general neglect of hyphens, they are often omitted in numbers like *sixty-eight* and *twenty-one,* careful usage calls for them. This is true also of fractions rendered in words: *four-fifths, seven-ninths.*

Hyphens with Phrasal Verbs   Hyphens often insinuate themselves into those combinations of verb and adverb that really are new verbs, like *cash in, hole up, pay off.* Confusion arises because some such expressions can be used as modifiers, and then the hyphen is required. Thus "The Communists *stepped up* infiltration" (a verb in two parts, no hyphen); and "A *stepped-up* campaign is planned for spring" (compound adjective modifying *campaign,* hyphen required).

To prevent misinterpretation, use of the hyphen must be based on good judgment. The distinctions necessary in the examples cannot be made in publications that ban the hyphen, without recasting the sentence. The no-hyphens rule is, of course, worse than the evil (too many hyphens) it would suppress, because it is likelier to alter the meaning. That is something the disease we might call hyphenitis seldom does, however much it may annoy the discriminating.

Hyphens with Prefixes and Suffixes   Hyphens, as we have noted, have a strong tendency to fade away. In certain common uses, they are called on for a time to link ordinarily separate elements. After a while people seem to get used to seeing those elements together, and the engagment, so to speak, is followed by a wedding; the elements are joined and the hyphen is forgotten. This is particularly true of prefixes and suffixes (like *pre-, bi-, anti-, co-, -down, -goer*). Thus *mid-summer* becomes *midsummer,* and *pre-war* becomes *prewar.* Yet many writers not only hang onto the hyphen like grim death in instances like these, but also wedge it into words like *react, intercede, excommunicate, retroactive,* and others where it has not belonged in the memory of living man, if ever.

The dictionary-makers are often thought of as stick-in-the-muds who don't catch up with accepted usage until thirty years too late. But they are far ahead of many of us when it comes to dropping hyphens that have served their purpose. It seems like a good idea to get rid of hyphens when usage has sanctioned it to the extent that the dictionaries agree. There is an easier solution to the hyphen problem than creating a morass of rules for individual combinations. Just shift the whole thing onto Webster's shoulders. The result will be a heap of discarded hyphens, which may be thrown away, combined to make dashes, or chopped up into periods.

For ready reference, here is a list of prefixes usually set solid: *a-, ante-, anti-, bi-, by-, circum-, co-, counter-, dis-, down-, electro-, extra-, fore-, hydro-, hyper-, hypo-, in-, infra-, inter-, mal-, micro-, mid-, multi-, non-, on-, out-, over-, pan-, post-, pre-, re-, semi-, sesqui-, sub-, super-, supra-, trans-, tri-, ultra-, un-, under-, uni-, up-.*

Prefixes usually hyphenated: *all-, ex-, no-, self-, vice-, wide-* (*wide-angle,* but *widespread*).

Suffixes usually set solid: *-down, -fold, -goer, -less, -like, -over, -wise.*

Suffixes usually hyphenated: *-designate, -elect, -odd, -off, -on, -to, -up, -wide.* Yet *headon, leanto, closeup, nationwide* are not merely on the way but already here.

The whole question of the hyphen is fraught, as they say, with peril, and the only point concerning it on which grammarians agree is that confusion reigns supreme. Many an open-minded person will go along with Webster on setting prefixes solid until he reaches something like *antilabor,* which may stick in his craw even after he figures it out as the consistent treatment of *anti-labor.*

John Dos Passos, with combinations like *welldressed, sportsclothes* and *panamahats,* may be so far ahead of the parade that it will never catch up. On the other hand, many British publications use *to-day.*

Is there hope for those who write *radio-active* for *radioactive, over-turn* for *overturn, thorough-going* for *thoroughgoing, re-admit* for *readmit, one-time* (single occasion) for *onetime* (*sometime* or *quondam*)? Not unless they can be persuaded to stop, look, and look up before striking the hyphen key. See also the discussion of word combining under *back yard.*

Let us close with a wistful comment from the Fowlers in *The King's English:* "Hyphens are regrettable necessities, to be done without whenever they reasonably may."

Hyphens in Titles   Hyphens are often confusingly used in corporate titles: "He was chief engineer-general manager of the concern." Not *engineer-general,* as appears at first glance, but chief engineer *and* general manager. If the form with *and* is too long, the dash would be better than the hyphen: chief engineer—general manager. Then there are such titles as *vice president-sales,* to which the same objection applies. Improvements: *vice president in charge of sales, vice president* (*sales*) or *vice president—sales.*

Hyphen with -ly   The principle that words ending in *ly* should not be joined to what they modify is fairly well known, though not so well observed (*an easily* [-] *grasped concept, a beautifully* [-] *executed painting*). The reason is that, as in the examples, *easily* and *beautifully* (like nearly all words ending in *ly*) are adverbs, and cannot modify anything but the adjectives that follow. Thus it is superfluous to link *easily* with *grasped* and *beautifully* with *executed. Almost* does not end in *ly*, but the principle is the same: "an almost-insuperable obstacle." The hyphen should be omitted.

The hyphen is widely used with other adverbs like *once, seldom, often* as well. This might not be worth notice except for the widespread absence of the hyphen from places where it is needed to make the proper sense.

Hyphens in Definitions   In consulting the dictionary, people sometimes mistake the dots used to divide syllables for hyphens (gob'ble·dy·gook). Hyphens intended as such are printed in their usual form in dictionary entries or sometimes as double hyphens (=).

Hyphen vs. Dash   Incredible as it may seem, there are those who do not know the difference between a dash and a hyphen. Briefly, it is that a hyphen is the shorter of the two (-), and serves to connect; the dash is the longer (—) and serves to separate.

Obviously, nothing meaningful can be conveyed on this subject if the hyphen is referred to as the dash, or vice versa. An example of this confusion occurred in a Senate hearing at which a stenographer, reading the transcript of a monitored phone call, noted that a dash occurred at a certain point.

She was interrupted by a senator, who presumably had a copy of the transcript before him. "Two dashes," he said.

"Two hyphens—yes, sir—a dash," was her slightly flustered reply.

The dash is formed on the typewriter by striking the hyphen twice, a fact of life that the stenographer had in mind but that was foreign to the senator.

Confusion on this point leads to hyphens getting into print in place of dashes. In print, of course, the dash is ordinarily a single line, at least twice as long as the hyphen. Sometimes, however, in very large type faces, the dash is constructed from two hyphens, as on the typewriter, and this is where trouble often begins when the difference is not recognized.

Superfluous Hyphens The befuddlement that prevails as to the hyphen's job is illustrated by a new and seemingly growing tendency to hyphenate phrases for no reason. Some examples (all the hyphens are superfluous):

These articles are *profiles-in-depth;* much can be accomplished through *word-of-mouth;* American women were given a *pat-on-the-back;* garbage pickups will be made *once-a-week;* that was the chancellor's *point-of-view;* the chart is updated *minute-by-minute;* the boy was *10-years-old* (but—attributively—a *10-year-old boy* is correct).

hypo- Solid as a prefix: *hypodermic, hypogastric, hypothyroid,* etc.

hysterical Often wrongly preceded by *an* rather than *a.* See *a, an.*

—I—

I (we) Columnists and others using an informal style sometimes self-consciously avoid *I* by simply omitting it and starting sentences endlessly with verbs, leaving the subject to be supplied by the reader: "Appeared on a television program last week, and . . ."; "Was embarrassed by some criticism . . ." When overdone, avoidance of *I* is even more conspicuous than its use. See also *Editorial We.*

-ic, -ics Is there a difference between a *dramatic* instructor and a *dramatics* instructor? It seems apparent that any instructor who used stage techniques in putting his lesson across would be a *dramatic* instructor, but that a *dramatics* instructor could only be one who taught dramatics.

The distinction between *athletic* and *athletics,* used as adjectives, is technically the same, but is less observed. On the sports pages, most athletics directors have long since become athletic directors, disregarding the fact that they may be paunchy and inert. The difference between an *athletic* director and an *athletics* director is the same as that between a musical critic and a music critic.

We often read of *electronic engineers,* who (or which?),

strictly speaking, would be robots, but this is not the meaning intended—nor even the one the reader assumes, if we are going to be honest about it. The writer has in mind *electronics* engineers; that is, engineers who are trained in electronics.

Politics, although capable of being pressed into service as an adjective, fortunately has a distinct and well-accepted adjective form, *political. Politic,* of course, is something else again.

Narcotics, cosmetics, and *economics* sometimes give the same kind of trouble as *athletics* and *dramatics*. Narcotics agents, who deal with drug-law violations, often see themselves referred to as *narcotic agents*. This designation, which describes them as "tending to stupefy," would better fit after-dinner speakers.

The point in all this is the difference between a true adjective (*athletic*) and a noun (*athletics*) that is being made to do service as an adjective. This matter of *-ic* vs. *-ics* cannot be pursued very far, because it has become puristic to insist on a distinction between, for example, *athletic director* and *athletics director*. There is about as much chance of impressing the difference on the sporting fraternity as there is of getting it to pronounce *athletics* in three syllables instead of four.

Names of studies or activities ending in *-ics* are singular: *mathematics is, athletics is, politics is, economics is* (not *are*).

IDENTIFICATION (OF PEOPLE)   See *Reference*.

identified with   Pretentious for *belongs to, member of,* or *works for*. See also *affiliated with*.

ideology   *Idealogy* is a variant, but so unusual that it is likely to be taken for an error.

idiosyncrasy   Sometimes misspelled *idiosyncracy*.

if, whether   The idea that these words are not interchangeable where they make sense is a superstition. "I do not know whether he will come" and "I do not know if he will come" are equally correct. It is sometimes said that *whether* is preferable to *if* when an alternative is stated (*we shall go whether it rains or clears*). This draws a pretty fine and arbitrary line, and finds no corroboration among authorities on usage. Nor does observation indicate that careful writers are conscious, generally, of any such distinction. Rhythm, as much as anything, appears to be the deciding factor in the choice between *if* and *whether*.

if and when   A pretentious redundancy fancied by many. An effect that is conditioned on *if* alone implies the idea of *when:* "If and when the conferees reach an agreement, the factory will reopen." Either *if* or *when.*

if I was, were   Anyone who wants to examine the tortuous expositions of the grammarians on whether the subjunctive in English is here to stay or gone forever may do so. The consensus is that it is disappearing. The use of the right form to express conditions contrary to fact is usually instinctive, and no space will be wasted on examples here. There is one case, however, where uncertainty is sometimes felt, and that is in the choice between *was* and *were.* The correct form continues to be *were: If I were king; If he were wise. If I was,* etc., is subliterate.

if . . . then   The use of *then* to begin the conclusion that follows a conditional clause starting with *if* usually makes for unnecessary emphasis and may indicate an immature style. "If he can't be a bullfighter right away then he'd like to be a steeplejack"; "If one Democrat deserts to a united opposition, then the vice-president can cast the deciding vote in the Senate." Delete the *thens.*

ilk   In spite of some objections, *of that ilk* is no longer strictly a Scottish expression meaning *of the same (name, surname, place).* Its use in the sense *of that kind (a development of that ilk; a swindler of that ilk)* is established, though facetious.

ill   See *sick.*

illegal operation   A euphemism, favored in journalism, for *abortion,* which everyone knows is meant.

illiteracy, illiterate   In their absolute sense, the terms refer to inability to read and write, but they are often extended to ineptitude or low ability.

illusive   See *allusive, elusive, illusive.*

illy   Although the word is in good odor, many have held their noses at it as an illiteracy. This may account for its being something of a rarity, or vice versa. The usual thing is to use *ill* as both adverb and adjective: *an ill-conceived plan; we do not think ill of it.*

imaginary, imaginative   *Imaginary* relates to what exists in the imagination in contrast to what is real: "Pink elephants are likely to be imaginary." *Imaginative* means *characterized by, or showing use of, imagination*: "The plans for the Civic Center are imaginative." Disregard of this distinction causes trouble: "A variety of imaginative space people have long thrived in the pages of science fiction." Did the writer intend to say that these people possess imagination, or that they are figments? He meant the latter, as the context showed, and thus the word should have been *imaginary* (or possibly *imagined*).

immigrate   See *emigrate, immigrate.*

imminently   Sometimes misused for eminently (which see). "Each of the three men proved himself imminently competent at solo performances." *eminently.*

impact   Equally the darling of the newswriter and of the composer of official prose. The newswriter likes it because it conveys the specious sense of drama and excitement on which he depends so much. *Impact* has a distinct suggestion of collision. Even allowing for figurative use, it hardly seems appropriate as a substitute for *effect* or *influence* in "For years scientists have recognized the impact of the immense Greenland icecap on the North Atlantic climate"; "The full impact of today's mortgage restrictions and tight money won't be felt until next spring or summer"; and "The president's advisers are concerned over the impact of high interest rates on school-building." The writer of gobbledygook likes to talk about *federally impacted areas,* meaning those in which the presence of federal activities have had noticeable effects on the local economy. This is true gobbledygook because it requires translation except for the initiate.

impeach   The word means simply to bring charges against an official with the object of removing him, not necessarily to accomplish the removal.

impeccable   A counterword of the music-reviewing trade.

Somehow considered preferable, in critical contexts, to *flawless* or *perfect*. See also *consummate*.

impel   Often misspelled *impell*.

implement   Recognized as a verb in the sense of *accomplish, fulfill, complete, carry out*: "The farm program will be *implemented* in the fall*.*" But it is so characteristic of gobbledygook that the fastidious shun it, and it is regarded by many as not having legitimate standing. The word is often considered a neologism, but it has been around long enough for Fowler to have cast a jaundiced eye at it.

imply, infer   To imply is to hint at, or suggest; to infer is to draw a conclusion. It may help to remember that only the speaker can imply, but either the speaker or the hearer can infer, though usually it is the hearer. *Infer* is often used where *imply* is called for, and although such a distinguished linguist as Kemp Malone has pointed out that this is long-established usage in English, the fact cannot be blinked that what is written with care maintains the distinction. "He *inferred* that we were rascals." The writer meant "He *implied* [*hinted, suggested*] that we were rascals," but the statement as made is open to misconstruction as "He drew the conclusion we were rascals."

impresario   Often misspelled *impressario*. The word has no relation to *impress*. *Impresario* comes from the Italian *impresa, enterprise; impress* comes from the Latin word meaning *press upon*.

in, at   Pointless efforts are sometimes made to prescribe one or the other, depending on the prescriber's prejudice, as the correct preposition to use with a place, such as a city, building, or street. Either *in* or *at San Francisco*, or *the Municipal Auditorium*, is correct. Some insist that a house is *in* a street, and, as a corollary, that people live *in* a street. Saying that people live *in* a street probably indicates conscious or unconscious imitation of British practice (*a house in Tottenham Road*), but it is not American idiom; in the U.S., *in* in reference to a street is usually taken to mean upon the roadway itself.

in, into, in to   *In* as a preposition, generally speaking, indicates presence; *into* indicates motion. "The girl was waiting in the room"; "He followed her into the house." *In* is now so commonly used where purists insisted (and perhaps still do) on *into* that it must now be accepted as standard, however. Webster recognizes this development in usage, equating *in* with *into* and citing *threw it in the fire; wouldn't let her in the house.* The choice between *in* and *into,* where there is motion, is a matter of rhythm, idiom, or the writer's preference. Precisians will stand by *into* in such instances. The preposition *into* should be distinguished from *in to* (the adverb *in* followed by the preposition *to*): "We dropped into coffee with the Smiths." *in to.*

in- Solid as a prefix: *inaccessible, inalienable, inboard,* etc.

in addition (to) Often roundabout for *besides.* See also *together with.*

in all probability Mushmouth (a language) for *probably.*

inasmuch as The correct form; not *in as much as* or *inasmuchas.* But *inasmuch as* is a clumsy expression whose idea can usually be expressed more neatly by *because, since,* or *for.* "Double sessions were instituted inasmuch as the school was overcrowded." *because.*

inaugurate Journalese for *open, begin, start.* See also *launch.*

in behalf, on behalf See *behalf.*

in back of A gaucherie for *behind. In front of,* however, serves a purpose that *before* does not: "The car was parked *in front of* the house." *Before* is possible here but less likely to be used. *Behind* might also be considered before *at the rear of* is set down. See also *upwards of.*

incarnate Repellent as the idea may be to Latinists, *incarnate* has long departed from the sole meaning *embodied in flesh;* it now means also *embodying an ideal form:* "The rural setting was peace incarnate."

in charge of Equally correct meaning *in the charge of* (*the program is in charge of Smith*) and *responsible for* (*Jones is in charge of entertainment*). The context always rules out ambiguity. "The children are in charge of a nurse" (in the charge of) ; "A nurse is in charge of the children."

incidentally, incidently   Webster now recognizes *incidently* as a variant of *incidentally*, but it formerly was considered an error, and probably continues to be so regarded by many.

include   Often inexactly used in the senses belonging to *comprise, consist of,* or *be composed of.* That which includes is not all-inclusive, careless use to the contrary. One should not say "The group includes . . ." unless he intends to omit some members of the group. In introducing an all-inclusive list it is preferable to be more explicit : "Members of the group are . . ."

incompetence, -cy   Both forms are standard, but the second is little used.

in connection with   Verbiage for *in,* as in "Two arrests were made in connection with the shooting." *in*

incredible, incredulous   *Incredulous* applies only to people, and means *skeptical* or *disbelieving*: "The testimony was given with conviction, but the jury was obviously *incredulous.*" *Incredible* may apply to people, but is used oftenest of things, and means unbelievable: "The alibi was *incredible.*" See also *credulous,* etc.

independent   Often misspelled *independant.* There is a choice, however, between *dependant* and *dependent* (which see) as either noun or adjective.

index, indexes, indices   *Indices* is the Latin plural of *index,* and some pretend it is the only proper form. But *indexes* was recognized as long ago as 1897, in the great *Century Dictionary.* Anglicized forms are likely to predominate.

indiscriminate   Not *undiscriminate.* Either *un-* or *indiscriminating* is correct, but *un-* is more usual.

indispensable   Sometimes misspelled *indispensible.*

individual   Not wrong, of itself, as a noun, as many seem to think, but undesirable where *person* will do. It is preferable only for emphasis of single identity. Thus "Several individuals accompanied the artist into the hall" is questionable, but "Individuals and organizations have different rights" is correct. The use of *individual* where *person* will serve is pretentious.

indorse   See *endorse*.

in effect   Should not be set off by commas: "The former president of the Ford Motor Co., in effect, told his congressional critics to put up or shut up." Usually the commas are merely superfluous, but in this instance they may be misleading, suggesting that the person referred to was only in effect the former president of Ford.

inequity, iniquity   Sometimes ignorantly confused; inequity is inequality, iniquity is evil. "Punishment is visited upon the sons for the inequity of the fathers." *iniquity*.

in excess of   The long way around for *more than*: "In excess of a thousand delegates will attend the convention." A pomposity.

infer   See *imply*.

INFINITIVES
Infinitives of Purpose   Reading "He made the trek in four days to arrive here exhausted" one might easily get the impression that the poor fellow had traveled with the intention of wearing himself out. That seems absurd, so the reader decides the writer really meant "He made the trek in four days, arriving here exhausted." It is usually possible to guess what is intended in spite of what is written. Indeed, the reader of some kinds of prose must become adept at a kind of steeplechase, because ambiguous constructions like the one illustrated are freely employed. They make reading a sporting proposition and may even transform a dull account into a moderately interesting game of chance.

Constructions like *to get* in "He went to the store to get some ice cream" are sometimes called infinitives of purpose. But it is not necessary to know what they are called to sense that they convey an intention. They should be saved for that purpose; if they are used when no intention exists, a double meaning results.

"Increased sales are announced by many companies, to confound the pessimists." One would think those diabolical companies announced increased sales just to confound the pesky pessimists. This idea is interesting, but hardly likely. What seems more probable is that the confounding of the pessimists was an unpremeditated sequel to the announcements, such as would be expressed by "Increased sales are announced by many companies, confounding the pessimists."

Here's a three-way weirdie: "George Fox, the itinerant preacher-mystic, defied Oliver Cromwell to found the Society of Friends in the seventeenth century." At first blush it seems as if Fox might have said something like, "Look here, Cromwell, you go founding any Society of Friends and I'll fix *your* clock." Fox, however, was himself the founder of the society, so this can't be right. Could it be that Fox defied Cromwell *for the purpose* of founding the society? Not much logic here, either. What the writer had in mind, of course, was "George Fox . . . defied Cromwell *by founding* the Society of Friends."

Moral: When you use an infinitive (*to arrive, to confound, to found*) make certain that you are not unintentionally indicating an intention or purpose.

Misleading Infinitives Infinitives find their way into places where they are obtrusive, ambiguous, or both: "It was the largest maneuver ever to be held in the South." This may easily be read as meaning "the largest maneuver that will ever be held" but the intention was "that has ever been held." The writer could have achieved his purpose explicitly by leaving out the infinitive *to be*: "It was the largest maneuver ever held in the South."

Sometimes an infinitive displaces a relative clause: "This is one of nineteen communities to have such a program." Here too there is an unintended suggestion of the future. The intended meaning was *that have* (rather than *to have*).

"One of the most determined suicide attempts to be recorded locally was a failure yesterday." Again, the infinitive does nothing but give a misleading suggestion of the future; it should have been omitted. *Ever* (*ever recorded locally*) would have supplied any desired emphasis.

"He was one of three speakers to address the meeting." Misinterpretation is unlikely here, although this might be misunderstood as "who were scheduled to address." The writer meant "one of three speakers who addressed" and might as well have said so.

These objectionable and unnecessary uses of the infinitive seem related to, or descended from, its occasional use to indicate the future: "He is to leave in the morning." Curme points out that this construction has some modal force, conveying the idea of necessity or compulsion. Very often, however, writers who use the infinitive in this way intend a simple future. They say, "I am to meet the 5:15" when they mean simply, "I will meet the 5:15." In no sense do they mean "I am required to meet the 5:15." A more glaring example: "The decision is to add $15 million to the cost." *will add;* possibly *is expected to.*

The use of *am to, is to,* and *are to* for *shall* or *will* should be discouraged. This usage is probably fostered by newspaper headlines, in which the convention is to indicate the future with the infinitive: "Statesmen To Meet in London." Headlinese, whose characteristics grow out of space limitations, often finds its way into text, where the limitations do not exist. It is easy to see how one might expand that headline into "Statesmen are to meet in London." But the preferable form would be "Statesmen will meet in London."

Split Infinitives One might think the revered Henry Watson Fowler had the last word on the split infinitive a generation ago when he divided the English-speaking world into five classes, namely:

"(1) Those who neither know nor care what a split infinitive is; (2) those who do not know, but care very much; (3) those who know & condemn; (4) those who know & approve; & (5) those who know & distinguish."

But no; here we are, still in doubt about the split infinitive, although his conclusion remains the consensus of grammarians today. In a nutshell: a split infinitive is not an error of itself, horrifying as this may sound to the dogma-damned fuddy-duddies who compile stylebooks. The acceptability of a split infinitive depends only on whether it damages the rhythm or meaning of the sentence.

Let's start from scratch. An infinitive is a verb form containing *to: to go, to run, to eat, to walk.* It is split when something separates *to* from its partner: *to* quickly *go, to* clumsily *run.* Splitting an infinitive objectionably is only one of the many ways a sentence can be spoiled by poor arrangement of its parts. Yet a big red flag has been hung on verb forms containing *to,* and unnumbered browbeaten wretches believe they will not enter heaven if they split the infinitive. They go to any lengths to avoid it, on all occasions, even though half the time the cure is worse than the disease.

Those who are impatient with grammatical definitions and distinctions, a category that seems to include most of us, may rely on the ear as a pretty good guide. If a sentence doesn't sound right, it isn't any good, whether the infinitive is split, rewoven, braided, or sawed in half.

These split infinitives are objectionable because they sound awkward: "I want to *consistently* enforce discipline"; "His purpose was to *effortlessly* be promoted"; "Jones was ordered to *immediately* embark." Such sentences call for recasting even if you don't know a split infinitive from an ablative absolute. The adverb (italicized) fits easily at the end in each instance.

But look at this: "Production of food fats is expected to *moderately* exceed domestic use and commercial exports." The nonsplit fanatic is likely to do one of two things with this. He may make the sentence read "is expected *moderately* to exceed," which raises a doubt whether the expecting or the exceeding will be moderate; or he may move *moderately* to the end of the sentence, but that's too far away from *exceed*, which it modifies.

This sentence was criticized as containing an undesirable split: "This will permit the nation to *quietly* drop her violent opposition to the treaty." Because there was no other comfortable place for the adverb, rewording was prescribed. Why? This kind of thing only illustrates Fowler's comment to the effect that reasons are not the strong point of the critics of split infinitives.

Life might be pleasanter if the existence of the infinitive were forgotten and if the mischief sometimes caused by splitting it were cured in each instance for its own sake. See also *Compound Verbs*.

inflammable   See *flammable*.

informal, informally   Words for which misguided fondness is often shown. Subjects of interviews have been known to be described, for example, as "perched informally on top of a desk." The absurdity of qualifiers is sometimes illustrated by substituting their opposites, which, presumably, the writer fears the reader might otherwise assume. We may ask, then, is it possible to perch *formally* on top of a desk? *Informal* and *informally* are all right to set the tone when necessary, but they are not necessary, and in fact are foolishly superfluous, when the tone has already been set by the words they modify. *Chats*, often described as informal, can hardly be anything else. "The president," we are informed, "makes some of his most informal cracks while posing for pictures." At the bottom of all this seems to be a democratic yearning to prove that the great, or at least the newsworthy, can unbend like the rest of us.

infra-   Solid as a prefix: *infrahuman, inframundane, infrastructure, infrared.*

in future   A Briticism; American idiom calls for *in the future.*

in (his, her) own right   The expression is ordinarily used by members of a family, and indicates individual ownership of something that might otherwise be held in common. If a man is a poet, it would be correct, in speaking of his wife, to describe her as a poet in her own right. But if a man is a religious leader, it is meaningless to describe his wife as following some other line of endeavor in her own right: "Each morning, the mystic's fourth wife, a poet in her own right, massaged him with oil for two hours in accordance with Hindu practice." Since the mystic was not a poet, his wife should have been designated simply as *a poet.*

INITIALS   The use of a single initial (*R. Roe, J. Doe, L. Witherspoon*) is considered an inadequate identification by most publications, which insist on a full first name (*Richard Roe*), at least two initials (*R. W. Roe*), or a combination of given name and initial. Preferably, the form should be that used by the owner of the name. Identifying people in writing by one initial, and even signing technical papers that way, seems to be an affectation around scientific establishments, like wearing beards.

ink a contract   A hopeless figure. Someday a sportswriter will tell of a player *signing* a contract, and will be acclaimed as a phrasemaker.

in line   See *on (in) line.*

in-migration   See *emigrate, immigrate.*

inoculate, vaccinate   These words for the process of immunizing by the injection of vaccine are interchangeable. *Vaccinate,* however, has been firmly established by custom as the word for immunization against smallpox. *Inoculate* is favored for immunization against polio and other diseases, such as diphtheria. *Inoculate* is often misspelled *innoculate*. The example of *innocuous* may have something to do with this.

in nothing flat   The ultimate, perhaps, in clichés as well as in speed.

in order, in order that   *In order*, when followed by an infinitive, as in "He bought the suit in order to impress his girl" can usually be omitted without loss. The same is true of *so as. In order that* should not displace *so, so that*.

in receipt of   Commercial jargon in such sentences as "We were in receipt of the shipment." *had already received*. Kin to *take delivery on* (which see).

in regard(s) to   See *regard*.

in respect to (of), with respect to   The idiomatic form of the phrase meaning *about* or *concerning* (which are preferable anyway because they are shorter and more direct) is *with respect to*. "Firm action was advised in respect to the Soviet Union." *with respect to; in respect to* may be understood *having respect for*, and thus makes this statement ambiguous. "Requirements for lighting are stringent, particularly in respect of allowable brightness levels." Fusty: *"particularly in allowable brightness levels"*; or, perhaps preferably, *"particularly in allowable levels of brightness."*

in routine fashion   An inflation of *routinely*.

inside   *Of* is superfluous with *inside* (and with *outside*): "inside of the hall." *inside the hall*.

insigne, insignia   The first is the singlar, the second the plural.

insist   Often loosely used in attribution, simply for variation, when there is actually no emphasis, and *say* would be more accurate. "You can study your game by examining the pattern your clubhead makes in the snow, insists one of the competitors." *says* or *points out*; no one was contradicting him. To save the sanity of the curious it may be explained that the sentence referred to an offbeat variety of golf played in winter. See also *contend*.

204

insofar as The proper form; not *in so far as, insofaras.*

inspirational As applied to speeches and writings, particularly, this descriptive should be used with care, for the knowing tend to associate it, through hard experience, with pap.

install In such constructions as "He was installed president," idiom calls for *as* with *install*: "He was installed *as* president."

instance Occurs in redundancies like *in the instance of;* see *Redundancy.*

insure See *ensure.*

integration See *desegregation, integration.*

inter- Solid as a prefix: *interflow, interjoin, intermingle, interwind,* etc.

interesting It is simpleminded to inform the reader that a fact being related is interesting. Interest is a subjective consideration, and the reader will make his own judgment about it. By being told he is expected to react with interest, he may even be deterred from doing so.

interfered Often misspelled *interferred,* perhaps by the influence of *inferred.*

interment, internment *Interment,* a favorite in obituaries, is burial. ("The good is oft *interr'd* with their bones.") *Internment* is a form of imprisonment and is generally used to describe what happens to aliens living in an enemy nation during wartime.

intermittent See *continuous.*

in terms of Generally a pomposity that would be better replaced by a simple preposition. "Owners of efficient ships would normally think in terms of lower rates." *think of* (*consider*) *lower rates.*

internecine This word has acquired a generally accepted meaning that departs from its strict sense. Basically, *internecine* means simply *destructive.* Fowler explained this, and went on to argue that the idea of mutuality (that is, *destructive of one another*), then becoming widespread in connection with the word, "is what gives the word its only value, since there are plenty of substitutes for it in its true sense—*destructive, slaughterous, murderous, bloody, sanguinary, mortal,* & so forth." The dictionaries now admit the idea of mutuality, but it is observable that good usage has gone one step further in restricting the meaning. World War II was certainly an internecine struggle, in the original sense, between the Allies and the Axis, but the word is not used in that way, and, if it were, it would be misunderstood. We now think of internecine war as civil war. ("An *internecine* war over the corpse of Karl Marx has threatened to split the party for decades.") The tendency of popular usage usually is to broaden meanings of words. In this curious instance, the meaning has been narrowed.

interpretative, interpretive Fowler preferred *interpretative* as conforming to the Latin derivation. The word is clumsy, however, compared with *interpretive,* which seems to have gained the majority vote. Preferences based on reasons like Fowler's in this instance have been steadily cast on the ash heap, very likely because there is hardly anyone around any more who can be affronted by distortions of Latin. See also *preventative, preventive.*

in the altogether See *altogether.*

in the course of Wordy for *during, in,* or *at.*

in the event that The long way around for *if.*

into A preposition that should be used with care in some constructions, which call for *in to.* "A man wanted as an Army deserter for fifteen years turned himself *into* the sheriff's office last night" suggests an implausible transformation.

in toto Often the victim of ignorance of spelling: "She said the story was ridiculous and denied it *en toto.*" This version has a French sound, but the phrase is Latin and the preposition is *in,* not *en.* It is questionable anyway whether a foreign phrase like *in toto* is suitable in most informal contexts.

intra- Solid as a prefix: *intracollegiate, intramural, intrastate,* etc.

intrigue Well established in the sense *arouse interest, desire, curiosity,* or *beguile,* despite carping by some pedants. "The handsome stranger *intrigued* her." Fowler scorned it as an interloper from France. Webster cites as examples "a tale that intrigues the reader"; "an intriguing smile"; "became intrigued with sketching."

inure The word means to become accustomed, not just to anything, but to something that is disagreeable, such as annoyance or pain. "For one inured to the singer's style, the transition is unsettling." *accustomed.*

invective(s) *Invective,* coupled with *hurl,* is a stock expression of journalese.

invent See *discover, invent.*

INVERSION See *Word Order.*

invest Has a strong connotation of an expected return, but often it is loosely used for *spend.* "The college will invest $13.8 million in new buildings over the next few years." It is arguable that a return in education is expected, and the return associated with *invest* need not be money; but this was simply a report on a construction program, with no philosophical implications.

in view of the fact that The long way around for *since, because,* or *considering that.*

invite As a noun, a barbarism: "The invites went only to contributors." *invitations.*

invited guest Redundant. Being invited is essential to guesthood. The uninvited are gate-crashers.

involve Inexactly used in place of *cause, result in.* "This involved a complete change of plans." *caused.*

in which Often dispensable, and when it is dispensed with, expression is improved: "Everybody is aware of the disorganized way [in which] the Senate and the House carry on their work." See also *Redundancy.*

irregardless   Often criticized when used for *regardless*. See also *regard; irrespective*.

irrelevant   Often carelessly pronounced *irrevelant* and consequently thus (or otherwise) misspelled.

irrespective   A synonym for *regardless*, and not, like *irregardless*, a freak in the form of a one-word redundancy. *Irrespective* probably prompted *irregardless*. No one has ever explained, however, why we need both *irrespective* and *regardless*. *Irrespective* once had a fine distinctive meaning, *lacking in respect*, but that sense is now obsolete.

-ise, -ize   With easily recognized exceptions, *-ise* is the characteristically British termination, *-ize* the American: *apologise, apologize*. This is not a matter of right and wrong, but of custom. Americans who use *-ise* on words that take *-ize* in the U.S. generally do so deliberately and are likely to be considered affected or precious in this respect.

Tacking on *-ize* is a convenient method of making a needed verb from a noun: *concertize*. But it should not be practiced when existing verbs will serve.

Israel, Israeli   See *Jew, Jewish*.

issue   See *noncontroversial issue*.

is to (am to, are to)   See *Misleading Infinitives* under *Infinitives*.

ITALICS   Used generally in carefully edited material for the titles of books, musical compositions, paintings, and other works of art, for foreign words, and to convey emphasis that would be conveyed by stress in speaking. One should be certain that italics are available in the typesetting equipment before indicating their use (which is usually done in typescript by underlining). Most newspapers are not able to set italics conveniently. When italics are not available, titles are often enclosed in quotation marks, although the growing tendency is to set them without any distinctive mark. Boldface is suitable in place of italics to denote emphasis, but not for foreign words or titles. When something that would ordinarily be set in italics occurs in what is already being italicized, the desired differentiation is indicated by reverting to Roman.

ITEMIZED PARAGRAPHS   When paragraphs constitute a sequence of related points this should be indicated in some unmistakable way. Sometimes it is attempted by indenting the body of the paragraphs, but the instructions to indent may easily be overlooked. Even when they are followed, this device may not be conspicuous enough.

Some publications follow the practice of numbering or lettering the paragraphs, or of using some such device as the paragraph symbol (¶). It is a growing practice, since such characters are often unavailable, to set off the related paragraphs by starting them with dashes. This has the advantages of not appearing to rank the points by importance, as lettering or numbering may do, and of facilitating the insertion of additional points if necessary.

Long lists of names are often arbitrarily broken into paragraphs to open up a column of type and prevent a gray, forbidding appearance. This is a good idea, but it is unnecessary to link paragraphs after the first one by starting them with *also*. The elegant way to handle long lists of names is to set them one under the other in two columns side by side.

"School bills passed by the Legislature this year affected adult education classes, financial reports, cafeterias, child-care centers, and electronic data processing.

"Also high-school honors, reading assistants, insurance, interdistrict attendance, and investment of retirement funds.

"Additionally, retirement, school property, elections, transportation, workmen's compensation, and special education programs."

The items might better have all gone into one paragraph instead of being separated and then artificially and obtrusively linked by *also* and *additionally*. This device makes a sophomoric impression.

it goes without saying   See *of course; needless to say.*

it is, there is   Use of the false subject is not wrong, but it can easily be overdone, and it makes for a muffled style. Sometimes such expressions as *it is believed* are used to avoid the personal pronouns: "I [or we] believe." This is a mistake unless there is an overriding reason to keep the statement impersonal; personal ones have more interest and immediacy. See also *there; Editorial We; one.*

it is I who (is, am)   In constructions like "It is I who am the nominee," strictly speaking the verb *am* agrees with the subject, which is *I*. But there is a strong tendency to use *is*, since *am* sounds artificial. Identical constructions with other pronouns fall naturally into place with no hesitation: "It was you who were," "It is they who are," "It is she who is."

its, it's   *Its* means *belonging to it:* "The cat is washing its fur." *It's* is the contraction for *it is:* "It's one o'clock." None of the possessive pronouns ending in *s* takes an apostrophe (*its, hers, theirs, ours*).

it's me (him, her, us)   Acknowledged as correct by all authorities. The nominative ("It's I") is stilted and thus avoided.

—J—

Jap, Japanese   *Jap* was freely used during World War II, with malicious satisfaction in the fact that it is derogatory. Since then, *Japanese* is carefully chosen nearly everywhere as both noun and adjective: *four Japanese; Japanese ships*. The derogatory implication of *Jap* is so clear it is avoided even in newspaper headlines, despite the pressure of small space. *Nip*, as a clipped form of *Nipponese*, is considered equally offensive.

jest growed   See *Misquotation*.

jetsam   See *flotsam, jetsam*.

Jew, Jewish   Much expostulation results from careless use of the terms in connection with Israel. Although that nation is closely identified with the Jewish race and religion, the expressions *Israeli* and *Jewish* are not interchangeable. Israel, like other nations, is composed of peoples of many races and religions, including a substantial number of Arabs and Mohammedans, and Christians of various races too. *Jew* and *Jewish*, then, in reference to the nationals of Israel, are called for only in the circumstances when those terms would be applied to the nationals of any other country. *Jewish* is not the name of a language; usually *Hebrew* or *Yiddish* is intended.

jeweler, jeweller   *Jeweller* is the British preference.

jewelry, jewels There is a superstition to the effect that *jewelry* is properly applied to what is in a jeweler's window, and that the same ornaments, when worn, must be called *jewels*. By this principle, the crown jewels, if on display, would have to be called the crown jewelry. *Costume jewelry*, it may be observed, is an invariable term, applied regardless of whether the jewelry is worn or displayed. If there is a distinction, it is that *jewelry* is a collective likely to be applied to items of the jeweler's art considered as a group, and that *jewels* is a plural applied particularly to gems.

Jewess Often considered derogatory.

jibe See *gibe, jibe*.

job, position Usage does not substantiate the idea that *job* necessarily connotes manual labor. It is the homelier word of the two, and certainly *position* would never be seriously applied to ditch-digging. *Job*, sometimes qualified by *big*, is applied casually to employment of all ranks. *Position* is sometimes suspect because it is used to confer a spurious dignity, and those who are sensitive to this avoid it, especially in reference to their own jobs. See also *wage, salary; rise, raise*.

jobless Once derided as an unnecessary invention, *jobless* long since has won its spurs, though the *Oxford Universal Dictionary* does not recognize it. The inventor doubtless was a frustrated headline-writer confronted with *unemployed* during the Great Depression.

join together Despite the example of the Bible, this redundancy may well be put asunder; *join* alone serves.

joke, -d See *quip, -ped*.

journalese, journalism, journalistic Before 1954, when pressure was successfully brought to bear against the G. & C. Merriam Co. by Sigma Delta Chi, the professional journalistic society, the definition of *journalistic* in the Merriam-Webster dictionaries was more or less equated with that of *journalese*; it was as if the words were really *journalese* and *journalesetic*.

Journalese is what linguists like to describe as a pejorative; that is to say, a word that depreciates. It applies to all that is bad in journalistic writing. *Journalistic*, on the other hand, properly means *pertaining to journalism,* and ought not to have any derogatory connotation. Nor does it, ordinarily. The old Webster definition of *journalistic* was "Characteristic of journalism or journalists; hence, of style characterized by evidence of haste, superficiality of thought, inaccuracies of detail, colloquialisms, and sensationalism; journalese." In the revised definition, the derogatory aspects were replaced by "appropriate to the immediate present and phrased to stimulate and satisfy the interest and curiosity of a wide reading public —often in distinction from *literary.*" The definition of *journalistic* in the Third Edition of Webster has been further revised, but the effect is the same and it remains neutral.

The Third Edition defines *journalese* first as a style of writing held to be characteristic of newspapers, and goes on with "writing marked by simple, informal, and usu. loose sentence structure, the frequent use of clichés, sensationalism in the presentation of material, and superficiality of thought and reasoning."

The *Dictionary of Contemporary American Usage* remarks that "As a term for all newspaper writing, *journalese* is a snob term. There is just as good and effective writing in the best newspapers as in the best books, and the faults that are commonly classed as journalese are to be found in all writing." This is a fair judgment, but something more may be said on the subject of snobbery. *Journalese* is seldom applied to all newspaper writing, and when it is, the tone is so bitter that there is little hope of bringing the critic to reason. The truly snob term is *journalism,* applied, as Webster had it, in distinction to *literature.*

Often, when used in this way, *journalism* is preceded by *mere: mere journalism,* says the reviewer, and thus consigns the subject of his comment to perdition. Such judgments are generally stupid, and amount to depreciating folk music by comparing it with classical music. Journalism and literature nurture each other, as do folk and classical music. Much that is unpretentiously journalism is superb, as for example the kind of writing found in *The New Yorker* and the *Reporter;* much that aims at being literary is atrocious.

Now and then *journalese* is mistaken for a neutral descriptive of newspaper style. An author of a book on English usage even misapplied it as the term for the cant, or technical terminology, of journalism.

Most inferior writing is cliché-ridden, but newspapering has developed its own clichés. In journalese, a thing is not *kept secret,* but *a lid of secrecy is clamped* on it; rain and snow do not *fall,* but *are dumped;* a river does not *overflow,* but *goes on a rampage;* honors are not *won* or *earned* but *captured;* divisions are too often *crack;* a reverse of any kind does not *threaten,* but *looms;* a development is not *unprecedented,* but *precedent-shattering* (as though precedents were glass, when everyone knows they are rubber); large buildings are not *extensive,* which despite its colorlessness still has more life left in it than the battered *sprawling.*

All such expressions have something in common besides extreme fatigue. If you can shake off, for a moment, the anesthesia they produce, you will see that originally they were dramatic. Even if they were too dramatic to suit the occasion— another characteristic of journalese, not necessarily related to clichés—the first few times they were used they piqued the readers' attention. But that was long ago. How, then, do they come to be used so much? The obvious explanation is laziness. These expressions and many equally tired ones have become fixed in the minds of the lethargic and unimaginative as the only ones that are suitably descriptive.

When reporters are taxed with the stereotyped flavor of newspaper writing, they sometimes offer as an excuse that much of their work must be done in haste, to meet a deadline. This does not happen to be a good excuse, however, for it would be easier and faster to use the plain language the clichés conceal. Thus if the lazy were even a little lazier, the results would be happier.

Plain language—the words the cliché expert uses himself when he is talking instead of writing—often looks surprisingly fresh in print. It will never wear out, as the clichés have, because it is the natural and inevitable currency of expression.

Faults that are described in this book as journalese are prevalent in news publications, but by no means peculiar to them, because they exert tremendous influence on usage generally. See also *Clichés; Overwriting.*

Jr., Sr. It is growing practice to omit the comma once commonly used before *Jr.* and *Sr.: Joseph Williams Jr.; Edgar Smithson Sr.* Omission has grammar on its side, for such designations as *Jr.* and *Sr.,* like *II, III,* in *William II, George III,* are after all restrictive modifiers.

judgment, judgement *Judgement* is the British preference.

jungle gym   The correct form for the playground apparatus; not *jungle jim*.

junket   Not a neutral equivalent of *trip, journey* or *excursion*, for the word has a derogatory connotation. One kind of junket is a trip taken by a politician at public expense, ostensibly on public business but primarily for his own enjoyment. The *Overseas Press Club Bulletin* for April 16, 1960, decreed: "The word *junket* will henceforth be taboo in the deliberations of the Foreign Press Association of New York. On motion of Britishers on the executive board it has been decided to substitute the term *facility trips*." *Junket* is generally applied by newspapermen to joyrides provided not to facilitate news coverage, but to create goodwill. There is a hazy line between these and travel provided at someone else's expense, for example the military services or a corporation, with legitimate news coverage in view. Some scenes of news cannot be reached except by courtesy of, say, the military. The Foreign Press Association apparently was not inventing a euphemism but attempting to discourage loose application of *junket* to trips for legitimate news coverage.

jurist   As a variant of *judge, jurist* is inexact, and its use resembles the substitution of *attorney* for *lawyer*. "Winners & Sinners," *The New York Times* critique, commented: "A jurist is merely one who is versed in the law. Therefore, although a judge is, or should be, a jurist, a jurist is not necessarily a judge." Nonetheless, there seem to be few opportunities to use the word in its explicit sense, and newswriters are so afraid of using the same word twice that *jurist* is likely to become established as an exact synonym for *judge*.

—K—

Kas., Kan., Kans.   Kansas, to the casual eye, is a peaceful enough place, but appearances are deceptive. For beneath the surface civil rebellion seethes. The bone of contention is how to abbreviate *Kansas*. Some prefer *Kan.*, which may be regarded as more or less the orthodox version; others favor *Kas*. The disagreement is not without a tinge of bitterness.

It was with a piece entitled "What's the Matter with Kansas?" that William Allen White first attracted national attention. His successors in Kansas journalism are demanding, "What's the Matter with *Kan.* (or *Kas.*)?" depending on their preference. As a journalistic controversy, this difference appears to date back at least to a 1952 meeting of Kansas members of the Associated Press. It has been debated at subsequent meetings, too. The trouble is that the Associated Press uses *Kan.* in the other forty-nine states, and Kansas members who see nothing wrong with it are irked by the confusion resulting from the intrastate use of *Kas.*, which is not uniform even in Kansas.

The chief proponent of *Kas.* is F. W. Brinkerhoff, editor and manager of the Pittsburg, Kansas (taking no chances), Publishing Co. Mr. Brinkerhoff concedes that the choice between *Kan.* and *Kas.* is a matter of taste, but adds, "Kansans themselves should say what the abbreviation should be. Kansas is independent and would not appreciate having the other states choose its abbreviation."

It is good to be able to report that democracy rules in this crisis, because the current use of *Kas.* by the Associated Press (in Kansas, that is) is the result of a vote by AP members.

Illustrious example figures on both sides of this affair. The *Topeka Capital* and the *Topeka State Journal*, it is said, have always used *Kan.* But the mighty *Kansas City* (Missouri, that is) *Star* uses *Kas.* If the *Kan.* and *Kas.* camps are not utterly unreconcilable, they may yet find common ground in the U.S. Postal Guide. Its version is *Kans.*

keep pace with The form of the idiom; not *keep in pace with.*

kerosene, kerosine People who read not for the usual reasons— pleasure or information—but only to see if they can find any mistakes may think they see one in the occasional spelling *kerosine.* It is not an error, however, but a legitimate, if rare, variant. In some parts of the country, kerosene is called coal oil, an expression all but unknown in other areas. See also *paraffin* (the British term for kerosene).

kick off Either as a verb (*kick off the campaign*) or as an adjective (*a kick-off dinner*), this frayed figure from the football field has been done to death.

kick over the traces Nearly everyone is aware in a general way that this means *to defy* or *escape restraint,* but a generation has grown up that does not know what traces are in this sense.

215

Well, Junior, they are the straps or chains by which horses used to pull wagons.

kids A generation ago, teachers busily instructed their pupils that kids could only be young goats, but the real goats were the kids who swallowed this pedantry. Some of them grew up to be editors with a prejudice against *kids* for *children*. The word is well established colloquially in this sense, however, and in many contexts *children* sounds stilted.

kind of See *sort of, kind of (a)*.

knocked up The difference in meaning of this expression as slang in Britain and America has yielded much merriment. The British senses are *make tired* or *awaken;* the American is *make pregnant;* as the latter is illustrated in Webster, "no girls get married around here till they're knocked up." (There are other senses, but they are not confused.)

knots Landlubbers sometimes find themselves at sea when they use nautical terminology; for example, *knots per hour* is a recurrent bit of flotsam. It's redundant, for a knot is a nautical mile per hour; the word is a measure of speed, not distance. A nautical mile is about one and one-seventh land miles.

kudos *Kudos* (from the Greek *kydos*, meaning *glory*) is one of the rare words unearthed and popularized by *Time* magazine in its early efforts to attract attention. *Kudos* is not a plural any more than *pathos* (from the Greek *penthos, grief*); thus one can no more speak of *a kudo* than of *a patho*. Neverthless, there was conferred upon a correspondent the dubious distinction of "a Congo kudo" for his work in that country. "Based on his compassion and perception, kudos are in order for Edmund Wilson." *is*. The misapprehension that *kudos* is a plural whose singular is *kudo* has been ridiculed so much that it is no less than flabbergasting to see the word used as a verb: *"Life* Kudos Capitol's Cast Albums." Let us now kudo famous men.

know-how The term must have the hyphen until it becomes one word: *knowhow*. "The man who has the know-how must know how."

—L—

la, le In proper names, see *de, du*, etc.

labor (a point) See *belabor*.

labour Should be thus spelled in reference to the British political party; otherwise, U.S. usage calls for *labor*.

lacerations See *Technical Terms*.

lady See *woman, lady*.

(a) large portion of Verbiage for *much, most:* "A large portion of his continuing popularity is due to habit." *Much of his* . . .

(a) large number of Excessive for *many:* "A large number of flamingoes were crowding to the gate." *Many flamingoes* . . .

Lafayette, we are . . . See *Misquotation*.

larynx Sometimes misspelled *larnyx*.

last, latest, past Some insist that *last* can only mean *final*, and that *past* must be used for *immediately preceding*, as in *during the past week, the past year*. This, however, is quibbling. As in *during the last week, the last year, last* is commonly used in the sense of *just past* without ambiguity, since occasions for referring to the end of the world are few. *Latest* is suitable in other references to mean *immediately preceding* where *last* could be misunderstood as *final:* "The *latest* issue is dated Dec. 15; the one to be published in January will be the *last*."

late Redundant in *widow of the late*.

Latin America There is no occasion for hyphening the term as either noun or modifier: *The economics of Latin America; Latin American literature*. Not *Latin-America, -n*.

latter Used to distinguish two of a kind, and generally coupled with *former* (which see). There is no occasion to displace

217

pronouns with *latter:* "No law can prevent a conflict of interest from affecting a government official. Though the latter [preferably *he*] may have divested himself of stock . . ." *Latter* may, however, refer to the last of three or more.

laudable, laudatory Occasionally confused; what is laudable deserves praise, what is laudatory confers it.

launch Journalese for *open, begin, start.* See also *inaugurate.*

law concern Not idiomatic; a better term is *law firm.* Otherwise, *concern*, like *firm*, is properly used in the sense of *business establishment.* See also *firm.*

lawman The term is most commonly used in Western stories and dramas and means *law enforcement officer.* It is appropriate for the cop, the sheriff, or even the federal marshal. It is not properly applied to lawyers.

lawyer See *attorney.*

lay See *lie, lay.*

layman The primary meaning is *of or pertaining to the laity, as distinct from the clergy.* It is well established, however, to designate one outside some other profession or field of endeavor. Thus *layman* may be used in contradistinction to *doctor, lawyer, engineer, teacher,* etc., as well as *clergyman.*

lb., lbs. The use of the abbreviations *lb., lbs.* for *pound(s) sterling* and similar monetary units is confusing and undesirable. George Mayberry's *A Concise Dictionary of Abbreviations* gives *lb., lbs.* as the abbreviation only for units of weight.

Derivation might support the use of *lb.* for the monetary pound, since the pound sterling originally was an avoirdupois pound of silver. But usage has attached *lb.* to the unit of weight. Whence *lb.* for *pound?* It stands for *libra*, the ancient Roman unit of weight from which our pound derives. Many typesetting machines carry the symbol for the pound sterling, £. When available, it should be used. When it is not, it is better to spell out *pounds sterling* (*25,000 pounds sterling*) than to use *lbs.* The pound sterling symbol, or something like it, can be produced on the typewriter by striking the hyphen over the *L.*

A sum given in pounds sterling or, for that matter, any

unfamiliar monetary unit, should be followed by the equivalent in United States dollars.

Lbs. is often used for the plural form. If the purpose of an abbreviation is to abbreviate, it should be *lb.* for both singular and plural. This applies to any abbreviation capable of being pluralized: *In.* (not *ins.*), *sec.* (not *secs.*), for example. Despite its logic, or maybe because of it, this principle is not much observed, especially for *lb.*

lead   The past tense of the verb is *led:* "They led us to the mouth of the tunnel." Sometimes it is rendered *lead,* perhaps by confusion with the name of the metal, which of course is pronounced *led.*

In the cant of printing, *lead* is a verb (as well as a noun) pronounced *led,* meaning to space out lines of type by inserting strips of metal. In a commendable effort to prevent confusion, the *Linotype News* invented the spelling *ledd* and *ledding.* Such efforts, no matter how well intentioned, seldom succeed, and it remains to be seen what will come of this one. There is a successful precedent, however, in *linage* (which see) as applied to space occupied by advertising.

leading question   Strictly, a question that suggests its answer, and not necessarily a significant or critical one. The original sense comes from the courts of law.

leaped, leapt, lept   *Leaped* is the favored form in America as the past of *leap*; *leapt* is chiefly British. *Leapt* is pronounced *lept* but not spelled that way.

LEAPFROG   A problem of reference is exemplified by a game we might call leapfrog. It is among the favorites of that fun-loving crew, the gentlemen of the press. In this form of leapfrog, the leaping is done by the reader, whether he likes it or not. The object is to see whether he can make the jump from one to the other of two related references that have been slyly separated by the writer. Here is an example:

"A prominent businessman criticized the city's proposals for off-street parking today as too expensive and poorly planned.

"Rensselaer van Wart spoke at a meeting of the Chamber of Commerce Traffic Committee, of which he is a member."

Is van Wart the prominent businessman? Of course, the writer might reply. How could it be otherwise? No one else has been mentioned. Yet the link between *prominent business-*

man and *Rensselaer van Wart* has to be forged by the reader. Depending on a variety of factors, such as the reader's familiarity with the name, more or less hesitation ensues when he encounters such a gap in identification. Neglecting to show the relation between things is an offense against clarity. Making the reader guess at, or assume the connection is a slipshod practice.

In the example, the second paragraph should have been tied to the first by something like "The businessman, Rensselaer van Wart . . ." or "The criticism was expressed today by Rensselaer van Wart at . . ."

Let us go on to a three-stage example of the same kind of error: "Senator Francis Case, for one, is going to be definitely chary. The South Dakotan has too long a memory. When the newly elected solon heard about the incident, he laughed." There was nothing in what went before to identify Senator Case as either a South Dakotan or newly elected. The reader was expected to jump to the conclusion that all three designations referred to the same man. No doubt the reader would jump to the right conclusion, after a confused moment or two. But why should be have to jump at all? He may have no stomach for leapfrog. Many readers might have preferred, after the first sentence, something like "The senator, who is newly elected from South Dakota, has too long a memory. When he heard about the incident, he laughed."

Another obstacle course: "The judge discharged a juror, after learning that William Roark was related by marriage to the defendant's cousin." Roark was the juror, but even an experienced leapfrogger could not be sure of this without looking for further clues.

Leapfrog appears to grow out of two other foibles—avoiding repetition of a word at all costs, including clarity, and painfully condensing sentence structure. See also *Variation.*

learn, teach   *Learn* for *teach* is rustic: *She learned us arithmetic.* To learn is to acquire knowledge, to teach is to impart it.

leave   See *furlough, leave.*

leave, let   Although *leave* (for *let*) *me alone* is widely seen and heard, a useful distinction is lost by neglect of *let. Leave* means *go away from,* and *let* means *permit* or *allow. Leave me alone* strictly means *leave me by myself; let me alone,* which is usually intended, means *don't bother me. Leave* has become popular, with a humorous tinge, in the imperative sense where *let* is called for: *Leave us go*. To corrupt George Washington: "Leave us raise a standard to which the wise and honest can repair." This is in fact a revival of an archaic usage. "About half the American people turned their clocks ahead for daylight-saving time, while the other half left their clocks alone." *let*. "This publisher leaves his editors alone, while he concentrates on business matters." Ambiguous as it stands; the editors are undisturbed, rather than in solitude. *lets*.

leisurely   Although both an adjective and an adverb, *leisurely* is used so seldom as an adverb that it has an uncomfortable sound: "He walked *leisurely* along." It seems almost as if it should be *leisurelyly*.

lend, loan   The idea that *loan* is not good form as a verb is a superstition. There is no basis for the prejudice, and in fact *loan* seems to be gaining favor. Part of the explanation may be that *lent*, the past tense of *lend*, looks funny, and even wrong, to some people, though of course it's correct.

lengthy   *Long* has apparently been barred from much prose in favor of *lengthy*; this is unobjectionable except that it is longer, or lengthier. What did *long* ever do to us that we should boycott it?

less   See *fewer, less*.

less   Wrongly joined to an adjective by a hyphen. See *much*.

-less   Solid as a suffix: *childless, conscienceless, tailless, waterless*, etc.

let   See *leave, let*.

LETTERS TO THE EDITOR   No great savvy is shown by publications that print letters containing accusations against themselves or challenges of their factual accuracy, and neglect to offer any comment or reply. The readers of such letters may be left with any of a variety of impressions, none of them complimentary. One is that the publication, although it condescends to publish the criticism, is too Olympian to reply. Another is that the charge is true, but the editors cannot think of anything to say in answer to it, or hope no one will notice.

Another is that the high command is not aware enough of the publication's contents to realize it is being criticized. An attack by a reader, when it impugns the publication's motives and does not merely express a divergent opinion, ought to bring forth a brief statement of justification. If a reader calls attention to an error of fact, the publication ought to be large-minded enough to make it clear he is right. Or, if he only thinks he is right, the publication owes it to all its readers to reaffirm the facts, rather than leave them wondering.

Even when the publication's own accuracy is not in question, an obvious misstatement of fact in a published letter might well be identified for what it is, especially when public questions are concerned.

A series of letters dealing with the same subject are best grouped under some inclusive heading, rather than scattered among letters dealing with other subjects.

level *Level a charge* (or *accusation,* or whatever) *against* has no apparent advantage over simply *charge* or *accuse.*

liable See *apt, liable, likely.*

liaison Often misspelled; *liason,* among other ways.

liberal It is misleading to capitalize the term as a political descriptive in the United States, for this may suggest the existence of a nationwide Liberal Party. (Some areas like New York have a local Liberal Party.) In Britain there is a Liberal Party and consequently there are Liberals. See also *conservative.*

lie, lay, laid The chief difficulty here is remembering that the past tense of *lie* is *lay*—"after dinner we all lay down"; "The book lay on the table"—and that the participle is *lain,* not *laid*—"The tools have lain on the grass since Sunday." *Laid* is the past tense and participle of *lay* (meaning *place down*): "She laid the silver in the closet." *Lay* and *lie* are often erroneously interchanged: "Let us lay down in the shade." *lie.*

lift Slangy or facetious in the sense *pick up, retain,* or *revoke,* just as it is in the sense of *steal.* It does not serve any purpose that is not met as well or better by standard expressions. "The new French premier has lifted most of his predecessor's program." *retained, adopted, kept.* Here *lift* has the unhappy (and unintended) suggestion of thievery. "The TVA has lifted the license of a luncheonette operator who refused to serve Negroes." *revoked*. See also *relieve*.

lightening, lightning   Lightening is the process of making bright or light (less dark or less heavy); *lightning* is the term for the electrical discharge in the heavens.

like   See *as, like; False Comparison*.

-like   Solid as a suffix: *childlike, lamblike, lifelike, tigerlike*, etc. But *bill-like* (after *l*).

likely   Fowler conceded that in American usage the word may appear without *very, most*, or *more:* "The concert will likely be a benefit." Even though this construction occurs fairly often, many writers still do not feel comfortable with it. See also *apt, liable, likely*.

limp into port   A grand old cliché as applied to disabled vessels. More recently it has been applied to partially disabled airplanes—in one instance to a four-engine jet with one engine out, even though the difference is not noticeable in flight.

linage, lineage   Though *lineage* is interchangeable with *linage*, the latter almost invariably has to do with printed lines, for example the measurement of advertising space. *Lineage* (never *linage*) has to do with line of descent. See also *lead*.

linguist   Ordinarily, the term would have been used a few years ago to mean only one accomplished in languages. This remains one sense, but another is becoming more and more common: a student of or expert in linguistics; that is, the science of language.

lion's share   Originally a whimsicality that has lost its whimsy. *Lion's share* once was a way of referring delicately to the whole hog; now that same share has shrunk to merely the larger part.

lisp   The rendering of a lisp, like the handling of such archaisms as *thee* and *thou* together with the verb-forms they take, is the downfall of many. Look at this hapless example: "Thirty days hath Theptember, and tho have all the othersth, I guessth." If thith kind of thing ith nethethary, let uth at leatht be conthithtent and pronounthable: "Thirty dayth hath Theptember, and tho have all the otherth, I gueth."

lit Standard as a past tense of *light* ("The lamps were lit") though it is sometimes superstitiously aspersed. *Lighted* is equally correct.

literal, -ly Unliterally used to mean (a) *figuratively,* (b) *almost* or *virtually,* or (c) nothing much at all. Seldom are the words employed in their exact sense, which is *to the letter, precisely as stated.* Some examples: "The actor was literally floating on applause." The word wanted is *figuratively,* unless levitation occurred. "George is the proud owner of a bristly, 20-pound porcupine that literally dropped out of a tree at his feet." The writer did not mean that was exactly what happened; and so adept have we become at translating such misuses that we are not likely to read it that way. "Flowing through the buttes and deep washes of South Dakota, the Missouri River literally cuts the state in half." *Literally* is excess baggage, for the sentence is more forceful without it. So also in "A marble bust of Tom Paine may soon leave Philadelphia, where it literally has been a controversial object for seventy-eight years." The habit of demanding that the reader be thunderstruck by commonplaces, which the meaningless use of *literally* exemplifies, is tiresome.

literature Sometimes the application of the term to sales brochures, or to the body of writing on a subject (*the literature on beekeeping*) is criticized as ignorant because such writing is not literary. This, however, is an established and useful sense of the term. No one except the pedant is misled about literary qualities, and he is perversely so.

little man, people In an author's note in *McSorley's Wonderful Saloon,* Joseph Mitchell wrote:

> The people in a number of these stories are of the kind that many writers have recently got into the habit of referring to as "the little people." I regard this phrase as patronizing and repulsive. There are no little people in this book. They are as big as you are, whoever you are.

The little man, a near relative, has incurred the distaste of the Canadian Press, whose stylebook enjoins:

Do not use the term *little man* in referring to the population generally or any segment of it. The term has no precise or defensible meaning in that connection and has long since become objectionable.

There is no question that both these expressions are patronizing, and therefore objectionable. Oddly enough, *little woman*, as a fond epithet for *wife*, is something entirely different, and seems unlikely to fall under any ban. Louisa May Alcott, come to think of it, got away with both *Little Men* and *Little Women*.

lives with his wife   The wording *He lives with his wife at* has an unhappy ring, because it seems to suggest the alternative of separate maintenance. Something like *He and his wife live at* or *The Tannenbaums make their home at* sounds more suitable.

livid   According to Webster, this is almost any color you can think of, or at any rate it can qualify any color (livid brown, livid pink, etc.). Basically it is gray or the color of lead. This latitude suits the phrase "livid with rage," for some people turn one color when enraged and some another.

Lloyd's (of London)   *Lloyd's* is merely the name of the place where the insuring takes place; the insuring is done on behalf of individuals who form syndicates, and they are properly described as *Underwriters at Lloyd's. Lloyd's* is the casual term of reference; *Lloyd's of London* gained attention from the movie of that name, and the fatal allure of alliteration did the rest. Neither *Lloyd's* nor *Lloyd's of London* is technically correct.

loan   See *lend*.

loath, loathe, loathsome   *Loath* is the adjective meaning *reluctant*, as "I am loath to criticize him." *Loathe* is the verb meaning *detest*, as "I loathe spinach." "Officers have been loathe to make arrests in such cases." *loath*. It's *loathsome*, not *loathesome*.

locate, situate   It was once deemed improper to say "The house is *located* [rather than *situated*] on the wrong side of the tracks." *Situated* is as correct as it ever was, but *located* is usual in such contexts. *Located* is also both usual and acceptable in the sense of *settled* or *living:* "Where are you located now?" *Locate,* of course, also means *find,* or *fix the position of,* as "You can *locate* the North Star by finding the Big Dipper." In the sense of *situated,* however, *located* is often superfluous: "The house is [located] on the wrong side of the tracks."

lone   See *poesy.*

loom   Journalese in the sense *threaten, be expected.*

loose, lose   *Loose* is perpetually misused (or mistaken) for *lose:* "Don't loose your money." *lose. Loose,* though principally an adverb (*the gown hung loose*) or an adjective (*loose change*), is also occasionally a verb, but it then is the equivalent of *loosen, let go: loose the animals.*

loot   In its standard sense as both noun and verb, refers to ill-gotten gain. Its slang use to mean a large sum of money or valuables in general is disturbing because of conflict in sense and possible aspersion. Reference to an actor's income as *loot,* for example, carries a suggestion of misappropriation of funds. While this may be true as a species of dramatic criticism, the writer should be sure it is the meaning he intends, and, if so, convey it in some unambiguous way. "He will pay roughly a million and a quarter for the mansion, which contains that much loot in the form of tapestries and paintings." The writer meant simply *value;* the owner of the place is entitled to take offense, if not legal action, at the suggestion, though unintended, that his tapestries and paintings were stolen goods.

loss and gain   The comment that "Podunk's loss is Dogtown's gain," in tribute to a departing resident, is a hallmark of rustic journalism.

lot, lots   In the sense *a great deal* (*a lot of money, lots of people*), suitable to informal, conversational contexts. The writer who is practiced enough to wonder whether these expressions are appropriate in a given place is not likely to go astray. Very little writing now, furthermore, maintains a tone to which they would be unsuitable. (See *formal, informal.*) If there were something scathing to say about *a lot* and *lots,* Fowler surely would have said it, but he merely referred to them in passing as colloquial (which see) and concerned himself mainly with whether they take singular or plural verbs, a question whose answer now seems self-evident.

lulled into a false sense of security   A cliché.

luxuriant, luxurious   *Luxuriant* relates to *luxuriance,* and means *lush, thick, flourishing; luxurious* relates to *luxury,* and pertains to gratification of the senses: rich, lavish, choice, costly. A head of hair or tropical vegetation can be luxuriant but not luxurious; a dwelling or a meal can be luxurious but not luxuriant.

-ly   There is no need to add this ending to ordinals (*firstly, secondly,* etc.) but if it is done it should be done consistently: not *first, secondly, thirdly,* etc., but *firstly, secondly, thirdly,* etc.

    The hyphen is wrong after adverbs ending in *-ly* ("a luxuriously-equipped ocean liner"). An adverb or any other adverb can only modify the adjective following. This determined and superfluous hyphenation would be of no consequence except for the equally determined omission of hyphens where they are required to make sense.

—M—

mad, angry   The idea that *mad* cannot be correctly used to mean *angry* is now a nearly forgotten pedantry. The word retains its other senses of *insane, wildly enthusiastic, distraught,* etc. No valid question of usage arises apart from the academic one referred to because the context always indicates the sense intended. *Mad* is what comes most easily for *angry* in conversation; *angry* may come naturally in both talk and writing to those who think twice in choosing their words, and the consequence of this is that it has a faintly bookish flavor. In the sense *insane, mad* is now distinctly literary.

madam, madame   As a term of deference, as distinguished from the designation of the keeper of a whorehouse, *madam* has no plural; the French *mesdames,* usually placed in front of a series of names and abbreviated *Mmes.,* is often used, especially on the society pages. *Madame* is the French equivalent of *Mrs.*

maddening (madding) crowd   See *Misquotation.*

maintain   Often questionably used in attribution; what one maintains must have been previously asserted. See also *contend*.

majority   Expresses a distinction that seems worth preserving; that is, in its exact sense it means *more than half*. Many say *a majority of* when *most of* would be better. *Most* certainly is the stronger expression. *Majority* might well be saved for elections and the like, where its technical sense applies.

major portion of   Excessive for *most of*.

mal-   Solid as a prefix: *maladjusted, malapropos, malfeasance,* etc.

mania, phobia   A mania is a craze (*a mania for cards*); a phobia (*a phobia of snakes*). *Mania* takes *for; phobia* (like *fear*) takes *of*. Why *phobia* should be confused with *mania* is unexplainable, but it often is. "They had a phobia for cards." *mania*.

manner   Circumlocutions are often formed on the word in place of using an adverb: *in a patient manner* (*patiently*), *in a solemn manner* (*solemnly*).

manner, shape, or form   "He would not accept the honor in any manner, shape, or form." A pomposity.

(to the) manner born   Often misapprehended as *to the manor born* and used, accordingly, to suggest inheritance of wealth, taste, or gentility. The phrase comes, however, from *Hamlet*, Act I, Sc. iii, and refers to familiarity with local customs, not breeding.

MANUFACTURED VERBS   Although language is in a constant state of flux, so that some parts of speech take on the functions of others (nouns becoming verbs, etc.), deliberate wrenching of a word into a new role is to be discouraged as making for an artificial style. An example of this is: " 'My wife is upstairs pressing my suit,' jovialed Roy, a generous host," in which *jovial*, an adjective, has been uncomfortably miscast as a verb. See also *Utterance by Proxy* under *Attribution*; *-ise, -ize*.

mariage de convenance   If the French must be used, it had better be spelled thus, instead of the frequent mélange of French and English. But the English *marriage of convenience* is to be preferred.

marine Capitalization of *marine* in reference to a member of the Marine Corps, with all due respect to that force, seems unduly deferential. If *marine* is capitalized, *soldier, sailor*, and *airman* should be too. And if *Marine Corps* is capitalized, as it undoubtedly should be, consistency dictates capitalizing *Army, Navy, Air Force*, and *Coast Guard* as well.

marital, martial The easy transposition of letters that makes the one the other is the bane of proofreaders and editors, and the source of some unintentional humor, especially when what is intended to be *marital* comes out *martial*. Is it necessary to say that *marital* has to do with marriage and *martial* with arms and war?

married, was (were) married There is a delicate and fairly widespread conviction that the man *marries,* but the woman *is married to,* or rarely, *by.* The idea behind it is that the man is, or is supposed to be, the aggressor in marriage. In these days of equality of the sexes, however, there seems no warrant for preserving this polite fiction, and it appears to be disappearing. It attracts no notice to say a woman *married* a man, instead of *was married to* him. *Was married to* is unavoidable with both sexes to express the idea of duration: "He *was married to* the actress from 1945 to 1950." "He was then married and divorced by two heiresses." As to divorce, of course, the identity of the aggressor is usually a matter of legal record. Sometimes there is regrettable clumsiness: "After World War II, Markevitch married a second time, to Donna Topazia Caetani." *Married to* is hardly defensible; even the supposedly feminine version, *was married to,* would be preferable.

The phrases *married his wife, married her husband,* are open to the objection that the wife and husband acquire their status by the act of marriage; the expressions cited suggest they already had it. This can be avoided by saying simply, "He *married* [or *was married*] in 1933" instead of "He married his wife in 1933." "He and his wife *were married* in 1933" may be technically open to the same objection but sounds less objectionable. "The actor wants a divorce *from his current wife* on the grounds of adultery" illustrates the love of superfluity. The italicized words should be cut out.

marshal, marshall   There is no such word as *marshall;* noun and verb are both *marshal.*

masterful, masterly   Although some dictionaries show these words as synonyms, careful usage preserves the distinction that *masterful* means *domineering* and *masterly* means *skillful.* "This book contains a collection of *masterful* photographs." *masterly.*

masthead   See *Newspaper Terms.*

material, materiel   The second is a military term for supplies and equipment as distinguished from personnel; *material* and *materiel* are not interchangeable.

materialize   Means to take material, or physical, form. As a pretentious displacement of *develop, arrive* or *appear,* it is journalese: "The clear skies expected for the weekend failed to *materialize.*" *appear.*

may   See *can.*

may, might   *Might* is one of the few distinctive forms of the subjunctive in use; sometimes *may* is mistakenly used in its place: "The Bible ought to be banned; then it may be read instead of gathering dust on shelves." *Might* is necessary to express a condition contrary to fact. "If property owners had not seen the new sign erected during the night they may not know they are officially part of the county." *might.* "If the committee had had all the facts, it may have changed its report." *might have.*

maybe   Not the best usage as a modifier: *a maybe erroneous decision; a maybe enjoyable occasion. possibly.*

may or may not   This expression overstresses the uncertainty: "The matter *may or may not* be presented to the City Council tonight." *May* alone fully poses the alternatives.

M.C.   (for *member of Congress*). See *M.P.*

MEANING   Perhaps the most widespread of established superstitions embraced by many whose business is writing and editing and should therefore have risen above such ignorance before they left school is that there is one "primary" or "basic" meaning of every word, and that other meanings are suspect if not actually erroneous. The significations of some of the simplest and commonest words run on for columns in unabridged dictionaries. The most that can be said with any validity is that some meanings are older than others; in many instances, the form from which a word developed is traced back in the dictionary to an original in another or a predecessor language (Latin, Greek, Middle English, etc.). Those who hold the primary-meaning delusion likely would say that the most reputable sense is that which most closely approximates the root word. But in many instances that sense is obsolete. Usage and acceptance are what establish meaning, and any sense given in a dictionary without a qualifier such as *dialectal, substandard,* or *slang* is regarded as standard.

Perrin points out that no one can tell whether *check,* by itself, is noun or verb or adjective, much less which of its forty senses is meant. Fowler (under *spiritism*) referred to an "extravagant theory that no word should have two meanings— a theory that would require us . . . to manufacture thousands of new words." The word *set* has been shown to have 286 different meanings. Ninety per cent of all words have one meaning; the average is three meanings each. This means that the relatively small number of common words have large numbers of meanings.

It is also often wrongly assumed that the order in which definitions of a word are entered in a dictionary indicates preferential standing. There is no basis for this idea. See also the entry *Dictionaries.*

Medal of Honor   The correct form; not Congressional Medal of Honor (which see).

media, medium   *Media* is in increasing use to refer to the means by which advertising, particularly, is disseminated ("The *media* used were newspapers, magazines, and television"). It is not always recognized, however, that *media* is the plural of *medium,* and thus *medias* is impossible. Nor should *media* be used as a singular: "In the debate over toll TV the mathematics peculiar to a mass media [properly, *medium*] have tended to run away with common sense." *Mediums* is good usage and perhaps preferable as a regular plural form.

mediate   See *arbitrate, mediate.*

mediocre   Whether we like it or not, this once weak word has grown muscles. Its strict sense, which is the only one yet recognized in dictionaries, is *average* or *commonplace*. But we may as well face the fact that *mediocre* means *lousy*—not *infested with lice*, but *pretty bad*. A musician described as having given a mediocre performance would be mortally affronted, and with good reason. If the critic means the performance was of average quality, he had better say so, and not allow himself to be betrayed by *mediocre*. Webster now admits for *mediocrity* the senses *poor worth* or *inferiority*. But the derogatory connotation has also attached to *mediocre*.

meet   There is an unreasoning prejudice against the use of *meet* as a noun. Yet it is unqualifiedly recognized by dictionaries in this sense. Usually the ban is imposed on the use of the word in the headlines, where it fits when *meeting* would not. In text, the use of *meet* is a matter of idiom, and rarely raises any valid question. In *track meet*, particularly, it is established and invariable.

meet, pass   Though carelessly interchanged with respect, for example, to trains on parallel tracks or to automobiles on the same highway, a distinction is worth encouraging, especially to make accounts of accidents clearer. *Pass*, in these connections, at least, might be reserved to mean *overtake*, or better, be abandoned in favor of *overtake*. The suggestion sometimes advanced that *meet* indicates a collision is nonsense; it indicates, as *pass* does not, that the vehicles are traveling in opposite directions.

MEETING NOTICES   These, unfortunately, constitute a large part of the content of many newspapers. This stuff often is of no interest to anyone but the members of the organizations concerned, who already know what it conveys. Much depends, of course, on the size of the town. In little places where everyone knows everyone else and every reader goes through the local news line by line looking for names, there is probably no way out but to announce and report inconsequential doings of organizations.

In larger places, however, just as slavish a policy is often followed. Editors in those places might well re-evaluate a practice that robs a large amount of space from the presentation of information of general interest. Any such re-evaluation is likely to be agonizing, however, because the editors and publishers themselves are likely to be members of one or more of the town's civic clubs and other groups.

True, people like to see their names in print, no matter how flimsy the excuse, and there is probably no arguing with any editor who uses this principle uncritically as a criterion of news. Sometimes it seems as if such editors might as well publish a page a day out of the city directory or the telephone book.

Still, meeting notices could be rid of some current excrescences, such as references to *guest* (or *featured,* or *principal*) speakers, *special* guests, *noon* luncheons, and *dinner meetings*. There is rarely more than one speaker at a club meeting, and he is almost always a guest. A luncheon, by definition, is at noon, and guests are special by virtue of their guesthood. A dinner at which members will gather is perforce a meeting.

"The Customs Service will be discussed (in a talk) by . . ." and "presided (at the meeting)" would be just as good, if not better, without the words in parentheses. The announcement that someone *will be the speaker at* can be tightened to *will speak at* or *will address. Elected to the board of directors* may as well be *elected to the board* or *elected a director.* Why list officers when elected, and again when installed? *Is affiliated with* is just a pretentious way of saying *belongs to;* this phrase is a vice of the society pages. And since co-chairmen are equals, how is it justifiable to speak of one of them as being assisted by the other? A dismaying characteristic of meeting notices is some such revelation as this: "Herman Aardvark, president, presided." Disregarding the unhappy repetition of sound, why should the president's name be dragged into account after account? Even when someone presides in his place, the fact is hardly worth noting.

Where to draw the line on announcements of no interest outside the membership of a group may be difficult to decide. But the *Schenectady Union-Star* drew it several years ago in front of *Refreshments will be served,* and suffered no shock.

memento Sometimes misspelled *momento;* the plural is *mementos* or *mementoes.*

menial As applied to jobs, the word means merely *unskilled, lowly,* or *humble;* but as applied to people and otherwise it means *servile, dull, sordid.* Most importantly, in these connections the word has a distinct connotation of contempt.

mental attitude Admittedly an attitude may be mental or physical, but the context always makes so clear which is intended that *mental attitude* may be set down as a redundancy.

mental telepathy It may be too late to point out this redundancy, but telepathy is thought transference, and so is inescapably mental.

merchandise, merchandize *Merchandize* is a correct but uncommon variant.

meretricious The word has something to do with merit, but in an adverse way; it means *appearing to possess merit but lacking it*. Not to be confused, though it is, with *meritorious*.

message Not used as a verb by those who choose their words carefully; it is journalese: "A military adviser messaged from the front that the village had fallen." *Sent a message.*

meticulous Once the term could be properly used only to mean *timid* or *overcareful*. The fact that Fowler devoted between 700 and 800 words, about a quarter of them examples, to indignant objections against the use of *meticulous* in the sense of *scrupulous* or *punctilious* showed, however, that the handwriting was already clearly on the wall. No very careful observation is needed to see that in general use the connotation of timidity has all but vanished, and Webster now designates that sense obsolete. *Meticulous* now may mean overcareful or fussy, but it also has a positive sense: commendably thorough or precise. The context must show which. Pigheaded insistence on preserving obsolete senses only cuts the line of communication between writer and reader.

Mexican, Spanish *Spanish* (or *of Spanish extraction, Spanish-speaking*) has become a euphemism for *Puerto Rican* in the East and for *Mexican* in the Southwestern U.S. Technically, any citizen of Mexico, regardless of ancestry, is a Mexican. Most Mexicans, however, are *mestizos*, in this case of mixed European and American Indian blood, possessing dark skin, black hair, and high cheek bones, and thus easily recognizable.

The large numbers of Mexicans who have settled in the Southwest have been the object of active discrimination, which, however, has noticeably diminshed, especially with respect to the second generation. *Mexican* continues, nevertheless, to have a derogatory connotation. In efforts to avoid any slighting implication, *Spanish* and the other terms cited are resorted to, but this is erroneous and misleading. It confuses Mexicans with Spaniards.

A member of a panel discussing integration in schools of a Western community, for example, delicately referred to students of Negro, Oriental, and Spanish descent. The number of Spanish descendants in the West is negligible; she meant *Mexican* but feared to say so.

In dealing with racial problems it seems best to face the facts head-on, and consequently it is desirable to use *Mexican* rather than avoid the term in favor of anything as misleading as *Spanish* or related evasions. The evasions are insulting in their own way because they suggest there is something wrong with being Mexican.

It must be conceded that *Mexican* is sometimes objected to by Mexicans themselves, but generally this is true only of the uneducated, just as some Finns are insulted to hear that the Finns have Mongolian antecedents. *Mexican-American* is a more exact term than *Mexican* for residents of the U.S.; *American of Mexican descent* is better yet.

micro- Solid as a prefix: *microbiology, microcosm, microfilm, microphotography,* etc.

mid- Solid as a prefix: *midday, midiron, midriff, midwinter,* etc.

Middle East, Mideast *Mideast* appears to be a coinage that grew out of the attention concentrated in recent years on what was formerly known as the Middle East. Its usefulness, especially to headline writers confronted with *Middle East* as an alternative, is hardly to be gainsaid. At a congressional hearing in 1957, Representative Walter H. Judd of Minnesota explained that *Middle East* originated in British military and colonial policy. In terms of distance from England, Asia Minor (mainly Turkey) was the Near East, beyond the Suez Canal through the Red Sea to India was the Middle East, and from there on was the Far East.

Midlands, Middle West, Midwest *Midlands,* originally applied to the middle counties of England, may be an affectation as applied to the central United States. *Midwest,* because of its concision, is preferable to *Middle West.*

235

might See *may, might.*

might perhaps Like *possibly may*, redundant; either *might* or *perhaps* will do.

military In spite of suspicions to the contrary, *military* properly applies to all branches of the armed forces, including the Navy. Such descriptives as *military and naval forces*, then, are redundant. It is true, however, that the word comes from one meaning *soldier*, and thus its application to sailors and airmen is an extension.

militate, mitigate To mitigate is to soften ("His apology *mitigated* the accusation"); to militate (with *against*) is to have an adverse effect on ("The rumor *militated* against her success"). Often confused.

million The plural of the noun is indifferently *million* or *millions; eighty million strong; sixteen millions.*

mills of God The quotation correctly is: "Though the mills of God grind slowly, yet they grind exceeding small" (a translation from the German of Friedrich von Logau by Henry Wadsworth Longfellow). Often given *mills of the gods, exceedingly small, exceeding(ly) fine*, though this is indeed an exceeding picayune matter.

minimize "Its influence on modern American architecture cannot be minimized." This says the influence is so small nothing could diminish it; the writer meant that the influence cannot be overstated or overestimated. See also *reverse*, etc.; *Reversal of Sense; undue; underestimate.*

minister See *Rev.*

minority, minority group The expressions have become euphemisms or perhaps catch-alls, in some respects, to indicate not merely a lesser number but also an outnumbered group that is racially different and discriminated against. The usual term is *minority group*, and in America it refers to Negroes, Mexicans, Chinese, Japanese, Filipinos, and others whose distinctive appearance has stood in the way of their assimilation, unlike the descendants of Europeans.

minus   Facetious in place of *lacking: minus a tire, minus three teeth.*

minuscule   Often misspelled *miniscule.*

mis-   Solid as a prefix: *misadventure, misinform, mispronounce, misqualify, mistranslate,* etc.

mislead, misled   *Mislead* is the present tense, *misled* the past. Why set forth anything so obvious? Because one often reads things like "The voters were mislead on this issue." *Mislead* and *misled* are analogous with *lead* and *led*. The error of using *mislead* as a past tense perhaps arises out of mispronouncing it *misled;* it is actually *misLEED.* See also *lead.*

MISQUOTATION   Most of us were brought up believing that Voltaire wrote, "I disapprove of what you say, but I will defend to the death your right to say it." Chances are that he would not only disapprove of our saying this, but also decline to defend it. For "I disapprove . . ." is only what S. G. Tallentyre (the *nom de plume* of E. Beatrice Hall, an English writer) thought Voltaire should, or might, have said. She expressed surprise when people regarded the words as a direct quotation, just because she had enclosed them in quotation marks in her book, *The Friends of Voltaire.* What great thinkers omit to express, industrious and imaginative biographers will put into their mouths.

Mark Twain and General John J. Pershing are also entitled to join the legion of those who complain of misquotation. And unlike the politicians who make up most of that shrill group, they would have a good chance of making their complaints stick. "Everybody talks about the weather, but nobody does anything about it" is usually ascribed to Mark Twain. Charles Dudley Warner, however, when he was editor of the *Hartford Courant,* wrote in an editorial: "A well-known American writer once said that while everyone talked about the weather, nobody seemed to do anything about it." This is not conclusive, of course, for Warner may have been ascribing the remark to Twain, who was his close friend. *Bartlett's Familiar Quotations* says in a footnote that it is often attributed to Twain, though not found in his published works. Burton Stevenson, editor of *The Home Book of Quotations,* was talked into changing the attribution from Twain to Warner in his book, and some other dictionaries also credit Warner.

Popular fancy has General Pershing striding down the gangplank at the head of the American Expeditionary Force, striking a pose, and declaiming to a throng of bug-eyed Frenchmen, "Lafayette, we are here!" But this *mot* belongs to a ringer, Charles E. Stanton, chief disbursing officer of the AEF, whom Pershing deputed to speak for him at the tomb of Lafayette in Paris on July 4, 1917. Pershing never offered a satisfactory excuse for having omitted to think up this immortal announcement himself. The public's assumption that he was its author, however, may well have taken the edge off the winning of World War I, as far as Pershing was concerned, while at the same time possibly having poisoned the life of Stanton.

"Baldness may not be pretty, but it's neat. ANON." read a magazine advertisement. Now, for one thing, the wording is not quite right, and for another, Anon did not say it. The original version is "There's one thing about baldness—it's neat," and the author was that wit and baldhead, Don Herold. Other approximations of this witticism turn up from time to time, but usually without a mention of Herold, even in most dictionaries of quotations. These words are unquestionably destined for the ages, and happily they are properly credited to Herold in at least one book, Evan Esar's *Dictionary of Humorous Quotations.*

"God rest ye, merry gentlemen" is the way we often see it, but not without an uneasy feeling that we have also seen it "God rest ye merry, gentlemen." This latter version does not quite seem to make sense, and *Bartlett's* puts the comma after *ye.* Charles D. Rice explained in *This Week,* "The comma should be placed after *merry; God rest ye merry* was a common greeting in early England." The *Oxford Dictionary of Quotations* concurs in the late comma.

Lord Acton is usually quoted as having said, "All power corrupts. . . ." but the uncorrupted version is "Power *tends to* corrupt, and absolute power corrupts absolutely." Consistency is often flatly called the hobgoblin of little minds, but it was qualified in Emerson's original to "A *foolish* consistency . . ."

Emily Kimbrough, in entitling a book *How Dear to My Heart,* did nothing to curb the prevalent misquotation of "How dear to *this* heart are the scenes of my childhood" (Samuel Woodworth). Thomas Hardy and Ernest Hemingway used more care in borrowing *Far from the Madding Crowd* and *For Whom the Bell Tolls,* respectively. Yet Thomas Gray is frequently supposed to have written it "Far from the maddening crowd," and John Donne's line is often pluralized to "For whom the bells toll."

Rudolf Flesch points out, in *The Art of Plain Talk*, that Churchill's famous wartime offer to the British nation, which is generally remembered as "blood, sweat, and tears" was in fact "blood, toil, tears and sweat." Flesch notes that Churchill's intention was to encourage people in the war effort, and that the popular distortion of what he said not only damages the original rhythm, but also ends on a defeatist note, *tears*.

Topsy is often invoked as a comparison with something or someone that "jest growed." Topsy's remark on this subject, however, was void of *jest:* "I 'spect I grow'd."

Cervantes said "Let the worst come to the worst," not "If worse comes to worst." It was a savage *breast*, not *beast*, that Congreve said music hath charms to soothe.

The cloud "no bigger than a man's hand" that has become the standard reference to a small but menacing omen was pristinely "There ariseth a little cloud out of the sea, like a man's hand." This is from the Bible, as are some other warped quotations. The "prophet without honor in his own country" is, more precisely, *"not* without honor *except* in his own country." Money is unduly berated as the root of all evil, but it is *the love of money* that the Bible warns against. This at least gives the rich more comfort than the pronouncement that it is easier for a camel to go through the eye of a needle than for a rich man to enter into the kingdom of God. "The voice crying in the wilderness" is more exactly "the voice of *one*." And it is not a fall, finally, that pride goeth before, as in the popular misconception; rather, "Pride goeth before *destruction*, and an haughty spirit before a fall."

Shakespeare, inevitably, has also been the victim of inexact quotation, sometimes involving the choice of prepositions: "Such stuff as dreams are made *on*" (not *of*); "Hoist *with* [not *by*] his own petard." Shakespeare *painted*, rather than *gilded*, the lily: "To gild refined gold, to paint the lily."

"Alas, poor Yorick," we hear it declaimed; "I knew him well." But the lines run "I knew him, Horatio; a fellow of infinite jest, of most excellent fancy." It was not "a poor thing but my own," but rather "An *ill-favored* thing, sir, but mine own." If somewhere Shakespeare's spirit is aware of what is happening, it may be muttering, "An ill-quoted thing, sir, but mine own."

Did it ever strike you that the idea of Cinderella wearing a glass slipper is an unhappy one? Poor Cinderella apparently danced the evening away in slippers made of one of the hardest and most unyielding of materials, since her day antedated fiber glass. And if that were not enough, attempts were made to force one of the slippers on hapless but hopeful maidens throughout the kingdom, when the prince set out to find her. Originally, that slipper was not glass at all. The idea of a glass slipper resulted from a mistake in translation, according to the *Encyclopaedia Britannica*. The English version of the story comes from the French tale, *Cendrillon,* by Perrault. Perrault wrote of *pantoufle en vair* (a slipper of fur), but the translator confused *en vair* with *en verre* (of glass). The idea of a glass slipper is too firmly associated with Cinderella now, however, to hope for any change.

Miss A curious lapse from chivalry, it seems, is shown sometimes in handling the names of unmarried women who are in trouble with the law. References to them are given as *the Smith woman* instead of *Miss Smith*. This is clearly an aspersion; *Miss* is simply a title that indicates spinsterhood.

Miss is properly applied to women, married or not, when they are named in connection with their careers, and whether or not, as is often so of actresses, they have professional names that differ from their legal ones.

missile Often misspelled *missle*. And, curiously, *missive* (a message) and *missile* (a projectile) are sometimes confused.

misspell Often, with ultimate perversity, misspelled *mispell*.

mitigate See *militate, mitigate*.

modern, modernistic As applied to design, the words have different meanings. What is modern is contemporary, more or less, by whatever standards apply to the art of field in question. *Modernistic* applies to a jagged, angular school of design that lived and died in the '20s and '30s, and the word now generally is derogatory.

MODIFIERS

Participial Modifiers One-word participial modifiers beginning a sentence are a peculiarity of the journalese style. This device exemplifies the clipped, telegraphic expression characteristic of the press. It is found only in low surroundings, and in the writings of those who are insensitive to jerkiness. Jerks, perhaps. Here are some examples: "Shortlived, the committee was a thorn in the growers' flesh"; "Married, he is the father of a young son." Handled with respect for the nuances of language, these sentences would have been put in some such form as: "He is married and the father of a young son"; "Although the committee was shortlived, it was a thorn in the growers' flesh."

Noun appositive phrases are used similarly, but perhaps are less objectionable: "A salesman, he spent a lot of time away from home." The worst thing about this pattern is that it is overdone.

The participial modifier should form a logical sequence with the rest of the sentence. This principle is often disregarded in biographical sketches: "Born in Illinois, he was admitted to a partnership in the firm at the age of 24"; "Married at 18, she was later named a regent of the university she had attended." Such dislocations will be avoided by a less frantic style and closer attention to the sense of what is being said: "Mr. Smith, who was born in Illinois, was admitted . . ."; Mrs. Smith was married at 18. After her family was grown, she was named a regent . . ."

Position of Modifiers It is preferable that modifying phrases and clauses should stand next to what they modify: "He has been executive vice president since 1952, an office that will not be filled immediately." The clause after the comma does not modify *1952*, and the structure would be improved by rearrangement along such lines as "Since 1952, he has been executive vice president, an office that . . ." or "He has been executive vice president since 1952; the office will not . . ."

"Nkrumah set out for the U.S. in 1935, where he spent 10 years studying." Better: "Nkrumah set out in 1935 for the U.S., where . . ."

Elision of Modifiers "This self-effacing, dedicated woman in her mid-40s bears one of the most delicate yet little-known responsibilities of anyone around the President." Adverbs that modify adjectives in parallel constructions should not be elided; the reader does not readily apply *most* to *little-known* as the writer intended, perhaps because *most little-known* is not idiomatic. *Most delicate and yet least-known*. See also *Ellipsis*.

Piled-up Adjectives The urge to condense, while generally commendable, is to blame for some odd effects that place an unnecessary burden on the already weary reader. Behold the puny noun, staggering under a load of adjectives so heavy it is all but crushed:

"He was arrested on *conspiracy and concealing stolen property* charges." (The modifiers are italicized.)

"Next on the docket were *two disturbing the peace* suspects."

"*Former San Anselmo County Sheriff's Deputy* Wolfgang Schmalz is in trouble again."

"*A 15 cent per $100 assessed valuation road tax* increase was proposed."

What price terseness? Howard B. Taylor, as managing editor of the *San Diego Union,* hit it off neatly in a memo to his staff:

"Mouth-filling strings of compound adjectives force the reader to go back and retrace the meaning of a sentence: 'The strikers presented *a 20-cent-an-hour wage-increase* demand.' The compound adjective is too big to swallow. Let's make it 'The strikers asked an increase of 20 cents an hour.' A wire story recently read, 'The strikers are seeking *a 25-cent-an-hour wage* hike, contending that *a 10-cent-an-hour* jump, which gave them *a $2.10 hourly pay* scale, is insufficient.' That's really making life tough on the reader.

"A string of titles preceding a name likewise is difficult to digest: 'Signers included *former Salt Lake City mayor* Albert Sprague.' Let's make it 'Signers included Albert Sprague, former mayor of Salt Lake City.' "

Another variation of this quirk gives us "a 9 A.M. February 26 meeting" instead of "a meeting at 9 A.M., February 26," and "the 1939 erection of the Oakdale School" instead of "the erection of the Oakdale School in 1939."

The AP Log told how a bureau chief who had been taken to task for *"Glass jar manufacturing heir John A. Kerr's divorce* decree" came back with:

"All I can say is it's a good thing for Associated Press members that Kerr's old man didn't invent the International Harvester Company's two-row cotton-picking machine."

Limiting Adjectives Limiting adjectives are often used in a way that has an ambiguous effect, especially in writing where concision is attained at the expense of exactness.

"His labor turnover is nominal, and he is proud of the loyalty of his nonunion workers." This sounds as if the man might have had two kinds of employees, union and nonunion, and as if only the nonunion ones were loyal. In this instance, however, all the employees were nonunion, so the writer should have said, "He is proud of the loyalty of his workers, who are nonunion."

"The reception was held in Mrs. Nelson's San Francisco home." Does Mrs. Nelson have homes elsewhere, as this seems to suggest? If not, it would better be "in Mrs. Nelson's home, in San Francisco" ("in Mrs. Nelson's home in San Francisco" —omitting the comma—would be open to the same objection as the example).

It is undesirable, for the same reason, to write "Burglars invaded the 424 W. Oak home of Al Fresco last night." Since this was Fresco's only home, it would have been better to say "the home of Al Fresco, at 424 W. Oak, last night."

Unnatural placement of modifiers also appears in other contexts: "Receipts were 25 per cent ahead of the same 1959 month." This is disagreeably unidiomatic; better, "the same month in 1959."

"The speaker cited Professor A. M. Low, Britain's inventive version of Thomas A. Edison." Here the adjective *inventive* has been dragged in to tip off the reader to the basis for the comparison, but the effect is to suggest that Edison was not inventive. A piece about the use of television to train teachers spoke of the program's *electronic objective*. Here the use of the adjective *electronic* is not misleading but merely obtrusive and silly, which may also be said of *inventive* in the foregoing example.

"General Motors turned out its first rear-engine Corvair shortly thereafter." The implication is that some Corvairs are rear-engine models and some are not. Actually, all have their engines in the rear. This could have been made clear by saying ". . . its first Corvair, a car whose engine is in the rear, shortly thereafter."

"The chain-smoking Cahan-Salvador has only one wryly humorous complaint." On the face of it, we could assume that Cahan-Salvador may have many complaints, but only one of them is wryly humorous. What the writer meant, as we suspect, however, is that in the circumstances referred to, C.-S. has only one complaint, which happens to be wryly humorous. The main point is that he has one complaint; that it is wryly humorous is secondary, or additive. What difference does it make, one may ask, whether the writer puts it as in the example, rather than saying, "The chain-smoking Cahan-Salvador has only one complaint, and it is a wryly humorous one"? The difference is that the reader cannot take the statement literally, but must rearrange what is stated into what the writer meant to convey. Writing that imposes this obligation on the reader is a poor job. It causes annoyance and sometimes ambiguity.

Nouns as Adjectives Any flat ban on pressing nouns into service as adjectives is foolish. One part of speech easily assumes the role of another; this is one of the most distinctive and useful characteristics of English. Sometimes, however, a bad taste is left with the fastidious when nouns are forced into the role of adjectives. These are undesirable examples: "The officer expressed reluctance to discuss the case for security reasons"; "The general was retired for health reasons"; "The architect warned that the situation soon may reach disaster proportions"; "The service will be discontinued for economy reasons."

It is noticeable that three of these four examples have *reasons* as the objectionably modified noun. Locutions of this kind are recognizable as journalese. The difficulty cannot be with the words used as modifiers, for *health, security, disaster,* and *economy* all sound acceptable as adjectives in other combinations: *health* insurance, *security* measures, *disaster* preparations, *economy* drive.

What's the difference? It looks as if (1) all these combinations have evolved from prepositional modifiers (reasons *of* health, measures *for* security) and (2) those in which the preposition is *of* cannot tractably be forced into the adjective-noun relationship.

In the first example, *reasons of security, reasons of health, proportions of disaster,* and *reasons of economy* sound undeniably better than *security reasons, health reasons, disaster proportions,* and *economy reasons.*

It should be possible to play by ear in these situations. Furthermore, *security reasons, health reasons,* and the rest can also be recast as *for the sake of security, for* (or *because of*) *his health, may amount to disaster,* and *for economy.* This often means more words, but nothing is more noxious than the idea that there is some all-redeeming virtue in brevity.

Repetition of Defining Modifiers Redundancy is evident in the useless repetition of defining modifiers. Once a man has been identified as a hotel porter he should be referred to as *the porter* rather than *the hotel porter.* (This is not to be interpreted as discouraging the use of *he* or *him* when possible.) The examples that follow illustrate other instances of excessive identification. The descriptives that should be omitted are in parentheses:

"George Jones was found guilty of second-degree murder today. A jury composed of seven men and five women returned the (second-degree) verdict after five hours. The (second-degree-murder) conviction carries a penalty of five years to life."

"A dinner will be held Sunday at 7 P.M. Reservations (for the dinner) may be made by telephone."

It is a mark of an undeveloped style to purposelessly review, sum up, or restate what has just been said. Summaries should be made deliberately, with a view to assisting the reader, and should not simply betray fuzzy-mindedness in the writer, as in these instances:

"He became pastor of the church when it was completed two years ago. Prior to accepting the pastorate, he was a student." Better: "Before that, he was a student."

"They tried to break a safe out of a 500-pound block of concrete. Failing to free the safe from the concrete, they fled." Better: "Failing, they fled."

"Sixteen people were killed in a tragic crush on New Year's Day. Those victims were killed when a tremendous crowd surged across a narrow bridge." Better: "Sixteen people were killed in a tragic crush on New Year's Day when a tremendous crowd surged across a narrow bridge." See also *Dangling Participles; Appositives* (misrelated); *Word Order; Ad Lingo; National Descriptives.*

Mohammed, Mohammedan, etc.   John Gunther, in *Inside Africa*, noted: "There are at least a dozen ways to spell *Mohammed*. Most correct is *Muhammad*, and do not forget the dot under the *h*. I am conforming to simplified American usage in saying Mohammed."

Moslems are said to object to the term *Mohammedan* as wrongly implying that Mohammed is the object of worship, that is to say, a deity, but the term is so firmly established without any derogatory intention that this specialized quibble is not likely to make any headway. *Moslem*, which Moslems prefer, means "those who submit to the will of God" *Muslim* is the version favored in Britain, and it is curious that the American Black Muslims should have adopted this spelling, except that it may have a more elegant sound. *Mussulman* is a variant of *Moslem*.

moisturize   *Moisturize* is an invention of the advertising gentry that, although it has been in use for a number of years, is recognized by no dictionary now current, including the Third Edition of *Webster's Unabridged,* which has been roundly criticized for lowering the bars to almost anything. *Moisturize* is superfluous, since we already have *moisten.* Nonetheless, *moisturize* is seeping out of the ads into other contexts: "When moisturized by fog it is transformed into sulphuric acid." *Moisturize* appears to have been synthesized to describe the action of certain cold creams and soaps that purportedly impart an abiding moistness to the skin.

momentarily, momently   Once differentiated to the effect that the first meant *for a brief time,* the second *from moment to moment* (*momentarily out of breath, momently expecting a telegram*); now often interchanged.

money is the root . . .   See *Misquotation.*

Money   See *Sums of Money.*

Mongolian idiot   C. W. Strong, in a letter to the *Pasadena Star-News,* raised the question whether the term *Mongolian idiot* should not be displaced as "illogical, unscientific, and especially impolitic."

"It seems strange," he wrote, "that a word which designates the world's largest race of human beings should be used by another race to specify a certain class of its abnormal births. Whether there is slight or close resemblance between the features of a child so tragically afflicted and those of the race indicated is hardly justification for the Caucasian ethnocentrism reflected in the expression *Mongolian idiot.*"

monster, monstrous   *Monster* is often criticized as an adjective in the sense *enormous: a monster celebration,* for example, is perversely interpreted as a celebration for (or by) monsters. What counts, however, is the sense conveyed, and no one is really misled. *Monster* as an adjective is acceptable, though noticeably avoided by the fastidious. *Monstrous,* however, may not be a good substitute, for it connotes unnaturalness.

moot   Almost invariably used as an adjective in the sense of *debatable,* and usually modifies *point* or *question:* "Whether the city had a case was a *moot* point." A *moot court*, however, is a mock court set up for law students to practice in.

more, most   Generally the comparative and superlative forms of adjectives are preferable, when they exist, to *more* and *most*: "the most knotty problems in its history." *knottiest*. See also *Comparison of Adjectives*.

more preferable   A sophomoric error; *preferable* is itself a comparative, and tacking *more* onto it creates a redundancy.

mortician   Possibly invented by undertakers to dignify their macabre trade, it has now taken on a facetious tone. *Undertaker* seems to be growing old-fashioned; the usual term now is *funeral director*.

Moslem   See *Mohammed, etc.*

most, almost   *Most* for *almost* is not a heinous crime, but it has a schoolgirlish sound: "Most anyone can participate." *almost*. *Almost*, an adverb, means *nearly; most*, an adjective, means *the greater part.*
   Most as an adverb should not be joined by a hyphen to adjectives it modifies: "his most-private thoughts." *most private*.

most times   A gaucherie for *usually, generally,* etc.: "Sterility is most times due to physical causes."

motif, motive   Interchangeable in reference to a recurrent theme, for example in music, but *motif* is predominant in that sense and may well be reserved for it.

motor   See *engine, motor*.

M.P., M.C.   M.P., for *member of Parliament,* has been solidly established for a long time, and its solidity is probably assisted by the fact that the letters are the usual form of reference. But the attempt to establish *M.C.* for *member of Congress* does not seem to have caught on, although some congressmen use it in signing letters. *M.C.*, unhappily for its sponsors, just does not happen to be used by itself the way *M.P.* is.

Mr.   Whether and when to accord the title *Mr.* is a tricky question on which there is disagreement. Publications that otherwise bestow it sometimes withhold it from two categories that usually have little in common, although they sometimes coincide: the famous and the infamous, or arrested.

Mr. is shorn from the famous on the reasoning, apparently, that they are virtually institutions and that such a commonplace designation would only diminish their stature. Thus we usually do not see "Mr. Bernstein," "Mr. Faulkner," "Mr. Nixon." Many publications use *Mr.* only for the president of the United States, out of the same special and perhaps overblown respect they show in capitalizing the designations *president* and *chief executive* even when they stand alone. Yet they lower-case *presidency*, which raises a question whether they regard the man as greater than the office.

Criminals and suspects lose their *Misters* in many journals that use the title for men in good repute, on the seeming ground that such undesirables have forfeited their right to the courtesy paid law-abiders. According to American principles of justice, a suspect should be allowed to keep his *Mr.* at least until conviction.

A well-advised exception sometimes is made by *Mister*less papers in handling obituaries. The last name alone gives an unfortunate impression of brusqueness and is capable of injuring the sensibilities of relatives and friends. *Mr.* seems like a small enough tribute at the last opportunity to pay any tribute at all.

Among the things that may be said against the omission of *Mr.* generally is that use of the last name alone tends to suggest familiarity or inferior station. This impression comes from the practice in the military services and also from the style of address used for servants. There are men whose hackles rise when they are addressed by their last names alone. There are also those, though this is irrelevant, who are irked by hearing men confer the title on themselves, as for example in identifying themselves over the telephone. For of course *Mr.* is a title of courtesy, and is properly applied only by—and to—others.

In any event, the general use of *Mr.* can do no harm. It affords a touch of courtliness in these rude days. Why should we withhold in print the courtesy we would unhesitatingly pay a stranger in a letter or conversation? The omission seems, in borrowed words, not to show a proper respect to the opinions of mankind.

Mr. is a proper designation for any member of the Protestant clergy, and has the advantage of sidestepping the difficulties in the correct use of *Rev.* (which see). *Mr.* is sometimes affixed to titles to create a formal term of address: *Mr. President, Mr. Secretary.*

Mrs. Strictly speaking, a married woman using the title *Mrs.* should go by her husband's given name, i.e. *Mrs.* John *Doe,* not *Mrs.* Mary *Doe.* Many publications attempt to make this a rule, but it is almost impossible to enforce because many women insist on using their own given names with *Mrs.* Some organizations even require it within the group. If a married woman uses her given name, the *Mrs.* might well be dropped on first reference, but used thereafter (with the last name alone). It is improper to follow *Mrs.* with a woman's husband's title: Mrs. Dr. Smith; Mrs. Prof. Jones. If the woman herself holds the title, she should be referred to by it or by the descriptive *Mrs.* alone, not by both together. See also *Titles; Dr.; Miss.*

much Often wrongly hyphenated; in this respect it is like adverbs ending in *-ly: a much-ballyhooed meeting.* It is unnecessary to indicate, by means of the hyphen, that *much* and *ballyhooed* form a unit modifier; *much,* as an adverb, cannot modify anything but the adjective *ballyhooed.* The same reasoning applies to *less* (*a less-frequent occurrence*), *most, almost,* and *sometimes.* See also *-ly.*

Much cannot properly modify plurals. "The committee chairman said he agreed with much of Burns' remarks"; "Much, if not all, of these developments were meaningless." *many* or *most.*

multi- Solid as a prefix: *multicellular, multimotor, multimillionaire,* etc.

mucus, mucous *Mucus* is the noun, *mucous* the adjective: *A secretion of mucus; the mucous membranes.*

munch Fondly fancied as a journalese variant of *eat,* especially with reference to sandwiches and other snacks.

murder With respect to specific crimes, other than musical ones and the like, application of the term *murder* is a matter of a legal determination involving the filing of a charge or the return of an indictment. *Killing* and *slaying* have no precise legal definition, and the acts may fall into various classifications as crimes, such as murder of different degrees or manslaughter. Speaking of a killing that has not been legally classified as a murder is, then, loose usage, and may be prejudicial or actionable if a suspect is named.

musical, musical comedy See *operetta*, etc.

music hath charms. . . . See *Misquotation*.

Muslim See *Mohammedan*, etc.

must Now well established as both noun and adjective: "Aid to education is a must on the administration's legislative program"; "The lawmakers have their own idea of must legislation." Apologetic quotation marks around the word are no longer necessary.

mutual Not restricted, as superstition would have it, to what is reciprocal, but applicable also to what is shared or held in common. Webster cites *a mutual friend, a mutual hobby, mutual effort, mutual advantage.* Some critics say *mutual friend* should be *common* friend, but this is capable of derogatory interpretation. Often used redundantly with expressions like *each other, exchange, both.*

my dear As a salutation, see *dear*.

myself The use of the reflexive (*myself*) where the objective (*me*) will serve is sometimes criticized: "The invitations will be signed by myself." In this instance *myself* conveys an emphasis that *me* does not. *Myself* is generally considered unsuitable in place of *I*: "She and myself attended the coronation." Webster recognizes both usages, however, quoting Fitzgerald, "Myself when young did eagerly frequent Doctor and Saint" and "My income supports my wife and myself." See also *Reflexives.*

—N—

naif, naive, naïveté, naivety Although *naif* is a standard variant of *naive*, it is seldom used and then in contexts that make it seem precious. *Naif* is actually the masculine form of the French from which both versions derive (just as *employe* is, or was, masculine and *employee* feminine, though this distinction has been abandoned in English). The masculine connotation of *naif* in English has been lost for centuries, and as long as a generation ago Fowler considered the form unnecessary. As for the nouns, the general acceptance of the Anglicized form (*naivety*) that Fowler hoped for has yet to come about: *naïveté* predominates. *Naive* generally carries a touch of scorn.

naked, nude   As applied to people, *nude* is at the same time something of a euphemism and, paradoxically, more suggestive than *naked*. The connotation of suggestiveness may arise from the awareness that *nude* has been selected to avoid the honest starkness of *naked*. In a poem entitled "The Naked and the Nude" which appeared Feb. 27, 1957, in *The New Yorker*, Robert Graves wittily recognized this, observing "For me, the naked and the nude . . . stand as wide apart As love from lies, or truth from art."

Nude is often unwarrantedly stretched in reference to stage shows, for example in Las Vegas, Nevada, where performers are merely bare-breasted. This misapplication raises false hopes of an American *Folies Bergère*. The descriptive in these cases should be *partly nude* or, more explicitly, *bare-breasted*.

namely   Often superfluous.

nameplate   See *Newspaper Terms*.

NAMES OF PEOPLE   Names make not only news, but also enemies, unless care is exercised in publishing them. It has been said that few things affront a man more keenly than seeing his name misspelled in print. The only safeguard against misspelled names is actual practice of the care that is incessantly enjoined.

A common impropriety is the identification of a person with only a single initial on first mention: *J. Anderson, R. Thompson*. This is objectionable because it invites confused identity and because many people are likely to feel slighted at having their names truncated. Publications whose standards are high have inflexible rules against the use of names with single initials. Two initials, a full first name, or some combination of given name(s) and initials are required.

In general, men are named in full on first mention, and

thereafter may be referred to by their last names alone, preceded, in courteous publications like *The New York Times*, by *Mr.* (which see). In recent years, however, the newsmagazines have adopted a curious habit of varying the form of *reference* (which see) as much as possible as an article proceeds.

Such designations as II, III after a name (George Evans III)—sometimes rendered *2nd, 2d, 3rd, 3d*—are restrictive modifiers and should not be separated from the name by a comma. For abbreviation of proper names, see *Abbreviations*. See also *Quotation; Possessives*.

naphtha   Often misspelled *naptha*.

narcotic, -ics   See *-ic, -ics*.

national   A national is a person belonging to a country or nation and the word should no more be capitalized than *citizen* or *countryman*. *National* has come into great currency in the phrase *Mexican national*, as applied to crop workers brought into the United States.

NATIONAL DESCRIPTIVES   There is a tendency to disregard the adjectives that are available to indicate nationality or identification with a country, especially in attributive use (that is, standing before the noun). For example, speaking wrongly of *a Belgium* (rather than *Belgian*) *colony*. Britain is misused in the same fashion: *a Britain arrangement* (rather than *British*) (*Speech by Acheson Stirs Britain Anger*). So is *Italy: an Italy treaty*. This mischoice often occurs in headlines, and it is not to be justified, like many barbarities there, by the excuse of cramped space when the adjectival form is no longer and sometimes is shorter than the noun. *Spain* vs. *Spanish* may be open to this justification, however, since *Spain* is shorter (*Spain Project Approved*).

Now and then forcing the noun into the role of adjective in this connection is misleading. A journalist visiting the United States was referred to as *an Africa news editor;* he was, in fact, an *African* news editor; the form used might have been understood as meaning that he was an editor whose job was dealing with African news.

native   A native of a place is ordinarily a person who was born there, a fact that ought to be clear by analogy with *nativity,* although it appears that many do not know that *the Nativity* means *the birth* (of Christ).

There is, however, a specialized use of *native*, in distinguishing inhabitants from visitors, that does not necessarily imply birth in a place. It is commonest in New England.

nature   The word (like *character*, which see) figures in many a fuzzy formula: *comment of an adverse nature* (*adverse comment*) ; *a mixture of a cloudy nature* (*a cloudy mixture*). "The neighborhood is of a restricted nature." *is restricted.*

naught   Now quaint for *zero*, like *aught* and *ought.*

nauseated, nauseous   *Nauseated* means *suffering from nausea; nauseous* means *causing nausea.* Sufferers from seasickness are nauseated; the illness itself is nauseous. Webster now allows *affected with* or *inclined to nausea* for *nauseous*, but other dictionaries do not. There is the likelihood of unconscious humor in using *nauseous* for *nauseated.* The distinction seems well worth continued effort to preserve, and confusions are often criticized, indicating a lively awareness of the difference. *Nauseating* equates with *nauseous* (causing nausea).

naval, navel   A ridiculous confusion, but nonetheless frequent, perhaps owing as much to slipshod proofreading as to careless writing and editing. *Naval* means *pertaining to the navy;* the *navel* is what is vernacularly called the bellybutton, and the word also is applied to a variety of orange that has a similar depression.

née   A French import oftenest seen on the society page; it means *born.* So far, so good. *Née* is invariably used with names: *Susan Warfield, née Smith,* indicating that Warfield is the woman's married name and Smith her maiden name; that is to say, the one she was born with. Often *nee;* see *Diacritical Marks.*

Assuming that they are not bastards, in the legal sense of the term, people are born with only their surnames: Smith, Jones, Winsocki. Consequently it is incorrect to say of a man who took a stage name that he was born George Williams, or to refer to our friend Mrs. Warfield as *née Susan Smith.* George was born Williams but christened George; Susan was born Smith but christened (or named, if you prefer) Susan.

needless to say   Why should one state what he has blackballed as *needless to say?* asks the pedant. Well, *needless to say* (like *it goes without saying* and *of course*) has become a conventional means of conceding that the reader may have drawn the conclusion or acquired the information unassisted; it is at once a small but advisable courtesy, and an escape hatch for the writer from giving an impression of pomposity or didacticism. Criticism of the expression, except for overwork, is quibbling.

negative   See *affirmative, negative.*

Negress   Often considered derogatory.

Negro   A certain amount of tightrope-walking is practiced in the use of racial terms. The most conspicuous development in this field in recent years has been the spread of rules against regularly identifying Negroes as such in the press. Editors have increasingly concluded that in general there is no more reason to characterize a person as a Negro than as a Jew, a Swede, or a Chinese.

There are instances, of course, when identification by race is essential or desirable, and sometimes it is hard to decide where to draw the line.

The consensus among responsible publications appears to be that racial identification is justifiable only when it is an essential consideration, as in describing a fugitive from the law, or when the race angle is what gives the account its point.

Some publications proscribe *colored* in the sense of *Negro*. *Colored* is not explicit, although in the United States there is little likelihood of its being misunderstood. But the reason sometimes given for banning it is that Negroes consider the word offensive. There seems no way to square this explanation with the use of the term in the name *National Association for the Advancement of Colored People*. In South Africa, *Colored* is applied to a special type of mulatto. Elsewhere, it may be applied to non-Caucasians other than Negroes, but this is not done in the United States.

The American College Dictionary's definition of *negrophile* is "one regarded as *too* [italics supplied] friendly to Negroes," but its definition of *Anglophile* is merely "one who is friendly to or admires England. . . ." To Webster, however, a *Negrophile* (with a capital N) is, disinterestedly, "One friendly to the Negro." What dictionary d'ya read?

Sometimes *Negro* is not capitalized, and some use this form to refer to people of mixed ancestry. This distinction has no recognized standing, however, and failure to capitalize the word may be interpreted as an intention to demean.

A newspaper that took great pains to avoid offense in racial matters found itself in a quandary over what to call a neighboring community regrettably named Nigger Hill. The problem was solved by rechristening the place Negro Hill as far as references to it in the paper were concerned—regardless of maps, general usage, and the befuddlement of its own residents.

(in the) neighborhood of   Redundant for *about, approximately*.

neither   As a conjunction, generally takes *nor*, but this is not so invariable as some rule mongers would have you think; Webster says usually *nor*, sometimes *or*. No hideous crime against civilization, morality, or even meaning is committed by using *or*, though *nor* naturally, because alliteratively, follows *neither*.

Neither as a pronoun (like *either*, which see) does not invariably take a singular verb. Often it occurs with a plural verb if it is followed by a prepositional phrase containing a plural: "Neither of us were embarrassed." In such cases, either a plural or a singular verb is considered correct.

new construction   See *Redundancy*.

new high record   See *record*.

new innovation   Redundant; an innovation is new of itself.

news   See *Collectives*.

newsman   There is no reasonable basis for the prejudice against the term in the sense of *newspaperman;* it is now recognized by all dictionaries.

newspaperman   A newspaperman is a member of the editorial department; that is, one whose duties are writing or editing. This is no aspersion on the other kinds of specialists whose services are necessary to the production of a newspaper, but there is a continuous, though ineffectual, attempt to arrogate *newspaperman* (or, on a tonier level, *journalist*, to which the same reasoning applies) by those who have no title to it. No

255

newspaperman, however, has ever been known to pass himself off as a member of some department other than the editorial.

NEWSPAPER NAMES Most publications now consider it excessive to enclose the names of newspapers and other periodicals in quotation marks. But those who persist in this rather old-fashioned practice will be better off if they determine the correct form of the names they are quoting. With newspapers, this is not always easy, for some newspapers incorporate in their names the names of their communities, and some do not. For purposes of identification, however, the community names are generally given regardless.

A political columnist, for example, steadily refers to *the New York "Times,"* and *the New York "Herald-Tribune."* No such animals; they're *The New York Times* and the *New York Herald-Tribune*—that is to say, *New York is part of the name* in both instances. He also animadverts upon *the Washington "Post"* but he can't fool us; we know he means *The Washington Post.*

The business of the definite article is tricky too; some papers use it in their titles and some do not. Forms of reference can be difficult; properly one should speak of "the *The New York Times* account of the episode" but the consensus probably would be that this is going too far.

The columnist cited also refers to *the Baltimore "Sun."* This is more nearly accurate, for the name of the paper is *The Sun.* *The Baltimore "The Sun"* does not sound so good. If the quotation marks are persisted in, the only out is *"The Sun" of Baltimore.*

The point of all this hairsplitting is that he who uses quotation marks around newspaper names is setting a trap or two for himself. (The?) *The New York Times Style Book* specifies no quotes and *The* (with a capital T) in all cases. It insists on *The Times of London,* not *The London Times.*

NEWSPAPER TERMS Certain such terms have mildly surprising histories. Who would have thought, for example, that a deadline was originally the line drawn around a military prison, beyond which a prisoner might be shot?

Tabloid had its genesis in a trademark registered in 1884 by Burroughs Wellcome & Co. of London, who used it for a pill, and attached to the term the idea of concentration. The expression passed into general use, and in 1902 was first applied to a newspaper format. Although a tabloid is no longer necessarily a pill, some tabloids have been described as hard to take.

The union of white-collar newspaper employees is the American Newspaper Guild. *Guild* had its first use in trade in the Middle Ages. At that time, guilds were associations of masters; that is, employers or owners, and not employees. Guild members of those days had objectives opposite those of modern union members.

Now consider *masthead,* often misapplied. The masthead, contrary to general assumption, is not the name of the paper as displayed at the top of the front page. That's the *nameplate,* sometimes referred to as the *flag.* The masthead is what used to be commonly found at the top of the editorial column. It usually contains a reduced version of the nameplate, the terms of subscription, etc. There is a tendency now to drop it in at random on an inside page. Time was when the information in the masthead usually included the names of the chief editorial executives, but that was before editors were put in their place by publishers and business managers.

It is not surprising that misused words should be so common in newspapers, considering the confusion that reigns in the terminology applied to their own operations.

Editorial, for example, is a confusing expression, especially as between newsdom and the laity. Within the craft, the application of *editorial* (as an adjective) is clear enough; it applies to the news aspect of the paper as distinguished from the advertising end. Consequently, the news department is often referred to as the editorial department. But the rub comes in the fact that to the nonnewsman, *editorial* may easily mean having to do with editorials, and thus he may conclude that the editorial department is the one that produces editorials.

Many readers do not differentiate between editorials and the rest of the paper's content, especially syndicated and other columns. They tend to apply the term *editorial* (as a noun) indiscriminately to columns as well as to editorials proper. Do these readers also confuse the views expressed in columns with the paper's own opinions? It seems likely.

The title *editor* is loosely used in the newspaper business, often with the aim of inflating to dignity some menial task like rewriting handouts in the real-estate field. An editor, it would seem, is properly either a news executive, or one who exercises selective judgment in preparing material for publication. The term hardly fits one who merely writes about a specialty, but the titles *science editor, labor editor, farm editor, music editor* are commonly used in such instances.

257

Telegraph editor is an anachronism; it is long enough since telegraphy was abandoned for transmission of the intelligence he deals with so that the term would have been superseded, except for the stick-in-the-mud temperament that delays many improvements in journalism—headline typography, for example.

Copyreader is singularly unsatisfactory; it is not descriptive of the job. Consequently, the term *copy editor* is sometimes substituted. But that title is sometimes also applied to a supervisor, e.g., a news editor or slot man, and thus becomes presumptuous, highfalutin, or misleading when applied to the lowly copyreader. We can be sure that the layman has no clear idea what a copyreader does (edit news copy and write headlines) and is not helped by the term to understand.

Rewrite man is another misnomer. One can rewrite only what has already been written, but that is a negligible part of the rewrite man's function. For the most part, he is fashioning stories from information he has obtained himself or been supplied with by legmen.

Chief editorial writer is often a misleading oddity, for generally it is applied to a chief who has no Indians; that is to say, when only one editorial light is shining from the ivory tower. Perversely, when there is a staff of editorialists, their chief usually holds the title of editor or editorial-page editor.

nice Only the pedant insists that *nice* means *exacting* and must not be used in the sense of *pleasant* or *agreeable*. It may mean either, and the context always shows which. The meanings attached to this word at various times have a long and tortuous history, which will not be gone into here. Suffice it to say that the word or its forebears have meant everything from *foolish* to *delicately balanced.*

nicety Preserves a specialized sense of *nice,* and does not mean something pleasant or agreeable. In general, a nicety is a detail or a minute distinction, as in "The niceties of formal etiquette are seldom observed today."

nickel Often misspelled *nickle. Nickel* is the term for both the metal and the coin (named for the metal, of which it is made).

NICKNAMES Reference to a person by his nickname in print suggests a familiarity that the subject may consider objectionable. If the owner is famous, the reader may regard this trick as a species of name-dropping; if the owner is an ordinary person, referring to him by his nickname may sound patronizing. This is no criticism of the practice, on first mention, of including in the identification a nickname by which a man is widely known, e.g., ex-Gov. Edmund (Pat) Brown; this is informative. The worlds of sports and entertainment, too, are laws unto themselves; more informality, if not downright chumminess, reigns in the reportage that concerns them. But casual reference in an otherwise impersonal account to a man by his nickname is likely to strike a false note.

There is no necessity to use quotation marks around a nickname. The usual practice is to introduce a nickname in parentheses, as indicated: Meyer (Mike) Berger. Thereafter, if the writer chooses to use the nickname, it is better simply *Mike*, not "Mike."

Nip   See *Jap, Japanese.*

no-   Hyphenated as a prefix: *no-ball, no-trump,* etc.

nobody, no one   See *somebody, someone.*

no exception   To particularize by describing something as no exception to a stated generality is to be trite: "The employees were underpaid, and he was no exception."

nohow   Although the word is recognized as having a standard use (Webster cites as an example "could nohow make out the writing"), the user is likelier than not to be considered illiterate unless he is employing it for dialectal effect.

noisome, noisy   That which is noisome stinks, and so does the use of this word to mean *noisy.* Its proper sense is *objectionable, annoying.*

non-   Solid as a prefix: *nonadhesive, noncommittal, nondefining, nonobservant, nonpolitical, nonneutral,* etc. But *non-African* (followed by a capital).

noncontroversial   A pertinent observation for this age of controversy was made by Robert M. Hutchins, the educator, in *Look:* "An issue is a point on which the parties take different positions. A noncontroversial issue, therefore, is as impossible as a round square. All issues are controversial; if they were not, they would not be issues." By the same token, the often-seen *controversial issue* is redundant. See also *controversial*.

none About the first thing any cub reporter learns, after being told the location of the men's room, is that *none* is singular and consequently always takes a singular verb. He must never write *none are, none were,* but always *none is, none was.* This is an article of faith, a first principle as firmly established as the delusion that it's a sin to split an infinitive. If the cub should question the invariable singularity of *none,* some kindly but condescending veteran will explain: "It's a basic rule of grammar, my boy. *None* comes from *not one,* and what else can *not one* be but singular?"

It's a persuasive theory, and the chances are that the cub will take the old hand's word for it and not look it up. This may be just as well, because if he did look it up he would get a surprise that might cause him to inquire into a number of other supposedly immutable principles and thereby discover that some of them are as soundly based as old wives' tales.

Let us assume that some less credulous cub does undertake to look up *none.* We might peek over his shoulder as he turns the pages:

"As subject, *none* with a plural verb is the commoner construction."—*Webster's New International Dictionary.*

"*None* may be considered singular or plural according to the implied meaning, but is generally used with the plural form of the verb."—Clark, Davis, Shelley, *Handbook of English.*

"*None* may be either singular or plural."—Woolley, Scott, Bracher, *College Handbook of Composition.*

"*None, most, some, such* may be singular or plural." Easley S. Jones, *Practical English Composition.*

"With the indefinite pronouns *all, any, none,* and *such,* use a singular verb if the group is considered as a unit and a plural verb if the members of the group are considered individually."—Sanders, Jordan, Magoon, *Unified English Composition.*

Fowler also concurred in this, or perhaps set the stage for it, since his comment was the earliest. But even before him, as he points out, the *Oxford English Dictionary* had described the plural construction as commoner.

Yet it is evident that somewhere, somehow, *none* apparently was anointed as singular, although the records of the proceedings seem to have been lost. Harry Shaw Jr., author of *Writing and Rewriting,* speaks of a "standard rule" that *none* requires a singular verb. But first he says that it may be used with either singular or plural and that studies of its use by good writers have shown that it is as often plural as singular. Even sour Ambrose Bierce in *Write It Right* hedged here in deference to usage.

NONRESTRICTIVE CLAUSES   See *Restrictive and Nonrestrictive Clauses.*

noon luncheon   Redundant. By definition, a luncheon is at noon.

no sooner   Followed by *than,* not *when,* in such constructions as "No sooner had the whistle blown *than* the workmen thronged out of the factory."

Nordic   See *Scandinavian.*

normalcy   Whatever his other sins, President Warren G. Harding has been unjustly held accountable for *normalcy* as an illegitimate coinage. *A Dictionary of Contemporary American Usage* points out that Harding was employing a perfectly good, though at that time little-used, word. Either the attention attracted to it by Harding and his critics or the inscrutable currents of language have given it far greater currency today, so that now it is not boggled at. *Back to normalcy,* however, is less likely to be rendered *back to normality* (the word Harding's critics thought he should have used) than *back to normal.*

North   As a part of the United States, by common consent (like East, South, West) usually capitalized.

not   Sometimes statements are unintentionally reversed in sense by ill-advised use of the negative: "Current discussions cannot be oversimplified merely by referring to the administration as antibusiness." Obviously the writer meant that discussions *could* be oversimplified by such a reference; he should have written *should not be* or *can be.* See also *overestimate; minimize; reverse,* etc; *Reversal of Sense.*

not, not all, not every   The problem of placement is similar to that of the placement of *only* (see *only, not only*). Fowler, who usually insists on exactitude and no nonsense, takes a liberal view in both instances, which may only illustrate that even oracles have their foibles. Perhaps this was his way of paying off some early teacher for what he considered pedantry in this connection. Those who wince at the misplacement of *not* wince oftenest, probably, at "All is not gold that glitters" (correctly, it's *glisters,* as Fowler quoted it, but no one says that any more). We all know, of course, what is meant; not, as might be perversely construed, that everything which glitters is not gold, but *"Not all* that glitters is gold."

A more modern example, outside the sacred precincts of Shakespeare: "Every story with an unusual feature does not call for a humorous headline." We all know here, too, what is meant: *"Not* every story with an unusual feature . . ." Fowler held it not worthwhile to make any great point of this misplacement. He predicted, however, that *all . . . not* for *not . . . all* would pass away in time. But the time is not yet. Careful writers put *not* where it belongs.

notable, noted, notorious, notoriety   *Notable* means *worthy of note, important, memorable,* and as applied to people is a synonym for *noted,* meaning *well known, eminent, celebrated. Notorious* is the one to watch out for; its commonest sense is, as the linguists like to say, pejorative; that is, a person who is notorious is well known for unfavorable reasons: *a notorious prostitute; a notorious deadbeat.* Unconscious slander is often committed in the use of *notorious* on the assumption it means *noted* or *notable.*

Notoriety, likewise, is not simply fame but, we may say, ill fame; the man who acquires it is famous for the wrong thing, for example criminal acts. *Notability* is the word often displaced by *notoriety.*

not about to   An odd colloquialism with the sense *not intend to.* It should be avoided in writing, for *not about to* has the literal sense *not on the verge of.* "The secretary said he isn't about to make another trip to press for an agreement." Ambiguous; the intention here was *does not intend to,* but the statement might easily be understood as meaning the secretary would not make a trip imminently.

not all that   "The comedian admitted he was not all that blasé about the award." *Not all that* for *not* or *not that* is a British mannerism that has been taken up lately in the U.S. It may be regarded as an affectation.

note   Such expressions as *strike a happy* (or *sour*) *note* pass for humor or cleverness among many writing about a subject that has some connection with music, no matter how remote or inappropriate the association. Obvious straining for effect kills the effect. See also *Attribution* for use of *note* as a verb.

not . . . not   Double negatives, even when consciously and correctly used, are to be avoided because they place on the reader the burden of sorting out the meaning, and may easily lead the writer to set down what he does not intend. "I would not be annoyed if they did not agree with me." Clearer: "I would not be annoyed if they disagreed with me." See also *Double Negative.*

not only   See *only, not only.*

not so . . . as   See *as . . . as.*

not so (as) much . . . as   The correct form; not *not so* (as) *much . . . but.* "*Not so much* sinning *as* sinned against."

not too   *Not too,* as the successor of *not very,* is a prevalent peculiarity that bears watching. To begin with, the legitimate meaning of *too* in this phrase, and the one likely to be assumed, is *more than enough. Not too* is clearly objectionable as it is often used. *Not very,* although it also may be open to objection, at least has established itself as an idiom, and conveys a clear meaning (*not very satisfactory; not very honest*). A case against *not too* may be constructed on the grounds that it is often illogical, sometimes misleading, and not found in careful writing. It appears to be a sample of the timid understatement favored by the mealymouthed. Let us look at some examples:
  "She testified that her husband was very restless and did not like to stay put too long."
  "The fact that the device will not accurately fix the position of an enemy plane is not considered too important."
  "The gross national product next year may not be too far below the peak."
  "Elsewhere, apparently, there was not too much resistance to the price-support program."
  "Since the primaries set a pattern, the new system should not mean too much change at election time."
  These sentences will strike the critical reader as open to a charge of absurdity. *Not very,* substituted for *not too* in each

instance, sounds more acceptable. But neither *very* nor *too* is necessary. As an experiment, strike the *too* out of the quoted examples: "She testified that her husband . . . did not like to stay put [too] long." Nothing meaningful is lost by the omission of *too,* and a certain directness is added.

There are sentences in which the lurking illogicality looms over everything:

"Mrs. Antoine's health is not always too good, either." Is it possible for anyone's health to be too good? Even one's enemies may stop short of conceding this. *Not always good* seems preferable.

"The candidate is not too prosperous." Much the same criticism applies here. If *not prosperous* is too blunt, how about *none too prosperous, prosperous but not rich,* or *only moderately well off?*

"The expert said farmers do not need too much rain, but some moisture would be beneficial." Too much rain would be a flood, or at any rate more than enough, and it takes no expert to say the farmers do not need it.

There are occasions when *not too* could be useful in a literal sense. But if someone says "It's *not too* hot out today," we may understand him as meaning either "It's not unendurably hot" or merely "It's not at all hot." We have reached the scene too late, for the spurious *not toos* have already made sentences like this hopelessly ambiguous.

"The dean of the University Medical School says the Asian flu may not hit this area too hard." *not* or *not . . . very.* See also *too.*

NOUNS AS ADJECTIVES See *Modifiers.*

NOUNS OF ADDRESS Should be set off by commas. "George I want to go home." *George, I want.*

now An adverb that is incorrectly joined by a hyphen to the adjective it modifies: *the now-bankrupt financier. now bankrupt.* It is old fashioned to set *now* off with commas: "Once there were only two great powers; now, there are several." *now there are . . .* See also *presently.*

nowheres Dialectal; not good usage. *nowhere.*

nth Fowler was in a testy mood the day he leveled his lance at the popular usage of *to the nth. N,* in the language of mathematics, he explained, "does not mean an infinite number, nor the greatest possible number, nor necessarily even a large number, but simply the particular number that we may find ourselves concerned with when we come to details; it is short for 'one or two or three or whatever the number may be . . .' "

Unless we are going to shut our eyes, however, we must concede that *to the nth degree* is now permanently established in the sense of *to the utmost* or *infinitely*. Webster gives us "extreme or utmost."

Let us steel ourselves while Fowler lays on the lash: "Those who talk in mathematical language about knowing mathematics go out of their way to exhibit ignorance." Aw, come on, H.W., technical terms are constantly being taken up by the populace, and out of either ignorance or blithe disregard of the properties are used to mean something different. That is what has happened here.

nubile Once the term (related to *nuptial*) meant solely *of marriageable age*, but it attracted more interesting connotations. The sense that predominates is the one given by Webster as "physically suited for or desirous of sexual relationship."

nude See *naked, nude*.

number Preceded by *a*, *number* is plural (*a number were waiting*); preceded by *the*, it is singular (*the number of voters was diminishing*).

NUMBER See *Collectives; Plurals; with; together with*.

NUMBERS

Large Numbers Big (or astronomical, as the cliché artist would have it) numbers seem here to stay. Everything is out of sight —government budgets, the explosive force of bombs, almost any figure dealing with the atom and its possibilities, and, as always, distances in the heavens, which, like other technical considerations, are appearing increasingly in print.

The least we can do is give the bedeviled, number-stunned reader a break and present these large totals as understandably as possible.

Large round numbers can easily be simplified. The zeros in 22,000,000 are forbidding enough, but in 22,000,000,000 they have to be counted. What an imposition on the reader! As a matter of fact, he usually refuses to be imposed on in this way, but lets the tails of such numerical comets swoosh past unheeded. How much easier it is to write, as well as to read, *22 million*, *22 billion*, or *billion-dollar industry*, rather than *$1,000, 000 industry*.

It has been argued that the zeroes should be allowed to stand in figures relating to government expenditures as a means of impressing the reader with their size, but this sounds foolish. It is politics, not diction.

The notion that an expression like *$8.6* million is likely to be read *eight and six-tenths dollars million* rather than *eight and six-tenths million dollars* does not stand up against scientific studies showing that words are comprehended in groups rather than singly. We do not read $8 "dollars eight."

The fact that an expression like *$8 million* may break at the end of a line, momentarily giving the reader the impression of *$8*, is considered objectionable in some quarters. This objection seems hardly more valid than complaints against the misleading sense that may occur at any line break. Some publications forestall this difficulty, real or imagined, by linking the elements with a hyphen: *$8-million*.

Rounding off is advisable for large figures in most contexts, unless there is some overriding reason against it; *$18,500,000* is preferable to *$18,478,369* and *18½ million dollars* (or *$18.5 million*) is preferable to either.

Useless Counting Many of us not only know how to count but are unduly proud of it. Of course, we may not be showing off but only trying to be helpful when we add up trifling, meaningless totals. Even so, ungrateful readers have been known to wish they could bite the hand that is feeding them these tasteless tidbits. What can it be about little numbers that holds such fascination? The following will be recognized at once as common examples:

"They were joined by their three children, John, Ruth, and Mary."

"He was referring to Egypt and Saudi Arabia, two nations that control much of the strategic Red Sea coast line."

"This facility and the one in Baltimore are two of the finest in the country."

"Sports and music are his two hobbies."

The love of little numbers also rears its stupid head in references like *the two*, *the three*, *the duo*, *the trio*, *the quartet*, *the quintet*, as used in avoidance of that simple word *they*.

266

Words like *duo, trio,* and *quartet* suggest an organization, as of performers; when they are used simply as variants for *two, three,* and *four,* they reflect adversely on the intelligence of the writer.

Sometimes the adding machine gets jammed, probably from overwork. Then we get "Four examination dates have been approved for the positions of fire captain, senior clerk, key-punch operator, and construction foreman." Four each, or one? Omit *Four.*

"Christmas Day will be observed with two festival services at 9:30 and 11 A.M." Four services or two? A comma after *services* would help, but why not just leave out *two?*

There are other ways to insult the reader's intelligence than by forcing second-grade arithmetic on his attention. One is to labor the obvious with something like "The river reached a peak of 30.7 feet, a little below the predicted crest of 31 feet"; or "Sales for 1954 hit $10.5 million, exceeding the previous year's total of $10 million." More judicious wording would be "The river reached a peak of 30.7 feet, as compared with the . . ." and "Sales for 1954 hit $10.5 million, a half-million more than the total for 1953."

Figures vs. Words There must be something fundamentally indecent about the use of figures in text, to judge from the way publications generally shy away from it. Some magazines even spell out numbers as large as *six hundred and fifty-three,* thereby demonstrating their scorn for economizing on space, and also their abhorrence of anything so revolting to the sensibilities as *653.* Book publishers tend to spell out numbers under one hundred, round numbers such as one thousand, a million, fifteen hundred, and to use figures for statistics, measurements, and percentages. All other numbers in a paragraph containing *any* number of three digits or more are usually set in figures.

Newspapers usually draw the line at *ten;* that is, numbers under *ten* are spelled out, and figures are used for the rest. A person's age, however, is invariably given in newspapers in figures, and words are used in a phrase with numbers that fall on both sides of the rule: *eight or ten inspections,* not *eight or 10. Ten* must have mystical significance as a great divider, for it is generally accepted.

The question of which numbers are to be rendered in figures and which are to be spelled out is, of course, a matter of the style of individual publications. And style is a matter of taste or preference, concerning which there should be no dispute. It seems that in handling numbers, however, things are often made unnecessarily difficult.

The rule of ten would be easy enough to follow if it were not for the usual legion of exceptions. Let us sample a few, chosen at random: ages, addresses, percentages, scores, dates, expressions containing mixed figures (*nine* or *ten*), statistical matter (what a bushel basket this one is!), height, time of day, decimals, betting odds, latitude and longitude, temperatures, humidity readings, barometric readings, sums of money, vote totals, page numbers, tables, dimensions, military designations, roll calls, rainfall measurements. These are often directed to be given in figures, regardless of size.

Some exceptions are freakish: give rain-gauge readings in figures unless they are not taken from the gauge and are under ten (fathom that one, if you can); spell out decades and sums that have been incorporated with words (whatever that means); use figures for temperatures except in such expressions as "There was a thirty-degree rise in temperature during the day."

The numerous exceptions, some of them footless and others incomprehensible, cause the copy-editor to stop and ponder when he encounters a number, and then, oftener than should be necessary for such a routine matter, to have recourse to the stylebook. Even then he will often not get a conclusive answer, as evidenced by the murky rules cited.

Such considerations as these suggest an earth-shaking reversal: Why not give up the losing fight against the use of figures? Permit the use of figures entirely, and in doubtful instances let common sense govern. The decision to rely on common sense would itself be a gain, for the present welter of arbitrary and conflicting rules certainly is not based on it.

Who would care? Not readers, certainly. Those who have some critical apprehension of the use of language are likely to be nettled by errors and banalities, but not by the difference between *six or eight* and *6 or 8*.

And yet, and yet—the experience of a publication that changed its style to figures entirely for cardinals and ordinals was a sorry one, and the experiment was shortly abandoned. It was bad enough to see things like "Sometimes it walked on 2 legs, sometimes on all 4s."

But there was worse:

"He got 1 of those new cookbooks for Christmas."

"Production was a 3rd more this season."

"The issue was submitted 1st to the board of directors."

To be sure, none of these latter is really a cardinal or an ordinal, and thus they do not fall under the rule. The *1* is the pronoun *one,* the *3rd* is a fraction, and the *1st* is the adverb *first.* But just try to knock such distinctions into the heads of copyreaders and proofreaders. Once the rule against anything but figures was put out, there was reason to believe they took a diabolical pleasure in changing everything possible to the hideous numerical versions. Things got as bad as *2wice.*

Apart from aberrations, however, it must be admitted that there is indeed something distasteful about the appearance of small figures in text. They give an impression of immature composition. Cardinals are bad enough, but ordinals are even worse:

"Both Rita and Aly were smiling and happy after their 1st reunion."

"The man was run over by the scraper and cut in 2."

"The freshman was the 2nd who paid tribute to the dean."

The best thing to do, apparently, is to retain a rule. The main complaint against such rules, anyway, is aimed at the confusion created by inconsistent exceptions. But there are more important things than consistency, and no rule should be permitted to flout good taste.

Figure at Beginning of Sentence The common rule against starting a sentence with a figure seems defensible enough, because a number coming first *does* look strange. The usual means of avoiding it are to write the number out or to recast the sentence so that something else comes first. The brewers of that intoxicating potion, style, however, have been known to recommend another way out: placing the word *exactly* (or *there,* which see) in front of the figure.

Thus "Six thousand, five hundred people attended the concert" would become "Exactly 6,500 people . . ." The objection to this ought to be apparent, because a round number like 6,500 obviously is an approximation. But even with figures that are intended to be precise, as in "Exactly 6,519 persons passed through the turnstile" the intrusion of *exactly* places an emphasis on accuracy that sounds strange when such emphasis is unwarranted. Recasting to move the number back is preferable to using a word that may give the sentence a peculiar tone.

See also *Sums of Money* and *Preposition with Numbers* under *Ellipsis;* for *a, an* with *hundred* and *thousand,* see *a, an; Roman Numerals.*

numerous Not standard as a noun: "Numerous of the banners were frayed." *many.*

—O—

O, oh *O* is generally restricted to invocations; this form of address is somewhat archaic: *O king, we beg thy favor. Oh* is an exclamation: *Oh dear, the stew is boiling over.* The forms are often used interchangeably, however.

OBITUARIES It has been predicted by Saul Pett of the Associated Press that the next war will be between reporters and copyreaders. Perhaps the one after that will be between those who hold that a man is survived by his *wife* and those who insist that he is survived by his *widow.* Stylebooks favor both sides of this disagreement. Nothing very grievous hangs from the choice between one word and the other, probably. Those who prefer *widow* argue that, once a man dies, a widow is what his wife incontrovertibly becomes.

The choice of *wife* can be supported by an examination of the word *survive,* which means *to remain alive.* She who remains alive was the wife rather than the widow.

But debates over points like this are useless. No one who has ever thought about the matter enough to have formed an opinion in favor of either *wife* or *widow* is likely to be budged an inch. Even so, the use of *wife* can be justified from another direction. A woman is likely see herself called a widow for the first time in her husband's obituary, and she can easily be spared this shock.

To press things a bit further, if a man is survived by his widow, why does one not speak of women as being survived by their widowers? Or of parents being survived by their orphans? Quite obviously those words, apart from other considerations, would seem to be laboring the fact of bereavement. Thus also with *widow?*

Unreasonably squeamish relatives sometimes seek to withhold from publication the age of a deceased woman. Reporters should press for it, however, because one's age, it has been well said, is the fullest possible description in the smallest possible space. Withholding the age of a living woman may be an act of chivalry, but after she is dead her sensibilities can hardly be affected. There seems no way this can hurt relatives, either.

The omission of any information about what the subject did for a living is a conspicuous fault of many short obituaries. This is the most interesting fact about a person.

The use of a nickname is an indignity, except in instances when a man is widely and publicly known by it. Even then, it should be used parenthetically with the full, formal version of his name. (See also *Mr.*)

The line *funeral arrangements are pending* seems to be a useless statement of what the reader can assume, especially when the practice is to publish those arrangements once they have been made. It is growing common to speak of the subject of an obituary as having been *preceded in death* by some other member of his family, but this expression smacks of the unctuous mortician. Like such euphemisms as *passed away* and *departed this life*, it is a fit subject for interment. And while we're at it, let's exhume that plain old word *undertaker*.

"Mr. Smith leaves three brothers, Frank of Ossining, George of New York, and Gerald of Los Angeles." Sometimes it's "a sister, Mary of Italy." Somehow, this puts one incongruously in mind of such grandiose designations as "William of Normandy" and "Lawrence of Arabia." A better form for the list of survivors might be "Frank, Ossining; George, New York; and Gerald, Los Angeles." If the *of* must be kept, it had better be preceded, in this instance, by the comma. And as for "Mary of Italy," she should become "Mary, *in* Italy."

object, objective The *object* is the purpose; the *objective* is the goal. *Objective* likely has a more impressive sound, and tends to displace *object*. "The objective was to tell the people about the record of Congress." *object*. When *object* will do, use it; the simpler and shorter are always preferable to the more complex and longer if they will serve.

OBJECTIVITY Often sacrificed through inept writing: "The district attorney took exception to the confusion psychiatrists create in the minds of jurors by their legal interpretations of insanity." Here the writer has aligned himself with the district attorney as a critic of psychiatrists in the courtroom. Such work often arouses charges of bias, but usually the real reason for it is stupidity. See also *Misleading Attribution* under *Attribution*.

observance, observation The word for marking a religious rite, holiday, etc., is *observance*: "The bank was closed for observation of Veterans Day." *observance*. *Observation* is looking, watching, noticing.

obtain *Obtain* is often pretentious for *get*. See also *got; secure, obtain*.

obtrusively, unobtrusively Unexplainably (but often enough to indicate a widespread misapprehension) misspelled *obstrusively, unobstrusively*.

occasion Often—and unaccountably, for it would appear to change the pronunciation—misspelled *occassion*.

OCCUPATIONAL TITLES See *Titles*.

occur, take place The consensus of usage is that what occurs is accidental and unforeseen ("The explosion *occurred* while shifts were changing"), whereas what takes place in planned or arranged ("The coronation will *take place* May 12"). *Occur* is equivalent to *happen*. *Occurrence* is sometimes misspelled *occurrance*.

octopus The plural is either *octopuses* or *octopi* (though the latter is falsely formed). Sometimes misspelled *octupus*.

oculist, etc. *Oculist* and *ophthalmologist* are equivalent; both are M.D.s whose specialty is the eye. The difference is a matter of derivation, the first term having developed from a Latin root and the second from a Greek. An *optometrist* is licensed to prescribe glasses and possesses the degree O.D. (doctor of optometry). Optometrists, while qualified to use the title *doctor*, seldom do so, and in some states must specify, if they do, that they are O.D.s. An *optician* does not administer treatment but grinds lenses and makes spectacles.

-odd Hyphenated as a suffix: *thirty-odd*, etc. Redundant with *some: Some thirty-odd soldiers*. Use one or the other. See also *some, -odd*.

of See *Prepositions;* with identifying phrases, see *One-Legged Comma* under *Comma; Obituaries*.

of between, of from, etc.   Doubling of prepositions is redundant with numbers indicating a range: "An appropriation of from six to eight million dollars" (*of six to eight*); "a rise in temperture of between three and five degrees" (*of three to five*).

of course   It is sometimes advisable to concede that the reader may already know what he is being told, lest the writer sound didactic; at the same time, the writer may not be able to risk omitting what he qualifies by *of course,* if it is essential to comprehension by those who do not know. Overly cautious writers, however, tend to slip in *of course* by reflex action, as a kind of running apology. Every *of course* should be weighed critically with a view to striking it out. This applies also to *as is well known* and *it goes without saying;* the critic may object that if it goes without saying, why not let it go unsaid?

off-, -off   Oftener solid than hyphenated as a prefix: *Offhand, offset, offshoot, offshore,* etc. But *off-color, off-white, off-peak.* Solid as a suffix: *cutoff, sendoff, blastoff, writeoff.*

offense, offence   *Offence* is the British preference.

offhand, offhanded, offhandedly   *Offhand* is both adjective and adverb; the other two forms are clumsy and superfluous; *an offhand gesture; he performed the trick offhand.*

officer   The idea that, with reference to policemen, *officer* should be applied only to those holding a rank, such as sergeant, lieutenant, or captain, may have merit, but usage does not support it. Police themselves might like to see *cop* (which see) supplanted by *police officer,* a term of much more dignity. At any rate, all policemen are officers of the law.

official, -ly   Overused in contexts where there is no occasion to think the action described could be unofficial, as for example the conduct of business by public bodies. *Official,* as might be expected, runs rife in officialese. Bureaucrats take deep satisfaction in speaking of their duties as *official business.*

off of   *Of* is superfluous with *off:* "He jumped off of the bridge." *off the bridge.*

offspring   The plural, as well as the singular, is *offspring* (not *offsprings*).

often   An adverb, and thus erroneously joined to adjectives with a hyphen: *often-warring elements. often warring*.

oh-oh   The *oh-oh* that is the equivalent of *oops* is hyphenated, as given here; not *oh, oh*.

O.K., okeh, etc.   Now and again some wounded scholar raises a plaintive cry in favor of *okeh*, accompanied by a denunciation of *O.K.* as impure. There are moving accounts of how *okeh* is the way Hiawatha, or some other literary Indian, spelled it. Woodrow Wilson, too, is said to have given his benison to *okeh*, possibly as a diverting interlude in the drafting of the Fourteen Points. *Okeh*, at least, has lasted longer than the League of Nations, that other monument to his fame. It is still with us, though failing fast.

The outraged proponents of *okeh*, who want it imposed on everyone by fiat, overlook an all-important point: people generally do not favor *okeh*, no matter how pure it is. What probably denied *okeh* a fair start in life is that it does not look as if it sounds like what everyone says.

The legalists in the audience may be interested to hear that the matter apparently was settled, as far as derivation is concerned, by Allen Walker Read in an article, "The Evidence on O.K.," in the July 19, 1941 issue of what was then known as the *Saturday Review of Literature*. Read traced *O.K.* back to the O.K. Club, a Democratic organization formed in New York in 1840 to promote the re-election of President Van Buren. The initials were those of Van Buren's birthplace, Old Kinderhook, N.Y. In 1936, five years before Read's research was published, H. L. Mencken listed ten versions of the origin of *O.K.* in *The American Language*, and showed remarkable perspicacity by leaning toward a hint of the explanation Read was to develop.

The latest Merriam-Webster dictionaries list *okeh* only as a variant, and cite Read's article. If Read's explanation is all right with Webster, it ought to be O.K. with the rest of us, especially since *O.K.* has general acceptance in its favor. And so farewell, *okeh!*

O.K., OK, and *okay* are all equally acceptable, though the initials are more used.

old   See *elderly*.

old adage   Redundant. Oldness is inherent in *adage*.

older   See *Ad Lingo; Comparison of Adjectives*.

old fashion, old fashioned   The correct form of the modifier is *old fashioned: an old-fashioned girl;* not, as is sometimes seen, *old fashion*.

Old Guard   (*The*) *Old Guard* is a collective that cannot properly be pluralized into *Old Guards* in reference to individuals. Make it "Members of the Old Guard."

oldster   See *elderly*.

OMISSION   See *Ellipsis*.

on   Standardization, by making mechanical parts interchangeable, gave the industrial age a big push. This process is also at work in language and has been for centuries. The specialists in that field call it not standardization but leveling. That is to say, diverse forms which do the same or similar jobs tend to merge, or to kill one another off. One evidence of this is the disappearance of *thee, thou, ye,* and the like from all but archaic or specialized usage. *You* has put them all out of business.

The losing fight being made by *whom* against *who* is an example of leveling that is under way in our own time. It seems predictable that *whom* will go the way of all flesh, in spite of the fact that people who are trying too hard to be correct sometimes make it displace *who. The New Yorker* calls attention to this from time to time under the heading, "The Omnipotent Whom." See *who, whom*.

The prize contender for omnipotence is probably neither *who* nor *whom*, but rather the preposition *on*. Like a bandwagon-climber who has scented a promising dark horse, one critic began some time ago to note down evidences of *on's* increasing popularity, especially in the press. It was found to be nosing out *about, at, for, from, in, into, of, to,* and *toward*. Drunk with success, it may easily press forward and knock all other prepositions out of the language.

Would this be a good thing? Some linguists regard as the most advanced those languages in which leveling has gone the farthest. Certainly it makes communicating simpler. In this instance, the effort now spent on choosing among prepositions would be saved. But *on*, despite its popularity in the press, is not being accepted as a proxy elsewhere. Let us see how *on* has gone berserk:

"His worried fans can be reassured on one thing, however." *about*, or perhaps *of*.

"The officer questioned the woman on her wounds." Sounds uncomfortable for the woman and downright inconsiderate of the officer, who might have settled himself elsewhere. *about* or *concerning*.

"The mayor was dismayed on the permit denial." *at* or *by*.

"Don't wait on me." This remark was addressed, not to a waitress, but to a friend by a man who did not want to be waited *for*. This is a Far-western barbarism, common in conversation. From there it oozes into print: "The trustees must wait on approval by the State Allocations Board." *await* or *wait for*.

"Complaints on dogs running loose are increasing"; "I'll call him on that." *about*.

"The man has an elephantlike memory on abuse he has taken"; "Support will be sought on the proposal." *of* and *for*.

"The wraps may be lifted soon on dramatic defense developments." *from*.

"Developments on Middle East problems dominated the session." *in*.

"The defendant was convicted on a charge of theft"; "A study on psittacosis has been undertaken"; "Complaints on violations of waterway rules have been received." *of*.

"Science is finding clues on possible causes." *to*.

"Little progress has been made on racial integration." *toward* or *in*.

"Apathy marks the public's attitude on government." *toward*.

And, finally: "The aim is to educate the populace on the proper use of English." Let's start now, if it's not too late.

On is unnecessary with days of the week, and to be used only as rhythm and idiom make it desirable: *He arrived* [on] *Tuesday; The play will be given* [on] *Friday*.

on-, -on   Solid as a prefix: *oncoming, onlooker, onrush*, etc. Hyphenated as a suffix: *come-on, head-on*, etc.

on account of   Preferable: *because of*.

on behalf   See *behalf*.

once   Often mistakenly joined to adjectives with hyphens: "a once-quaint area." Correctly, *once quaint area*. For an explanation, see *-ly*.

one   The editorial *we* (which see), *this writer, the present* reporter and the like are absurd under a by-line, as a means of sidestepping the forthright and honest *I*. We may as well add *one* to this list of pompous evasions.

"This program," a music critic wrote, "brought confirmation of the conviction that Mozart is one's favorite composer."

Which one's? Anyone's, it might be hastily deduced by the reader, who is generally on the run and therefore likely to seize the first sense that suggests itself. But he would soon decide it is unlikely that the critic suggested Mozart is the favorite of all.

Backing up for a new try, the reader would see that the critic really meant "My favorite composer." But *my* is a form of *I*, and horrors! one can't refer directly to oneself, even if one is expressing one's own preference. Better make it a circumspect if confusing *one's*. If a choice must be made between the reader's ease and the writer's Victorian sense of modesty, the devil take the reader.

"The artist is, one suspects, headed for international recognition." The suspicion belongs to the critic who wrote this, but by saying *one* instead of *I* he fraudulently suggests it is more widely held. If there are grounds for expressing a consensus, it should be done honestly: "It is generally agreed that this artist is headed for international recognition."

The use of *one* for *I* has three strikes against it: false modesty, quaintness, and ambiguity. *One* should be used, if at all, as an indefinite pronoun meaning *someone* or *anyone* or *a person: One does one's duty*, but not as a substitute for *I* or *me*.

One takes *a*, not *an:* "Such an one is readily available." *a; an* here is archaic.

-one   Distinction should be made between the pronouns *anyone, everyone, someone* and the adjective-pronoun phrases *any one, every one, some one: Anyone can do that; Take any one of the pieces; Everyone knew the story; They walked off with every one* (of something) *; Someone is on the phone; Some one of the books will have the answer*. Usually the indefinite pronouns refer to people, the phrases to things.

one and the same   The phrase has lost its force from repetition.

one of the (only, etc.)   "California is one of the only, if not the only, states subsidizing its college students." A clumsy way to handle matters because *states* does not go with *the only*. It is better to spin this construction out a little farther to get a smoother effect: "California is one of the only states subsidizing its college students, if not the only one."

one of those who (is, are)   Such sentences as "I am *one of those who* hope(s) for a peaceful settlement" agitate people who cannot decide whether the verb should be *hope*, to agree with *those*, or *hopes*, to agree with *I* and *one*. Strictly, the correct form is *hope*, since its subject is *who*, which refers to *those*. Nevertheless, a singular verb (*I am one of those who hopes*) is often found in constructions of this kind, and is regarded as acceptable.

oneself, one's self   Both forms are acceptable, but there seems no occasion for the latter, which is clumsy.

one that is   Generally excess baggage: "The situation is one that is ripe for controversy." *The situation is ripe* . . . In this instance, the phrase also disrupts the rhythm.

onetime, one-time   It is desirable to differentiate *onetime* (former) from *one-time* (single-occasion). "He is a *onetime* prospector" (at one time he was a prospector). "It was a *one-time* attempt" (the attempt was made only once).

on (in) line   When *The New York Times* said, "The reporter got on line and grabbed the premier's hand," some readers were ready to decide they had been wrong all their lives in thinking the expression is *in line*, because they were brought up to believe that if you see it in *The Times* it's right. They probably had seen *on line* here and there in other places, but dismissed it as a typographical error.

But Margaret M. Bryant's *Current American Usage*, a scholarly work based on geographical studies and other evidence, tells us that *on line* "is almost universal in all types of speech in New York City and the Hudson Valley. *In line* is found in all other areas and generally in formal written English." New Yorkers have a way of attempting to foist their provincialisms on the rest of us. Will we resist in this case?

On line reminds one of Christopher Robin in A. A. Milne's *When We Were Very Young*. Christopher, you will remember, carefully refrained from stepping on the lines in the sidewalk lest he become the quarry of bears whose natural prey standers-on-lines are. Perhaps some retribution awaits those who stand and write *on line*.

only, not only (not only, but also)   Fowler scathingly and surprisingly denounced those who would criticize "He *only* died a week ago" as a mistake for "He died *only* a week ago." Not that he would permit *only* to be dropped in just anywhere; he saved his scorn for those who would change its position when there is no chance of misunderstanding.

The placement of *only* is something that warrants close attention, however. This is illustrated by an example in *Word Study* attributed to Professor Ernest Brennecke of Columbia University: Seven meanings result from placing *only* in all possible positions in "I hit him in the eye yesterday." Let us spin this exercise out: *"Only* I hit him in the eye yesterday" (I alone); "I *only* hit him in the eye yesterday" (I did no more than hit him); "I hit *only* him in the eye yesterday" (him, no other); "I hit him *only* in the eye yesterday" (just in the eye); "I hit him in the *only* eye yesterday (he had just one eye); "I hit him in the eye *only* yesterday" (as recently as yesterday); " I hit him in the eye yesterday *only*" (yesterday, no other day).

Yet authorities agree that too much fuss has been made over the placement of *only*. Its strictly logical position is before the element it modifies, and surely no one will be criticized for meticulously placing it there. Perhaps the thing to do, if you are bound to be meticulous, is to keep your preference to yourself.

Meticulousness is advised, if only because it's a good habit in writing. Laxity with *only* will likely lead to trouble with *not only . . . but also*, and here carelessness is more damaging. "The strike has created problems for the company in maintaining not only the goodwill of its customers but also of the general public." *Customers* should be balanced off against *general public*, and the only way to do it is: *"not only* of its customers *but also* of the general public."

George Orwell, a highly self-critical writer, permitted himself to say: "Mr. Auden's brand of moralism is only possible if you are the kind of person who is always somewhere else when the trigger is pulled." Nigglers would insist on *possible only*.

The problem of the placement of *only* is similar to that of the placement of *not*. See *not, not all*. See also *Poesy* for the displacement of *only* by *lone*.

on the order of See *order*.

on the part of Generally involved wording for *by, among*. "There is less studying on the part of high-school pupils these days." *by*.

operation The fad of giving projects names like "Operation Breakthrough" originated in World War II, when military operations were so designated but with code names carefully chosen to give no inkling of what they referred to. "Operation Overlord," for example, was the designation for the Allied invasion of France. After the war, military and other undertakings were widely designated "Operation This" and "Operation That," usually with names intended to indicate their nature: "Operation Spring Cleanup" This practice has grown extremely tiresome, especially when writers resort to it casually: "The Legislature began Operation Adjournment this week."

operetta, light opera, musical, musical comedy *Operetta* is now an old-fashioned word applied to an old-fashioned genre, for example the works of Gilbert and Sullivan, and in America, those of Victor Herbert (*Sweethearts, The Red Mill, Babes in Toyland*), Rudolf Friml (*Rosemarie*), and others of that era. Musical comedy is applied to more modern works of the same kind (light music, spoken dialogue), such as Rodgers and Hammerstein's *South Pacific* and *Oklahoma!* and Lerner and Loewe's *My Fair Lady. Musical* is simply the clipped form of *musical comedy. Light opera* is a term alternatively applied to what has been identified here as operetta, but virtually never to musical comedy.

opine In the sense *express an opinion*, the word has come to be quaint and facetious; never intended seriously any longer except in newspapers.

opposite See *reverse*, etc.

optician   See *oculist,* etc.

optimistic   Optimism is a cheerful or hopeful frame of mind, and thus *optimistic* can be properly said only of a person. It is miscast for *favorable* or *encouraging* in "He cited several optimistic factors." See also *pessimistic.*

optometrist   See *oculist,* etc.; *Dr.*

or   Should not be followed by a comma at the beginning of a sentence or clause: "Or, the tables may be turned." *Or the tables* . . . See *Comma After Conjunctions* under *Comma; Subject-Verb Agreement.*

-or, -our   When there is a choice between these endings, *-our* represents British practice and *-or* American.

oral   See *verbal, oral.*

orchestra, band   The basic distinction, as applied to groups playing classical or light classical music, is that an orchestra contains stringed instruments and a band does not, being made up entirely of woodwinds and brasses. As applied to jazz ensembles, however, *band* implies no such distinction.

order (on the order, of the order)   *On* (sometimes *in*) *the order* and *of the order,* followed by quantities, are inflations of the technical writer. They sound as if they have some deep and precise connotation to the initiated, but they are merely ostentatious displacements of *about* or *approximately.*

Apparently *on the order* and *of the order* are offshoots of the concept *order of magnitude,* which does have a precise technical meaning. Webster's *Third New International* gives it thus: "A range of magnitude extending from some value to ten times that value (two quantities are of the same *order of magnitude* if one is no larger than ten times the other, but if one is one hundred times the other it is larger by two orders of magnitude)." There are other mathematically specific applications of *order.*

Now for some derivative pomposities:

"The number of troops is estimated to have increased sharply, to something on the order of 10,000." *something like* (or *approximately* or *about*) *10,000.*

"The budgetary deficit is still on the order of $150 million." *about*.

"Public estimates of the bomb's effectiveness are on the order of thousands of square yards, much less than a square mile." *are about* (or *run to*) *thousands of square yards*.

"The price tag for the program is on the order of $1 to $2 million." Omit *on the order of*.

ORDINALS   Forms like *1st, 2nd, 14th* are out of fashion and unnecessary in dates: *Feb. 1, March 2, April 14*. Ordinals of small numbers, particularly, are preferably spelled out: The award was his *tenth* (not *10th*). See also *Numbers*.

ordinance, ordnance   An ordinance is a law; the term is usually applied to those passed by legislative bodies on the local level, such as city councils and county boards. *Ordnance* is the general term for military weapons and ammunition.

orient, orientate   Both forms of the verb are acceptable in the senses *ascertain bearings* or *gain sense of direction*, or in others. But as in all such instances, the simpler form is recommended: "We used to *orient* ourselves by the tall tree on top of the hill."

orphan   Incorrectly applied to a child who has lost one parent. Webster now recognizes only the sense "a child deprived by death by both father and mother; parentless child."

oscillate, osculate   Absurdly though not uncommonly confused. Oscillate means *flutter* or *move to and fro*; a pendulum oscillates. *Osculate* means *kiss*, and the word now is heavy humor. Readers are occasionally amused by references to *osculating fans*.

other   "He has more readers than any financial writer on a New York newspaper"; "I am more interested in the capture of my wife's murderer than any person on earth." In both instances, logic requires *any other*. As pointed out in Perrin's *Writer's Guide*, the rule is that *other* is required in the comparison of things in the same class. *Other* is often used superfluously when there is no need to differentiate: "Three small children and a young woman were killed, and three other children were almost asphyxiated"; "The pilot made the mission in a huge Sikorsky helicopter. Three other persons accompanied him." *Other* should be omitted in both instances.

Ambiguity should be guarded against with *other(s)*: "The Russian woman was the twelfth person orbited in space. Six others were Americans." This may be taken as referring, all told, to 18 astronauts. The second sentence would have been better put "Six of them were Americans."

ours   Sometimes ignorantly given *our's;* there is no such form.

out-   Solid as a prefix: *outargue, outdo, outfox, outkitchen, outsmart, outperform, outtalk,* etc.

out-migration   See *emigrate, immigrate.*

outside   *Of* is superfluous with *outside* (and with *inside*) : "Outside of the hall." *outside the hall.*

over-, -over   Solid as a prefix: *overabundance, overrate, overpopulate, etc.*
Solid as a suffix: *carryover, hangover, runover, turnover,* etc.

over   Among the sturdiest of superstitions is that there's something wrong with *over* in the sense of *more than.* Webster gives one meaning of *over* as "more than; as, it cost *over* five dollars." *Over* is also defined as "beyond or above, or in excess of a certain quantity or limit; as, boys of twelve years and *over.*" The *Oxford English Dictionary* specifies this sense too. Nevertheless, *over* for *more than* is noticeably avoided in careful writing.

Some harbor the delusion that it is wrong to say a man was hit *over* the head, unless the blows missed him. This is a standard sense of the word ("down upon from above"), however, and instantly clear except to those who willfully misunderstand. Those perverse ones would probably insist that a person could not wander over the face of the earth except in an airplane.

Over, however, sometimes *is* called into play illogically, as in "Considerable reductions over single-performance prices are again being offered." These reductions, it seems plain, are *from,* not *over,* which suggests an increase.

overall, over-all   Some yearn to preserve, or more likely establish, a distinction that *overall* is the garment and *over-all* the term meaning *inclusive*. Webster gives both senses as one word, however, and it is impossible to imagine how they could be confused since one is a noun and the other an adjective, and in American usage the garment is *overalls*.

Lord Conesford, that captious and often muddled critic of American usage, wants *over-all* (the adjective) expunged from the language altogether, as an unnecessary addition, but no one seems to have paid any attention.

OVERWRITING You can often tell a news story, if in no other way, by the supercharged effort that has been exerted to make it sound bright and lively. The rawest cub learns at once to strive for this effect. To the old hand, an awareness of that goal, if not its attainment, has become second nature. "Brighten it up" are the words that have accompanied innumerable news stories as they were handed back by the city editor for rewriting. Now, in view of all this, how can we explain the discouraging fact that only the rare news story sounds bright to the reader?

Easy. It's a variation on the old story about the boy who hollered "Wolf!" too often. People got tired of coming to the rescue just because he liked the excitement. Finally, when a wolf really did appear, they ignored him and he was wolfed. Many have yet to learn that they cannot brighten writing by using words whose color or vigor are too much for the occasion. In a given instance, this only creates a faintly ridiculous, overstrained effect. When it is done repeatedly, the reader quickly comes to disregard the overwrought verbiage altogether. Thus the usual state of affairs is that the writer has his tongue in his cheek and the reader has his fingers crossed.

We are on difficult ground here, for the exercise of restraint in writing is one of the things that contribute to making it an art. It seems foolish to have any artistic pretensions or aspirations about newswriting, for example, considering the exigent conditions under which it is generally done. About the best that can reasonably be expected is workmanlike communication of facts, leavened as far as possible by felicitous touches of description, bits of humor, and pointed insights.

Obviously, it is easier to write in conversational language than to overwrite. A conversational tone is easier to read, too.

Criticism by and of public officials may range from the mild to the severe. Little account seems to be taken of the tone of the criticism, however. It usually comes out *attacked, blasted, flayed, lashed out at, lambasted,* or *scored*.

"The jury might order him imprisoned for life or flung back into the arms of his family." If the flinging should kill him, as seems likely, he might prefer life imprisonment. The breakup of a three-man stage act could have been reported in those terms, instead of *the trio was shattered. Toss* is a great favorite. Often it is substituted for *throw*, which in fact is stronger, not weaker. But we read of a diplomat tossing a treaty to a conference, of the National Broadcasting Company tossing colors into costumes for TV shows, and of a tax cut tossing a budget into the red.

Is the reader diverted or stimulated by this shrill stuff? Not at all. He's bored stiff, when he is not revolted, and what interest he feels is inspired solely by the factual content. Things are worse when, as is so often true, the attempt to enliven is made with clichés—*hurl* for *make* (an accusation), *smash* or *shatter* for *break* (a record), *slash* for *reduce* (prices), *soar* for *rise*. Life's not that exciting most of the time, and when it is, the circumstances will speak for themselves.

In a survey of the American press, *The Times* of London commented:

> It is this fundamental striving to attract the attention of, as well as to inform, the normally indifferent citizen which gives modern American journalism some of its most striking characteristics. Notably, it is the cause of its tendency to oversimplify political and diplomatic situations and developments to the point of distortion; to heighten personalities and the part played; to describe complex events in vivid, breathless, exciting prose so that the regular reader must live with a perpetual state of crisis or develop a deliberate indifference as a protection against it.

Jacques Barzun has taken note of the overexcited tone of much journalism by referring to reporters as "writers whose professional neurosis is to despair of being attended to and in whom, therefore, a kind of solemn ritual clowning is inevitable." See also *Technical Terms*.

owing to   See *due to*.

—P—

pachyderm Want to pick up some easy money? Make a few bets that a horse is a pachyderm. Refer your takers to Webster, and then collect. The unwritten law against using a word twice, no matter what absurd efforts are necessary to avoid it, has so firmly ensconced *pachyderm* as the synonym for *elephant* that many consider it the basic term and use *elephant* as *its* synonym. The fact is that *pachyderm* (*thick-skinned*) is equally applicable to the rhinoceros, the hippopotamus, the tapir, the pig, and perhaps even the politician. See also *Variation*.

packing A cliché of weather stories in reference to winds: "A hurricane packing 75-mile-an-hour winds . . ."

painful As descriptive of a beating or injuries, sometimes criticized as superfluous on the ground that there is no such thing as a painless beating or injury. This objection seems captious, since *painful injury* conveys a graphic meaning.

painfully (hurt) See *badly hurt*.

pair, pairs Interchangeable as the plural form: "Eight pairs [pair] of sox."
   Pair is logically a plural in reference to people: "The pair were [not *was*] surprised in the act." See also *Collectives*.

pajamas, pyjamas *Pyjamas* is the British preference.

pan- Solid as a prefix: *panatrophy, pangenesis, pansophism,* etc. But the most common combinations with *pan-* are proper names, with the result that the hyphen is used and both elements are capitalized: *Pan-Arabic, Pan-American, Pan-Pacific.* Exception: *Panhellenic, -ism.*

pander, panderer Although *panderer* is favored by the press, headline writers, who are always up against it for space, will be glad to hear that *pander* is equally correct as the noun and in fact is the basic version.

para- Solid as a prefix: *paratroop, paramilitary, paramarine,* etc.

paraffin, kerosene, coal oil What is called kerosene in America is called paraffin in Britain; in America, paraffin is a kind of wax used mainly to seal preserves. In some parts of the U.S., the term *coal oil* is used for kerosene. See *kerosene.*

PARAGRAPHING See *Itemized Paragraphs.*

PARALLELISM Parallelism is the name for following the same pattern with constructions that naturally fall into it. It makes for ease in reading and, therefore, is to be encouraged. Most offenses against parallelism consist in switching verb forms: "It is a matter of letting tavern owners know their rights and to avoid confusion." *Of letting* should be matched by *of avoiding.*

"Benson said the only real answer to the dairy-surplus problem seems to be to push consumption of butter through regular marketing channels and encouraging farmers to get rid of inefficient cows." *to push . . . to encourage.*

"The unit will contain air-to-ground voice equipment for transmitting traffic-control instructions and to obtain position reports from aircraft." *for transmitting . . . for obtaining.*

"Vladimir Petrov was reported as having asked for and was granted asylum in Australia." This construction not only flouts parallelism but also shifts awkwardly from the active to the passive voice. The best phrases would be *having asked for* and *having obtained; having been granted* would be acceptable, however.

"Stringfellow had returned to Ogden, Utah, became a radio announcer, gone into politics, and been elected to Congress." Either *had returned, had become, had gone,* and *had been;* or *returned, became, went,* and *was elected.*

"A welcome will be extended by Joe Blow, and Wolfgang Ethier will speak on 'My Reform School Career.'" An awkward shift from the passive to the active: "Joe Blow *will extend* a welcome, and Wolfgang Ethier *will speak on . . .*"

"The state suspended sixteen driver permits, and one was revoked for vehicle violations." *suspended sixteen . . . and revoked one.*

Parallelism is desirable in other instances than those involving verb forms:

"Mr. Ziegfeld selected girls for their good looks, personality, and good figures." *personalities.*

"The fight ends when the losing cricket breaks away from his conqueror and is promptly removed from the cage by its owner." Either *his* or *its* should be used consistently.

"One of the officers was suspended for ten days, and the other for a five-day period." *for ten days, and . . . for five days.*

"The production models will have a speed of 85 miles an hour, a range of 150 miles, and carry 800 pounds." and *a capacity* of 800 pounds.

"The people of this state recognize that we have to set aside wilderness areas as well as meeting commercial needs. *as well as meet* (the infinitive is required to pair with *to set*).

"Although published in 1960 and receiving numerous laudatory reviews as a top reference work, the book has leaped into controversial prominence in the last month." *"Although it was published in 1960 and received . . ."*

PARENTHESIS   The problem here is the relative position of the period and the closing parenthesis. If an entire sentence is enclosed, the period comes first. If the enclosed matter is the last part of the sentence, the parenthesis comes first. (This and the following sentence will illustrate.) Such problems, however, are usually left to the printer or proofreader (sometimes inadvisedly).

PAROCHIAL TITLES   See *Rev.*

partially, partly   That these words should be synonyms in one sense, that of *in part,* is unfortunate, because *partially* has another and widely divergent sense that can cause ambiguity if care is not used, namely, *showing favoritism.* "The testimony was *partially* recorded" may be read as meaning either that it was recorded in part, or that it was recorded in a biased way. The writer who wants to stay out of trouble with these words will use *partly,* not *partially,* to mean *in part.* It is preferable also because it is simpler.

PARTICIPIAL MODIFIERS   See *Dangling Participles; Adjectives; Participles and Time Sequence* under *Time Elements.*

PARTICIPLES, DANGLING   See *Dangling Participles.*

party   *Party* for *person* is legalese and telephone cant (*the* *party of the first part; your party does not answer*). Otherwise the word is inappropriate unless it is used humorously. "Firemen helped police remove the injured parties from the car" is objectionable. *people.* Some fancy the word as giving tone to their utterances, but it is merely pompous.

pass   See *meet, pass.*

pass away, on   For *die,* a euphemism that is growing quaint.

passed, past   *Past* is sometimes confused, perhaps because the pronunciations are alike, with *passed:* "My era has past." *passed. Past* is a noun (*the glorious past*), adjective (*all that is past*), and preposition (*past the boundary*) but not a verb. "My era is past" is correct.

passion flower, fruit   It may show something of the preoccupations of our age that, by common consent, these are assumed to be aphrodisiacs. But *passion* here is used in reference to the passion of Christ. The name was given because portions of the flower resemble the cross. Figurative use (*my little passion flower*) perversely always has a sexual connotation.

PASSIVE VOICE   The use of the passive voice ("The door was *opened*" rather than "Someone *opened* the door") is a favorite object of excoriation in stylebooks, usually without further qualification or explanation. Sweeping indictments of this kind are meaningless, but they are nevertheless characteristic of the vaporings of self-appointed stylemasters, especially on newspapers.

Critics say the passive is undesirable in description or narration. The real issue is whether the subject brought into prominence by use of the passive voice is of any consequence. "The door was closed quietly" and "The issue was discussed for an hour" are hardly objectionable if the closer of the door and the discussers of the issue are of no moment.

As a device for varying sentence structure, however, the passive is not only objectionable but also conspicuous. In any biographical sketch "Further education was received at Brown University" is absurd because it places an unexplainable emphasis on *further education.* "France and Germany were visited next" illustrates the same fault.

For other considerations involving the passive, see *drowned,*

*was drowned; married, was married; graduated, was gradu-
ated.*

past Redundant with *history, experience, records, precedent,
achievements, accomplishments.* See also *last, past; passed,
past.*

patio Purists have inveighed, with the usual results (none),
against the American use of *patio.* Properly, a patio is an enclosed court open to the sky. But the patio that is almost
standard equipment with modern houses is seldom enclosed
in the sense of being a courtyard, and usually is covered.

pedal, peddle To pedal is to operate something worked by
pedals, such as a bicycle; to peddle is to hawk or distribute
some item or idea. "The government back-peddled fast when
it looked as if pressure groups were beginning to frown."
back-pedaled.

peer, peerless The noun *peer* seems to many to have two meanings: *equal* and *superior.* If so, this is a sad state of affairs,
for plainly those meanings are mutually exclusive.

   Peer in fact means *equal.* The man who is tried by a jury
of his peers is tried by his equals (in rank). The confusion of
sense has arisen from the application of *peer* to members of
the British nobility. Since they are indubitably the upper
classes, the impression has been created that *peer*, at least in
this connection, means *superior.* Not so; peers are so designated not to indicate that they are superior to anyone, though
of course they are, at least in pretensions, but to indicate that
they are *equals to each other. Peerless*, then, does not mean
without a superior, but *without an equal.*

   Peer in the sense of *equal* is part of the jargon of sociology
and education: *peer groups*, etc. The contexts in which such
expressions are found often seem intended to obscure rather
than convey meaning.

   For a long time, and perhaps even yet, members of the
British nobility on trial for felonies or treason had to be
judged by juries of their peers; that is, juries composed of
other noblemen. If found guilty of a capital crime, a peer was
hanged with a silken rope. Rank has its privileges, as the
Navy holds, a principle often condensed to the acronym RHIP.
A convicted peer would progress from the status of RHIP to
that of RIP.

A writer of a letter to an editor, making the point that human worth varies, worked up to an impassioned but befuddled climax by exclaiming, "Some people are not my equals; they are my peers!"

penny It is an illustration of how far the compilers of stylebooks can carry absurdities that some of them forbid *penny* for *cent*, holding that a penny can only be the British coin. *Penny* is so thoroughly established in America that even a stylebook compiler would be startled to hear his child ask for a cent, disregarding the fact that inflation has pushed the minimum of such requests up to at least a nickel.

people See *persons, people.*

per *Per* for *a* or *an* is technical and thus inappropriate in casual use: "He used to call for me twice per day." *a.* "The news comes on once per hour." *an* or *every. Per* belongs in connections like *miles per hour, population per square mile, gallons per second.*

per cent, percent Either form is correct. Technically an abbreviation for *per centum,* which prompts some to write it *per cent.,* but the period is so long gone in general usage that its use must be set down to fussiness.

It is easy to be ambiguous in constructions like "The measure would lower the rate from 3 to 2 per cent." Here the reader must decide whether 3 and 2 per cent are the present and proposed rates, or the proportion by which the rate would go down. The intention here would have been unequivocally expressed by "The measure would lower the rate from 3 per cent to 2 per cent."

percentage *A large percentage* in place of *most* or *many* and *a small percentage* in place of *few* are mushmouthed.

(a) period of Usually verbiage before a specified interval, as in *a period of five years.*

period of time A redundancy for *period* or *time: a short period; a long time* (not *period of time*).

permit of As in *statements that permit of no denial,* accepted usage, but it has a fusty sound, and may even be taken for an affectation, since the meaning is not touched by omitting *of*. "I felt my job was too demanding to permit [of] other involvements."

perpetrate, perpetuate Many readers must have done a double-take when they saw the quoted citation that accompanied the award of an honorary degree. It praised the recipient as "a worthy perpetrator of an illustrious tradition." *Perpetrate* means *commit something evil*. And then there's *perpetuate*, which means *give enduring character to*. These words may have something in common, however, in that both a perpetrator and a perpetuator may be thought of as carrying on.

perquisite, prerequisite A perquisite is an advantage, often in addition to pay: "The *perquisites* of the office include the use of an automobile and a place to live." A prerequisite is something required as a condition. In schooling, basic courses are prerequisites to advanced ones. Hard work, it is said, is a prerequisite to success (though success does not necessarily follow, and some succeed without really trying).

per se "Some of them feel that college students per se live in a vacuum for four years because they are engrossed in study." *Per se* itself is not often the occasion for error; this sentence is quoted to illustrate the point that foreign expressions are often resorted to in the hope that they will sound impressive and without awareness of their meaning. The overriding principle is that the skillful writer puts down nothing about whose meaning he has the smallest doubt. It is easy to pick up mistaken ideas of the sense of unusual words if one relies on notions created by occasional encounters with them. The only safe plan is to look up the meaning of everything that is out of the ordinary, especially foreign expressions, if one is not positive of their sense. *Per se* means "of, by, or in itself or oneself or themselves." Applying the definition to the example, it is impossible to imagine what the writer had in mind; "college students *as such*," perhaps, but this is something else.

persecute, prosecute Occasionally confused. To persecute is to afflict, harass, or annoy: "The Nazis *persecuted* the Jews." To prosecute is to carry out the legal procedure against one accused of a crime: "Trespassers will be *prosecuted*." Prosecution may be persecution, or regarded as such; the reverse is never true.

persistence, -cy The words are equivalents, and the only reasonable basis for choice between them is the rhythm of the sentence.

personal, personally *Personal* is often obtrusively used to qualify things that can be nothing but personal: *friend, charm, opinion* are the leading examples. *Great personal charm* has become a tiresome set phrase. An employer was described as *personally popular with his workers.* There is something distasteful about the idea these examples suggest, that friendship, charm, and popularity have been so devalued as qualities inseparably associated with the person that they must be specifically identified with it. Potentates and presidents seem to require *personal* physicians; the impersonal ones who treat us ordinary folk apparently will not do. But here the meaning is really that the physician has only one patient.

  Personally is often used to give a meaningless emphasis: "It has never been possible for him to attend a board meeting personally." *attend a board meeting.* Attendance is not possible other than personally. Opinions are often stated in some such way as "Personally, I believe . . ." This is unnecessary except in the rare cases when one may have differing personal and official or public opinions.

personnel It is a puristic fiction that the word cannot be preceded by a number, although, since it is a plural, one would not speak of *one personnel.* Webster cites *34,000 personnel in the expanded operation.* Phrases like *three military personnel* are irreproachable and convenient. The term is stiff and official when it displaces *people.*

persons, people The superstition is still pretty vigorous that *people* cannot be used freely as the plural of *person* and that *people* correctly denotes only a nation or a large and indefinite group, as in *the British people* or *We, the people.* According to this law, which usage has in fact repealed, one may not speak of *sixteen people,* or any other definite number, but must say instead *sixteen persons.* The *Dictionary of Contemporary American Usage* says, however, that the use of *people* in this way "is now fairly standard English, and is generally preferred to the word *persons.* We may now say *three people were present* or *three persons were present,* as we please. Most people now prefer the first form, and *persons* now sounds pedantic or bookish."

Or, it might have added, newspaperish. The basis for these conclusions is perfectly evident, apparently, except to newspaper editors, whose feeling for usage often is about two generations in arrears. Foolish rules have a way of running amuck, leading to such absurdities as "The job of the comedian is to make persons laugh."

Often *those* may be more comfortably substituted when either *people* or *persons* is used in a general sense: "Persons who expect different have a surprise coming." *Those*.

In a strange coincidence, three press associations made *persons vs. people* the subject of comment in their bulletins within the space of a month. The first comment, in *Copy Talk*, put out by the Canadian Press, could have pointed the way for the other two, because it reasonably followed the example of usage and criticized a couple of curious examples that came of going hog wild with the case-hardened rule: *elderly persons of Ivor* and *an elderly persons' party*.

"*Persons* is perhaps defensible," *Copy Talk* noted, "but people just don't think or talk that way. *People* and *people's* would have been better and more natural."

Not long afterward another press-association bulletin dogmatically recited the old rule at the behest of a subscribing editor, adding its own blessing. That was too much for two other subscribing editors, who offered indignant rebuttals in the next issue. One of them correctly identified the problem as one of changing usage, rather than misuse, and the other used words like "snobbism" and "stultifying" to describe the attitude of the diehard who had started it all.

A few days later this ukase appeared in a bulletin issued by a third press association: "Ten persons may be killed in a fire, but not ten people." And that was all. Ah, the splendid isolation of it—isolation from usage, from common sense, from observation, from everything but hand-me-down "grammar." Yet this bulletin quickly recanted in the face of concerted objections, many of them from members of the press association's own staff.

perspicacious, perspicuous To put it briefly, *perspicacious* describes an attribute possessed by a person; it means *discerning*. *Perspicuous* means *easily understood* or *seen through;* an explanation may be perspicuous, and so may a simpleton, though the term is seldom applied to people. The related nouns are *perspicacity* and *perspicuity*.

persuade, convince   The displacement of *persuade* by *convince* flouts idiom. One is convinced *of* a fact, or *that* it is so. This is the customary form of use, and the meaning of *convince* is *to create belief in*. *Persuade*, on the other hand, means *talk into* or *induce*. One may be persuaded *of* a fact, or *that* it is so, and in these constructions the sense shades into that of *convince*. It is in the strict sense of *talk into*, when *persuade* is followed by an infinitive, that the confusion arises.

Note these examples of incorrect usage: "The director of the museum had convinced Brancusi to part with the sculptures for awhile"; "The decree of nationalization has all but convinced Western capitalists to zip shut their billfolds"; "We can only hope Congress can be convinced to finance the dam and the canal at the same time"; "He hopes he has convinced the prime minister to await developments."

In each instance, the word should be *persuade*, or else the infinitive object must be recast to read (*convinced*) *that he should part with, that they should zip shut, that it should finance*, and *that he should await*. Since the revisions are clumsy, it may be assumed that the word wanted in each instance was *persuade*.

pessimistic   Like optimism (see *optimistic*), pessimism relates to a state of mind, and the word applies properly only to people. "At this pessimistic juncture in East-West relations" would better be "At this *discouraging* juncture."

petite   Too much of a favorite, perhaps, in connection with brunettes. Why can't blondes be petite?

phase   See *faze, phase*.

Ph.D.   See *Dr*.

phenomenon, phenomena, phenomenal   The first is the singular, the second the plural. *This phenomena*, then, is incorrect; it must be *these phenomena*. *Phenomenon* and *phenomenal* are often misspelled *phenominon, -al*, perhaps by the suggestion of *nominal*. Remember that the base noun is *phenomenon*.

Philippine(s)   One of the most misspelled geographical designations: *Phillipine*(s). The correct form is the first mentioned.

phobia   See *mania, phobia*.

phone, 'phone   It may once have been desirable, if not necessary, to indicate that *phone* is a clipped form of *telephone,* but no longer, any more than it is desirable to apologize for *auto* as the clipped form of *automobile.*

phony, phoney   The predominant spelling of the slang expression meaning *not genuine* is *phony. Phoney* may come from some imagined connection with *phone.*

PHRASAL VERBS   See *Hyphen.*

pick, choice   *Pick* is loosely interchangeable with *choice* or *selection,* but its use in this sense is avoided in careful writing, except in such set phrases as *take your pick, the pick of the crop.* "We are studying American authors, and you are my pick" is a disagreeable construction. Sportswriters, when they gaze into their crystal balls, like to speak of their *picks* as the victors in forthcoming contests, but the word sounds no better here either.

PICTURES   One picture, says the Chinese aphorism, is worth more than 10,000 words (or 1,000 or 100,000, depending on the rate of exchange). This notion, if nothing else, may justify the 500-odd words expended herewith on some random observations about pictures and related matters.

It seems to be standard practice to describe any woman in the news, particularly a crime story, as *pretty, attractive,* or even *beautiful.* This device, employed not as reportage but to titillate the reader, regardless of the truth, is certainly effective in bringing to life an otherwise moribund account. But it may be one of those tricks that should have gone into the ash can in view of the increasing maturity shown generally by the press in recent years.

On more than one paper the editors have grown so conscious of, and nettled by, the unremitting parade of beauties in the news that standing orders have been given to delete all appraisals of women's looks. The reason is that when women who are described as beautiful in one edition are pictured in the next, they often turn out to be dismal crows. The use of such descriptives as *pretty* or *beautiful* with a picture seems simpleminded. Judgments in such matters vary, and when the evidence is at hand for the reader to decide for himself, why not let him do so?

Cutlines present some hazards. (It may be appropriate to

comment on the tendency to apply the word *caption* to the explanatory matter beneath pictures. Properly speaking, a caption is a heading, not a legend.) Pictures, which show something in the process of happening, seem to demand the utmost immediacy in the accompanying text. But need we be jolted by the recurrent absurdity of coupling the present tense with a past time element? It comes out this way:

"General Wilford Jones and Japanese Prime Minister Shigeru Yoshida meet for a private chat in the general's hotel suite yesterday"; or "William Willis stands aboard his balsa raft as it moves off the Peruvian coast late last month." How much more sensible it would sound to say "General Jones and Prime Minister Shigeru Yoshida *met* [or *are shown as they met*]" and "William Willis stood [or *is pictured standing*]."

Then we have the tiresome occupations of *looking on* or *standing by*, assigned to supernumeraries who happen to be in a picture and, since they cannot be cropped out, must be identified. The truth might be diverting: "Those other two guys just muscled into the picture."

piece   Sometimes pointlessly criticized in reference to a literary composition, but it is good idiom (*a piece in the newspaper*). Ordinarily it is applied to nonfiction.

pier   See *dock*.

pinch hitter   So often debased from the original sense that any attempt to rehabilitate it seems hardly worthwhile. In baseball, where the expression originated and still holds its original sense, it means a replacement sent to bat with the expectation he will do better than the man he is substituting for. In other connections, alas, it now means merely a replacement, sometimes an inferior one.

pistol, revolver   A pistol is a hand-sized gun; a revolver is a type of pistol with a revolving cylinder from which the cartridges are fired.

plan   The fulcrum for a number of redundancies. The act of planning must relate to the future; thus *plan ahead, advance plans,* and *future plans* are all generally redundant.

plane, plain   A plain is a flat stretch of ground; a plane is a level. "A high ethical plain." *plane*.

planned withdrawal   See *Euphemisms*.

play (wreak) havoc   Clichés.

plead, pleaded, pled   *Pleaded* and *pled* are both acceptable past forms of *plead*, although *pled* sometimes is considered wrong. The suspect pleads (guilty, not guilty) *to* a charge, and *of* the offense itself; that is, "He pleaded guilty *to* a charge of drunken driving"; "He pleaded guilty *of* drunken driving." See also *dismiss against*.

    People who have been charged with crimes are often described as pleading innocent, but technically there is no such plea. What they plead is *not guilty*. A lawyer correspondent of "Winners & Sinners," *The New York Times* critique, wrote, "If a man were let aver that he is innocent, he might be required to prove it, and it is fundamental that no man is required to prove his innocence."

    In some journalistic quarters, however, *plead innocent* is encouraged lest the *not* should be accidentally omitted in *not guilty* and the publication thus be exposed to action for libel.

pleasantry, unpleasantry   *Pleasantry* in the sense of *pleasantness* or *pleasure* is archaic. "An increasing number of patrons have discovered the pleasantries of this resturant." *pleasures*. In its modern sense, *pleasantry* means a joke or banter ("They exchanged pleasantries about the rigors of campaigning"). *Unpleasantry* is a rarity but standard and means an insult or disagreeable incident: "There have been no acts of disorder, no disturbance, and no unpleasantries at our schools."

please be advised   A Victorian pomposity of correspondence that is better discarded, together with "Yours of the 18th inst. received . . ." and the like. Don't ask your correspondents to be advised; simply tell them what's on your mind.

plenty   A noun, and properly takes *of*: *plenty of brains, plenty of talent* (not *plenty brains*, etc.).

plow, plough   *Plough* is the British preference.

PLURALS   Idiom, that perverse old dictator, requires that the singular—rather than the plural, which would be logical—be used in expressions like *a ten-year-old boy, a six-mile race, a three-month investigation* (not *ten-years-old, six-miles, three-*

months). The possessive is acceptable (*a three months' investigation*) but this construction seems to be fading away.

Likewise, it was a *10-foot* pole Ed Wynn, the comedian, used for not touching things. Idiom calls for the plural, however, when the modifying phrase follows, rather than precedes, the noun. None but the rustic speak, or write, of *a man 6 foot tall*, or *a ditch 9 foot wide*.

Some compounds develop mixups in their plurals. *Court-martial* (actually, a martial, or military, court) becomes *courts-martial*, not *court-martials*. The tendency to make it one word, *courtmartial*, does not help matters. Likewise, *right-of-way* becomes *rights-of-way*, *passer-by* becomes *passers-by*, and *son-in-law* becomes *sons-in-law*. Such is the inconsistency of English, however, that the possessives of such expressions are formed on the last element: *court-martial's finding*, *mother-in-law's temper*.

Names of people that end with *s* (Jones, Dithers, Adams) call for the addition of *es* to form their plurals. Thus the Jones family are the *Joneses;* not, as we too often see, the *Jones*, the *Jones'*, or even the *Jone's*.

Proper names ending a sibilant (*sh* or *ch*), *x*, and *z* also form their plurals by the addition of *es*, not an apostrophe. The plural of *Bush* is *Bushes;* of *Church*, *Churches;* of *Rich*, *Riches;* of *Wilcox*, *Wilcoxes;* of *Broz*, *Brozes*.

Conservative usage still calls for the apostrophe in plurals of letters, figures, signs (the *B's*, the *1940's*) and the like, although there is a strong trend away from it. There is nothing wrong with *1940s* or *GIs*. An inflexible rule calling for omission of the apostrophe will lead to trouble now and then, however, as in *As*, which comes out more intelligibly *A's*. This is an argument not against the apostropheless forms, but against inflexible rules, which are likely to lead to trouble anyway. Even when the apostrophe is dropped in plurals like *GIs*, it is needed to indicate possession (the *GI's uniform*) and seems desirable in verb forms like *O.K.'s* and *O.K.'d*.

When something more than *s* or *es* is deemed necessary to indicate the plural of a sign, symbol, or other nonword, the apostrophe should be used: *the A's, the 1920's*. The hyphen is wrong: "Some misleading statements were circulated by the anti-s." *Anti's* or *antis*. More and more, the *s* alone is used in such circumstances unless it is misleading: *the 1960s, the Ds*.

Another curiosity is the use of plurals when there seems no reason for it, and when, in fact, the singular would be more exact. Consider, for example: "Church services were held at

11"; "Charges of vagrancy were lodged against the transient"; and "The dedication ceremonies were canceled." In the foregoing, the reference is to a single service, a single charge, and a single ceremony. The plural usage seems fairly prevalent and probably does no harm for the most part, except perhaps when the mistaken impression may be given that more than one charge is lodged. How, we may wonder, did this quirk get started? The tendency to inflate things larger than life size may be the answer.

plus To be avoided in place of *and;* best saved for the idea of arithmetical addition.

P.M. See A.M., P.M.

POESY The gentlemen of the press are sometimes eager to prove that the often humdrum task of reporting the news has not entirely numbed them to the finer things in life. They do this with random poetical touches, like *'twas, 'tis, 'twere,* and *'twill.* Such ornaments may be calculated to make the throat of the reader tighten, but if this happens, it is most likely because he is retching. *Lone* is a more prevalent example of poesy; it has all but supplanted the homely *only* or *sole:* "He cast the lone dissenting vote." That must have been the vote against lyricism in inappropriate contexts. Fowler, under the heading "Vulgarization," cited *save* (in the sense of *except*) and *ere* as examples of words abandoned to the journalists, who, he said, had not yet ceased to find them beautiful. Nor have they yet, especially sportswriters. But perhaps *'twas, lone, ere,* and the like are the only poetry that enters their lives, and to forbid them such delectations might be cruel.

(the) poet " 'Breathes there a man with soul so dead,' the poet wrote . . ." In this case, the poet was Sir Walter Scott, and referring to him simply as *the poet,* in the favored device of editorialists, leaves the impression that (a) the writer did not remember who wrote the line and could not be bothered to look it up; (b) he did not remember and did not know how to look it up; (c) there was only one poet, who was responsible for all the poesy in English literature; or (d) the writer thinks so. If a man is worth quoting, he deserves the dignity of naming, unless he happens to be the great Anon.

poetess Now quaint; *poet* is applied to both sexes. See also *Feminine Forms.*

poetry, verse   *Poetry* and *poem* are loosely applied to any writing in verse form. The discerning, however, use the terms only for what has some artistic merit. The general and neutral term for what has meter, rhyme, or both is *verse*. It is well to make the distinction for what obviously has no artistic pretensions, as for example limericks and humorous quatrains. Lack of judgment may be indicated by calling *verse* (a neutral, technical term) poetry, but not by calling poetry *verse*. In brief, all poetry is verse, but not all verse is poetry. See also *Verse*.

point out   See *Misleading Attribution* under *Attribution*.

political pot   To speak of the political pot as boiling, bubbling, simmering, or whatnot is to use one of the creakier clichés of journalese.

politics   Singular, though some are confused on this point: "How honest is [not *are*] American politics?"

poll tax   In Texas and other parts of the South, the annual collection of poll taxes is referred to, in a curious regionalism, as a *sale*, and the act of paying such taxes is referred to as *buying* them, or *buying the receipt*. There is no logic in this.

polyglot   Things are seldom, as Captain Corcoran observed, what they seem; *polyglot*, for example, is not what it seems to some who venture to use it. But no one who has a feeling for derivation will go astray here, for the word literally means *many-tongued*. A man who speaks a number of languages may properly be described as a *polyglot*, and there are related senses. But how now: "Most of the valley is a verdant and prosperous polyglot of cities." Perhaps the writer was reaching for *complex*. A city can be described as polyglot, if many languages are spoken there. But how cities could *constitute* a polyglot is unaccountable. Sometimes polyglot is misused in the sense of *mixture*.

pom-pom, pompon   The first is the designation of two kinds of artillery; the second is the ornamental tuft often seen at football games, and the variety of dahlia resembling it. Webster defines pom-pom girl as *pickup, prostitute. Pompon girls* (often referred to as *pom-pom girls*) in the Western United States, at least, are the high schoolers who flourish pompons as part of cheerleading ceremonials. *Pom-pom* (or *pompom*) is very commonly used in the sense of *pompon*.

POMPOSITY   This is not the curse it once was, the apostles of clarity and simplicity having got their message across in many quarters. Nonetheless, eternal vigilance is required to preserve those qualities. The examples given here are intended merely to illustrate the vice of using more or longer or harder words than necessary; they hardly scratch its surface. But for anyone who develops a critical awareness of pomposity, the battle is half won.

"One thousand dollars was voted *to help defray* [toward] expenses *in connection with* [of] the celebration." (The bracketed expressions might have been used in place of the italicized ones they follow.)

"About 200 youngsters were turned over to probation authorities last year. This year the number will be *far in excess of that figure* [much higher]."

"Authorities awaited the results of *toxicological tests on tissue samples* [tests to discover any sign of poisoning]."

"The lower tax rate *is attributed to elimination of* [results from dropping] the special high-school tuition charge."

"This equipment *was received in a nonoperative condition* [would not work when it arrived]."

"The group was organized *to render assistance in the placement of veterans in employment* [help veterans find jobs]."

"The woman who had shot herself refused to *divulge her reason* [say why]."

"Gradually the boy learned to *function more adequately* [behave better] both at home and at school." (*Behave better* was precisely the meaning, as the context showed.)

"The defendant was placed on probation on condition he *refrains from consuming alcoholic beverages* [does not drink]."

Some common phrases are mushmouthed: *voice* as a verb inspires some of them. *Voice objections* usually would better be *object; voice approval* would better be *approve. Is employed by* is more dignified, perhaps, but longer than *works for; resides* is ostentatious for *lives; position* is highfalutin for *job* and often applied to employment of no pretensions. *Adequate in size* has dignity, but *big enough* is better.

But what can we expect of an age when garbage men are sanitation specialists and janitors are maintenance engineers?

pore, pour *Pore* (usually with *over*) means *read studiously;* *pour* means *tip out of a container*. One *pores* over a book, but *pours* water. The usual error is something like *pour over a book,* which raises the question what could have been poured over it, and why.

portland In relation to cement, not a proprietary designation but a generic term growing out of the fact that this type of hydraulic cement was regarded by its inventor, Joseph Aspdin of Leeds, England, as resembling stone quarried on the Isle of Portland. Nearly all cement used today is portland cement, and the term is not capitalized.

position See *job, position*.

POSSESSIVE FORMS Have you, too, sometimes puzzled over forming possessives, especially of words that already end in *s?* It's all very simple. To decide whether you want just the apostrophe, or apostrophe plus *s*, you need note only:
    1. The number of syllables in the word.
    2. Whether the accent (primary or secondary) falls on the last syllable (the penult), the antepenult, or elsewhere.
    3. Whether the last syllable begins, or ends, or both begins and ends with an *s* sound.
    4. Whether the word falls into certain categories of ancient classical, Biblical, or foreign proper names.
    Then all you have to do is apply the right one of the half-dozen or so rules prescribed for various combinations of these conditions.
    Haw. Is there a revolver in the house?
    As usual when rules run rampant, confusion is the only thing that clearly emerges. Words like *antepenult* are an affront to those of us too lazy to look them up, and may even be obscene. But pronunciation alone can be relied on for a rule of thumb in forming the possessives of both singular and plural forms. If you add an *s* sound in speaking the word in its possessive form, add apostrophe *s;* if the pronunciation is unchanged, add just the apostrophe.
    This gives us, by way of examples, *the boy, the boy's bike; the boys, the boys' bikes; Louis, Louis's pencil; Dulles, Dulles's memorandum; Moses, Moses' tablets* (you would not say *Moseses,* which is how *Moses's* would sound); *the boss, the boss's order; the bosses, the bosses' orders.*

The rule of letting the pronunciation govern is not only easy to follow most of the time, but also conforms to the predominant trend of usage. There may be legitimate differences about pronunciation. Some argue that they would not add another syllable in speaking such possessives as *Dulles'* and *Dickens'*. These forms are acceptable, and furthermore the possessive of *any* name that ends in *s* may be formed by adding only the apostrophe: *Louis', Doris', Thomas'*.

It is also considered correct to form the possessive by adding only the apostrophe to words that end in *s* sounds, though not in the letter *s* itself: *Dr. Schultz's office, Mr. Chance' car, Cortez' discovery, innocence' evidence*. These forms, however, have a strange look, and carefully edited writing seems to be consistent in using apostrophe *s* rather than the apostrophe alone in such instances. This follows the sensible rule of letting the pronunciation govern.

Funny examples will turn up. Few writers would make it *Illinois's*, because the basic word properly pronounced does not end with an *s* sound. The *s* sound is added, of course, in speaking the possessive, which leads to the fleeting notion it should be written *Illinoi's*. But that way madness lies.

A prevalent solecism of suburbia is displayed on countless fancy mailboxes and front-yard lamp posts in the form of the householder's name bedecked with a misplaced apostrophe. *The Smith's* is what the scrollwork usually announces; the proud owner is apparently unaware that this does not quite make sense. It might better be *The Smiths* or *The Smiths'*. This little bobble is even more prevalent on millions of imprinted Christmas cards (*The Glotz's,* for example, rather than *The Glotzes*).

It is generally considered objectionable to make possessives of the names of inanimate things (*the water's temperature; the sky's color*). *The temperature of the water* and *the color of the sky* are smoother and more idiomatic.

Double Possessives The attentive writer is conscious of redundancy in such expressions as *a property of the Joneses', a friend of my uncle's, an opinion of the teacher's*. Why the possessive (indicated by the apostrophe), he will wonder, when ownership has already been shown by *of*?

Such constructions are avoidable, often by simply changing the form of the possessive noun. *A friend of my uncle* sounds neater and more logical to many than *a friend of my uncle's*, which is known among grammarians as a double genitive or double possessive. If the context leaves *an opinion of the teacher* ambiguous, the idea can be conveyed by *one of the teacher's opinions*. If *a property of the Joneses* is unsatisfactory, it can be changed to *a property belonging to the Joneses*.

Double genitives, however they may offend some ears, are not considered wrong; they are long-established idiom. There is no reason, apart from personal preference, to avoid them. But some critics feel the double genitive may raise a question in the reader's mind: *a friend of my uncle's what?*

The construction in which a double genitive follows the relative pronoun *that* is unquestionably repellent: "Their idea is the same as that of the tariff commission's"; "The footprint is fully as long as that of a large gorilla's." In such instances surgery is indicated. It does not matter whether the possessive or *that of* is cut away: "Their idea is the·same as that of the tariff commission" or "the same as the tariff commission's"; "as long as that of a large gorilla" or "as long as a large gorilla's." Ending with the possessive is conversational and not unsuitable for informal writing.

When the possessive is a pronoun instead of a noun, the double genitive causes no annoyance: *a friend of mine, some books of yours, a hat of his,* though such expressions are structurally identical to *a friend of my uncle's.*

False Possessives Now let us take up a dido that might be called a false possessive. Many modifiers end in *s* and, especially when they are proper names, some feel compelled to regard them as possessives and clap apostrophes on them. Note these examples:

"He accepted a *General Motors'* scholarship."

"The applicant was a *United States'* citizen."

"The scene did not pass muster with the *Hays' Office*."

There is really no idea of possession here, and so the apostrophes are uncalled for. *General Motors, United States,* and *Hays* are being used simply as adjectives. like *roads* in *roads appropriations* and *athletics* in *athletics director.*

This brings us to a shadowy realm inhabited by names once regarded as possessive forms, but now often written without the apostrophe: *Odd Fellows*['] *Lodge, Lions*['] *Club, Taxpayers*['] *Association, master*[']*s degree, in ten years*['] *time,* and even *Hell*[']*s Canyon,* from which the federal government removed the apostrophe by ukase. It looks as if such words are coming to be felt primarily as describing, and not as indicating possession.

305

The apostrophe is still considered necessary in strict usage in such expressions as *three years' imprisonment* and *nine days' wonder*, but there is a noticeable tendency to drop it.

POSSESSIVE PRONOUNS There are no apostrophes in the possessive pronouns ending in *s: its, hers, ours, theirs.* "Its fur was mangy"; "The purse was hers"; "The slaves are ours"; "The automobile is theirs." *Her's, our's,* and *their's* are marks of ignorance. There is such a form as *it's,* but it is the contraction for *it is,* something wholly distinct from *its.*

possible, possibly *Possible* is impossible in such phrases as *a possible fractured jaw, a possible serious fire, a possible serious accident. Possibly,* or recasting, is called for.

possibly may Redundant. *May* alone conveys the idea of possibility.

pound(s) sterling See *lb., lbs.*

power corrupts. . . . See *Misquotation.*

powerful As descriptive of the House Ways and Means Committee and like legislative groups, all that remains is for *powerful* to be incorporated into their official titles.

practicable, practical What is practicable is capable of being accomplished, as "Scientists now consider a rocket shot to Mars *practicable*"; what is practical is useful or adapted to use: "*Practical* solutions are better than theoretical ones."

practically Not used by careful writers in the sense of *almost:* "The oranges are *practically* gone." It is used by so many others in that sense, however, that its strict meaning, *in practice* or *in effect,* has been all but eroded away. Aside from this, *practically* is a pomposity for *nearly* or *almost.*

practice, practise *Practise* is the British preference in spelling the verb ("The girl was *practising* on the piano"), but *practice* is the preference in both Britain and America for the noun ("The doctor has a large *practice*").

pre- *Pre-* has become the darling of the adwriters' frantic prose (*precooked, preheated*), and true to the frantic tradition it becomes attached to words where it is redundant: "The secretary of state denied that the president had made a foreign ministers' meeting a precondition to a treaty"; "Preregistration for the course is scheduled for Tuesday"; "They bought a house in the area after having pretested it on several summer vacations." *condition, registration, tested. Preplanning* is an asininity; planning cannot be anything but *pre-*.

Pre- is solid as a prefix: *prearrange, preempt, preheat, preprint,* etc.

precede, proceed, procedure   Subject to a variety of confusions, including being mistaken for one another. To start with, *precede* means *go before; proceed* means *go* or *move forward.* The commonest error is spelling *preceding preceeding.* Sometimes *proceed* is given *procede. Precede* may appear as *preceed. Procedure* occasionally is misspelled *proceedure.*

predicate   A latter-day superstition has it that *predicate* (as a verb) is incorrect in the sense *found* or *base on,* as in "Several senators had predicated their misgivings on what effect it would have on European security." All four of the newest desk dictionaries, and *Webster's Unabridged,* give *based* or *founded* as one sense of the word. The worst that can be said of the example, and it may be bad enough, is that *predicated* is pretentious and *based* would have been simpler.

predominately, predominantly, predominant   *Predominately* is not necessarily an error, for it has found its way into the dictionary. Nonetheless, it is a rare bird, and when you see it you can lay ten to one the writer was aiming at *predominantly,* the only form to be found in most dictionaries, and missed. *Predominate* as an adjective (*the predominate criticism*) is an error for *predominant.*

preempt   Now one word, after an uneasy transition through a siege of dieresis (*preëmpt*) and hyphenation (*pre-empt*). See *Diacritical Marks.*

preface   See *foreword.*

prefer   The idiomatic forms with *prefer* are illustrated by *prefer this rather than that; prefer this to that; prefer doing this to (doing) that.* Not *prefer this than that;* nor *prefer to do this than (to do) that.*

PREFIXES Will be found in their alphabetical places together with information on whether they are hyphenated or set solid. See also *Hyphens*.

premise, premises In the sense *building* or *real property* only the plural form is correct ("Trespassers were warned from the premises.") A premise (whose plural, naturally enough, is *premises*) is a basis for reasoning or argument. "It will not be necessary for us to visit your premise to make this change in telephone service." *premises*.

preoccupy One word; not *pre-occupy*.

preparatory to Inappropriate when it displaces *before;* what is *preparatory to* should *prepare*.

PREPOSITIONS Prepositions are often unexplainably displaced by modifiers like *both* and *either*:
"The Soviet bloc and most of the Arab states refused to pay either for the Middle East or the Congo operations."
"The speech had been reviewed both by the President and the Secretary of Defense."
"All this has a familiar ring both to U.S. exporters and to U.S. Treasury officials."
"The work affords the musical basis for both moments of power and reflection."
The better order would be *refused to pay for either* (not *either for*), *by both the President* (not *both by*), *to both U.S. exporters* (not *both to*), *for moments of both* (not *for both moments of*). In every case, *both* and *either* modify the objects of the prepositions, and their proper position is behind the prepositions. There is danger, as the examples were written, that the force of *both* or *either* may be directed elsewhere than where it belongs and thus confuse the sense.

Prepositions Repeated Needlessly Prepositions are often repeated needlessly before a series of objects:
"If you're the average American motorist, every 9.2 years you're going to get a ticket for running a red light, for speeding, or for reckless driving." There is no reason to fear that the force of the first *for* will not carry over to *speeding* and *reckless driving: for running a red light, speeding, or reckless driving*.
"So far, the blame has been placed upon the players, the

coaches, the overemphasis on athletics at American universities and on the moral laxness of our times." *On*, as more idiomatic, would have been better than *upon*, and it would not have been necessary to repeat it where the shift was made to *on*.

"If the President actually manages to convey his message with conviction and with persuasion, the meeting will be worthwhile." The second *with* is superfluous.

There are places, however, where a preposition must be repeated to prevent ambiguity:

"He was fined for lack of character and *of* reliability." Without the second *of* the fine is for reliability rather than its lack.

"The paper's independence from pressure groups, lack of opportunism, and timidity were not sufficiently emphasized." A Freudian lapse, possibly; *and of timidity* was intended.

Prepositions with Numbers   It must be an uncontrollable passion for exactness that causes us to pile up prepositions, or in some instances to use them when they could be better omitted altogether. Doubled prepositions often occur when a range is specified: "Its control spreads into between 25 and 30 per cent of the economy." Such constructions are clumsy because the reader must figure out that the object of *into* is the whole six-word phrase beginning with *between*. "Into 25 or 30 per cent" reads more easily.

"The airlift is expected to speed the delivery of mail by from twenty-four to forty-eight hours" would be smoother going with *from* left out.

"Investments of from two to four million dollars were reported." Here, too, *from* is superfluous.

"The clerk estimated that from 40 to 45 per cent of the city's voters would cast ballots." Delete *from*.

"The weatherman predicted a low temperature of between 75 and 80 degrees." In this instance *of* seems expendable.

Weather stories seem especially hospitable to intrusive prepositions. The words in brackets would never be missed in "A low temperature [of] near 45 degrees is expected" and "The Sierra received [from] 2 to 4 inches of slushy snow." *At about* may be trimmed to *about*: "About nine o'clock last night."

Some extra prepositions do not fall into any readily apparent category, but are none the less objectionable: "The Justice Department is expected to keep hands off in the dispute." *off the dispute*. This looks like a variant of *off of*, scorned of old and no more reputable now than before.

Preposition at End A couple of professors of English were mountain-climbing on vacation, when all at once they saw an avalanche bearing down on them.

"Heaven help us," cried one. "We're done for."

"For God's sake, Henry," returned the other, "don't end your last sentence with a preposition."

This may be funny enough on the surface, but it is a joke that could not have been made up by a grammarian. (If, in fact, any joke could.) The *for* in *done for* is not really a preposition but an adverb that has merged with the verbal modifier *done* to form a new expression, whose meaning depends on both words taken together. Anyway, who could imagine an English professor, even on vacation, using a colloquialism like *done for?*

The notion that it is wrong, or undesirable, to end a sentence with a preposition has been flayed by Fowler and many another authority on language. The most telling blow was struck by Sir Winston Churchill, who, when accused of ending a sentence with a preposition, is said to have replied: "This is the type of arrant pedantry up with which I shall not put."

You can show that sentences with the preposition at the end are more forceful than those that have been recast to avoid it; you can cite masters of English prose from Chaucer to Churchill who employ end prepositions freely and consciously; and you can prove that such usage is established literary English, but the superstitious will still wince at it.

In writing, as distinguished from rule-reciting, the avoidance of the end preposition is most evident, perhaps, in structural detours that start with a preposition followed by *which*. Few care about making the world a better place *to live in,* but nearly everyone wants to make it a better place *in which to live.* "The car she was riding in," after editing with zeal and ignorance, becomes "The car in which she was riding."

The use of circumlocution to find another place than the end for the preposition not only weakens the sentence but gives it a stilted sound. "What are we coming to?"; "There was nothing to talk about"; "It was something he had always dreamed of"; and "The situation was too much to contend with" are perfectly good English in any context. Shame on him who wads these sentences up into "To what are we coming?"; "There was nothing about which to talk"; "It was something of which he had always dreamed"; and "The situation was too much with which to contend."

The origin of the superstition forbidding the preposition at the end of a sentence is sometimes considered a mystery, but actually it came from applying Latin rules of grammar to English. In Latin, it is said to be all but impossible to detach a preposition from its object. Linguists now, however, have decided that the rules of one language make a Procrustean bed for another.

Sometimes jesters cite the little boy's complaint, "What did you bring that book up to be read out of for?" as the ultimate in putting the preposition at the end. Maybe it is a shame to spoil their fun, but only the final *for* functions as a preposition here (its object is *what*). *Out of,* together with *to be read,* form a phrasal verb, and the *up* that precedes is an adverb.

See also *Word Order* for misplaced prepositional phrases; and *Parallelism.*

prerequisite See *perquisite, prerequisite.*

prescribe, proscribe, prescription, proscription To prescribe is to lay down a directive; to proscribe is to forbid, denounce, or outlaw, generally by formal action.

present incumbent *Present* is redundant.

presently *Presently,* in the sense of *now* or *at present,* seems to be excising an increasing fascination. To those who can remember it from fairy tales, it may come as a surprise that it can properly mean anything but *by and by* or *before long.* As Webster is our judge, however, this is one of those unhappy instances in which the same word has contradictory senses. But *presently* in the sense of *by and by* always occurs with a future verb: "The roll will be called *presently*"; in the sense of *now,* it always occurs with a present verb. Although the dual meaning thus does not cause confusion, the fondness for *presently* often results in needless obtrusion of a time element. For example, "He is presently superintendent of parks," says nothing that "He is superintendent of parks" does not. Likewise, the time elements in "He is *now* living in Brooklyn" and "The children are being cared for *at present* by neighbors" are superfluous, unless there is some reason to contrast the present condition and some other. *Currently* is often used in the same way.

The overuse of *existing* (which see) is closely related to these redundancies. We read of "The provisions of *existing* law" instead of "The provisions of the law."

present(-ed) with   Frowned on in some stylebooks as excessive in the sense of *give,* and *present* by itself is recommended instead: "He was presented a token of esteem." This is faulty advice, however. *Presented with* is good idiom; *present* alone grates on the ear. The real case against *present with* is that it is slightly pretentious. Those who are prejudiced against it would do well to use *give* instead. This, of course, will lead to *was given* (which see) which is afflicted with a prejudice of its own.

present writer   See *Editorial We.*

preside   See *Meeting Notices.*

pressman   Only in Britain is *pressman* the equivalent of *journalist;* in America a pressman is a mechanic who runs a press. Thus A. J. Liebling's choice of *The Wayward Pressman* for the title of a book dealing with the vagaries and shortcomings of the press was not a happy one. (The book, incidentally, is most instructive and entertaining; and more newspapermen, particularly managing editors and publishers, should read it.) Mr. Liebling got caught in this trap because his book was based on articles published in *The New Yorker* under the heading, *The Wayward Press.* The title of the book suggests a recalcitrant printer rather than a newspaper critic. What Liebling wanted, perhaps, was *The Wayward-Press Man;* this, at least, would have come closer to the mark.

pressure   *Pressure* as a compression of *put pressure on,* in the sense of *exert influence,* is newly arrived in the dictionaries: "The mayor was *pressured* to fire the chief of police." Even so, the use of *pressure* as a verb in the literal, physical sense is questionable: "A muffled concussion pressured the eardrums."

presumptuous   Often misspelled *presumptious,* perhaps under the influence of *presumption.*

pretense, pretence   *Pretence* is the British preference.

pretension Often misspelled with two *t*'s (*pretention*), apparently by analogy with *pretentious*.

PRETENTIOUSNESS See *Pomposity*.

pretty Fully established in the senses *somewhat, moderately, considerably: a pretty good bargain, a pretty reasonable explanation,* pedantry to the contrary.

prevent See *avoid*.

preventative, preventive *Preventative* is sometimes said to be the noun, *preventive* the adjective. But *preventive* is preferable as both. Examples: "He took *preventive* measures"; "This medicine is a *preventive*." *Preventative,* said to be an incorrect formation, gets thumbs down from Fowler.

previous to Like *prior to*, generally the long and pretentious way around for *before*.

prexy College slang for *president;* it is out of its element when applied to other than college presidents.

pride goeth before a fall. . . . See *Misquotation*.

principal, principle Often confused. *Principal* is an adjective meaning *chief* or *leading,* as *the principal reason;* it is also a noun meaning *chief,* as *the principal of the school. Principle* is a noun only, meaning *a rule,* as *a principle of conduct.* "Kazakstan includes a principle grain region of the Soviet Union." *principal*.

prior to Stuffy for *before*. More at home in a legal document than in everyday discourse. True also of *prior* as an adjective in the sense of *previous* or *earlier; a prior conviction for drunken driving*.

private industry People who leave government jobs are often described as going into *private industry* (or *business*). Since *industry* or *business* alone have no connotation of government ownership, however, they should suffice by themselves.

privilege Often misspelled *priviledge* (sometimes *privelege*); but a privilege by derivation is a private law (*lex, legis*), not a private ledge.

pro- Hyphenated as a prefix meaning *favoring*: *pro-slavery, pro-liberalism*. Otherwise, in the senses *before, forward, substituting, projecting*, usually solid: *pronucleus, prognathous, procathedral*.

probate Sometimes criticized but nevertheless standard as a verb meaning *place on probation*; either a prisoner or a sentence may be spoken of as probated. The older use was in connection with proving (probating) wills, and an erroneous assumption has developed that the newer sense is incorrect. *Probate* as a verb is chiefly an Americanism in either sense.

probe May be unavoidable in headlines, but not the best English in text in the sense of *inquiry* or *investigation;* or, as a verb, for *inquire into* or *investigate*.

proceed to *Proceeded to open the meeting* is an overblown way of saying *opened the meeting*. The principle holds in the combination of *proceed to* with other verbs. The phrase should be used only to mean *take steps toward,* when some preparatory action is indicated.

procure Pretentious for *get:* "They interrupted their house-hunting long enough to procure a marriage license." See also *get; secure*.

PROFANITY Profanity and vulgarisms have gained considerable access to the printed page during the last quarter-century or so. Few newspapers, for example, now hesitate to print *hell* as a quoted expletive, or even as a casual comparison (*a hell of a time; hot as hell*) to say nothing of using the term as a true place-name.

Similar freedom is evident with respect to *damn*. The name of the Lord is facilely taken in vain: "God knows." Irreverent allusions to Christ are less common, but fairly frequent in quoted matter: "For Christ's sake, shut up."

The vulgarism *son of a bitch* (and its abbreviation, S.O.B.) has been admitted to the columns of some of our most august journals, which might have felt like resisting if these expressions had not turned up in utterances by two presidents of the United States, Harry S Truman and John F. Kennedy.

Other vulgarisms have gained a surprising currency in the news pages; *bull,* for example (as in " 'That's a lot of bull,' he said"). This, obviously, is a variety of synecdoche, the figure of speech in which the whole takes the name of a part. *Bitch* as a verb (*Soldiers always bitch*) is not unusual in the press, nor as a noun applied to a woman.

This latitude palely mirrors what has been happening in the world of literature, where the four-letter words descriptive of defecation, breaking wind, urination, and copulation have become relatively common. It may be well to bear in mind, however, that some of these words occur in Shakespeare, Chaucer, and the Bible.

Webster's Unabridged offers an interesting commentary on how far opinion has progressed, or retrogressed, as the case may be, in this department. The Second Edition, published in 1933, omitted numbers one, two, and four in the preceding list. The public temper, at least among that segment likely to consult a dictionary, was such that nobody missed them. The editors of the Third Edition, which appeared in 1961, almost entirely overcame the squeamishness of their predecessors except, as one reviewer put it, for the most important of the four-letter words. Presumably people are going to have to guess what that one means; they will get no help from Webster. At least two dictionaries of slang (although four-letter vulgarisms are not really slang) illuminate this point frankly, however.

The be-all and end-all of English dictionaries is, of course, the great *Oxford*. It is for the most part considerably older than Webster's Second Edition, but unexpectedly enough, in view of the era that produced it (1888-1933), it contains all the four-letter vulgarisms except the one that has consistently stuck in Webster's craw. There is something ingratiating about Oxford's starchy and yet indulgent descriptions of the vulgarisms it does include: "Not now in decent use." These words invest the soiled terms with a certain retroactive dignity, which certainly is not spurious, for there were times when they were freely employed in polite society, just as *ain't* once was used freely and considered correct by the cultivated.

A few years ago the Associated Press was curious enough about modern receptivity to profanity to run a little survey on what happened to the quotation, *A damn lie,* that appeared in one of its stories. Of 30 papers checked, two deleted *damn,* one changed it to d---, and 27 used the phrase as sent.

In 1964 the epithet *son of a bitch* was used in a trial having nationwide interest, and the Associated Press again ran a survey. Of 111 papers checked, 52 used the phrase, 30 substituted dots or dashes, 19 abbreviated it, and 10 deleted it. This appears to indicate growing conservatism in these matters. Then again, it may merely reflect a more marked reaction to a grosser expression.

Not so long ago (at least, if you are middle-aged, it does not seem so long) the closest any newspaper would come to printing *hell* in any context was h———. What appeared after the *h*, please notice, as well as in such renderings as G—— d——, was an elongated solid dash.

Refinements were gradually introduced, to the extent that some of the letters were replaced by hyphens: h---, G-d d--n. The theory behind the hyphens is possibly that the susceptibilities of the young are being spared. But the expressions might as well be spelled out frankly and in full, because no one old enough to read can miss the import of such easily decoded evasions.

Some publications, it must be noted, continue to quail at vulgarity and refuse even to give us the strong hint of the initial letters: "She called me a --- -- - -----." This probably looks nicer; still, readers are bound to work out such little puzzles, often with assiduity.

Sometimes, however, this device does tax the reader's ingenuity: "We had someone say to her, 'You rotten -----,' to test her reaction." Bitch? Whore?

This field has other peculiarities. Some apparently feel that *damn* is less profane if the *n* is omitted, in this fashion: "America's done *dam'* well." Or perhaps the idea is to indicate the pronunciation. But who pronounces the *n* in *damn*, and how? On the other hand, *dam'* may be a contraction of *damned*. *Damnedest* is sometimes telescoped to *damndest*. Why not *damndst*? Likewise, *darnedest* becomes *darndest* (*Kids Say the Darndest Things*).

Haphazard researches have yielded some diverting sidelights on this subject. Profanity is often against the law, particularly when directed at a policeman. A Cranston, R.I., man was charged with disorderly conduct for, as the Associated Press delicately put it, questioning the parentage of the officer who had stopped him for speeding. (This could have referred to use of the term *bastard*, but did not.)

The judge dismissed the charge, commenting that the epithet resorted to by the defendant had become "something of a presidential expression." No doubt the disposition of the case was in accord with public opinion. But what seemed particularly interesting was the judge's assumption that presidents necessarily set an example in linguistic matters. Vulgarity aside, they have not all shown the adeptness and discrimination in expressing themselves that would warrant imitation.

In April, 1958, *Editor & Publisher* reported that the advertising executives of the four (at that time) San Francisco dailies felt called upon to rule on the propriety of using the movie title, "The Respectful Prostitute," in advertising. This work became something of a contemporary classic in drama.

The *Examiner* and the *News* decided to remove the word *prostitute* from the title, perhaps to protect the sensibilities of readers not sufficiently hardened by free use of *rape* and circumstantial accounts of sex crimes in the news columns. The *Chronicle*, which for a long time has had a reputation as a sophisticated and civilized newspaper, stood fast, together with the *Call-Bulletin*.

The odd thing about all this was that *prostitute* and *prostitution* were already widely accepted as genteelisms for what the Bible calls *whore* and *whoring*. See also *Euphemisms*.

profession   The professions once were more or less agreed to be medicine, law, the clergy, and teaching. *Profession* now is often loosely used as a synonym for *calling* or *vocation*: "People of many professions were summoned to the meeting." This is harmless enough, but since the word suggests learning and distinction, strenuous efforts are made to apply it to occupations of no great standing.

Whether *profession* applies to a given vocation the reader will have to decide for himself. The American Newspaper Publishers' Association once argued that newspaper reporters qualify as professionals; the object was not to raise their status but to keep from having to pay them more money under a federal law that exempted professionals.

Those who hope to acquire dignity by labeling their work a profession might consider the requirements Webster sets forth in the definition that prescribes: "A calling requiring specialized knowledge and often long and intensive preparation including instruction in skills and methods as well as in the scientific, historical, or scholarly principles underlying such skills and methods, maintaining by force of organization or concerted opinion high standards of achievement and conduct, and committing its members to continued study and to a kind of work which has for its prime purpose the rendering of a public service."

Although architecture was not one of the original professions no one is likely to argue that it does not qualify. Engineering, science in all its branches, and other learned occupations do too.

By profession is often used redundantly, as in "He is an architect by profession." A descriptive of this kind is called for only when a distinction is made, as in "He is an architect by profession and an artist by avocation."

professor The title is properly reserved for one who holds the rank; it is not to be indiscriminately applied to college teachers. Some colleges do not have professorships. For much the same reasons that apply in the use of the title *Dr.* (which see) in the academic world, professors often prefer to be called *Mr.* In general, the more distinguished or qualified they are, the more likely this is. As usual, those whose entitlement to rank is questionable are most insistent upon the recognition it confers. Application of the title *professor* at random to teachers of music is an old-fashioned, small-town quirk that has all but disappeared, and usually now is humorous.

programed, -ing Music, computers, and much else are programed these days, and the preferred spelling calls for one *m.*

prohibit Takes *from,* not *to:* "The audience was prohibited to smoke." *prohibited from smoking.*

promptly In many contexts, it is driving *at once, immediately,* and *right away* to the wall, and not entirely justifiably. Promptness implies meeting a demand or limitation of some kind: "We pay our bills *promptly"*; "Meet me at the theater *promptly* at eight." *Promptly* seems inexactly used of an act that merely follows upon something: "When he won the lawsuit, he promptly tore up the contract." Is *promptly* worth preserving in the sense of meeting an obligation or requirement? Choosy writers, to judge from the way they use the word, seem to think so.

prone It is nit-picking to insist that *prone* can mean only *face downward,* even though that is one sense of the word (as distinguished from *supine,* meaning *face upward*) and the one favored by derivation. Modern dictionaries, however (the Merriam-Websters, *Webster's New World,* the *Standard College,* and *The American College*), while recognizing the distinctive sense, also equate *prone* with *flat* or *prostrate.* The *Oxford Universal Dictionary* gives prone as (loosely) meaning *lying flat*, as if opposite to *erect*. This volume dates back to 1933. In the absence of any other hint in the context, *prone* can no longer be depended on to convey the sense *face down.*

PRONOUNS Pronouns are among the handiest gadgets in the language, but we often tend to shun them in favor of unnecessarily naming our subject again. Ambiguity, it is true, can result from using pronouns carelessly. But when the reference is unmistakable it seems a shame to forego the terseness, naturalness, and ease of expression that come from writing simply *he* instead of *the official, she* instead of *the housewife*, and *it* instead of *the proposal under discussion.*

Fear of pronouns is related to another idiosyncrasy, love of epithets. This takes the form of a *tour de force* in which the writer sets out to astound the reader with the number of different names he can think up for the same thing. The reader may be more revolted than astounded by such a shallow trick, but he is, after all, defenseless against it. Thus a game becomes successively a *contest*, an *event*, a *match*, a *set-to*, a *tilt*, an *encounter*, and a *tussle* in the references of as many paragraphs. (See *Variation.*)

Sometimes repetition of a word grates on the ear and is therefore to be avoided. This problem is explored *ad infinitum* by Fowler under the headings "Elegant Variation" and "Repetition of Words or Sounds" in his *Modern English Usage.* The gist of it is that a dozen sentences are spoiled by straining to avoid repetition for every one that is spoiled by repetition itself.

Getting back to fear of pronouns, let us retire to the laboratory and dissect a few specimens:

"Three governors planning to attend the conference have stated their intention of turning public schools over to private hands. The three are . . ." Why not "*They* are . . ."?

"A mechanic's helper shot and killed his estranged wife with a shotgun while she slept with one of the couple's three children." When the writer set down *the couple's* instead of *their*, he not only fled from the smoother construction to the more awkward one, but also risked raising the question whether the children were those of the mechanic and his wife or of some other couple.

"A spokesman said the group gave a vote of confidence to the negotiation committee and endorsed the latter's stand in refusing a wage increase." Why not *its* instead of the clumsy *the latter's?*

It is advisable, though not a rule, that pronouns should be preceded by the nouns they refer to. If not, the writer must guard against ambiguity: "The senator was the true heir, if indeed he had an heir, of Lyndon Johnson." The senator, true, would hardly be referred to as his own heir, but the reader may be momentarily confused by relating *he* to *senator* instead of to *Lyndon Johnson*. Rearrangement will improve matters: "The senator was the true heir of Lyndon Johnson, if indeed he had an heir."

proof As applied to alcoholic content, a puzzler that everyone pretends to understand until asked to explain it. It is the percentage of alcohol multiplied by two. Thus *200 proof* would be pure alcohol, *180 proof* 90 per cent alcohol, and so forth.

-proof Solid as a suffix: *waterproof, acidproof, fireproof, shrinkproof*, etc.

PROOFREADING AND EDITING SYMBOLS These should be distinguished. There is no point in running corrections in typescript out to the margin, as on proofs; this is merely confusing. Typescript corrections should be entered at the point where the change is desired; manuscripts are double-spaced to leave room for emendations. A table of proofreaders' marks is to be found in *Webster's Collegiate Dictionary*.

propellant, propellent Acceptably interchangeable as both noun and adjective: a new type of *propellant* (*propellent*); a *propellent* (*propellant*) force. *Propellant* is preferred as the noun, especially in technical writing.

prophecy, prophesy Often confused. *Prophecy* is the noun ("He uttered a *prophecy*"), and *prophesy* is the verb that describes what the prophet does: "He *prophesied* rain." "It takes no gift of prophesy to see the outcome." *prophecy*. Confused only in writing, for *prophesy* ends with "sigh" and *prophecy* with "see." Mastery of the spoken distinction will help prevent written errors.

prophet without honor. . . . See *Misquotation*.

proportion, proportions *Proportion* figures in a number of pretentious redundancies, which usually would better be replaced by *most: the greater proportion, the larger proportion, by far the largest proportion*.

Proportions is correct in the sense of *dimensions:* "It was a storm of cloudburst *proportions.*" But it is often criticized as wrong, perhaps because in the singular it denotes merely a relationship, having nothing to do with size. Many are unduly fond of it, however, as a substitute for *size, dimensions, extent, magnitude,* and the like. The example cited will be recognized as journalese.

proportional, proportionate Fowler threw up his hands at any effort to differentiate between the words, and since the tendency is almost always in the direction of less discrimination rather than more, any such attempt at this late date would be futile. Fowler also included *proportionable,* now designated archaic by Webster. *Proportional* is in more common use than *proportionate,* especially in set phrases like *proportional representation.* But in general the terms must be considered equally acceptable, and this is true also of the adverbs *proportionally* and *proportionately.*

proposition As a verb ("The woman said she had been *propositioned* in the bar"), *proposition* is slang for *make an indecent proposal to,* and had best not be used in the decent sense of *make a proposal to* when there is any danger of ambiguity.

prosecute See *persecute, prosecute.*

proselyte, proselytize Equally acceptable variants, although the vote here always goes to the simpler form in such cases.

prostate, prostrate *Prostate,* the name of a male sexual gland, is sometimes ignorantly rendered *prostrate,* which means *prone.*

protagonist The natural assumption is that *protagonist* is the opposite of *antagonist,* and that since *antagonist* means *fighter against, protagonist* means *fighter for.* But such an assumption is enough to make purists, especially those who know Greek, writhe. It happens that *agonistes,* the root of both words, has two meanings. One is *fighter* and the other is *actor.* *Antagonist* (*fighter against*) developed from the first sense, plus *anti,* and *protagonist* (*leading actor*) from the other sense. *Pro* here does not mean *favoring,* but rather is *prot* from *protos,* meaning *first.*

Chances are, however, that even when *protagonist* is used

in its correct sense of *leading actor,* it will be understood in the sense of *fighter for,* so prevalent has the misuse become. Lost and losing causes are the sad lot of the purist. The most irretrievably lost causes of all may be those based on the knowledge of a language that has become the property of a handful of pale classicists, and has long since ceased to be the distinguishing mark of an educated man.

protégé The press has come forth with a curious euphemism, *protégé,* as applied to girl friends, mistresses, and the like. Its most conspicuous use has been in connection with teen-agers who take up with aging matinee idols. This application is not technically wrong, because the word means "one under the care or protection of another."

Protégé is usually understood, however, as referring to a person being cared for or assisted by some established practitioner of the arts, for the purpose of developing talent. The art of love may come under this heading. But some newspapers have shied away from *protégé* for *girl friend,* and have more explicitly substituted *girl friend, companion,* or some such. *Mistress,* of course, may be actionable.

Like *fiancé, protégé* is a masculine form, strictly speaking; the feminine is *protégée,* and this is what should have been used in the cases referred to. *Fiancé* and *fiancée* have retained their distinctive forms, though in most places they have lost their accents. So have *protégé* and *protégée.*

protest As a noun preceded by *in,* takes *against* or *to* rather than *of:* "The group was organized in protest *against* racial discrimination" (not *to*). A protest is made *to* in the sense of being presented: "Numerous protests were made *to* the city council."

Protestant The religious connotation of the word is so strong that it may be best avoided or at least used with great care in the generic sense of *objector.* True, *Protestant* in the religious sense is capitalized, but proofreading is not always all it might be, and the reader often feels called upon to supply his own capitals.

prototype Means the original or model after which something is copied; an experimental model of an airplane may be the *prototype* of the production model. It does not mean merely a predecessor, instance, sample, or example. "Miss Smith, who is in charge of a program marking National Secretaries Week, is a prototype of the businesswoman being honored." The writer of this strained for a word he did not understand; he might better have said that Miss Smith *exemplified* the businesswoman.

proved, proven A notion has been set afoot and fostered, largely in stylebooks, that *proven* is incorrect. Both forms are acceptable, however, ·and *proven* is the more often used. The *Dictionary of Contemporary American Usage*, which is very canny about national distinctions, reports that *proved* is preferred in Great Britain. The *Oxford English Dictionary* recognizes *proven*, although Fowler aspersed it as not the regular past participle.

provide, provided, providing Connote desirability; what is provided fills a need. The word is often misused of what is unwanted: "A few of the sightseeing guests provided problems." *presented, created.*

Provided is often considered preferable to *providing* in the sense of *if*, but there is no valid basis for this. He who is tempted to use either *provided* or *providing* in this sense, however, should try *if*, and if it fits, use it.

psychological moment Fowler deplored the fact that this expression had come to mean *the nick of time*. The substitution neatly exemplifies how much we love the pompous and the apparently technical.

pupil, student It is sometimes represented that *pupil* may be applied only to one attending an elementary school, but neither usage nor definition supports this. The best that can be said is that ordinarily those attending elementary schools are called *pupils* and those attending high schools are called *students*, but *high-school pupils* is often heard and hardly objectionable.

PURIST The purist generally is an authoritarian in his attitude toward language; he wants someone else to make decisions for him, preferably a long time ago. When the dictionary does it on the only reasonable basis possible—the consensus of literate usage—he is unlikely to accept decisions he recognizes as representing change.

A purist, further, is anyone whose ideas of grammar and usage stand to the right of those held by the user of the term.

It is, of course, a deprecatory epithet, much like *Puritan* on the lips of a libertine. In this book, *purist* and *purism* are used for the most part concerning rules and distinctions that have no standing in usage and no effect on meaning.

PURPLE PASSAGE Purple passages are characterized by (a) brilliance or (b) ornate, highly rhetorical writing; *purple* does not mean risqué, as in: "The novel had difficulty finding a publisher. because of some *purple* passages." This was a case of confused colors, for *blue* has the meaning, in a literary sense, that was intended.

purpose "*With* [or *for*] the purpose of advancing," or whatever, is redundant for "to advance." See *Misleading Infinitives* under *Infinitives*.

—Q—

qua Latin for *as,* and properly used, Fowler said, to distinguish something in one aspect from its qualities in another aspect. There seems no real occasion for *qua,* however, since *as* will take its place with no loss in meaning and with a gain in clarity, at least to those for whom *qua* is a dubious quantity.

qualified expert Redundant. An unqualified expert is no expert.

quandary, quandaries Often misspelled *quandry, quandries.*

quartet Journalese as a collective in reference to four of anything whether they have any relationship or not. The criticism applies to indiscriminate use of *duo, trio, quintet,* etc. See *Useless Counting* under *Numbers.*

quasi Usually two words with a noun: *a quasi contract; a quasi difference; a quasi American.* Hyphenated with an adjective: *a quasi-historical play; a quasi-humorous speech.*

QUESTIONS The indirect restatement of a question does not make the restatement itself a question: "He asked the director of the museum whether the paintings on display were originals?" The question mark is wrong. This error appears also with speculative statements, as "I wonder whether my application has been considered?" The statement is declarative, not interrogative, although it describes a state of indecision. Another example: "What he would like to know is how the police found out about this?" "Guess what I did today?" is an imperative, not a question.

quiet, unassuming   The descriptives are so often linked as to be truly a cliché.

quintet   Journalese as a collective reference to five of anything whether they have any relationship or not. *Duo, trio, quartet* are misused in the same way. See *Useless Counting* under *Numbers*.

quip, quipped   "The actress gave her age as thirty-seven, but later quipped to newsmen, 'Confidentially, I'm fifty-seven.'" This use of *quipped* amounts to digging the reader in the ribs with a big fat thumb and saying, "It's a joke, kid—get it?" *Quipped* with any direct quotation is a fit candidate for outlawry. Perhaps there is a place for it in those rare instances when the reader has no way of knowing the speaker is joking. Even then, it seems, some more explicit indication of levity is called for. Otherwise, if a quip is too weak to stand on its own legs, why bother to quote it?

Quip is generously applied to nonquips: "This street has gone to pot,' the mayor quipped." Not a pun, jest, japery, witticism, or joke; merely a doleful judgment.

Cracked, as a truncated form of *wisecracked,* is in the same league with *quipped,* like *wisecracked* itself, *joked, jested,* and *gagged.* "Questioned whether Italy's long siestas have anything to do with its overpopulation and housing problem, Scelba cracked, 'In Italy, a siesta is a time for rest, not work.'" Look, Ma—Scelba made a funny! Instead of beating the defenseless reader over the head with them, let us take the standing advice of the *Chicago Tribune*'s "Line o' Type" column: "Hew to the line, and let the quips fall where they may."

quite   The lexicographers say that formally *quite* means *entirely, wholly,* or *altogether*; colloquially, it means *fairly, somewhat, moderately.* We may as well concede that the colloquial sense has all but driven the other out. "I was *quite* happy with the editorial," said a legislator who had received an accolade. Although the purist might accuse him of ambiguity, everyone else will understand immediately that the

325

legislator was pleased though not carried away. Thus also in "The franc is *quite* stable"; "These big ships are still *quite* vulnerable"; "Christian Dior has done something to the female bosom that might prove *quite* startling." Yet careful writers tend not to use *quite* in any sense but *entirely*.

Quite (like *rather*, which see) is sometimes ineptly used to diminish the force of a modifier: "He managed to get past this quite huge stumbling block." Was it really huge, and the writer was too timid to come right out with it, or was it only moderately large? When *huge* is knocked down by *quite*, we cannot tell.

QUOTATION

Excessive Quotation The quotation mark is hopelessly overworked. This probably reflects a morbid anxiety lest the writer appear to be taking the responsibility for opinions or other questionable utterances. Often it will not do to take a chance that the reader may think the writer is talking.

Quotation marks are often used unnecessarily with what are referred to as fragmentary quotes, when only a word or a phrase is quoted in a sentence that already contains an attribution. The quoted words may have been the ones used by the speaker, but since he has already been credited as the source of the information, there is usually no reason for placing quotation marks around them. The press associations are especially fond of fragmentary quotations. Some stories are so peppered with them the writer can hardly call a word his own. Let's look at some examples:

He declined to say what "action" would be taken.

The department said "some" improvement is expected.

The secretary of commerce said the coming year would be one of the "most prosperous" in American history.

That, he said, would "delay" victory.

It is hard to see what is accomplished by the quotation marks in any of these sentences. Perhaps the writer considered it illegal or immoral to use any word from the direct quotation he was paraphrasing without acknowledging a prior claim, so to speak. Nothing is gained by quoting minor fragments like these, and the quotation marks clutter things up. They also interfere with readability, for the reader necessarily pauses at a fragmentary quote to decide why the quotation marks are there. If this becomes too confusing, he may give up.

Are all fragmentary quotations, then, undesirable? By no means: *He accused the senator of making "mean, untrue, and dastardly" statements.* No objective account would take the responsibility for such hard words, and even though the statement is cast as an indirect quotation to begin with, the words in quotation marks warrant unmistakable attribution.

In general, however, only especially striking or significant matter should be quoted, and then preferably in complete sentences. Using complete sentences minimizes the danger of giving the wrong impression through quoting fragments out of context. The cure for quote-craziness is to try leaving the quotation marks off fragments. Generally this test will show they add nothing.

Another misuse of quotation marks appears occasionally, but it is rarely seen outside remote backwaters, and so seems hardly worth mentioning. This is the use of quotation marks around words the writer mistakenly regards as cute, clever, or used in a special sense. Few things are more exasperating to the reader.

When a word is indeed used in some other than its expected sense, *so-called* is superfluous with a term that has been placed in quotation marks: the *so-called "black list."* Either *so-called* or the quotes will suffice. If slang suits the writer's purpose, let him use it forthrightly, and not in quotation marks, which protest too much that he is stooping from another level of diction.

Quotation marks are justified around a word or phrase to indicate that it is to be understood in some other than its literal sense. *Management officials said yesterday they won't budge from their "last offer."* Many a purported last offer is succeeded by another in labor negotiations. The quotes tell the reader that the words enclosed are not to be taken at face value.

For many years, Kansas was a "dry" state. An ironical use of *dry,* as made clear by the context, which explained that at the time when Kansas was legally and technically dry, it was in fact illegally and sopping wet.

Fragmentary quotation is a handy device for the person who wants to give the flavor of a remark without reproducing at length context that does not suit his purpose. But it is a device whose use requires some skill, rather than the shotgun technique that is so common. It is well not to quote short fragments, and above all single words, lest the reader misunderstand and think they are not to be taken literally. When a writer must use a portion of a quotation, he should at least cut off a big enough slice for the reader to get his teeth into.

She and her advisers think their party might pick up "ten to fifteen seats in the coming election." No reason for the quotes; readability would be improved by leaving them off.

The chancellor announced a "meeting" would be held. A meeting is a meeting is a meeting; why the quotes?

He said the market is so "sensitive" it can be influenced by various factors. The quotes are inexplicable and confusing.

Doctors have told him that his body, at 77, is that of "a man of 50." The quotation marks are superfluous. It is noticeable, however, that any word coming from a doctor or a hospital is reverentially though stupidly set off in quotes by the press: *The victim's condition was reported "good."*

The senator urged the use of "force." Real force, or something else? Such are the questions raised in readers' minds and rarely answered in the heedless and irrational use of fragmentary quotes.

The secretary of the treasury told Congress today that the nation "will get into serious difficulty" if the present tax burden "is continued over a long period." He added that "the country should shape its affairs" to cut taxes "at the earliest possible moment," but stressed that America in the world situation still has a "pistol" pointed at her head.

The "reader" of "this" tortured "stuff" will "wish" he "had" a "pistol" pointed "at" the "writer's" head.

Apologetic Quotes The first thing students in speech classes learn is that a speaker should never apologize for his speech. Doing so leaves him no way to explain why he is giving it. Similarly, placing apologetic quotation marks around an expression leaves a writer no way to explain why he used a word he is ashamed of.

Quotation marks should not be placed around slang or colloquialisms. It is the writer's duty to choose the word that suits the occasion. When a slang or colloquial term fits, he should have the moral courage to use it without apology, and without any foolish misgiving that the reader must be put on notice. Such punctuation makes for a mincing style, and constitutes a form of writing down to the reader. The apologetic quote is the mark of the writer who lacks both skill and self-confidence.

The approach of many newspaper writers to their craft is apologetic, accounting for the prevalence of uncertain, fragmentary quotations in their work. They are not quite sure what they are about, and when encountering a word or phrase that is new to them (and there are so many) they clap quotation marks around it. They are afraid of offending the discriminating by a misuse, but instead they stamp their writing as unpracticed and themselves as ill-read.

Some "swapping" may be necessary. Swap, though colloquial for *trade,* is universally understandable. If *swapping* is beneath the writer he should use *trading* or *exchanging;* otherwise, he should forthrightly leave the quotation marks off *swapping.* Their use gives him away as timid.

Basic English has received a great deal of attention, especially since Winston Churchill gave it a "plug" over the radio. Plug, true, is colloquial for *favorable mention,* but the word is eminently suitable in connection with broadcasting. No one could misunderstand. By putting it in quotation marks, the writer is cozily telling the reader, "I'm really too fastidious for this, but . . ."

The senator's wife admits having "pressured" him for her pet projects. Pressure as a verb is colloquial, but pretty appropriate in political contexts, and could not be misapprehended. The writer may have invoked the quotation marks to indicate that *pressured* was the word the senator's wife used, but one he would never stoop to. Is this chivalry?

Superfluous apologies in the form of quotation marks are bad enough, because they create a fussy, irksome effect; but what about people who don't know when they are using standard English, and apologize for that, too?

The professor is likely to "hedge" in his answers on this subject. Hedge in the sense of *qualify* is neither colloquial nor slang, but standard. By putting it in quotation marks, the writer exposes his ignorance of this fact and also gives himself away as hopelessly addicted to apologetic quotation.

The usefulness of "summit" conferences is questioned by many diplomats. Summit conference is good, inescapable English. This writer no doubt has much to apologize for, but it does not include the use of *summit* in this sense.

William protested that the Army was "gagging" Lawton. Does the writer fear that *gagging* is something less than standard (which it is not), or is he intent on unmistakably attributing the choice of that word to Williams? Either way, or both, he is ill advised; the protest is already attributed, and the quotation marks do nothing but unnecessarily interrupt the reader.

Gone are the days when the private could "snub" the general off post by keeping his hands at his sides. Why the quotes? *Snub* for *slight* is standard.

The question arises whether any popular president can "transfer" his political strength to a candidate. The quotation marks around *transfer* are a baffler. Breathes there a writer with brain so dead he thinks there is something below par about the word?

Wrong Person in Quotation "Mr. Truman smilingly conceded that he 'feels more kindly toward newspapermen, now that one is about to become a member of his family.' " Obviously, the word he used wasn't *feels,* unless he said, "Mo'nin' y'all. Ah feels more kindly toward newspapermen."

Writing in "Winners & Sinners," Theodore M. Bernstein thus impaled one of the vices associated with quote-craziness, namely, the mishandling of fragmentary quotations so that the speaker appears to be talking about himself in the third person. Quotation marks, until the rules are changed, are supposed to enclose *the exact words* of the speaker. Any change in the form of those words leads to things like the example and worse.

" 'In point of fact,' the historian remarked, 'he couldn't bear to go—he was too immersed in the production of his fourteenth book.' " This, culled from a leading news magazine, is a prize example of confused quotation. The historian, believe it or not, was intended to be referring to himself. This kind of thing can cause more uncertainty than when the village atheist married the preacher's daughter. "The board acted on the basis of an appeal by Haymes that 'somebody pretty high had made up his mind to get him.' " To get whom? Well, Haymes; but Haymes must really have said "to get *me.*"

Some fragmentary quotations are such a mixture of direct and indirect discourse it is a hopeless task to untangle them: "The defendant told the judge he 'didn't allow people to grab his arm,' " and "Stevens said he 'feels in his heart that the responsibility was entirely his.' "

"The neighbors said she had 'a whole mob of cats that would fight, cry all night and sit on their cars.' " Sounds like those fat cats we hear so much about, but the speaker must actually have said *our cars.*

QUOTATION MARKS   In American practice, quotation marks go outside periods and commas, and inside colons and semicolons. In British practice, quotation marks generally stand inside periods and commas. This is a matter of printing practice, not of sense or grammar.

There is a tendency to drop, as superfluous, the quotation marks that once were generally used (in lieu of italics) around titles of books, plays, works of music, names of publications, and the like.

When a quotation is longer than one paragraph, closing quotation marks are omitted at the ends of intermediate paragraphs. Each paragraph in a continuing quotation starts with quotation marks, and the last paragraph ends with them.

Quotation marks or italics rather than commas are called for to set off a word as a word: "Sometimes he used the term, ecliptic, incorrectly." "the term *ecliptic*" or *the term "ecliptic."*

quote, quoted   One may quote a person (by repeating what he has uttered), or quote the utterance itself, but *quote* alone is not considered good usage in attribution: " 'There was no connection between that charge and my administration,' the President was quoted." *quoted as saying.* The shortened version is so prevalent and convenient, and the objection to it is so obviously sheer prejudice, however, that this usage can be expected to make its way.

quotes   Fowler disparaged the term as a clipped form for *quotation* marks; more recent critics have had at *quote* and *quotes* as clipped forms for *quotation* and *quotations.* But the tendency to make long words more convenient by abbreviating them is irresistible.

—R—

racket, racquet   The first is the commoner form for the tennis bat though the second is sometimes reserved for that sense. There is no hard and fast distinction in usage.

radio   *Radio* as a prefix is doggedly hyphenated by many, but it is not given thus in any dictionary, and carefully edited publications observably set it solid. The commonest combination, perhaps, is *radioactive* (one word). Other examples are *radiotherapy, radiotelephone, radiotelegram, radiothermy.* It's different, of course, when *radio* is an adjective: *radio tube, radio station, radio spectrum.* When in doubt, use the dictionary.

raise, rear, rise It is grammatical folklore that children are reared, animals are raised. *Reared,* however, has a flossy sound. Speaking of children as raised is sound American idiom and beyond cavil.

   Raise as a verb is transitive, *rise* intransitive: "The curtain will raise." *rise* or *will be raised.*

raise, rise Sometimes confused in connection with increases in pay. The established form is *a raise; a rise* can be defended, but is little used in America. In Britain, *rise* is preferred.

rampage Constructions like *go on a rampage* are cast-iron journalese in reference to overflowing rivers.

rarefy Often misspelled *rarify.*

rassle Or *wrastle, wrassle, rassel, rastle* are regarded as dialectal or colloquial forms of *wrestle,* growing out of the vernacular mispronunciation of the term. An attempt was made in a California lawsuit, however, to establish *rassling* as the descriptive for professional wrestling. The proponents described rassling as a combination of vaudeville and tumbling, with a prearranged conclusion, and added that professional wrestling is now a form of satire, having deteriorated as a sport.

rather Often called upon to do too big a task. In the sense considered here, it is the equivalent of *somewhat; a rather cold day* we understand to be a chilly but not unendurable one, colder than its fellows but not remarkably so. The word is a mild qualifier, and is often coupled with too strong an adjective. The impression is left that a milder modifier would have been more suitable in the first place.

   "The revelation was rather astonishing"; "The contradiction was illustrated in rather amazing fashion"; "He suffered a rather staggering loss" exemplify this. *Astonishing, amazing,* and *staggering* are all too wild to be tamed by *rather,* and the attempt leaves the reader in a fog as to the force intended.

   Rather and a strong descriptive tend to cancel each other.

332

What is rather astonishing obviously is not astonishing at all, but something more nearly approaching *surprising*. *Rather amazing* comes down to much the same thing. Losses that are *rather staggering* appear to have been severe but no more.

Those who use *rather* in expressions like these want to have it both ways; they yearn for impact, and very likely *amazing*, *astonishing*, and *staggering* by themselves would convey the true state of affairs. But then, Nice Nellys at heart, they are frightened by the verbal power they have unleashed, and so they timidly invoke *rather* as a counterbalance. What they end with stops pretty much on dead center, and they would have been better advised to stick with their first choice, undiminished.

Slightly is often misused in much the same way, though sometimes a humorous effect is intended. *Slightly amazing*, however, and similar expressions are often set down seriously. It may be deposed that *slightly amazing* comes under the same heading as *slightly pregnant*.

"The official hailed the year as 'a rather spectacular one for the union.'" What will you have: *spectacular* or *rather*? See *very; quite*.

ravage, ravish To ravage is to damage or destroy; to ravish is to rape, abduct, or enchant. A building may be ravaged by fire; a woman may be ravished, ravishing, or ravaged (ordinarily by age).

rave As an adjective applying to enthusiastic reviews of entertainments, a dismal cliché. Or, one might say, a journalistic shout-word. See also *adequate; consummate*.

re In the sense *concerning* (a form of the Latin *res*, thing), *re* is not an abbreviation and thus does not take a period. This applies also to the legal phrase *in re* (*in the matter of*). *In re* is perhaps best reserved for legal documents.

re- Nearly always solid as a prefix: *reconvert, redo, retell*, etc. Formerly it was hyphenated when followed by *e*, but there is a strong tendency now to set it solid even then: *reecho, reelect, reenact*. The hyphen continues to be used to distinguish *re-creation* (another creation) from *recreation* (amusement) and *re-collect* (collect again) from *recollect* (remember).

readjust, -ment "For the time being, certainly, it had been found necessary to make a readjustment of rations (Squeaker always spoke of it as a 'readjustment,' never as a 'reduction') . . ." *Animal Farm*, George Orwell.

"Speaking of taxes, Treasury Secretary Dillon recalled that in the past year he had frequently stated that the central element in the reform measure would be a proposal to readjust the rate structure.

" 'I had not thought it necessary to spell out the fact that readjustment necessarily meant readjustment downward,' he added." *The Associated Press.*

Readjustment, it is clear, is a favorite euphemism for *reduction* among Big Brotherly and bureaucratic types, when they are not using *downward revision.* Preferable in these contexts: *cut.*

See also *adjust, readjust; Euphemisms.*

real, sure The use of *real* and *sure* as adverbs in place of *really, surely,* or their equivalents is acceptable, perhaps, in conversation, but even there they may mark the user as slovenly or untrained in his habits of expression: "Being in the White House sure does change your point of view"; "The performance was real good." Not found in careful writing except for a deliberately folksy effect.

realistic See *Euphemisms.*

realize, realise *Realise* is the British preference.

realtor A designation properly belonging to members of the National Association of Real Estate Boards, which registered it in 1916. Though it has come into wide use applying to property salesmen generally, perhaps *real-estate dealer* or *broker* is preferable. Many more people than members of the association are engaged in the realty business, and the proportion was estimated in 1963 at 75,000 out of 500,000. This aggravates the difficulty of restricting the use of *realtor* to those who legally own it.

rear See *raise, rear.*

reason is because, due to *The reason is that* is better usage than *the reason is because* or *is due to.*

reasons Often clumsily modified by nouns that have been forced into the role of adjectives; the commonest of these expressions is perhaps *for health reasons.* "For expediency reasons he limited his criticism." *For reasons of expediency.* See also *Nouns as Adjectives* under *Modifiers.*

rebut See *refute.*

receipt, recipe Usage has differentiated them to the extent that it now attracts slightly surprised attention to use *receipt* to mean a formula for cooking, although this sense is technically correct. The word for the formula is now almost invariably *recipe; receipt* is all but exclusively used to mean a written acknowledgment, as *a receipt for a payment.*

receive See *suffer, sustain, receive.*

receptive See *acceptable.*

recipe See *receipt, recipe.*

reconvert Threatens, as a redundancy, to drive out *convert,* especially in connection with the adaptation of buildings to new uses. Homes, for example, are erroneously spoken of as being *reconverted* to apartments. What is *reconverted* must already have been converted. *Reconvert* gained currency after the war, when industrial plants that had been converted to war production were reconverted to their original uses.

record *All-time, new high,* or even *new* is redundant with *record* in reference to an unprecedented level.

recur, reoccur There is no occasion for *reoccur, reoccurence; recur, recurrence* serve more neatly.

recurrency A false form; *recurrence.*

red-faced The expression may have some virtue as the invariable substitute it has become for *embarrassed,* but, if so, the virtue is not apparent. Account might be taken of the fact that most people may be embarrassed without blushing.

redhead, redheaded Curiously aspersed in some stylebooks as not properly applicable to someone with red hair, on the basis that only the hair, not the head, is red. Both common (and choice) usage and dictionary recognition of these terms show this criticism to be pedantry. For that matter, no hair, except perhaps that of a clown, is red, strictly speaking.

REDUNDANCY The sportsman does not use a shotgun when a rifle will do. When it comes to writing, the rifle can't be beat. He who closes his eyes, pulls the trigger, and lets fly with a barrage of words ought to be told that somehow they lose their force in bunches. A single, well-chosen shot will bring the quarry down. In general, the fewer the words the better the writing.

The soporific habit of using several words where one will serve may be illustrated by *a sufficient number of* vs. *enough*, *at the present time* vs. *now*, and *in the immediate vicinity of* vs. *near*. These woolly expressions, which occur so often they pop unbidden into the mind, are readily used by the uncritical writer. Hunting them down and nailing them to the wall is a salutary exercise.

An excellent dictum on redundancy was set forth by William Strunk Jr. in *The Elements of Style:* "A sentence should contain no unnecessary words, a paragraph no unnecessary sentences, for the same reason that a drawing should have no unnecessary lines and a machine no unnecessary parts."

A repulsive pair of expressions has grown onto *future*: *in the near future* and *in the not-too-distant future*. Translated, *in the near future* means *soon*, and *in the not-too-distant future* can mean *before long, eventually, finally, next year, sometime,* or *sooner or later*. The reader, poor fellow, must decide.

Case is the progenitor of a hardy breed of villains that seem impervious to attack: *in case* (*if*), *in most cases* (*usually*), *if that were the case* (*if so*), *not the case* (*not so*), *in the case of* (which often may be omitted entirely, and if not, replaced by *concerning*), and *as in the case of* (*like*).

"It is possible that this material may become mixed with clouds in some cases and induce rain sooner than otherwise would have been the case." Stripping this down to what counts, we get: "This material may become mixed with clouds and induce [cause?] rain sooner."

"This station will be able to track more satellites over longer distances and do more observations than is the case with most other tracking stations in the world." Omit *is the case with.*

Instance sometimes appears in place of *case: in most instances,* etc.

Some redundancies have become classical targets of critics: *"at the intersection of* Market and Main" (*at*); "consensus *of opinion"* (*consensus*); *"entirely* destroyed" (*destroyed*). Also undeservedly popular are *despite the fact that* (*although*), *due to the fact that* (*because* or *since*), *during the period from* (*from*), and *for the purpose of* (*for*).

Redundancy is a vast and overfertilized field. Among its varieties, as classified by scholars, are pleonasm (using more words than necessary), tautology (repeating an idea in different words), and circumlocution or periphrasis (talking around the subject). The point of this preachment is not so much to urge the outlawing of the particular expressions cited as to encourage the critical sense. Nevertheless, the examples have been chosen for their prevalence, and anyone who does forgo them will certainly not harm his writing.

Ignorance of what common words mean, or unwillingness to trust them to do their job unaided, is responsible for some specimens of redundancy. *Experience, records, custom,* and *history* come only from the *past;* thus there is no occasion for *past experience, past records, past custom,* and *past history. Gifts* and *passes* are by definition *free,* even if the advertising gentry cannot be made to see it. An *innovation* is by its nature *new,* as are a b*eginner* and a *tyro*; and an *incumbent* is inescapably of the *present. Plans* are willy-nilly of the *future,* as must be *prospects* and *developments. Planning* can be nothing but *advance.*

What is *friendship* if it is not *personal?* And what is *business* if not *official,* O bumbling bureaucrats? *Both agreed* offends the thin-skinned, for *both* is two taken together and *agreement* is a coming together. *Equally as* is a horse of the same color. *On account of* is distasteful for *because of,* and *in excess of* is even worse for *more than,* because it is not only redundant but pompous.

"In order to balance the budget," or what have you, might better be simply *to balance. In back of* is a gaucherie for *behind,* though *in front of* (a building, for example) serves a purpose that *before* does not. *Advance reservations* seem to be getting ahead of themselves. *In which* is often superfluous, as in "Each candidate will be given fifteen minutes [in which] to express his views." An accident victim is taken to a hospital *for treatment,* inevitably; why labor it?

New construction is Navyese for a ship abuilding; why

apply it to structures, when nothing is more self-evident than the newness of what is under construction? These random examples show, if nothing else, that the pen is mightier than the pitchfork.

redwood   Now and then Californians are startled to hear it said that *Sequoia gigantea,* the big tree of the Sierra, is not a redwood. There are two species of sequoia in California: *S. sempervirens,* otherwise known as the coast redwood, and *S. gigantea.* Precisians who hold that the term *redwood* applies only to the coastal variety will find some comfort in Webster. But this is a bookish distinction supported by neither general nor expert usage.

re-enforce, reinforce   The second is predominant, as in *troop reinforcements, reinforced concrete.*

refer   See *allude, refer.*

refer back   A redundancy for *refer.*

REFERENCE   It was once considered sufficient to identify a person by his full name, to begin with, and then to use the last name for subsequent references. Something of a fad, however, has sprung up in recent years to see how many different ways the subject can be styled. This may have been inspired by the mania for variation in reference to other things (*pachyderm* for *elephant, white stuff* for *snow;* (see *Variation*).

Richard Nixon, for example, was thus identified in an article about him. In the middle of things, however, he suddenly became "Dick Nixon." A page later, unaccountably he emerged fullblown as "Richard Milhous Nixon." Sometimes the subject will, for no apparent reason, be referred to here and there by his nickname alone. This skipping around from one form to another can become as confusing as a Russian novel, where the characters all seem to have twelve polysyllabic names and are referred to indiscriminately by any of them. No wonder many readers never make it through *War and Peace.*

Some of this trickiness is traceable to *Time* magazine, which once went out of its way to dig up little-known middle names of well-known people and startle its readers with them. Middle names may be interesting, but they can be presented unobtrusively: "John D. (for Davison) Rockefeller." There is no excuse for flaunting such small facts or leaving the reader in doubt what the usual form of the name is.

For ordinary purposes, it would seem preferable to name a person at the outset in the style by which he is generally known, which is also usually the way he signs his name. Some people use and are known by three names (Richard Harding Davis, Norman Vincent Peale) and it is misleading to refer to them as Richard H. Davis or N. V. Peale. Random reference to public figures by their nicknames is objectionable because it may sound patronizing or unduly familiar, but there are exceptions here, too, when people are better known to the public by their nicknames than otherwise or when the tone of the writing calls for familiarity. Once identification has been established, it seems sensible to stay thereafter with a standard form—usually the last name, but in some circumstances the nickname or first name. Switching forms of reference when there is no apparent reason for it tends to rattle and annoy the reader. For other problems of reference, see *Pronouns* and *Leapfrog*.

referenda, referendums The English plural is now in such wide use as to make the Latin (*referenda*) sound affected.

refined See *culture, cultured.*

refuse To refuse is to decline to accept; *refuse* is not a synonym for *disobey*. "The students were tried under a law making it a misdemeanor to refuse an officer's order to disperse." See also *decline*.

refute To refute an argument is to disprove or demolish it, not merely to contradict, rebut, or disagree. "The president refuted reports that he would flee the country." He could refute them only by remaining; not, as in this case, merely by denying he intended to flee.

regard *Regard* leads us to two barbarisms: *irregardless* and *in regards to*. *Irregardless* is beyond the pale, and no more need be said, except perhaps that it comes from heedless analogy with *irrespective*. *In regards to* is an illiterate variant of *in regard to*. *In regard to, with regard to,* and *as regards* are not actually crimes, but the writer who is neat will eschew all three for *regarding, concerning,* or *about*.

"National politics are different in some regards from state

politics" will offend the discriminating, who would prefer *respects*.

Regard in the general sense of *consider* takes *as*. Fowler expressed concern over the omission of *as* ("He was *regarded* a bum"), but this fault appears to be rare, having been succeeded by the unwanted pairing of *as* with *consider* (which see).

regular Redundant with any word that indicates periodic recurrence: *a regular weekly meeting, a regular monthly review. a weekly meeting, a monthly review.*

reign, rein Sometimes confused, perhaps because reins, the leather straps used to control horses, are unfamiliar in an automotive age. "The new superintendent was given free reign." *free rein; reign* is rule, as of a monarch.

relation, relative As the word for *kinsman, relative* is preferable because it is favored by usage. *Relation* is acquiring a tinge of quaintness, though it remains established in set phrases like *poor relations* and *friends and relations*.

RELATIVE CLAUSES See *Restrictive and Nonrestrictive Clauses; Ellipsis*.

RELATIVE PRONOUNS See *that, which* under *Restrictive and Nonrestrictive Clauses*.

relieve *Relieve* in the sense of *deprive of* or *take away from* sounds facetious, but its users are not always aware of this. "The city initiated action to *relieve* the bus line of its franchise" and "The pickpocket *relieved* several tourists of their wallets" are examples. *Relieve* in the first example is so inappropriate it must have been used unwittingly. See also *lift*.

religion, religious editor The religion editor is the one who handles religious matters; he may not himself be religious and consequently *religious editor* is ambiguous as a job description.

religious As a noun ("Two religious were kneeling in prayer" and "The pilgrimage was made by a party of religious and laymen"), the word is churchly cant, so seldom seen in ordinary contexts as to cause a moment of puzzlement.

remainder See *balance*.

remains Probably regarded by its users as a euphemism for *corpse*, but the term is distasteful to many, and beyond that has grown quaint. *Body* generally is preferable.

remind "Taxes will be due April 1, the collector *reminds*." This leaves the reader up in the air, groping vainly for the missing object, for *remind* is transitive. The correct use is along these lines: "Taxes will be due April 1, the collector *reminds property-owners*."

remunerate Highfalutin when *pay* will serve. But if it must be used, let it not be spelled *renumerate*, which means *renumber*.

renaissance, renascence Although they are synonyms and generally interchangeable, usage has pretty well settled on *renaissance* for the great revival of learning and things associated with it, and *renascence* for rebirth in general.

render It is not true, as stylebook superstition would have it, that only lard is rendered. The word is correct in the sense of *sing* or *play* ("render a vocal selection"), but this use is now both pretentious and quaint.

rendezvous Sometimes aspersed as a verb ("The searchers *rendezvoused* at Horner's Corner"), but its use in this way is reputable, even though an English ending has been grafted onto a French word. It probably gained popularity from frequent use in naval operations during World War II.

renown, renowned The first is the noun, the second the adjective. "The climate of California is world-renown"; "Chicago's re-known columnist." A common lapse; *renowned*. Sometimes misspelled *reknown, reknowned*. Pronounced *re-NOWn*.

reoccur, reoccurrence Needless variants of *recur, recurrence*.

repast See *banquet*.

repeat again A redundancy for *repeat*.

repellant, repellent Interchangeable as both noun and adjective: *an insect repellant* (*repellent*); *his manners were repellant* (*repellent*). *Repellant* is favored as the noun, however, and *repellent* as the adjective.

repertoire, repertory   More or less interchangeable in the sense of a supply available for performance, though *repertoire* is almost invariably used in reference to music: "Her thread-bare repertoire included only a few arias." *Repertory,* as both noun and adjective, is favored in association with the theater: *a small repertory house.*

REPETITION   Is it true, as it seems to be, that newswriters do not trust the reader to remember what they have just told him? If not, why can't they be content to allow what they have set down to stand, without repeating or restating it in some obvious way a few lines later? It may be taken for granted that what has been said in the lead paragraph, especially, is likely to stick in the reader's mind, for that is what makes him decide either to read on or to turn to something that interests him more.

Bald repetition of phrases and sentences seems to imply a lack of confidence that they have sunk in. This is no tribute to the reader's intelligence, nor does it reflect any credit on the writer's. Footless iteration like the following is often encountered:

"The president, smiling broadly, said today that ever since he was five years old his brother has been criticizing him." O.K. But two paragraphs later, we get this warmed-over dish: "Smiling broadly, the chief executive replied that his brother had been criticizing him since he was five years old."

As garnish, perhaps, the broad smile has now been moved forward; the president is interestingly referred to as the chief executive; and *has been* is changed to *had been* for some mysterious reason. Do these changes warrant the rehash?

"The lumber strike is over, and the president of the union calls it 'a draw.'" Passing by the unnecessary quotes around *a draw,* let us proceed to the second paragraph: "'We neither won nor lost the strike. It was a draw,' said George Willard. . . .'" All right, it was a draw, as the union president saw it. But after having established this, why not let it go at that?

And again: "She's tall, she's tanned, and she says the new Dior 'flat' look 'came just in time to save me.'" Four paragraphs later: "'I think Dior came just in time to save me,' she said." But what will save the account from the flatness that comes of meaningless repetition?

"He said last night that never before in the history of astronomy have the scientists been able to study a satellite which has traveled as fast as the Russian earth moons.

" 'We've never had this in astronomy before,' said Dr. Whipple." Maybe not in astronomy, but we've had it in print.

Here's not just duplication, but triplication:

"The White House said today it does not know whether reports of a Russian-manned rocket flight are true or not." (There were quotes around *true or not,* compounding the felony.)

" 'We have no knowledge of the truth of these stories,' the press secretary told reporters.

"Hagerty persisted in his refusal to comment on the reports 'because I don't know whether the story is true or not.' "

And so to bed, to bed, to bed.

See also *Ellipsis; Repetition of Defining Modifiers* under *Modifiers; Variation.*

replace   Means either *put back in the same place* or *substitute;* if the context does not clearly indicate which, recasting is called for.

replica   The commonest misuse is in the sense of *model* or *miniature;* it should be kept in mind that a *replica* is a copy in the same size. The word has a specialized application in the fine arts, meaning a copy by the person who made the original.

reportedly   *Reportedly* has been sneered at and even proscribed on the ground it was not to be found in dictionaries. Now, the fact that a word is not in the dictionary is no reason it should not be used. If everyone took this attitude there would be (a) no words, and (b) no dictionaries; for, of course, words come first and dictionaries later. Until 1960 or so, *reportedly* was indeed hard to find in dictionaries, though Webster's Second Edition did list it in small type at the bottom of the page. The word is so useful it was included in the Third Edition as well as at least two recent desk dictionaries. Some newspaper editors asperse *reportedly* on the ground that only verifiable fact should be reported, arguing that this leaves no place for it. Such views are matters of policy and have nothing to do with the virtue of the word. They would also rule out *allegedly,* *supposedly, reputedly,* and other speculative expressions. Publications that print only verifiable fact, incidentally, must be pretty bleak propositions. The important thing is to distinguish between fact and speculation, which is what *reportedly* handily does.

republican, Republican   The capitalized form should be reserved for references to the political party, the other for references to the form of government. See also *democrat; conservative; liberal.*

resides   Pretentious for *lives* in most circumstances.

resin, rosin   *Rosin* is not, as is sometimes supposed, an error for *resin;* rosin is a form of resin used to make the bows of string instruments tacky, among other purposes.

respective, -ly   Often used unnecessarily: "They returned to their respective homes." The reader will not otherwise assume that they returned to each other's homes. *Respective* (and *respectively*) should not be called into play unless there is a need for sorting out. An example: "Mrs. Jones and Mrs. Smith selected carnations and snapdragons, *respectively,*" which correctly matches the women with the flowers in the order given. But words like *former, latter* (which see), as well as *respective, -ly,* which oblige the reader to match things up, are to be avoided.

"Shavers big and small will thus get a chance to compare the respective blades." No need for *respective.*

(the) rest   See *balance.*

restauranteur, restaurateur   A generation ago one way you could tell a cub from a seasoned reporter was that the seasoned reporter knew there was no *n* in *restaurateur.* If this test was inconclusive, you could try *Court of St. James's;* everything hung on getting *James's* in just that form. *James'* was grounds for excommunication. The court was the address of the American ambassador in London; at any rate, it was not important to know this; it was important only to know how to write the term. *Court of St. James's* was unlikely to loom very large in the writing of reporters other than those assigned to London, but that didn't matter either.

Restaurateur, admittedly, had a wider use, especially in

places when it was likely to be applied to the operator of a hamburger stand. Such is the force of attraction of *restaurant,* however, that the forbidden *n* often crept in. So often, in fact, that Webster made a new dispensation: both *restaurateur* and *restauranteur* are now considered correct. Still, this does seem like a shabby way to treat those platoons of reporters whose self-respect has hinged so long on knowing the spelling *restaurateur*. There may be some balm in the fact that none of the new desk dictionaries other than the Merriam-Webster admits the *n.*

rest easy   The form of the idiom; not *easily,* which evidences overcorrectness.

RESTRICTIVE AND NONRESTRICTIVE CLAUSES Lovable Miss Pennypacker, who tried so diligently to pound the difference between restrictive and nonrestrictive clauses into our thick heads, must be ineffably saddened when she reads a good deal of what appears in print, including the polished but sometimes pockmarked prose of the newsmagazines. The difference seems more honored in the breach than the observance (to misconstrue Hamlet). Miss Pennypacker might conclude that many of those who write and edit do not even know it exists.

Yet this is not one of those puristic distinctions evident only to those who enjoy separating the flyspecks from the pepper. On the contrary, it is something that directly affects meaning. Thus it is important to everyone interested in exact, unequivocal expression.

The trouble is that words like *restrictive* and *nonrestrictive* (or *defining* and *nondefining,* which mean the same thing) have the ugly smell of formal grammar about them and by themselves are enough to frighten off all but the hardiest seekers after truth. But if you will hold on a minute, we will try to part the grammatical foliage and point a safe and simple path through the wilderness.

The problem arises with relative clauses. You can always recognize a relative clause as one starting with *that* or *which, where* or *when,* or *who, whose,* or *whom.* And the question is whether such clauses should be set off by commas.

Consider a sentence like "I waved at the girl who was standing on the corner." Do we want a comma in front of *who?* It depends on what we mean. As the sentence stands, commaless, the speaker waved to a girl who is identified for the reader by the fact that she was standing on the corner. Let us put a comma in front of *who*. Now the fact that the girl was standing on the corner becomes merely incidental information. The *who* clause no longer identifies her. While it was originally restrictive, or defining, it now has become nonrestrictive, or nondefining, and *may be dropped*.

The important point to settle is whether the clause is essential to the meaning. If the clause is essential, the comma should not be used; if it is not essential, the comma is required to set it off. This is the law on the subject. If you have any doubt whether the clause is essential, try leaving it out. Obviously, you cannot leave out the *who* clause in the commaless version of our example without changing the intended sense. The girl would no longer be identified.

"No woman, whose attire makes her conspicuous, is well dressed." Preposterous, of course, with the commas. For if we leave out the *whose* clause, as the commas indicate we may, we get "No woman is well dressed."

"Every high-school district in the county, which called for a bond issue this year, has won voter support." This was intended to mean that bond issues carried in every district where they were proposed; not, as might be concluded, that every district in the county proposed bond issues and won approval of them. You cannot leave out the *which* clause without changing the intended sense; thus the commas are erroneous.

"The rule exempts commercial lots where there is no restriction on all-night parking." The writer wanted to indicate that commercial lots are unaffected because they do not restrict all-night parking, but what he did, by leaving out the comma before *where*, was to say confusingly that the rule affects some commercial lots and not others. A period could have been placed after *lots;* the rest is merely explanatory.

The careful writer asks himself, every time he writes a clause starting with *who, whom, which, when,* or *where* whether it should be set off by commas. The common error is to neglect setting off nonrestrictive clauses, thus misleading the reader as to the sense.

The question should also be asked if the pronouns listed are preceded by a preposition: *to whom, from which,* etc.

There are borderline cases in which the comma may be dropped. These generally are instances in which the relative clause bears on a proper name, as in "I feel sorry for Miss Pennypacker who tried so hard." But careful writers still use the comma here.

that, which   The question of nonrestrictive and restrictive elements inescapably involves the choice between *that* and *which*. To start with, elegance has nothing to do with it. Those who carefully substitute one for the other on this basis —opinion differs as to which is the more high-toned—are on a fool's errand.

Usage and grammarians alike agree that *that* should be used to introduce only restrictive clauses. Nonrestrictive clauses, as we have seen, are set off by commas; restrictive ones are not. Save *that* to introduce restrictive clauses. *Which* is all right with either kind, but is preferred with the nonrestrictive.

A rule of thumb may be useful here. If *that* will fit comfortably, it is correct, and furthermore the clause is restrictive. *That* introducing a nonrestrictive clause is a blunder: "The sun, that had a murky orange color, soon burned off the fog." He whose ear does not tell him *which* is required here in place of *that* has no ear. This construction once was regarded as correct, but now is a conspicuous anachronism. In "It was easy to find the house which was on fire," *that* can be substituted for *which,* and in accordance with our rule of thumb it thus is preferable. A corollary is that a clause starting with *which* should be set off by commas; one starting with *that* should not.

The prejudice against *which* with restrictive clauses is just that, however—a prejudice. The chief use of the distinction given here between *that* and *which* is that it helps in distinguishing between restrictive and nonrestrictive clauses, a far more important matter.

As a general rule, *that* may refer to either persons or things, but *which* refers only to things.

result   Takes *in,* not *with:* "The program is likely to result with a collapse of confidence in the city council." *result in.*

retro-   Solid as a prefix: *retroactive, retrocession, retrofit, retrograde,* etc.

reveal   See *Attribution.*

Reverend   It is an axiom that clergymen are touchy customers; among the shortcomings that are likely to make them grieve is the misuse of their own descriptive title, *Reverend. Reverend* is an adjective meaning *deserving of reverence,* and strictly speaking should never be used with the last name alone, as in *Rev. Jones* or *the Rev. Jones*. The correct form is *the Rev. Mr. Jones*.

For the first reference to a preacher, either *the Rev. John Jones* or *Rev. John Jones* (using the first name) is acceptable, although *the Rev.* is considered preferable by sticklers. Thereafter, references should be in the form *the Rev. Mr. Jones*, or more simply, Mr. Jones, which is easier to remember and equally beyond criticism. Just plain *Jones* is acceptable, too, even to ministers themselves, although we are not likely to be so blunt with our spiritual mentors.

Insofar as hatred is consistent with the Christian virtues, many preachers say they hate to be addressed as *Reverend*, as one addresses a physician as *Doctor*. This is a problem of speech, rather than writing, but the related peccadillo, *Rev. Jones*, turns up in both speech and writing.

This lapse not only inspires righteous indignation, but also causes preachers to break out into verse. At least three poems have been inspired by it. To be frank, they are pretty painful specimens, whose own infractions of rhyme and meter seem to overshadow the offense they deplore. They also show an alarming lack of restraint at such a venial sin. One of these puristic poets declares the error rends his heart, another hates it like the devil, and a third is ready to punch in the nose the transgressors responsible for it.

In spite of all this, *Rev. Jones* is spreading like repentance at a tent revival. Furthermore, many spiritual leaders are practicing Christian charity toward sinners in this department of usage. The editors of a half-dozen leading church journals who were asked for their opinions agreed that they have seen the handwriting on the wall and are ready to defer to it. The nub of the matter is that the layman can see no reason why Reverend should differ in its application from *Mr., Senator, Professor*, or *Doctor;* or why, if you can call a senator *Senator* and doctor *Doctor*, you can't call a preacher *Reverend*.

The layman, in the end, is the one who sits in the seat of judgment on these questions anyway, and the decisions of grammarians, theological and otherwise, are likely to be scattered forth like dust if they run counter to the popular will.

Reverend, as a term of deference and respect, is no more to be applied by a man to himself than *Mr.* (which see).

Referring to a cleric as *the reverend* is rustic: " 'The results far exceeded our expectations,' the reverend said." *minister, pastor*, or whatever is appropriate.

REVERSAL OF SENSE   Often occurs as the result of inattention. Two examples once appeared in a single issue of *The New Yorker* in the newsbreaks it uses to fill out columns:

"And quite suddenly this young pianist of tired mien is immersed in the business of producing sounds of such high-voltage individuality as to quickly dispel any notions that the evening would be anything but routine." The writer apparently has been carried away by his determination to create an effect. Perhaps haste (since the quotation is from a newspaper) prevented a critical second reading before the words were committed to print. Obviously, he meant "dispel any notions that the evening would be routine" or "to quickly give rise to notions . . ."

The other example: "Not even a blizzard prevented friends of the former ambassador and his wife from missing their cocktail party yesterday in honor of a former Washingtonian here from London on a holiday visit." *prevented . . . from attending;* or *was enough to make friends . . . miss.* Involved construction probably helped lead the writers astray in both instances. Similar mischances are dealt with under *reverse,* etc.; *Double Negative; minimize; underestimate; undue.*

reverse, converse, opposite, vice versa   These terms are sometimes applied to what is not logically or unequivocally capable of reversal: "There's no need to be a blackguard to be successful. In fact, the reverse is true." Here are three possible reversals of the statement: there's a need to be a blackguard to be successful; there's a need to be a blackguard to be unsuccessful; there's no need to be a blackguard to be unsuccessful. But, the reader will object, we know what was meant: It is necessary not to be a blackguard, etc. Yet confusion is possible, and at any rate the reversal is unclear.

Consider also: "This is Voltaire in reverse: I agree with everything you say but reject your right to say it." This a logical reversal, for Voltaire (in the popular misconception) disagreed, but would defend the right to say. The effect of devices like *the reverse* and *vice versa* should be instantly evident, as in an example cited by Webster: "It was with vast relief that we came upon a man pretending to be a machine, rather than *vice versa.*"

Herbert Depew in *Tortured Words* cites "We thought the law would punish him, but the reverse took place." He punished the law? Of course not; it would have been both more concise and more explicit to have said "but it did not."

"A fare increase will cause loss of bus patronage; the reverse would also be true—a fare reduction would increase the use of buses." Reversal is placing things in an opposite relation, and that is what happens in this case: fares up, patronage down; fares down, patronage up. *Reverse* is more often used in physical rather than abstract connections (*the reverse of a coin, reverse a motor*) and it makes us uneasy to see it in the abstract sense. *Converse* would be equally acceptable here, perhaps more so, because it always goes with abstract relations. *Opposite* would also do, if homelier English is acceptable. See also *Reversal of Sense; minimize; underestimate; undue; Double Negative.*

review, revue   Confusion of a sort appears in applying *review* to a stage show. Though it is technically justifiable, usage has fastened *revue* to such performances.

revise, revision   *Revise* is often loosely and improperly used for *rearrange, reorganize.* Revision has to do with changing or amending something that is written; printers' proofs and laws may be revised. "The lower courts were revised in California in 1953." *reorganized.*

right   Dialectal for *very much* or *greatly* or *much:* "We were right surprised." *very much* or something else.

right-to-work laws   It is generally realized that this is a political euphemism, concocted to make a kind of law that labor considers repugnant palatable to the voter. As a result, carefully edited publications now designate such legislation as *so-called right-to-work laws.* The purpose of such laws is not to preserve any right to work but to outlaw the union shop. See also *fair-trade laws.*

rime, rhyme   *Rhyme* is the established preference and *rime* in this sense, though technically correct, is an affectation. Thus it was in Fowler's day, and it is all the truer now. *Rime* is best reserved to mean *hoarfrost* or *frozen mist.*

Rio Grande River   See *Sahara.*

rise   See *raise, rear, rise.*

robbery   See *burglary.*

rock, stone Some say that *stone* must be used concerning what is of small size, for example what can be thrown, and *rock* concerning only a large mass, for example a boulder or mountain. Literary usage, especially in England, pretty well observes this distinction (*Rock of Ages*). But in the U.S. *rock* is indiscriminately applied to all sizes. *Stone* has also been reputably used for objects of considerable size, for example in reference to the stone that was rolled away from the sepulcher of Jesus.

Roman Catholic Although the descriptive *Roman* has been objected to by spokesmen for the Church, mainly on the ground that it dates back to an era when it was used derogatorily in England, no such connotation can be said to attach to it today. The adjective makes a distinction that is useful or it would not have endured, for there are, among other varieties, Greek and Anglican as well as Roman Catholicism.

ROMAN NUMERALS The ability to read—or even decipher—Roman numbers larger than, say, X (for *ten*) is now possessed by so few that their use may be considered a deliberate attempt to obscure. There was a time when the year of copyright of books was often given in this manner, but that practice has now happily been abandoned in favor of the Arabic numbers everyone can read.

Roman numerals continue to be used ceremonially, however, for cornerstones and often to indicate the volume number of periodicals. (The number is changed annually, by some publications at the beginning of the year, by others on the anniversary date of their establishment.)

The *New Haven Journal-Courier*, confronted by its 191st year of publication, had to consult a classical scholar at Yale before it could decide whether to give the volume number in the classical style (CXCI) or the early Roman style (CLXXXXI). An office boy who asked why not just use 191 and forget the whole thing was told, according to an account in *Publisher's Auxiliary*, to shut up. That may have been an example, of which many more significant ones could be cited, of hidebound tradition speaking to a public that wants a fighting chance to understand what it is reading. Habit and the reluctance to change or even examine it play an astonishingly large role in publishing, though perhaps no larger than in many other endeavors.

If Roman numerals must be used, *one* is represented by I,

not by the Arabic 1. Often such mixtures as X11 are seen in both typescript and printed material.

romance   Those who would criticize it as a verb must differentiate its senses. With the meaning *exaggerate, invent,* it is a reputable term whose use goes back to 1671. "The clergyman's wife had nearly been romanced out of a $203,000 inheritance," although aspersed by one critic, was certainly both clear and acceptable in its use of *romance.* It may be that the word was interpreted by the critic in the sense *make love,* but obviously the meaning intended was that the money was nearly lost to a storyteller. *Romance* for *make love,* as "There is much romancing in the moonlight," is sometimes regarded as Hollywoodese and slangy, but this sense may easily gain status.

root of all evil. . . .   See *Misquotation.*

rough   Slangy in the sense of *difficult:* "Congress will have a rough time in the next session."

round   See *around, round.*

rout, route   *Rout* means *drive out:* "The troops prepared to *rout* the invaders"; *route* means *select,* or *send along, a path:* "Hannibal planned to *route* his army through the Alps." The past tense (*routed*) is the same for both words.

routine training mission, flight, exercise   Usually redundant. Drop *routine.*

rules and regulations   A sententious coupling; one or the other should suffice, especially when they cannot be told apart.

RULE OF TEN   See *Numbers.*

rustic   Has acquired a specialized sense in the lingo of Western real-estate dealers and, perforce, their customers. To them, a rustic home is not one charmingly countrified, but one having wood facing, as distinguished from stucco or brick. This usage is spreading to the East.

—S—

Sabbath Not necessarily Sunday; to Jews and Seventh-day Adventists it is Saturday, and to Mohammedans it is Friday.

sacrilegious Often misspelled *sacreligious* through a mistaken connection with *religious,* and there is an association here, to be sure. By derivation, sacrilege is the theft of sacred things; its senses include profanation and desecration.

Sahara Those versed in Arabic, and some others, are aware that *Sahara Desert* is redundant, for *Sahara* means *desert.* Similarly, to those in the know, *Sierra Nevada,* the name of the great rocky spine of California, means *snowy mountains,* and *Rio Grande* means *Big River.* Some are distressed by the illegitimate but common plural *the Sierras,* rather than *the Sierra.* But those who would trim down *Sierra Nevada Mountains, Rio Grande River,* and *Sahara Desert* might as well forget it. It is pedantic to insist on distinctions based on knowledge of the languages from which these terms have emerged into English. Those who do so should consistently object to *City of Minneapolis* and *City of Indianapolis* as redundant too, since the suffix *-polis* means *city.*

said *Said* as an adjective in the sense *aforementioned* (*the said editor, said contractor*) is legalese and distasteful in other than legal contexts, but *aforementioned* is hardly to be recommended, either. Almost always, the definite article (*the*) suffices in reference to what has already been specified. "The editor of the local newspaper, together with members of the clergy, refused to take a position in the controversy. Said editor would not give his reasons, however." *The editor.* See also *Attribution.*

said in a statement Redundant in attribution, unless it is essential to indicate that the quotation was made in a formal statement rather than in a speech or by some other means; a pomposity of the press. See also *Attribution.*

salary, wage It is sometimes said that a job pays a wage and a position pays a salary. The distinction between *job* and *posi-*

tion (see *job, position*) is not, however, what it is often thought to be. In general, *wage* is applied to the compensation for work at the lower end of the scale in prestige. A teacher may get less than a truck driver, but the teacher's pay is not likely to be referred to as a wage, though that of either may be referred to as a salary. See also *job, position.*

saloon See *bar, saloon.*

same, the same *Same* as a pronoun ("He collected the money and deposited *same*") is not the best English; it bears an unwholesome odor of the world of commerce. The usage achieved a species of immortality and perhaps even an appearance of sanction from "Sighted sub, sank same," the laconic and famous report of an aviator in World War II. Kipling, too, had Tommy Atkins say, "We 'ave bought 'er the same with the sword and the flame." But the military are noticeably fond of adopting commercialese. In good usage, *the same* becomes *it.* "The publication will be mailed regularly and costs for same will be chargeable to member organizations." Omit *for same;* it is not just commercialese but superfluous.

Samson The name of the Biblical strong man is often misspelled *Sampson.*

sanatorium, sanitarium, sanitorium He who still seriously argues for a difference between *sanatorium* and *sanitarium* is putting misplaced dependence on a general knowledge of Latin. By derivation, the first is a place to restore health and the second a place to preserve it. Not only are these words easily confused, but the distinction seems of little use. So little has it been used, in fact, that Webster cites *sanatorium* and *sanitarium* as synonyms, although generally a preference is shown for *sanatorium* in names of institutions for the treatment of tuberculosis. *Sanitorium,* once an error, is now recognized as a variant spelling.

sank, sunk Both forms are standard for the past tense ("The boat sunk in 20 fathoms") but there is a noticeable preference among the discriminating for *sank.*

savant As a random variant for *professor, scholar,* or *scientist* (or anyone who knows more than the writer, which may not be much), *savant* is journalese.

save See *poesy*.

saving, savings As modifiers, these words have distinctive uses in two common connections. It's *savings bank* (a bank where savings are kept) ; but *daylight-saving time* (time that saves daylight). Thus *saving bank* and *daylight-savings time* are both wrong.

saw, see Scholars will have to tell us whether the uses of *saw* (and, less often, *see*) noted here are indeed dialectal, as they seem to be. At any rate, they are questionable.

"Winds up to 20 miles per hour are expected to see a recurrence of the dust storms today." *bring* or *cause*.

"He disbanded his chorus after nine seasons that saw more than 1,500 concerts around the world." *included*.

"Subsequent proceedings saw the closing of the place and the sale of its equipment." *resulted in*.

"The fiscal year saw a total of 300 million dollars appropriated for highways" is sanctioned, however, by one dictionary meaning of *see* (*witness as present or contemporary*), which apparently has been stretched to cover the other examples cited here.

Scandinavia, -n The Scandinavian countries are Sweden, Norway, and Denmark; the term does not apply, as is often mistakenly assumed, to their neighbor, Finland. The Scandinavian countries are linked by, among other things, languages so closely related that the person who knows one can understand the others. The Finnish language is totally different, and is related to Estonian, Lappic, and Hungarian. Iceland is sometimes regarded as one of the Scandinavian group. What is said here about *Scandinavian* also applies to *Nordic*.

scarcely Takes *when*, or rarely *before*, not *than:* "Scarcely were the words out of his mouth *when* the music began." *Scarcely* is a negative and should not be used with *not*: *not scarcely enough. scarcely enough.*

scattered in all directions Redundant for *scattered*.

scent, sense (trouble) According to one stylebook, a man does not sense trouble, he scents it. But what about the kind of trouble that doesn't smell?

sceptic See *skeptic, sceptic*.

scholar The word tends no longer to be used of pupils, for example the ten o'clock scholar, but is more and more reserved to specialists at universities and the like who are deep in their subjects.

scientist See *engineer, scientist.*

Scot, Scotchman, Scotsman, Scotch, Scottish Much as the inhabitants of San Francisco object to having their city called *Frisco,* inhabitants of Scotland object to being called *Scotchmen. Scotchmen,* however, is a reputable term, and the only reason for avoiding it is to keep from giving umbrage to Scotsmen (the term they prefer). *Scot* is the original name for a native of Scotland. For practical purposes, *Scot, Scotchman,* and *Scotsman* are synonyms. Scots generally reserve *Scotch* for things (*Scotch whisky, Scotch plaid*) and *Scottish* for people. This conforms with general usage, for *Scottish whisky* is unheard of.

In the sense *extirpate, obstruct,* and the like ("He Scotched the rumor that the farm was for sale"), *scotch* has nothing to do with *Scots* and thus should not be capitalized; *scotched.* See also *welsh.*

scrip, script Certificates used temporarily in place of money, and certain other fiscal documents, are known as *scrip,* not *script.* ("The workers are paid in scrip.") *Script* has a number of its own senses, none of which give difficulty.

sculp Standard though uncommon as a verb meaning *to create a sculpture; sculpt* is more usual. *Sculpture* is also acceptable: *sculpture a bust.*

seasonable, seasonal What is seasonable comes at the right time; what is seasonal is connected with a season. Snow in winter is *seasonable;* some jobs are *seasonal.* "The unemployment rate is always seasonably adjusted." To meet a deadline? No, season by season; that is, *seasonally.*

secular, sectarian *Secular* means *worldly* or *temporal,* in contradistinction to *religious; sectarian* means *pertaining to a religious sect or sects.*

secure, obtain *Secure* in the sense of *obtain* is an old and reputable use, though often denounced. But, as the Evanses comment, *get* is often preferable to *secure, obtain,* or *procure.* "The reporters *secured* complete details from the police." Pretentious for *got.* See also *get.*

see   See *saw, see.*

seldom ever   A redundancy; *seldom,* or *seldom if ever.* This common lapse puts one in mind of the supercautious small-town character who expressed doubt with, "You never can always sometimes tell."

self-, -self, self   Hyphenated as a prefix: *self-assured, self-government, self-reliant,* etc. Pronouns ending in *-self* (known as *Reflexives,* which see) should not be set off by commas: "The auditor, himself, was at the track." *The auditor himself was* . . .
   Self is not good usage for *I* or *me*: "Please reserve tickets for self and family." *me* (*myself*) *and my family.*

semi-   Solid as a prefix: *semiarid, semireligious, semitropical,* etc. Usually hyphenated when followed by *i: semi-idle, semi-intoxicated.*

senior citizen   A distasteful euphemism to many, including some seniors (that is to say, old people) themselves. Sometimes ineffectual attempts to avoid it are worse: "a nine-story apartment designed for senior persons." *elderly* (or perhaps *retired*) *people.* See also *elderly.*

sensual, sensuous   Often used interchangeably. When a distinction is made, it is that *sensual* connotes grossness, *sensuous* something more refined.

sententious, sentient   Although *sententious* has the sense of "terse and energetic in expression; pithy," it is used almost entirely in the derogatory sense of "marked by pompous formality." It may be said that only this latter meaning effectively survives; we can hardly expect a word to bear two nearly opposite senses. *Sententious* is sometimes unhappily confused with *sentient* (*capable of sensation*). Neither word means *wise,* as is sometimes assumed.

separate, separation   Often misspelled *seperate, seperation.*

SEQUENCE OF TENSES   Many an absurdity is committed in the name of a widely misapplied rule of grammar, the one governing sequence of tenses. The general idea is that the tense of the verb in the main clause of a sentence governs the tense in a subordinate clause. Sometimes this is called attracted sequence; that is, the tense of the verb in the clause that follows is attracted to the tense of the verb in the main clause.

So far, so good. Let's look at an example to make clear what we are talking about: "He *said* he *was* tired of everything." The verb in the main clause, *said,* is in the past tense, so the verb in the dependent clause, *was,* naturally falls into the past tense. Most of the time, this is not the kind of rule it is necessary to stop and think about. Here are some other examples of normal sequence of tenses:

"The man *wore* a pained expression as the officer *forced* his car to the curb."

"The motorist *explained* that he *tried* to buy a replacement for his defective headlamp."

"She *promised* that she *would be* there."

Some of us seize upon the rule of sequence and follow it out the window—or, just as bad, into the next sentence. The rule has an important exception, which can be relied on to forestall a good deal of nonsense, to-wit: The *present* tense, rather than the past, is used in the subordinate clause to express a continuing or timeless state of affairs. Consider: "He *said* the world *is* round." Applying the basic rule of sequence, *is* here would be *was* because the main verb, *said,* is in the past tense. But that would make it sound as if the world no longer were round. (A sentence concerning the roundness of the earth is invariably cited in discussions of sequence of tenses, and it may even be illegal not to do so.)

In the name of common sense, exceptions to the rule are properly made to describe any condition that continues in effect at the time of writing. Here are some examples:

"The surveyor *reported* that the terrain *is* [not *was*] rugged."

"Hoover *pointed* out that there *are* [not *were*] seventy-five to eighty independent government agencies, each of which *consumes* [not *consumed*] the President's time."

"The girl said yesterday she was a virgin." Was then, or said then?

Although the rule applies properly to one sentence at a time, succeeding sentences are often attracted into the past tense, sometimes with preposterous results. Here is an example:

"The chances of Richard Roe, candidate for Congress, *were considered* good. Roe *was* a Catholic from a predominantly Catholic district."

Since Roe's candidacy continued at the time of writing, this gave the unintended impression that he might have changed his religion. Lapses like this, which can be prevented by knowing when to make an exception to the rule, have drawn indignant protests to editors, to say nothing of having confused readers.

For all this, sequence of tenses is still good for a battle royal. One such battle raged for weeks in the bulletin circulated by a press association among its customers. It concerned this sentence:

"Nehru *said* he *would go* before the U.N. tomorrow to seek a vote on Hungarian intervention." Obviously, the disagreement revolved around whether it should have been "Nehru said he *will go*." Although the disputants freely made use of pious appeals to "good grammar," only one of them seemed to have a clear idea of what the grammar of this situation really is.

Who won? Well, nobody did. Considerable spleen, righteous indignation, sarcasm, and the like were vented, but when the smoke had cleared the situation was left, if anything, more confused than before. Now, which is correct—"Nehru said he *would go*" or "Nehru said he *will go*"? Both versions are. But the use of *will* is a modern trend. The rule of sequence, as we have noted, requires the tense in a subordinate clause to correspond with the tense in the main clause. Consequently, the past-tense *said* requires a past-tense *would go*. But several participants in the discussion held that "Nehru said he *will go*" is more direct and thus preferable. They could find some support in a pronouncement by George O. Curme, a grammarian's grammarian. In his *Syntax*, regarded by scholars as a classic, he took note of "a tendency in indirect discourse to break through the old sequence when a more accurate expression suggests itself."

One of the more interesting aspects of the debate was the confusion over the function of *would* in *Nehru said he would*. Several of the disputants mistook it for a subjunctive form indicating uncertainty. They seized on this as affording a wonderful excuse in the event Nehru did not carry out his intention.

A certain type of editor loves to hedge. The reasoning seemed to run like this: Suppose Nehru failed to appear and some reader came roaring in with a complaint that he had been misled. The editor who had used *would* could point it out, saying, "See? We said Nehru *would* appear—not *will*—*would*, that is, unless something prevented him. We're in the clear."

Would in this instance, however, is not a subjunctive form, but simply the past tense of *will*. Of the half-dozen-odd participants in the debate, only one appeared to recognize this. "I *would* if I could" illustrates the subjunctive, indicating a conditional state, but "I said I *would*" illustrates the past indicative, indicating simple intention.

sequoia   See *redwood*.

sergeant   Sometimes misspelled *sargeant* and otherwise as a result of pronunciation (*sarjent*).

serial comma   See *Comma*.

service   As a verb meaning *provide service to,* the expression is well established and in some connections has no convenient synonym, as when we speak of servicing an automobile. Its use is questionable, however, where *serve* will serve, as in "The bus line services the northern suburbs." *serves. Service* also has an agricultural meaning (as a synonym for *breed*), a fact the city-bred are not always aware of, and one that should discourage its indiscriminate use. Readers of John Steinbeck's *The Grapes of Wrath* are not likely to forget this:

> See that sign 'longside the road there? Service Club. Luncheon Tuesday, Colmado Hotel? Welcome, brother. That's a Service Club. Fella had a story. Went to one of them meetings and told the story to all them businessmen. Says, when I was a kid my ol' man gave me a haltered heifer and says take her down an' git her serviced. An' the fella says, I done it, an' ever' time since then when I hear a business man talkin' about service, I wonder who's gettin' screwed.*

sesqui-   Solid as a prefix: *sesquicentennial, sesquipedalian,* etc.

set, sit   *Set* for *sit* is dialectal: "The worst part of it is that his child is setting right there." *sitting.* Sitting is the act of resting on the haunches in a chair, etc.; *setting* is the act (among others) of placing something down. *Set* in this sense requires an object.

* John Steinbeck, *The Grapes of Wrath*. New York: The Viking Press, Inc., 1939. Used by permission.

settlement   Takes *of*, not *to:* "Look for a fast, easy settlement to the steel wage talks." *of*.

Seventh-day Adventist   The denomination prescribes this usage; not -*Day*.

sewage, sewerage   Much is made by the finicky of the distinction that *sewage* is what is carried off, and *sewerage* the system that carries it off, the act of carrying it, or the descriptive applying to either. As a practical matter, however, *sewage* is predominant as both noun and adjective ("The *sewage* is treated in four plants"; "A *sewage* system has been installed"). *Sewerage* is rarely seen as a noun ("The sewerage was faultily designed"); the choice in this sense generally is *sewage system*. *Sewerage* is falling into disuse, but no harm is being done, for the distinction between it and *sewage* serves no useful purpose and, what is more to the point, is little observed.

Shakespeare   This form is so widely used that *Shakspere* and other variants may be considered affectations.

shall, will, should, would   If you paid attention in school, you learned a little formula for the use of these verbs. It went like this: To express the simple future, or let us say to indicate a simple intention, use *shall* with the first person and *will* with the second and third persons.

This gives us "I shall grow old one day" and "You [he, she, it] *will* grow old one day." Plurals follow the same pattern: "We *shall* . . ." but "You [they] *will* . . ."

Then, to express determination, or insistence, the pattern is reversed: "I *will* demand my share, no matter what they say" and "You *shall* obey the law like everyone else."

The mass mind that decides on questions of usage appears to have rejected this method of making the distinction between simple future and determination, however. Even the textbooks, although they carefully recite the formula to stay within the law, are conceding that usage now largely ignores it.

For better or worse, *shall* and *should* have taken on a distinctly flossy overtone, at least in the United States, and few can use them without a twinge of self-consciousness, except in certain circumstances. We mentally note down the person who says, "I shall take the 5:15 home as usual" as putting on the dog, linguistically speaking. Those who insist that they use *shall* not as an affectation but as the unconscious result of careful training can only be insensitive or uncommonly resistant to what they hear all around them.

Shall reportedly is losing face even in England, although it continues to be much more frequently used there than in America, especially on the literary level. The purists among the English lump Scots, Irishmen, and Americans together when they fix the blame for the downfall of *shall*.

"The story is a very old one," writes Sir Ernest Gowers, "of the drowning Scot who was misunderstood by English onlookers and left to his fate because he cried, 'I will drown and nobody shall save me!' " Fowler mentioned the same story, calling it much too good to be true. The time may now have arrived when it is necessary to explain that the Englishmen, construing their grammar strictly, understood the Scot as insisting that he was determined to drown and would allow no one to save him.

Shall, then, seems well on the way to extinction, much like the hapless Scot, except in certain constructions where it is used idiomatically without hesitation; e.g., questions, like "Shall I answer the telephone?" and "Shall we dance?" *Shall* also remains firmly entrenched as a means of expressing compulsion or obligation, especially in legal contexts: "The sum shall be repaid in monthly installments."

To the ignorant, *shall* has a tonier sound than *will*, and this causes them to put it in impossible contexts: "I look forward to the time when delegates like yourselves shall meet in every country of the world." *will*.

Should has fallen under much the same shadow as *shall*. "I should like to attend the premiere" and "If the price fell, I should buy the property" grate on the ears of most Americans as high-toned. *Should* is generally used now only in the sense of *ought to:* "We should put the car in the garage before it rains."

The nice distinctions of determination vs. simple future that once hung on the choice between *shall* and *will* are now made in speaking by the tone of voice and in writing by a choice of words that cannot be misunderstood ("you *must*" rather than "you *shall*").

A curious misquotation of, or perhaps attempt to improve on, Winston Churchill turned up in a television panel discussion in which an Englishman was criticizing American usage. According to this critic, Churchill said, "Give us the tools and we shall finish the job." But what Churchill really said was "Give us the tools and we *will* finish the job."

In announcing the British nation's intention to finish the job of defeating the Nazis, Churchill was giving expression to the determination that carried Britain so far, if not quite so far as he expected at the time. Thus, in strict correctness, he said *will*. Some precisians determinedly keep alive the dying distinction between *shall* and *will* by going overboard with *shall*. They are like the shopgirl who has a hazy idea that *me* and *us* are often misused for *I* and *we*, and then goes too far by saying, with a mistaken notion of elegance, "Don't wait for we girls."

shambles   It is sometimes said that this word may be correctly used only of a slaughterhouse, or, by extension, a scene of carnage. Dictionaries, however, now recognize it also in the sense of *a scene of destruction or wreckage*. The really valid criticism is that newspaper writers and many others like *shambles* too well.

shan't   Correct as a contraction for *shall not* but uncommmon in the U.S.

sharp, sharply   In reference to time, idiom calls for *sharp*, not *sharply: At 7 o'clock sharp.*

shatter   Journalese at its most histrionic, as used in *shatter a production record, shatter a precedent.*

she   In reference to nations, the use of the feminine pronoun is now somewhat quaint. It is subject to exceptions even by those who continue to fancy it, and sometimes suggests absurdities. The growing practice, and the unexceptionable one, is to use *it, its* in such connections. This is true also of references to ships and cities.

shear, sheer   *Shear* means cut off: "The runaway car *sheared* [not *sheered*] a power pole." *Sheer* as a verb is most commonly used in the sense *veer away*: "The wheels hit a rock, and the car sheered away from the cliff."

shekels   Wooden whimsy in reference to money or dollars, but at least it should not be misspelled *shekles,* as so often happens.

shepherd Don't ask why, but in the sheepraising areas of the West the man who tends the flocks is not a *shepherd*, but the comparatively clumsy variant, *sheepherder*. *Shepherd*, for some mysterious reason, seems on the way to becoming literary.

shipshape "Cities like Chicago and Milwaukee plan to spend millions to get their docks in shipshape" may give an old salt a touch of seasickness, for *shipshape* is an adjective, not a noun. *Make their docks shipshape* would be better. Analogy with *in shape* is false.

shop Widely used as a transitive verb; that is to say, one does not shop at, or in, the stores, as of yore; one shops the store itself, or the merchandise. He who is really *au courant* shops the better stores. Those who live far from the madding admen can shop the mail-order catalogs. Yet this use is unlikely in careful prose.

should, would See *shall, will.*

shrouded *Shrouded in fog* (or *secrecy*) is a cliché.

sick, ill The idea that *sick* means only *nauseated*, or *sick at the stomach*, reflects British usage, not the realities of American speech. In the U.S. *sick* and *ill* mean the same thing. *Ill*, however, has a stilted sound, and in an everyday context may seem affected.

sidewipe, sideswipe Some stylebooks prescribe the first form, which, however, has no standing, and represents either a dialectal variant so restricted in scope as not to warrant inclusion in dictionaries, or the effort of certain editors to impose their prejudices on the language.

Sierra Nevada See *Sahara.*

sight, site, cite *Sight* is vision, or something seen; a *site* is a location (*a five-acre building site*); *cite* is a verb meaning to give as an example or charge with an offense. The commonest confusion is *sight* for *site*; it is so unexplainable that taking note of it may sound like invention of a horrible example. But here is an example, and it was not invented: "We have no assurance an on-sight inspecton would succeed." *on-site.*

simian   The journalese variant for *monkey, ape*. See *Variation*.

similar   Means *resembling,* and should not be used in place of the *same* or *identical:* "Rice exports through the first seven months of this year were 20 million pounds greater than during a *similar* [actually, *the same*] period last year." The writer did not mean any seven months last year, but the same seven. In comparing periods of time, *corresponding* is perhaps preferable to *same* and certainly to *similar* or *like*. If two men were accused of skulduggery and one of them were exonerated, it would be inexact to speak of the dismissal of a similar charge. It would be an *identical* charge.
  "The cottages are occupied by children of similar age and sex." Fuzzy, if not ridiculous; "Each cottage is occupied by children of the *same* age and sex."

similar(ly) to   *Like* is preferable to *similar(ly) to* in such constructions as "The oboe has a double reed, similar to the English horn and bassoon." *like*. See also *as, like*.

simple reason   *For the simple reason that* is redundant for *because*. There is usually no occasion to point out the simplicity of a reason when this phrase is used; its effect often is to make the reader feel patronized.

since   It is a delusion that *since* may be used only as an adverb in a temporal sense ("We have been here since ten o'clock"). It is also a conjunction meaning *for* or *because:* "Since it is raining, we had better take an umbrella." See also *as, since*.

-sion   See *-tion, -sion*.

sir   The British title is correctly used only with the full name or the first name, never with the last name alone: *Sir Winston Churchill* or *Sir Winston,* never *Sir Churchill*. The wife of a knight enjoys the designation *Lady* used with the surname (*Lady Churchill*).

situate   See *locate, situate*.

skeptic, sceptic   *Skeptic* is predominantly the American, *sceptic* the British version.

skid road, row   Which is it, *skid row* or *skid road?* This question will have little interest in New York, where it's *the Bowery*. Elsewhere, in a nation increasingly socially conscious, more and more references are being made to the quarter of town where bums, winos, and migrant crop workers forgather, and there is disagreement over what to call it. *Bowery* has spread beyond New York, for that matter. This term is applied in Duluth to the district that is the hangout of waterfront toughs. *Bowery*, incidentally, comes from the name of a street, which in turn comes from *bouwerij*, a Knickerbocker word for *farm*.

Skid road comes from lumbering operations in the Northwest, where logs are slid down a kind of channel made of other logs that have been peeled and sunk in the ground. The connection between such a slide and a resort for derelicts is none too clear. It seems, rather, that the resort should be *skid row* instead of *road*, the *skid* derived from *on the skids* and the *row* from the sense of a street and its buildings, as in *Rotten Row*. Regardless, *skid row* is more prevalent than *skid road*, which is what counts. Dictionaries of slang tend to favor *skid row*, when they do not give both versions.

Herb Caen, when he was writing for the *San Francisco Examiner*, coined the picturesque expression *Skid Rowgue*, which seemed to be a vote for *skid row*. But otherwise he referred to *skid road*, perhaps in deference to the *Examiner's* style. If this is the explanation, it is plain that wit is not always in style.

The Webster files show *skid row* to be commoner in the East, and *skid road* in the West, especially in Los Angeles and Seattle. But in Los Angeles an official city commission on slum clearance even incorporated *skid row* in its name. In Seattle, however, or for that matter the whole states of Washington and Oregon, the use of *skid road* seems to be practically a religion. Its high priest is the author, Stewart Holbrook, who, if he had not gained fame otherwise, might have won it by his incessant and impassioned public endorsements of *skid road*.

Webster cross-references the terms as synonyms, but relates *skid road* to loggers and defines *skid row* in the general sense of a rundown district.

skiing   One word; not *ski-ing*.

slash   See *Overwriting*.

366

slate Undeservedly frowned on in the sense of *schedule*. The verb, in any event, has a legitimate sense of *register on a slate* and does not mean solely *censure* or *reprimand*, as the folklore of stylebooks would have it.

slightly See *rather*.

sloe-eyed Means either "having soft dark bluish or purplish black eyes" (from comparison with the fruit named *sloe*) or "having slanted eyes," according to Webster; take your choice. What is unmistakable is that the expression connotes exotic beauty, despite wrongheaded efforts to link the descriptive with the taste of the fruit (sour).

slough, slew The body of water is *slough* (pronounced *slew*); the verb meaning shed or cast off is *slough* or infrequently *sluff* (both pronounced *sluff*). The verb meaning to skid sideways is *slew* (or *slue*).

slow, slowly *Slow* is equally an adverb and an adjective, so that *go slow* is just as correct as *go slowly*. An Englishman was outraged by a road sign that read DRIVE SLOW. Reacting violently and misguidedly, as people often do when their linguistic prejudices are crossed, he knocked it over. When he was haled before a magistrate for damaging public property, he pleaded that the sign was ungrammatical—it should have read DRIVE SLOWLY. As it happened, the magistrate was enough of a scholar to be able to show him he was all wrong and had the additional pleasure of fining him.

small in size Redundant; omit *in size*. Similar to *large* (*small, many*, or *few*) *in number; rectangular* (etc.) *in shape;* and the like.

smog In its pristine sense, smog was a mixture of smoke and fog. The term originated in the East. What has plagued Los Angeles and other parts of California is not smog in this sense, but a substance generated by the action of sunlight on pollutants in the atmosphere. St. Louis and Pittsburgh had smog, in the true sense. This is offered only as curious linguistic lore, for everyone knows only too well what smog is, and if Los Angeles did not have the original title to the word, it has certainly earned one.

smoky, smokey   The first spelling is widely preferred.

smut, smutty   The presence of these words in a criticism of the decency of a literary or dramatic production almost invariably indicates Comstockery at work. Those of prudish bent have taken these expressions for their own. Others are more likely to say *risqué* (which, to be sure, sounds titillating), *dirty, obscene,* or *pornographic,* as the spirit moves them and the occasion requires.

so   As an intensive, may sound unpracticed or feminine: "It's so hot"; "You're so funny"; "The Western European nations have accomplished so much in the last ten years." So much that what? *So* implies a comparison.

   So as a conjunction should be succeeded by *that:* "The present estimates so completely overlook the precious assets of nutrition, health, and food *that* they must be considered inadequate."

   So at the beginning of a sentence should not be set off by a comma. "So, the event began." See also *Comma after Conjunctions* under *Comma.*

soar   Journalese as a synonym or variant for *rise,* as in "the budget soared," "the temperature soared." See also *Overwriting.*

so . . . as; not so . . . as   See *as . . . as,* etc.

so as to   Verbiage for *to* with the infinitive: "We took the train [so as] to make better time." See also *in order to; for the purpose of.*

so-called   Excessive with an expression that has been placed in quotation marks (the *so-called* "blacklist"). Either *so-called* or the quotation marks will suffice.

social disease   A euphemism for *venereal disease* or for one such disease (syphilis, gonorrhea, etc.). The phrase is growing quaint.

Socialist   See *Communist, Socialist.*

solon   This term, which comes from the name of the Athenian lawgiver, is journalese in the sense of *legislator.* It may be inescapable, and thus grudgingly admissible, in headlines, where *legislator, senator,* or *representative* will not fit, but in text it is to be avoided.

some, -odd With numbers, the words indicate an approximation. They are inept, therefore, with anything but a round number: "Some sixty-nine horsemen" and "Waco is 94-odd miles south of Dallas" have a foolish sound. The naive are inordinately fond of *some* with numbers, and the trouble is that they have been impressed by the word as imparting a certain elegance. It is misleading and thus unsuitable as a device to keep from starting a sentence with a numeral. "The sailors unloaded some ninety-two cases from the ship" sounded to one critic as if some of the cases were unloaded but not all. When any other indication of inexactness is given, as by *about, approximately, estimated,* and the like, either *some* or *-odd* is superfluous.

some, somewhat *Some* for *somewhat* is dialectal and not good English: "The weather warmed up some"; "The wounded Nicaraguan leader was reported to be some better." *somewhat*.

somebody, someone It is superstition that one of these synonyms is preferable to the other; rhythm, however, may control the choice. The same is true of *nobody, no one.* For the number of verbs with these pronouns, see *everybody, everyone.*

some of us Which possessive pronoun is used with *some of us* depends on whether the speaker regards himself as part of the group designated: "Some of us lost *our* heads" is correct if the speaker lost his head and is willing to admit it, but if not, he would properly say "Some of us lost *their* heads."

something, somewhat (of a) Although sometimes sanctioned as interchangeable in such expressions as *somewhat of a coward,* it is noticeable that *something* is preferred in careful writing. The reason may be that *somewhat* as a noun is obsolete and sounds out of place.

some time, sometime, sometimes *Some time* is an adverbial phrase denoting an interval or period: "He stayed *some time* [not *sometime*]." *Sometime* is an adverb indicating an indefinite occasion: "He will come *sometime,* I am sure." *Sometimes* means *occasionally* or *at one time or another:* "Some-

times it rains in the summer in the desert, but very seldom." *Sometimes* is often wrongly joined with another modifier: *a sometimes-fatal disease*. It is unnecessary to indicate, by means of the hyphen, that *sometimes* and *fatal* form a unit modifier; *sometimes*, as an adverb, cannot modify anything but the adjective *fatal*. See also *almost; much*.

Sometime and *sometimes* are archaic as adjectives: "It was his sometime preoccupation"; "the sometimes waste of foreign aid." *occasional*.

somewheres   Not standard; *somewhere*.

son of a gun   An innocuous and once popular expression that has fallen overboard, perhaps since Harry Truman put the presidential seal on another breed of son. It is said that in the days when ladies of easy virtue were brought aboard warships for the diversion of the crews, they were always entertained on the gun deck, and consequent offspring, officially fatherless, came to be referred to as sons of guns. In those days *son of a gun* were fighting words.

sonic wall   The Style Guide of the Aerojet-General Corporation says:

> An example of a misused word that contributed to confusion among both technical men and laymen in recent years was 'the sonic *wall*.' When pilots first approached the speed of sound, they found that aircraft control was difficult and uncertain. The difficulties were first referred to as 'obstacles' to supersonic flight, then as a 'barrier,' and finally as a 'wall.' This last term became so popular with journalists that, after the speed of sound had been exceeded repeatedly, they felt called upon to announce the 'discovery' that there was no 'sonic wall.'

sophisticated   Once upon a time—and not so long ago, either— *sophisticated* was applied only to people. In recent years it has been unsettling to some to see devices and methods frequently characterized by this word: "These are sophisticated chemical reactions"; "Our technology is more sophisticated than theirs." This is not an innovation but merely the introduction of an old and respectable technical sense into everyday contexts.

sort of, kind of (a)   Not considered choice language as adverbs:

sort of cold, kind of stingy. somewhat, rather. In such constructions as "What kind of a dog is that?" and "This is a sort of a celebration" *a* after *of* is unnecessary and not considered good usage.

so . . . that   No comma should be used before *that*: "The car was so badly damaged[,] that it had to be towed away."

sound barrier   See *sonic wall.*

South   As a part of the United States, by common consent (like North, East, West) usually capitalized.

Southland   *Southland,* in California, means *Southern California,* which is practically a separate state, if not an empire. Used in California as a synonym for *the South* (the Ole South, that is), *Southland* will cause either confusion or indignation.

sovereign, -ty   *Sovereignty* is supreme political power, and is enjoyed only by autonomous states; that is to say, nations. The term is often misused by Southern states in efforts to assert their authority against the federal government. No state of the American republic enjoys sovereignty or anything approaching it, despite such presumptuous designations as "the sovereign state of Maryland." "This is an example of how each of the 50 states can be deprived of its sovereignty." Nonsense; they have none to be deprived of.

Spanish   See *Mexican, Spanish.*

spat   A trivial, usually brief, quarrel; the term is generally applied to skirmishes in the war between the sexes. Often inappropriately applied to differences of larger dimensions, as for example an incident in which a man was assaulted to the extent that his attacker was fined $100 and sentenced to 30 days in jail. See also *tiff.*

spearhead   Journalese for *lead, head, direct:* "Dr. Russ will spearhead the studies of alcoholism." Excessive use has blunted its point.

specie, species   *Specie* is coin: "The payment was made with a combination of *specie* and paper money." *Species* is a distinct scientific category of animal or plant: "Monkeys of this *species* are found only near the equator." *Specie* is often given when *species* is meant, but *species* is both singular and plural.

special Overused to confer a specious distinction on an event, act, or occasion: "A special invitation was extended to wives"; "The supervisor made a special presentation of a resolution." The word should not be used unless there is some indication of how the invitation or presentation was special.

Speech Tag See *Attribution.*

speed Properly modified by *high* or *low,* not *slow* or *fast.*

SPELLING Remember the spelling demons back in grammar school? Those were the words some statistical pedagogue had ascertained to be the most troublesome from one grade to the next, and how we were drilled on them! Anyone who has served much time editing knows that writers are beset by their own legion of demons. The most indestructible of them all is *accommodate.* Two *m*'s after two *c*'s seem to be just too much to expect.

But before trotting out the horrible examples, let us muse on some peculiarities. Newspapers dearly love to insist on their own spelling preferences. The press is nearly unanimous in favor of *cigaret* over *cigarette* and *employe* over *employee.* These forms probably are specified because they are the naturalized versions of what were originally foreign words and because they are shorter. Yet the joker is that, although newspapers unquestionably command a wider readership than any other printed medium, they have failed to unhorse *cigarette* and *employee* from favored usage generally.

That absolute tyrant of the language, the public, seems remarkably conservative in its resistance to variant spellings. Brevity and convenience seem to count for nothing; witness the hard sledding of such simplified forms as *tho* and *thru.* Americans, though they are likely to look up to the English as mentors when it comes to language, reject their handily telescoped forms like *spoilt* and *connexion* and *learnt.*

It is apparent that any attempt to influence spelling appreciably in the direction of simplicity is doomed. Periodicals that attempt this are likely to accomplish nothing more than to inconvenience their staffs and make their readers smile. The fact that not one of the *Chicago Tribune*'s millions of readers commented on its virtual abandonment of fonetic (oops) phonetic spelling in 1955, after years of persistence in such oddities as *frate* for *freight* and *sofomore* for *sophomore*, seems to indicate the subscribers thought they were seeing typographical errors all that time.

But large-scale, consistent efforts to simplify spelling are more logical, at any rate, than the random, freakish deviations found in some stylebooks. An example of this is the insistence by one periodical for many years until recently on *hight* for *height*. *Hight* is in the dictionary as a dialectal variant, but its presence there at all stunned every new staff member. Copyreaders delighted in working *hight* into big headlines, where readers took it for a glaring typographical error.

Here's a list of words that seem to give the most trouble: *Accommodate* (not *accomodate*), *accordion* (not *accordian*), *anoint* (not *annoint*), *exorbitant* (not *exhorbitant*), *existence* (not *existance*), *fictitious* (not *ficticious*), *fluorescent* (not *flourescent;* the word comes from *fluorine*, not *flour*) ; *inoculate* (not *innoculate*), *liquefy* (not *liquify*), *marshal* (not *marshall;* there is no such word), *nickel* (not *nickle*), *objet d'art* (not *object d'art*, if you must show off your French), *Philippines* (not *Phillipines*), *rarefy* (not *rarify*), *resistance* (not *resistence*), *restaurateur* (not *restauranteur*), *skulduggery* (not *skullduggery;* the word is an American version of the English *sculduddery* and apparently is not related to *skull*, for its origin is said to be obscure), *violoncello* (not *violincello*, though the long form is disappearing in favor of *cello*).

Rules for spelling English are so complicated and beset by exceptions that it is easier to learn to spell the words than to master general principles. There is, however, one familiar and useful rule:

> *i* before *e*
> Except after *c*
> Or when sounded like *a*
> As in *neighbor* or *weigh*.

Some exceptions: *either, neither, inveigle, seize.*

British Preferences British preferences in spelling are conspicuous when used in America, and the writer who favors them may be suspected of affectation. British preference is for *ou* in certain words where American usage calls for *o*: *behaviour, labour,* for *behavior, labor*. Other such words: *ardour, clamour, colour, dolour, favour, honour, mould, moult, odour, smoulder, splendour, valour, vapour, vigour.* Note, however, that *glamour* is preferred to *glamor* in both Britain and America. Other British preferences:

ce is used where Americans use *se: defence, offence, pretence.*

ss is used where Americans use *s: biassed.*

A terminal *e* is used where Americans drop it: *axe.*

que is used where Americans prefer *ck: cheque.*

xion is used where Americans prefer *ction: connexion, inflexion, reflexion.*

oe is used where Americans prefer *e: homoeopathy, oecumenical, oesophagus.*

ough is used where Americans prefer *ow: plough.*

s is used where Americans prefer *c: practise.*

e is used where Americans prefer *a: grey.*

y is used where Americans prefer *a: pyjamas.*

ise is used where Americans prefer *ize: apologise, capitalise, focalise, visualise.*

dge is used where Americans prefer *dg: abridgement, acknowledgement, fledgeling, judgement.*

re is used where Americans prefer *er: accoutrements, centre, fibre, lustre, metre, sabre, sceptre, spectre, theatre.*

ae is used where Americans prefer *e: aeon, aesthetic, aestivate, anaemia, encyclopaedia.*

ll is used where Americans prefer *l: apparelled, councillor, counsellor, empanelled, jeweller, quarrelled.*

l is used where Americans prefer *ll: dulness, enrol, fulfil, instal, skilful, wilful.*

Spelling as Humor

In his preface to *A Subtreasury of American Humor*, E. B. White transfixed a foible that he noted particularly, he said, in the humorous writing of fifty to one hundred years ago. It is still to be seen in print today, however, particularly in comic strips and stuff of the folksy or old-home-town persuasion.

Mr. White wrote,

It occurred to me that a certain basic confusion often exists in the use of tricky or quaint or illiterate spelling to achieve a humorous effect. For instance, here are some spellings from the works of Petroleum V. Nasby: he spells 'would' *wood,* 'of' *uv,* 'you' *yoo,* 'hence' *hentz,* 'office' *offis.* Now, it happens that I pronounce 'office' *offis.* And I pronounce 'hence' *hentz,* and I even pronounce 'of' *uv* . . .

the queer spelling is unnecessary, since the pronunciation is impossible to distinguish from the natural or ordinary pronunciation. . . .*

He had something there. Not only is such spelling pointless as humor when spoken words, rather than written misspellings (e.g., *Dere Mable*), are being represented, but it may strike many readers as simpleminded.

Variant Spellings Until recently, the first entry in the dictionary (if the versions appeared side by side) or the one under which the definition was given (if they were separated) was considered the preferred spelling. Webster's Third Edition, however, departs from the practice of indicating a preference. Variant spellings are generally set in alphabetical order; all versions given without a qualifying label are regarded as standard. If the variants are not in alphabetical order, the first is "slightly more common." This general principle is being followed by other new dictionaries.

The choice among variant spellings, then, is a matter of taste, not correctness. Publications often govern the choice by rule, so that their content will not show an inconsistency that might distract the reader or give the impression of inattention to mechanical details. For the same reason, writers do well to practice such consistency.

Misspellings It is easy to collect lists of misspelled words. Many such have been made for special purposes; for example, to single out the words most commonly misspelled by students at various grade levels, as noted above. The misspellings dealt with in this book are those that appear frequently in print.

Thorstein Veblen fairly described English spelling and at the same time offered the reason for overcoming its difficulties: "It is archaic, cumbrous, and ineffective; its acquisition consumes much time and effort; failure to acquire it is easy of detection."

SPLIT INFINITIVE See *Infinitives*.

SPLIT-VERB CONSTRUCTIONS See *Compound Verbs*.

spokesman A spokesman is one who speaks on behalf of others. The writer who told of "a fluent *spokesman* of idiomatic English" meant "a fluent *speaker*."

* By permission; copyright 1941, E. B. White and Katharine S. White.

sport   As a verb, *sport* is appropriate only of something that would be displayed or flaunted; a man might sport a moustache, or a red necktie, but hardly thick-lensed glasses, as a magazine reported. He who sports something exhibits it jauntily. *Sport* as a verb, in any event, is overused in newswriting.

sporting   As an adjective in the sense of *pertaining to sports, sporting* is now quaint. *Sporting editor* is redolent of a generation that is gone; the sporting editor's successor is the sports editor. *Sporting* in the sense of *sports* may prompt a snicker because it suggests the sense of *sporting house.* That term, however, is also an anachronism. Yet all this does not impugn such expressions as *a sporting proposition.* And *sporting goods* survives without a shadow.

SPORTSWRITING   Is there anything to the assumptions that sportswriting is more creative than other kinds of newswriting and that the sports page has been the launching pad for numerous literary rockets? One cynic said nothing more is needed to demolish this idea than to lay a number of sports stories beside other kinds of news stories, all selected at random, and compare them for evidences of creativity. It is true that sportswriters generally enjoy more latitude in choice of language, and in exhibiting individuality, if any, in their work. What use do they make of this latitude? We have two opinions, separated by more than thirty years. One of them was expressed by H. W. Fowler in *Modern English Usage* in 1926 under the heading *sobriquets:*

> . . . games and contests are exciting to take part in, interesting or even exciting also to watch, but essentially (i.e. as bare facts) dull to read about, insomuch that most intelligent people abandon such reading; the reporter, conscious that his matter & his audience are both dull enough to require enlivening, thinks that the needful fillip may be given if he calls fishing the gentle craft, a ball the pill or the leather, a captain the skipper, or a saddle the pigskin, & so makes his description a series of momentary puzzles that shall pleasantly titillate inactive minds.

The following comments were made by Bergen and Cornelia Evans in *A Dictionary of Contemporary American Usage,* under the heading "sports English":

> Because it deals with struggle, sports writing is required to be vigorous, and because it scorns formality it

must be slangy and colloquial. But slang is particularly unfitted for frequent repetition and sports writing is, above any other type of contemporary writing, repetitious, laden with clichés. The wretched sports writer, with slight material and often (one suspects) even slighter interest, is compelled to assume concern he does not feel and to conceal his yawns under forced shouts of excitement. . . . No one, apparently, using only the normal resources of the richest language known, can make sports interesting. . . .

A legend has grown up that the sports pages have produced an immense number of writers who have gone on to literary triumphs. But as Nunnally Johnson asked, after Lardner, Broun, Kieran, Pegler, Gallico, Reynolds, and Considine, who is there? Johnson's characterization of sports writing is not flattering. "Bad writing, grammar-school humor, foolish styles, threadbare phrases, spurious enthusiasm and heavy-footed comedy . . . nauseating sentimentality and agonizing slang . . . [and] above all, breeziness, breeziness, breeziness!"

sprawling The greatest love affair of all time is not that between Romeo and Juliet, nor that between Abélard and Héloïse, but between reporters and this word, as used to describe an extensive building.

sprightly, spritely *Spritely* appears in the dictionary as an archaic variant of *sprightly;* it is thus out of place in a modern context. "A collection of spritely verse." *sprightly*. The adverb is *sprightlily;* a clumsy word, to be sure, and seldom used.

square Should be carefully placed in dealing with dimensions or areas. *Twelve miles square* means a square twelve miles on a side, or 144 square miles; *twelve square miles* is what it says.

stabilize Often a euphemism as applied to prices; stabilization in this connection is not necessarily aimed at keeping prices steady (the true meaning), nor at preventing them from rising, but at keeping them from going down.

stage Survives in the West as the name for the vehicle that is called a bus elsewhere. It is applied only to vehicles in interurban service. Even the California Public Utilities Commission employs the term *stage lines* in reference to bus lines in its official documents.

As a verb, *stage* is journalese for *present, exhibit, offer, put on, perform.* There is a tendency to discourage its use except in reference to performances that are given on a stage, and this appears to be the most acceptable sense. *Stage a comeback* is a cliché. *Stage* as a verb in the senses under discussion here is so worn that it might as well be avoided.

stake out, stakeout   These terms, referring to surveillance of a place or area, continue to be police argot to the extent that their use is discouraged in well-edited publications intended for a general audience.

stalk   Outworn in connection with death personified, as "Death stalked the highways," which is warmed over and served up after every holiday.

stalling for time   Redundant. Stalling is inevitably for time.

state   Implies a formality inappropriate to its usual use in attribution. Not a casual synonym for *say*.

STATE DESCRIPTIVES   The official forms of reference for residents of states are Alabamian, Alaskan, Arizonian, Arkansan, Californian, Coloradan, Connecticuter, Delawarean, Floridian, Georgian, Hawaiian, Idahoan, Illinoisan, Indianian, Iowan, Kansan, Kentuckian, Louisianian, Mainer, Marylander, Massachusettsan, Michiganite, Minnesotan, Mississippian, Missourian, Montanan, Nebraskan, Nevadan, New Hampshirite, New Jerseyite, New Mexican, New Yorker, North Carolinian, North Dakotan, Ohioan, Oklahoman, Oregonian, Pennsylvanian, Rhode Islander, South Carolinian, South Dakotan, Tennessean, Texan, Utahan, Vermonter, Virginian, Washingtonian, West Virginian, Wisconsinite and Wyomingite. (Webster, however, also sanctions Alabaman, Arizonan, Arkansian, Floridan, and Louisianan.)

stationary, stationery   *Stationary* is the adjective that means *standing still* or *in a fixed position;* a stationary engine is mounted. *Stationery* is the noun that means *writing paper.*

statuesque   Excessively used to describe beauties of larger-than-average size.

statutory charge, offense   Euphemisms now less used than at one time for charges or offenses relating to sex, such as rape, sodomy, and incest. The expressions are carefully nondistinctive in themselves, for all crimes are defined in statutes of one kind or another. The result of using *statutory* only in connection with sex crimes is that the expression comes to be taken as applicable only to such crimes.

steam shovel   A number of stylebooks solemnly enjoin something like this: "Don't write *steam shovel*. The steam shovel is obsolete. Make it *power shovel*." But *steam shovel* has gone into the language, and thus serves a purpose even if most mechanical shovels are no longer run by steam. Steam is out of style for steamrollers too, and next we can expect someone to insist that legislation which fits the description is power-rollered, rather than steamrollered, through.

  Lead pencil is even more of an anachronism than *steam shovel,* because probably no one can remember when lead really was used in pencils, rather than graphite. What about *cable?* No effort is made to distinguish between messages actually sent by cable and those sent by radio. Any such effort would, of course, be ridiculous. Since *steamroller, lead pencil,* and *cable* have escaped the wrath of style dictators, it seems only fair that *steam shovel* should be excused too.

sterling   As applied to silver, sometimes regarded as meaning *pure,* but this is not quite right. It means 92.5 per cent pure (silver), or a little less so than Ivory soap.

still   As an adverb, should not be joined to a succeeding adjective with a hyphen: *the still-effervescent stock market. still effervescent.*

still and all   See *well and good.*

still continue, still remain   Redundant for *continue, remain.*

stink   The ordinary past form is *stunk; stank* is literary or facetious or, perhaps, euphemistic.

stomach   See *abdomen.*

stomp   Until recent years, *stomp* was the name of a dance, or a dialectal variant of *stamp.* Now the press no longer remembers that *stamp* exists, and everything is *stomped.*

stone   See *rock, stone*.

stormy petrel   This, once a numerous species, appears to be extinct as a metaphor. Too bad. One could imagine them angrily dipping and screaming in the troughs of the waves that bring the tempest. Is it possible that Gen. Billy Mitchell was the last of the stormy petrels? Latter-day petrels seem less stormy than petulant.

straightened, straitened   *Straitened* means squeezed: "A man may get into financial straits, in which case we say he is in straitened circumstances." *Straightened*, on the other hand, means *stretched out*, or, by extension, *set in order*. A man may get things straightened so that he no longer is straitened.

straightforward   One word; not *straight-forward* (or *strait-forward*.)

strategy, tactics   Technically, strategy is the overall plan, and tactics the specific means by which it is carried out. But the terms are often loosely interchanged in casual use, with no loss, especially when there are not two levels of activity, nor any occasion to distinguish them.

stratum, strata   *Stratum* is one of the handful of words that retain their Latin plural forms; the plural is preferably *strata*, though sometimes *stratums*.

streamline, -d   Interchangeable as adjectives: a *streamline* (*streamlined*) *train. Streamlined*, however, seems predominant.

stress   Often loosely used in attribution, simply for variation, when there is no actual emphasis. See *Attribution*.

stricture   In the physical sense, a stricture is a contraction or narrowing, as in a tube; in the nonmaterial sense, it is censure or adverse criticism.

student   See *pupil*.

stunning   Has become a counterword of high approval, especially in music reviews, but also in other kinds of criticism.

380

style   There are two fairly distinct though often confused applications of the word in literary connections. The commonest relates to a manner of expression, as would be described by *an informal style, an elegant style, a polished style,* etc. This is the style of which Buffon said it is the man. The other sense is quite different, relating to a code of mechanical practice governing such details as capitalization, abbreviation, and spelling (insofar as there are reputable choices). Many publications compile stylebooks to ensure consistency in such matters. The word *style* in the title of this book refers to both concepts at one time and another.

STYLEBOOKS   Are stylebooks here to stay? Not necessarily, a perfunctory survey indicates. The shocking fact is that some exceedingly well-edited journals get along without them. In any event, the apparent necessity for a uniform code to govern details of capitalization, spelling, and other mechanical matters on which opinions differ is surely one of the curses of the publications field, especially when the stylemongers grow drunk with the power that corrupts. (This article deals with internal stylebooks of newspapers, not published authorities.)

Meditation and prayer lead to the conviction that the best style is the one which governs least. As far as readers are concerned, even the uneducated among them encounter a great variety of practices in what little they read. The variety is so much greater for the educated that inconsistencies of editorial details even within a given publication are likely to pass unnoticed. But in the editing of newspapers we have, among lesser deviations, the Up Style and the Down Style. To a varying extent, from one publication to another, there is what might be denominated the Upside-Down Style. This shows itself in "grammatical" rules that have no basis in grammar, in random off-base spellings and hyphenations, and in weird but prescribed syntactical constructions.

Publications that enforce rules having no standing in accepted practice, either journalistic or linguistic, are setting up obstacle courses for their staffs. On some style-crazy newspapers, it is necessary to take wire stories apart and carpenter them into an unnatural shape to satisfy some such rule. This situation is analogous to that in a washing-machine plant where bolts and nuts would have to be rethreaded, for some mysterious but useless reason, before the machines could be assembled. Such nonsense only adds to the difficulty of the job without affecting the quality of the product.

It is observable that a publication can be far gone in style-craziness and still exhibit no intelligent or effective control over what really counts: excising of clichés, fining down of fuzzy expressions, squeezing the water out of redundancies, and tightening of construction. Indeed, there may well be a high correlation between style-craziness and poor editing in general. The forest is lost sight of in picking through the leaves, and a pathetic and hopeless reliance is placed on special rules to do a job that can be accomplished only by the continuous application of good judgment.

The attention that stylebooks give to grammar and usage could be all to the good, but many of them also serve to keep alive countless superstitions of usage, all too often peculiar to newswriting. Some favorite stylebook rules were, indeed, once grammar; others never were. Some of them have not enjoyed any reputability among the discerning for the last generation or two.

One such stylebook, used by a newspaper requiring rigid conformity to a farrago of absurd rules, many of them invented by its editor of seventy-five years ago, encourages writers to cultivate "snap and ginger" in their prose. The objective is fine, but how sadly that choice of language dates the thinking behind the book!

Style that goes beyond general principles enabling writers and editors to do their work expeditiously only gratifies someone's idiosyncrasies.

Let us consider some more practical aspects of this question. The stylebook of the *Los Angeles Times* leaves the left-hand pages blank for notes and addenda, and runs the text only on the right-hand pages. The usual practice, if any blanks are left at all, is to put them at the end of the book. The advantage of interspersing them should be obvious: Notes can easily be placed opposite the stuff they apply to and are more likely to be entered and referred to. It's also a good idea for a stylebook to be loose leaf, like that of the *Chicago Tribune,* and to possess an exhaustive index, or better yet, to be organized alphabetically on a dictionary plan.

Such memoranda as are necessary to supplement the stylebook should not merely be issued in loose sheets. In this form they are quickly mislaid, disregarded, and forgotten. They should be issued in such a form as to facilitate inclusion in an alphabetical file, perhaps on arch boards or in card-file boxes. One such file should be maintained at the copy desk, and at least one more at some central point in the city room. This supplemental material should be incorporated in the stylebook as it is revised. If a particular dictionary is designated as a publication's stylistic authority, it is well to forgo arbitrary exceptions to its advice. Short-circuiting the dictionary with special spellings, hyphenations, and the like only overloads the stylebook and sets up pointless artificial hazards to the process of editing.

sub- Set solid as a prefix: *subaudible, subarid, subhuman, subtotal,* etc.

subfreezing See *freezing, subfreezing.*

SUBHEADS By common consent, it is desirable to let air into long columns of type by using one typographical device or another. The most popular of these is the subhead, usually set in the bold or bold caps version of the body face. Stars or asterisks are sometimes used. We are concerned here primarily not with considerations of design but, as usual, with what affects expression.

Copy editors know that subheads are intended to open up the column, and thus tend to regard them entirely as mechanical devices. Consequently they often pay little attention to whether the subheads say anything worth saying. Readers, however, look for meaning in subheads, and when they find little or none may be justly annoyed.

Some newspapers require that a subhead be based upon the paragraph immediately beneath. There is no good reason why a subhead should not summarize all of what appears beneath it, if this is feasible. But it is not advisable to base the subhead on some fact near the bottom, which may be dropped or lost in make-up.

Newspapers, because of their peculiarities of format, are often torn between considerations of sense and of appearance. The flush-left headline was a great leap forward because it facilitated a compromise between such considerations.

The conflict of sense and looks also affects subheads. For the sake of appearances, the practice is to insert subheads at regular intervals, usually every three or four paragraphs. But this arbitrary spacing often causes a subhead to illogically interrupt a smoothly running account. The intelligent copy editor takes sense and sequence into consideration in the placement of subheads.

The most arrant offense against logic in the sense of subheads, however, consists of placing the subhead or other separating devices, such as stars or asterisks, between a colon and what follows, like this:

"In telling the world what we were doing in the space race, the United States has been forced to admit:
SPACE PROJECTS STRUCK
" 'Nothing much. Our space workers are on strike.' "

SUBJECT-VERB AGREEMENT "Many a company is unable to obtain funds to put in the new plant and equipment that *is* [correctly, *are*] necessary." *Plant and equipment* add up to a compound and thus plural subject. Inattentiveness is usually the cause of such errors.

Pronouns referring to compound subjects should be plural: "I see the unrest and turmoil that hold the world in its grip." *their grip.* Two singular subjects joined by *or* take a singular verb: "An increase or a decrease is [not *are*] no better."

"Less clear is [correctly, *are*] the politics of defense spending and the pressures generated in Congress." Inattentiveness again: the subject is the sum of *politics* plus *pressures.* See also *together with; with; Collectives; what.*

subliminal This word, as used to describe advertising flashed on a screen so quickly the watchers don't consciously perceive it, often is printed *sublimal.* This is going from the subliminal to the pediculous as far as spelling is concerned.

subpoena Although *subpena* is also correct, *subpoena* predominates, defying the tendency to abandon digraphs like *ae, oe* (which see).

subsequently Pretentious for *later; subsequent to* (for *after*) is the evil twin of *prior to* (which see).

such Possible as a pronoun, but some such uses jar the ear. The Bible says "the father of *such* as dwell in tents" and "Suffer little children to come unto me, and forbid them not, for of *such* is the kingdom of God." This usage is still current, though it has a faintly archaic flavor.

The examples that follow are conspicuously unidiomatic or at least awkward: "Dues are used for political purposes, but a dissenting member or minority group is without protection against such." *this* or *such practice.* "As long as stores sell toys that encourage violence, and parents place such in children's hands . . ." *them,* or *toys of this kind.* "The government will grant asylum to members of the crew who solicit such." *it.*

It is difficult to say just why some uses of *such* as a pronoun are acceptable while others stick in the craw. Fowler high-handedly solved the problem by citing objectionable ones and terming them illiteracies.

Such as an intensive is feminine: "We had such a good time."

such as Should not be followed by a comma: *musical instruments, such as*[,] *French horns, flutes, and clarinets. Like* is often more comfortable than *such as:* "Sudden and totally unexpected upheavals such as that in Guatemala." *like.*

such stuff as dreams . . . See *Misquotation.*

suddenly There is frequent discouragement against applying *suddenly* to death on the curious ground that death is always sudden. Not so; it often approaches by obvious degrees. The meaning of *suddenly* in this context is *unexpectedly,* and when the occasion requires, there is no reason why *suddenly* should not be used. All dictionaries define *sudden* as *unexpected* (and some of them vice versa). Webster and the *Standard College Dictionary* both also have *sudden death* entries equating *sudden* in this connection with *unexpected.* This is not to say that the expressions cannot have somewhat different connotations; *unexpected* has some that *sudden* does not. *Webster's Dictionary of Synonyms* says *sudden* is distinguished from *unexpected* only by "added implications of extreme hastiness or impetuosity."

suddenly collapsed Redundant. Suddenness is the essence of collapse, unless the word is otherwise qualified (*collapsed by degrees*).

suffer, sustain, receive Properly speaking, people suffer *injuries,* and such wording as "The driver *suffered* a broken leg" is frowned on by some critics because they think it means, in effect, that the driver suffered a leg. Such criticism has dubious foundation, for the writer said *broken leg,* i.e., *the breaking of a leg,* and that is how all but the captious will read it. "The driver *received* a broken leg" offers no refuge from these critics, who have been known to respond to such intelligence with "How? By parcel post?" In any event, such sentences seem open to improvement: "The driver's leg *was broken.*" There is no good reason why one should not write "The driver *suffered* [or *received*] a fracture of the leg," however. See also *break, broke,* and *had.*

It is sometimes held by those who have never looked up the word that *sustain* means only *hold up.* It is a proper synonym for *suffer* or *undergo.*

sufficient(ly) May sound pretentious when *enough* will do, as in place of *a sufficient amount.*

SUFFIXES Suffixes are entered in their alphabetical places in this book together with information on whether they are hyphenated. See also *Hyphen.*

suffocate Cannot be relied on by itself to indicate fatality. *Suffocated to death* may sound like a redundancy, and indeed it is, in view of one meaning of *suffocate.* But another meaning is merely *to stifle* or *choke. Suffocate* in its fatal sense, then, should be used only in contexts that indicate a fatal result.

suggest It is a common affectation, especially among those who shy away from direct statement, to use *suggest* instead of *say.* " 'The dam would not have great enough capacity,' he suggested." A suggestion is tentative; *suggest* is not suitable for a declarative statement like the example.

"The regulatory agencies, the commissioner suggested, are manned by ordinary men who yield too quickly to pressures." *said.*

"He suggested that the supposed difficulties will be nonexistent in actual practice." *predicted.*

"I would like to suggest my views on the Metropolitan Transit Authority and its proposal to tax property-owners." *offer, present, give.*

suggestive(ly) So preponderantly used in the sense of *indecent(ly)* that he who wants merely the simple meaning of *giving a suggestion* had better beware of ambiguity or unconscious humor. "Why doesn't someone write a book suggestively entitled 'The Greatest Photographs'?" This is not a flagrant example, but the reader may complain, what would be suggestive about that?

suicide Slangy as a verb: "The prisoner suicided in his cell." *committed suicide.*

suit, suite   *Suit* for *suite* (*a suite of rooms, a musical suite*—pronounced *sweet*) is ignorant.

SUMS OF MONEY   Logically considered singular, not plural: "The delinquency was $56 million, of which $44 million were owed by the Communist bloc." *was owed.* The writer was misled by the plurality of *$44 million,* but a sum is properly regarded as a unit.

Redundancy is often created by the designations *cents* and *dollars* when the units already have been indicated: *$.22 cents; $5 million dollars. Cents* is redundant by virtue of the dollar-sign and the decimal point; *dollars* is redundant by virtue of the dollar-sign. Correct: *$.22, 22¢, or 22 cents; $5 million* or *5 million dollars.*

There is no good reason to write *$30.00* rather than *$30;* the extra characters only increase the chance of error. See also *Numbers.*

super   Solid as a prefix: *supercargo, supercharge, superhighway,* etc.

supersede   Often misspelled *supercede.*

supply   See *furnish.*

suppose to, supposed to   The second is the correct form. "We were suppose to fall in a half hour before the signal sounded." *supposed.*

supra-   Solid as a prefix: *supraliminal, suprarenal,* etc. But usually hyphenated when followed by *a: supra-abdominal.*

sure   See *real, sure.*

survive   See *Obituaries.*

survival of the fittest   This phrase and concept were originated not by Charles Darwin, to whom they are generally attributed, but by Herbert Spencer, from whom Darwin took them up, not omitting to credit him.

suspect, suspicion   *Suspect* is either verb or noun; *suspicion* is only a noun. *Suspicion* for *suspect* is substandard: "Police suspicioned the vagrant." *suspected.*

suspected   Injustice is done by referring to a person accused of being a spy, for example, as a *suspected* (or *accused*, or *alleged*) spy. The implication is that the person *is* a spy, and not simply accused of being one. See also *allege, -d, -dly*.

SUSPENSIVE MODIFIERS   See *Commas*.

sustain   See *suffer, sustain, receive*.

swam, swum   *Swam* is the preferred form for the past tense: *We swam daily*.

swing into high gear   As a figure of speech, this expression unmistakably shows its age.

—T—

tabloid   See *Newspaper Terms*.

take   See *bring, take*.

take a fling   "After studying speech at Wesleyan, she spent a brief but futile fling at the footlights in New York." Idiom calls for *took a fling*.

take delivery on   A mercantile pomposity for *receive, be delivered*.

take it easy   An idiom; not *take it easily*, which is mistaken overcorrectness.

take off   There can be no reasonable objection to extending this term beyond its primary sense relating to aircraft, but it is overworked in place of *leave, depart*, and in addition has a slangy flavor. That, however, may be what its users want.

take place, occur   See *occur, take place*.

tar   Some sailors on liberty once got into trouble with the police, and the headline on the resulting story referred to them as *tars*. Now, as it happened, they were Negroes, and a delegation from the local Negro community shortly appeared in the editor's office, demanding an apology for what they considered an unnecessary racial slur. They got it, too. But although *tar* and *tarbrush* sometimes have a racial connotation, it does not figure in the use of *tar* for *sailor*. The expression is variously described as a shortened form of *tarpaulin* and as a reference to the tar sailors once smeared on their pigtails. See also *Negro*.

taunt, taut   *Taunt* means *jeer at* or *tease:* "The losing team was *taunted* by the students." *Taut* means *stretched tight:* "The clothesline was not *taut* enough." *Taunt* is often misused for *taut*.

A strange confusion is possible in references to ships. In the Navy and otherwise, the common expression *a taut ship* refers to one that is well disciplined, in good order. Sometimes the phrase *a taunt ship* is regarded as an error, but it has a different sense, i.e., tall-masted. The origin is unknown, and since masts are obsolescent, so is the expression.

taxpayer   One word; not *tax payer* or *tax-payer*.

Tchaikovsky, Tschaikovsky, Tschaikowsky   There is no right or wrong here, for the differences are matters of opinion in transliteration from the Cyrillic alphabet used for Russian. In modern practice, however, there is a nearly unanimous tendency to settle on the first version. The other two are likely to be found in older writings.

technic, technique   Though these forms are interchangeable, *technique* has a long running start. In any event, the word is always pronounced tek*neek*. *Technic* may as well be abandoned.

TECHNICAL TERMS   In everyday communication, should we use technical terms that are not common currency in preference to readily understandable substitutes? Experts on readability would probably say no. Nevertheless, the use of technical language, or of the cant belonging to a specialized field, is a temptation to those who think it will make their stuff sound learned and impressive.

The use of technical terms is hard to avoid in writing that deals with advances in physics, medicine, and the other sciences, and often no satisfactory synonyms are available in plain language. The writer who keeps his audience in mind, however, will be careful to follow the unfamiliar technical

389

terms he must use with definitions in as simple language as possible.

Science writing, a special case, is usually handled by writers who make it a specialty and have no need to be warned of such pitfalls. But what about writing that deals with such everyday subjects as automobile accidents? These accounts often abound with *contusions, abrasions, lacerations, fractures,* and other terms redolent of the hospital. Everybody knows, of course, that a fracture is a break, although that's not what everybody ordinarily says. Lacerations are cuts, for practical purposes, although the doctor may mean something more complex by this expression. It is doubtful that *contusions* presents any clear picture to the layman. What's wrong with *bruises* instead of *contusions, cuts* instead of *lacerations,* and *sewing* instead of *suturing?* This much is certain: although many readers may know what some medical terms mean, there are many more who do not.

Hemorrhage is certainly inexcusable for *bleed* in anything but a medical journal. *Coronary occlusion, carcinoma, thrombosis,* and *first-, second-,* and *third-degree burns* all require translation for the ordinary reader.

Some writers, having learned the meaning of some technical terms, are so proud of themselves they cannot resist showing off. Others never bother to find anything out, and lazily relay what has been given them by scientists. It is a good principle not to send the reader to the dictionary, but to send the writer there instead. Let the reader relax.

In one city, an outbreak of sleeping sickness (encephalitis) was attributed to the *culex tarsalis* mosquito. Newspaper stories on the subject, which caused considerable public alarm, ran for weeks before anyone thought of describing *culex tarsalis* and its habits, and giving some idea how common this variety was among the dozen or so in the area.

In another instance, the term *low low water line* was used again and again in connection with an important waterfront project. Yet no one but seafarers knew what that line was, and the newspapers failed to give any help to the others. See also *Overwriting.*

teen-age   The word and its derivatives (*teen-ager, teen-aged*) are properly hyphenated.

telecast, televise   The technical distinction that *telecast* means to broadcast by television and *televise* to record by television apparatus and then to broadcast may be useful to those in the field, but they are the only ones aware of it.

temblor The correct and usual form of the noun that means *earthquake;* although *tembler* is considered acceptable, it is likely to be taken for an error. Often misrendered *tremblor.* The analogy with *tremble* is correct but the spelling is not.

tempo Has to do with rate of speed or rhythm; its commonest application is in music. Often used ineptly: "The Berlin crisis will mount in tempo." Obviously the writer did not really mean that the crisis will grow faster. A rule of thumb is that *tempo* suitably applies to what is in motion.

tenable, tenet, untenable To start with, a tenet is something one holds to—a principle, doctrine, or belief. What is tenable, then, is something that can be held—abstractly, such as a doctrine, or physically, such as a battle line. What is untenable cannot be held. "Under such circumstances, living as a hermit is untenable." Unacceptable, undesirable, impossible, perhaps, but not untenable. (*Tenable* also has the sense *habitable,* but that does not figure in the confusion dealt with here.) *Tenet* is often mispronounced and thus sometimes misspelled *tenent,* perhaps by confusion with *tenant.*

TENSES See *Sequence of Tenses; Pictures; Time Elements; Participles.*

tenterhooks These are hooks on which curtains are stretched, and the term was once applied to hooks from which poultry was hung in a shop. The word is now usually used figuratively in the phrase *on tenterhooks,* meaning *in suspense,* and sometimes misrendered *on tender hooks.*

term as See *consider.*

than, than whom *Than* is now standard as a preposition, in addition to being a conjunction; consequently, such sentences as "He is taller than me" are correct. So is *than I. Than whom* has always been considered a correct form ("An architect than whom none is more reputable") though the construction is clumsy.

than is, than are See *as is, as are.*

thanking you in advance Oddly, more than one critic of language considers this rude or inconsiderate, on the ground that the writer is attempting to escape expressing appreciation at the proper time; that is, after the favor is done. They miss the point; those who thank in advance are, if anything, overcourteous. They hope that the expression will grease the way. It could be interpreted as presumptuous, but nobody does so. The phrase is, however, overeager and perhaps sophomoric.

that Although almost any stylebook you pick up will contain the admonition to leave out *that* as a conjunction ("He said *that* he was starving") when possible, it's actually good advice, in contrast to many stylebook dicta, which are likely to be (a) Victorian purism, (b) superstition, (c) prescriptions for decapitation as a cure for dandruff, or (d) nonsense.

Often, however, we encounter instances when essential *thats* have been omitted; they have been left out not only when possible, but also when impossible. That's the big trouble with rules, even good ones. We tend to clutch them like a life preserver and jump overboard.

The question of where *that* is called for and where it is not yields only to the capricious reign of idiom. Idiom is something that must be felt. *That* should be retained, in any event, to mark the beginning of a subordinate clause when a part of the clause otherwise may be wrongly associated with some part of the main clause. Often a time element will cause confusion if *that* is left out.

"Metzman said on Jan. 1 the fleet stood at 1,776,000 cars." The speaker was citing the size of the fleet on Jan. 1, but it is an open question, without a *that* after *said,* whether Jan. 1 was not the date on which he made the statement.

"The speaker said last November the outlook improved." This is another example of the same problem. *That* is needed after either *said* or *November,* depending on what the time element is intended to modify. It may be argued that the context is likely to supply the answer to this question, but the reader deserves to be spared even momentary doubt.

Sometimes the omission of *that* sends the reader off on the wrong scent as to the force of the verb: "He added the proposed freeway could follow the existing route." "He added *that* . . ." would read unequivocally, but the first version may appear, for the moment, to make *freeway* alone the object of *added.*

At least one *that,* and preferably a pair of them, should be used with coordinate clauses: "The deputy foreign minister said last night that Panama does not receive its fair share of Panama Canal revenues, and sentiment for a 50 per cent increase is likely to grow." Now, who is to say whether the words about growing sentiment for a 50 per cent increase were a part of the deputy foreign minister's statement, or an observation by the writer? The sentence should have read ". . . and *that* sentiment . . ."

The first *that* of a pair like this is sometimes dropped, perhaps out of the general eagerness to dispense with the word: "The board was told the point is really one of economics, and that if the ordinance were repealed, meat markets would be driven out of business." On the whole, however, the two clauses are more clearly balanced if both are set off by *that* (". . . was told *that* the point . . . and *that* . . ."). See also *Parallelism*.

Before a complete direct quotation, as distinguished from a fragment, *that* is clearly excess baggage: "The Point Four director in Iran reported that 'More than half the population of the village have been killed under the falling walls of their homes.'" *That* in this position—or inside the quotation marks, for that matter—smacks of an earlier age.

"The official was so incensed over developments, he vowed to remain in the city until the matter was settled." When *that* can be omitted, no comma is necessary to mark its place.

"It is hard to realize that as he lives in quiet retirement at the age of 88 *that* a generation is coming up that knows him only by historic reputation." The italicized *that* is excessive; it tends to raise the clause it begins to the same rank as the first *that*-clause, whereas it is really a subordinate element.

But that sometimes sticks in the craw of the critical, in such sentences as "I do not doubt but that society feels threatened by homosexuality." Technically, *but* is excessive here. Yet usage by good writers as well as those not so good has gained it a respectable place. See also *that, which* under *Restrictive and Nonrestrictive Clauses*.

that of Often useless: "One of the most popular hobbies is that of building boats." What of? The hobby of, obviously; so we get "One of the most popular hobbies is the hobby of building boats." The lyricist of "Home on the Range," observing the stars, wonders "if their glory exceeds that of ours." What of? Or, indeed, what of it? But *exceeds ours* would not fill out the meter, a better excuse for *that of* than the prose writer who uses it can muster.

"The department said the ship would not take any action other than that of observing the freighter." *other than observing.*

Sometimes *that of* is used with no referent whatever: "Nothing is more pathetic in sports than that of the fading, sagging veteran who goes to the well too often." *than the fading.*

See also *False Comparison; Double Possessive.*

that, which   See *Restrictive and Nonrestrictive Clauses.*

the   The notion has got around that opening sentences, particularly in newspaper stories, would be the better if they did not start with *the.* The idea, as once explained, is that the article conveys little or nothing and only stands in the way of the reader, who is panting to get at the meatier words.

Fortunately, this dictum appears to be falling from favor. But like the lie that runs twice around the earth while the truth is lacing up its shoes, it persists, and prejudice against— or neglect of—*the* is still to be found in odd corners.

The unhappily missing article is nearly always *the;* leaving off *a* or *an* has an even more indigestible effect than leaving off *the.* Some writers, conscious of the prejudice against starting with articles, and at the same time unwilling to commit abortion, cunningly rearrange their sentences so that some other element comes first. But in this labor there is no profit, and there may even be a loss, if the rearranged version is less readable or direct.

It is not true, of course, that articles convey nothing. If this were so, they would be dropped from conversational speech, especially at the least literate level, which hews to essentials. *The* particularizes what it precedes; *a* and *an* designate one of a class. Meaning of a sort *can* be put across without these subtleties, but not the sort of meaning that is the most readable and lucid.

Does it really speed the reader on his way to leave an article off the beginning of a sentence? Surely not if he pauses, as he will, to wonder what happened to it, and finds himself obliged to choose between possible shades of meaning. The writer's job has been foisted on the reader, and he has every right to feel irked.

"Crux of the situation is belief expressed by board members that legislation should govern the use of the reservoir by the public." If the aim is to be telegraphic, why not go whole hog: "Crux of situation is belief expressed by board members that legislation should govern use of reservoir by public"?

As a sidelight, we may note that *the* has been dropped in popular use of the name *Congress*. Who can say why? Certainly it never occurs to anyone to drop the article from *the Supreme Court, the Cabinet,* or *the Senate.* It is noticeable that recent Presidents have meticulously referred to *"the* Congress."

Alexander Sloan of the *Newark News* kindly calls attention to an interesting commentary in the introduction to *The President, Office and Powers,* fourth edition, by Edward S. Corwin, (New York: New York University, 1957).

Professor Corwin noted that the Constitution says *the Congress* twenty-six times and *Congress* only five times. Although the Congress established by the Constitution was the last of a succession of congresses, "no sooner did the Constitution go into effect than the term *the Congress* was scrapped by all and sundry." Washington, Jefferson, and Chief Justice Marshall, among others, all said *Congress.*

Professor Corwin attributed the recent reversion to the archaic form "to which Presidents Truman and Eisenhower and Chief Justice Warren have all succumbed," to Franklin D. Roosevelt, "who was never disinclined to resort to the bizarre when it was calculated to focus attention on himself; besides, FDR may have reckoned that his pious revival of the original expression ought to stop the mouths of the critics of his Court-Packing plan."

It is a tortuous business to generalize about the places where *the* is or is not normally required. The matter is governed by idiom, which does not yield to rules, anyway. Let's admit this: We all know very well when we are leaving out a desirable *the;* it is never done by accident.

Careless use of *the* may confer a distinction that is either inaccurate, unintended, or both. Referring to John Jones as *"the* vice-president of the Smith Corporation" implies that the corporation has only one vice-president. "Laurence Olivier, *the* actor" is acceptable on the assumption that he is well enough known so that his name will be recognized. On the other hand, referring to a movie starlet, Hazel Gooch, lately of Broken Bottle, Iowa, as *"the* [rather than *an*] actress" leaves the reader with a rattled feeling that he has not recognized a name he should know, although in fact his ignorance of Miss Gooch is nothing to be ashamed of.

theater, theatre *Theatre* is the British preference in spelling; in America, it is an affectation of theatrical folk.

thee, thou Some foreign languages have two forms for *you:* the familiar, used for intimates and subordinates, and the polite, used for others, especially those toward whom respect is intended. In German, for example, these forms are *du* and *Sie.* Sometimes the familiar form is translated into English as *thou.* This is technically correct, since in Middle English and later *thou* was a polite form in English. But the more modern translation of *du* (and its equivalent in other languages) into *thou* is wholly misleading, for the connotation of the term to us is now Biblical, poetic, or reverential. *Life* magazine, for example, translated the title of a German periodical publication, *Du,* as *Thou,* but it would have come closer with *Hey You.* Moral: translate *du, tu,* etc., as *you,* and explain if necessary that the familiar form was used.

Thou is the nominative form and *thee* is the objective; the difference is the same as between *I* and *me,* or *he* and *him.* "Thou hast not found favor in my eyes; I will smite thee." Quaker usage is specialized, however, and calls always for *thee.* See also *-eth.*

theft See *burglary.*

their, they In reference to technically singular pronouns, like *everybody, everyone, each,* etc., *they* or *their* is often used, particularly in speech, and is considered acceptable: *Everybody washed their own clothes.* Careful writers are likely to use the singular, however: *Everybody washed his own clothes.*

their's An error; the correct form is *theirs.* See also *Possessives.*

there Max J. Herzberg, as the editor of *Word Study,* found that three subjects got his readers' dander up higher than anything else: the split infinitive, proposals to dispense with the apostrophe, and the use of *there is* or *there are* to begin a sentence. This latter construction is often criticized as objectionably indefinite and a product of lazy thinking. Nonetheless, it is frequent in good literature, particularly the Bible: *"There were* giants in the earth in those days"; "Now *there arose* up a new king"; "The fool hath said in his heart, '*There is* no God'"; and *"There were* in the same country shepherds . . ."* Other examples have been cited: *"There is* a pleasure in the pathless woods" (Byron); *"There is* the smack of ambrosia about it" (Lowell).

It seems apparent that the construction is used thoughtfully, rather than lazily, in these examples, to avoid an undesirable emphasis on the true subject that would come of placing it first. "Giants were in the earth in those days" would lay an undesired stress on *giants*. In any event, the rearrangement kills the rhythm and force of the line. If "Now there arose up a new king" became "Now a new king arose up" *a new king* would take emphasis from *arose up*. Considerations of rhythm also enter here.

The *there* construction may be clumsy and objectionably indirect after a passive auxiliary: "As in the previous ruling, there was no jail sentence imposed." Surely "no jail sentence was imposed" would be better. "Yesterday there were four more cases of polio reported." Better: "Yesterday four more cases of polio were reported." The clumsiness is aggravated when *has* or *have,* as auxiliaries in passive constructions, follow *there:* "There have been thousands of people killed"; "There have been two surveys taken."

It is not considered good practice to begin a sentence with a figure, and there is reason to believe that the rule against it causes some writers to shy away even from starting a sentence with a number that has been spelled out. They resort to the *there* construction: "There are eleven organizations representing health, welfare, and youth groups in the county"; "There were nineteen military experiments connected with the explosion."

This timidity in the presence of numbers unnecessarily carries over to those beginning clauses, rather than sentences: "At present, it is said, there are 102 of the county's 167 dairies shipping milk into the area." *There are* only defeats the prominence that *102* deserves, and gives the sentence a woolly sound. Besides, the verb *are shipping* is unidiomatically divided by the submerged subject. Unidiomatic division of verb forms also figures in the unhappy sound of the passive constructions cited earlier. Care is necessary in determining the number of the verb following *there*: "There is six flowers in the vase." *are;* the true subject is *flowers:* "Six flowers are . . ."

Whether any ground has been gained in this review of the problem the reader must decide for himself. These points may be made, at any rate: The *there* construction is not to be condemned out of hand; it is both idiomatic and common in the best literature; it is clumsy and to be avoided with a passive verb; and in view of the prejudice against it, the writer who uses it should take heart and be prepared to defend himself, for defense is indeed possible. See also *Numbers*.

therefor, therefore   *Therefor* is usually found in legal or other fusty contexts, and it means *for that* or *for it:* "He explained the cause of action and the basis *therefor*" (that is, *the basis for it*). *Therefore,* a familiar friend sometimes displaced by *therefor,* means *consequently, as a result:* "The conclusion, *therefore,* is that we have no case."

these, this   See *this, these*.

these kind   An error in number; *these* is plural, *kind* is singular. Correctly, *these kinds* or *this kind,* depending on the circumstances. "*These kinds* of citrus *fruits* grow only in the subtropics"; "*This kind* of *orange* is the sweetest." The following is incorrect: "These kind of social attitudes are harmful." *these kinds.*

think   See *feel*.

this, and this   Use of *this, and this* to introduce a subordinate clause is quaint: "It certainly is gratifying to see a group of property owners joined in civic interest and pride, this despite all the talk we hear of overburdened taxpayers." *interest and pride despite all the talk.*

"Talk among the pickets themselves was that the strike would be short-lived—and this because of the strategic nature of the plant's production." *short-lived, because of . . .*

this, these   There are two misuses of *this* as a pronoun. One consists in using it at the beginning of a sentence or clause in reference to a noun or pronoun, rather than to the general idea, preceding. "The Senussis established what has been called a theocratic empire, spilling over political frontiers. This [better *It* or *The empire*] was then broken up." An example of correct use: "Because of inherited venereal disease, their population remains static. *This* worries the elders of the tribe."

Otherwise, the demonstrative *this* should not be used in place of personal pronouns. "We were much impressed by the chief. This [better, *He* or *This man*] is an able and progressive citizen." "Since 1927 he has lived in his studio, and it has long been his wish that this [better, *it*] be kept as a museum af after his death."

These as a demonstrative pronoun tends, like *this*, to be misused in the place of personal pronouns. "Her heartbeat tripled and her rate of breathing was three or four times normal, but as the rocket reached its orbit, these [better, *they*] tended to return to normal." "She digs up whole pages of evidence and serves these [*them*] hot." "I get all the oysters I want at home, but *these* taste like brass doorknobs." The demonstrative *these* is proper here because the writer was contrasting the oysters at home with others.

this writer   See *Editorial we*.

tho   *Tho,* like *thru* and *altho,* has yet to win its spurs, and generally is confined to the hastier variety of personal correspondence and to signs and advertising.

thoroughgoing   One word; not *thorough-going*.

though,   See *although, though*.

thrifty   In careful writing, applied to people: *a thrifty housewife*. Adwriters, however, loosely and liberally apply it to products: *a thrifty shortening, a thrifty toothpaste*, a usage that is distasteful to the discriminating, who would use *economical* in such contexts. Whether this distinction will be done in by the brevity and breeziness of *thrifty* vs. *economical* remains to be seen.

thru   Though there is much to be said for simplified spelling, forms like *thru* have gained no real acceptance.

thus   See *for, thus*.

thusly   Unnecessary and somewhat quaint for *thus*.

tidelands   In the original sense, this was the area exposed by low tide, but the term has been extended to the location of offshore, underwater oil deposits.

tiff   A tiff, like a spat (which see) is a petty quarrel. The term has been known to be misapplied—for example, to a race riot in which 16 persons were injured and 40 were jailed.

till, til   *Till* and *til* are faintly poetic (*til* more so, perhaps) for *until*. Consequently the choice is a matter of suiting the word to the tone of the context. *Till* and *til* are not contractions; there is no occasion for *'till* or *'til*.

tilting at windmills Don Quixote's avocation of mixing it with windmills is the basis for a popular metaphor usually rendered "tilting with windmills," but it should be "tilting *at*." The tilting here is the military exercise of charging with a lance; it has nothing to do with pinball.

TIME ELEMENTS

Misused Tenses in Time Elements Excessive and pointless caution seems to be at the bottom of the use of the past tense in places where it tarnishes the freshly minted news. This foible is especially conspicuous in some newsmagazines, which seem to be fearful lest the situation at the time of writing may change before the account is read. It is less prevalent, though not unknown, in newspapers.

"A seaplane with seventeen persons aboard *was* missing south of Japan, the Navy said today." Conceivably, the plane might have been found before the newspaper reached the reader. But is it really necessary to pussyfoot like this, or may the reader be left to assume that the paper is stating the facts of the time of writing?

Many news stories deal with conditions that will unquestionably persist between the time of writing and the time of reading. Take, for example, an account in a newsmagazine that began: "Connecticut *was* in for a wide-open and exciting election." Why *was*, since the election was a long way off, and there was no indication the situation might change? Having started with the past tense, however, the writer had to stick with it, thus giving a musty flavor to something that could have been kept fresh by the use of the present tense. How much more immediate "Connecticut *is* in for a wide-open and exciting election" sounds!

Those who insist on using the past tense where the present tense seems preferable might at least take care not to disconcert the reader by changing horses in the middle of a stream: "On the drawing boards are a physical-science center, a classroom and office building, a music building, and a student dormitory. It was all part of a $48 million building program." The inexplicable shift from *are* to *was* sounds as if the building program is no more, although the plans are still on the boards.

"There was a machine that chewed up old fluorescent tubes,

and another that keeps the air in the factory dry." *kept;* or *is,* *chews,* and *keeps.*

Here's a general principle that will brighten things up: Avoid the past tense except in narrating completed events. Use the present, as far as possible, to describe conditions in effect at the time of writing. Nothing is lost by saying "A seaplane with seventeen persons aboard *is* [rather than *was*] missing," and something is gained: immediacy. Use the present tense, too, for general statements, and stand clear of such absurdities as "The men who did the most to break the Solid South in the election were Democrats and they intended to remain Democrats," when in fact they still *are* and still *intend.*

There was once a disagreement between a reporter who wrote, "Officers elected last night *were* . . ." and an editor who thought it should have been *are.* Although, of course, either is correct, an arbiter seriously argued for *were* on the ground that the reporter could justifiably state only the fact as he knew it, and could not assume that the officers would survive until the next morning, when the paper carrying the account of the election would appear. See also *Sequence of Tenses.*

Antiquarians among newswriters, who are devoted to the past tense at the cost of brightness and clarity, often are not content until they have taken yet another step backward, into the past perfect—also known as the pluperfect. The past perfect (*had gone, had been,* as distinguished from the simple past, *went* and *was*) is useful in establishing a time previous to one already specified. But care should be taken not to confuse the sequence, nor to imply a nonexistent sequence. Often, for no apparent reason, the past perfect is used in place of the past.

When a sentence contains both a past and a past perfect tense, the reader is entitled to assume that the occasion described by the past perfect came first. "A doctor recently discovered the nail in a bronchial tube and had recommended surgery." *Had discovered* and *recommended* would be more logical, but *discovered* and *recommended* are what come naturally, because the train of events is self-evident.

"Many of the professionals in the audience had been in the Center Theater when Ballet Theatre started out on Jan. 11, 1940." The presence of the professionals in the theater did not precede the starting out, but coincided with it; *had been* should be *were.*

Much the same difficulty arises in sentences containing a

past time element and a past perfect verb: "He had been the youngest member of the College of Cardinals when he was elected in 1946 at the age of forty-six." This is nonsense, for he could not have been the youngest member until he was elected. Instead of *had been, was* or *became* is required.

"Only yesterday Adenauer had predicted an accord." *Predicted* would have served better; *had predicted* gives a fuzzy impression the prediction was made sometime before yesterday. "Another futuristic device, a converti-plane, actually had been flown in December." *Was flown* is what the circumstances called for.

"She had been eighteen when they were married." If so, she had also been seventeen, sixteen, etc. The writer intended "She *was* eighteen when they were married." "In 1899, Joseph Pulitzer Jr., four, sealed a copper box into the cornerstone of a new building. Last week, filled with mementos of nineteenth-century journalism, the box had tumbled out of the wreckage." This sounds as if the tumbling out occurred sometime before last week; *box tumbled* is what was meant.

Other peculiar pluperfects follow more or less naturally on the strange ritual of using the past tense, instead of the present, to report continuing conditions. Biographical sketches are often the habitat of clumsy past perfects where past tenses would read more smoothly.

"In the eighty-two years of his life, Bill Green had moved from a poor coal-miner's home. . . . His career had been anything but meteoric. . . . But it had been his unspectacular character . . ." Why not the easier "Bill Green *moved* . . . His career *was* . . . But it *was* . . ."? The writer probably set this tense-trap for himself by beginning with something like "Bill Green *was* dead today" (having died the day before). Devotion to the perfect is commendable, but the passion for the past perfect is to be discouraged.

Placement Newspaper writers could stay out of some of the grammatical swamps they get into if they would follow the example of Grampaw in "Annie Get Your Gun" and just do what comes naturally. Reporters who would never say "I today went downtown" will write in a news story, "The City Council last night voted a street-improvement program."

The natural place for the time element is generally after, rather than before, the verb, and often at the very end of the sentence: "I went downtown *today*"; "The City Council voted a street-improvement program *last night*." We don't really need to be told this; everyone, even the illiterate, realizes it instinctively. Why, then, don't we write accordingly?

There are at least two reasons for the misplacement of the time element in newswriting. One is overemphasis on the W's formula—the idea that the lead paragraph should tell when, who, what, where, why, whence, wherefore, which, wherein, and whither—but above all *when,* to impress on the reader what fresh intelligence he is getting. A revolt is now under way, however, on the ground that all this may be too much to expect the reader to assimilate all at once and that the lead really should be the nub of the story in the simplest and most direct terms. The new gospel is "Damn the W's—full speed ahead."

Another reason for the misplacement of the time element is that a moment of thought may be necessary to select the most suitable place for it. Thinking, as has been said, hurts the head, and to prevent pain, reporters heedlessly drop the time element in where it breaks the natural flow of the sentence: "The Air Force pressed tonight the search for a missing plane." Goofy as it sounds, this kind of disarrangement is nearly standard practice. There seems to be a silent conspiracy, even among those who know better, against putting the time element where it belongs.

When the time element is indispensable (and often it is not, as we shall see) it should be put in a place where it does not stick out like a sore thumb. Let us look at some examples of sheer clumsiness in this respect:

"An American novelist, who has written powerful novels of violence and death, was awarded today the Nobel Prize for literature." (". . . was awarded the Nobel Prize for literature *today.*") Why newswriters should fear to put the time element at the end when it fits there smoothly is a mystery.

"It was his own brother who last year spoke out against his political tactics." (". . . who spoke out *last year* . . .")

"Negotiations to end the crippling railway strike reportedly reached today their most crucial stage." (". . . reached their most crucial stage *today.*")

The placement of the time element in "World War II veterans next year will collect $220 million in dividends on their government life insurance" is defensible if the writer had intended to emphasize *next year,* perhaps in contrast to some other year. But such emphasis was not intended, and if it had been, *next year* should have come first. The writer might have chosen among "will collect $226 million *next year,*" or "in dividends *next year*," or "on their government life insurance *next year*." There were so many other places for *next year* that the most awkward one seems to have been chosen deliberately.

Care in placement of the time element is advisable not only to prevent clumsiness, as in the examples, but to keep it from modifying the wrong word or phrase. "The Indian prime minister arrived in Saigon after visiting Communist China today." *Today* belongs after *Saigon,* because it is intended to fix the time of arrival. As the sentence stands, *today* may be taken as fixing the time of the visit to China.

"Legislators working on the president's blueprint for the revised atomic-energy law today faced two major obstacles." *Today* might be omitted here, and *faced* changed to *face*. If *today* must be kept, it would be better at the end.

Shifting the time element or any other part of a sentence away from its natural position lays emphasis on it. This should only be done intentionally. Newswriters seem to be curiously insensitive to emphasis as gained by word order.

Possibly newswriters may be deliberately misplacing the time element to call attention to the freshness of their product. If so, it probably leaves no impression on the reader, except as another irritant. If they really want emphasis, why not put the time element at the beginning of the sentence, which is the most emphatic place for it?

Today   *Today*, we know, is the magic word of the diurnal press. It sums up the hopes and fears of newspapering—the hope that the reader is getting the news from one's own newspaper first, and the fear of having been scooped. There is a powerful yen to impress on the reader that what he is reading about happened, or at least was first consigned to print, *today*, that no expense or effort has been spared to bring him the news expeditiously, and that nothing could be fresher. This is the reason, no doubt, for the prevalence of *today* in the leads of news stories.

Consider wire stories. All are datelined, and few newspapers drop the date. What purpose is served by datelining if the reader must be prodded again with the time element in the form of *today* within a line or two? Even newspapers that drop dates from datelines carry the date of publication in their folio lines. It may be assumed that the reader is surer of few things than of the date of his paper, even without looking.

Often *today* is out of place, dateline or no dateline. It defeats its purpose and detracts from the immediacy of a story dealing with a continuing condition rather than a specific event. The way it is usually used, with verbs in the past tense, gives an old-hat flavor to stories that could be made to sound bright and fresh by omitting *today* and using the present tense.

Instead of "Another month of hot, dry weather was in prospect today for the already arid Southwest" how about "Another month of hot, dry weather *is* in prospect . . ."?

"A group of California Democrats *was* lined up today against a tax measure being pushed by their Republican colleagues" is improved by making it "A group . . . *is* lined up" since, as the story made clear, the alignment was not just a phenomenon of that day alone.

In summary, *today* is usually unnecessary in any lead that is datelined, and omitting it is the simplest way to solve the problem. Some such leads, however, would be improved by omitting the time element and changing the verb from the past tense to the present perfect. Here is one of them: "A Canadian inventor patented this week a way to make the garden grow better." Compare it with "A Canadian inventor *has patented* a way to make the garden grow better." Not only is it hard to find a comfortable place for *this week*, but the words serve no useful purpose in the lead anyway.

Sometimes the time element would be better left out because it misleads or confuses. "The Soviet Communist chief is in trouble today. He is fighting valiantly to hold together the empire left him by his predecessors." *Today* here is not only obtrusive but ludicrous, because it suggests that a long-continuing situation is of only a day's duration. The same is true of "The competitive athletic program here is on the rocks today because of á decision earlier this week to close the school gym" and "An eighty-year-old nun stood firm today [*is standing firm*] against plans to turn her little nation into a Communist state."

Datelines The datelines on wire stories in morning papers carry the date of the preceding day, and *today* in those stories is *yesterday* to the reader. This is consistent enough as far as it goes; the reader has the dateline to which he can relate all subsequent time elements in a given story. But let us consider a wire story about an event that will take place "tomorrow"; that is, the day the reader reads the story. What does the headline say? It says the event will happen *today*, but headlines relate to the date of the paper itself, not to the datelines of the

405

stories. The *today* in a local story in the next column, however, is the reader's *today*. It seems as if the sensible cure of this mishmash is to leave the dates out of datelines, thus clearing the way for a consistent treatment of the time elements in both wire stories and local stories.

Day of the Week   A peculiar effect is created when the day of the week is named: "John Jones Thursday shot his mother-in-law." Some newspapers follow this style, instead of saying *yesterday*, on the theory that the time is then more exactly specified, and for other reasons. Certain captious critics have said, however, that the likes of *John Jones Thursday* may leave the impression that *Thursday* is John's last name. At any rate, this construction is still open to the same criticism that applies to misplacement of *today* and *yesterday*—clumsy word order.

We may speculate on what might happen in some hypothetical news story dealing with the cunning Sergeant Friday, or with Robinson Crusoe's famous sidekick, who was just plain Friday. Readers very likely would be favored with something like "Sergeant Friday Friday started a new investigation," or "Friday Saturday helped Robinson Crusoe store provisions."

Participles and Time Sequence   Modifying phrases containing present participles often become structural atrocities in the hands of inexpert writers. There can be no gap between the time of such a phrase and that of the main part of the sentence. The timing must be either that of a connected sequence, or of simultaneous occurrence:

"Going to the door, he turned the key." (*Connected sequence*.)

"Laughing gaily, she turned to go." (*Simultaneous occurrence*.)

If there is an interval between what happens in the participial phrase and what happens in the main part of the sentence, a past participle should be used, or some other change should be made.

"Joseph Doakes is a graduate of Columbia, receiving his degree in 1960." This is painfully awkward for *"having received* his degree in 1960." The linkage here is not close enough for the present participle to fit happily. Recasting to *"who received* his degree in 1960" is, of course, another solution.

"The mother said her daughter fell out of the car, apparently opening the door when no one was looking." Here, similarly, *having opened* is required to indicate the sequence and perhaps even the agent.

"Eriksson has been a resident of the city for fifteen years, coming here during the war as a naval architect." *having come.*

"He has been in the service since 1927, starting as a clerk." *having started.*

Often a participial phrase inadvisedly subordinates an element that is of equal rank with the main part of the sentence.

"The Van Gilders were married on Christmas Day, 1907, in Anabel, Mo., moving to the West Coast shortly afterwards." This would be improved by substituting *"and moved* to the West Coast . . ." A phrase containing a present participle cannot be used to convey a time *after* that of the main clause.

"By 1918 he was president, moving up to the chairmanship in 1940." Same trouble: *and he moved up.*

"Miss Jones began her studies at the college in September, 1956, receiving her degree last June." *and received her degree.*

"This is one of the most sensational of the many revelations coming from behind the Iron Curtain in several years." *that have come.*

times less "This procedure is 100 times less effective." This does not convey a clear meaning, since *times* implies multiplication, not division or diminution. Better: *one one-hundredth* (if that is what it was) *as effective.*

"The new star is probably 25,000 times fainter than the sun." Baffling. *One twenty-five thousandth as bright;* or "The sun is 25,000 times brighter than the new star." See also *almost more.*

tinker's dam, tinker's damn The first version is said to derive from dams used by tinkers in soldering; the second from tinkers' purported habits of idle cursing. But the *Oxford English Dictionary* says the connection with soldering is "an ingenious but baseless conjecture." Further, it unquestionably represents an effort to Nice Nellify. *Damn* appears to be more used, and is certainly more effective.

-tion, -ion Repetition of this sound is to be avoided. "The education of the population of the nation is substandard."

'tis See *Poesy.*

TITLES

Occupational Titles   A wanton bestowal of titles, outdoing even the generosity of fraternal orders, is noticeable in much printed matter. Occupational descriptives, instead of being made appositives, as is customary in less frenetic prose, are often placed in front of names, on the model of true titles like *Dr., Mayor, Health Officer,* and *Dean.* Thus are hatched such characterizations as *Italian soprano Renata Tebaldi, carnival concessionaire Eddie Crews, registered nurse Edith Hampton,* and *Rome tailor Angelo Litrico.*

One problem in the use of such descriptives is: Should they be capitalized? Some authorities think so, by the analogy with true titles. The weight of opinion, however, seems to be that capitalization should be reserved for true titles, such as denote offices, and for established designations like *Dr.* Forms like *Italian Soprano Renata Tebaldi* and *Rome Tailor Angelo Litrico* seem to connote a status that does not exist, and to most people the capitals only look silly.

Time magazine appears to have been the fount and wellspring of the false-title foible. In extenuation, *Time* at least has diverted us with inventions like *cinemactress.* Apart from diversions, however, it remains more comfortably intelligible to use full-fledged appositives: *the Italian soprano, Renata Tebaldi;* or *Renata Tebaldi, the Italian soprano.*

Some feel self-conscious, or the word may be guilty, about telescoping what they know in their hearts to be the more readable form. Yet they cannot bring themselves to spurn altogether what they consider the fashionable form, having seen it so often. And so they compromise, placing the descriptive in front of the name and omitting the article, but retaining the comma of the appositive form, as a compromise to readability. These are typical results: *Italian Soprano, Renata Tebaldi; Nacionalista Party candidate, Carlos P. Garcia; art dealer, Joseph Duveen; Civil War Hero, Gen. William Tecumseh Sherman.*

The followers of this school, like the barefaced falsetitlers, cannot agree on capitalization either, as the examples indicate. Compromises are sometimes worse than the evils they would palliate. That is so in this instance, at least. The wedding of the false title and the legitimate appositive is certainly one of the sorriest mismatings journalese has brought forth.

It is a good idea to shun false titles entirely as one of the inventions that tend to make writing sound like the text of a telegram. By omitting what is desirable for clarity, or by distorting natural forms, these devices, however cute, demand unnecessary effort from the reader.

Sometimes there is an attempt to have it both ways, including mixed capitalization, in the same sentence: "Art Dealer Joseph Duveen was once trying to sell a painting to millionaire collector, Samuel H. Kress, whose interest was only lukewarm." Those who like it that way can have it. Others will prefer "Joseph Duveen, the art dealer, was once trying to sell a painting to a millionaire collector, Samuel H. Kress, whose interest was only lukewarm."

The false title is so entrenched in journalism there is no hope of uprooting it. But this advice at least may be offered: do not capitalize ordinary occupational designations; do not follow them with commas; and, most important for readability, avoid descriptives that are made up of more than one word.

Doubled Titles   It is objectionable to double titles. This is good practice in Germany (*Herr Dr. Kurt Weiss,* the equivalent of *Mr. Dr. Kurt Weiss*) and in England (*General Sir Hugh Borrow*), but not in America. Doubling usually occurs in such instances as *Superintendent of Schools Dr. Gerald Pedant, City Librarian Miss Tillie Bookworm, Councilwoman Mrs. Edna Gleason.* If it is desirable to give both designations, clumsiness may be avoided by writing *Dr. Gerald Pedant, superintendent of schools; Miss Tillie Bookworm, city librarian;* otherwise, simply *Superintendent of Schools Gerald Pedant, Librarian Tillie Bookworm.* Doubled titles are doubly objectionable when there is more than one mention of the name; in such examples the office can be specified on first mention and subsequent mentions will take care of *Dr., Mrs., Miss,* or whatever.

The world record for piled-up titles may have been set by "The speaker was former Assistant Secretary of Commerce for International Affairs and Occidental College graduate H. C. McClellan."

It is generally considered good form to dispense with titles in designating the author of a book (especially in the book itself) and in identifying public performers such as singers and actors. See also *Capitalization; Rev.; Dr.; Miss; Mr.; Mrs.*

-to   Hyphenated as a suffix: *lean-to, set-to,* etc.

to all intents and purposes   A windy way of saying *in effect.* "This state, to all intents and purposes, has had a one-party system in recent years." *in effect.*

to be   See *Misleading Infinitives* under *Infinitives*.

today, to-day   *To-day* is an odd fish in America, but it may be of interest that even back in his time, Fowler commented on the lingering of the hyphen in this word as singular conservatism. Its persistence may reflect a last-ditch effort by the British to preserve linguistic individuality. See also *Time Elements*.

together with   Under old-fashioned doctrine, *together with* and what follows it did not change the number of the subject from singular to plural: "The apple, together with the orange, *was* [not *were*] shrunken." But the point is moot; if the subject comes to have a plural feeling, *were* is surely more logical than *was*. Hairsplitters love to haggle over this kind of thing. The sensible will write what sounds natural. That goes also for the similar connectives *along with, as well as,* and *in addition to*. See also *Subject-Verb Agreement; Collectives*.

tome   A conspicuous journalese variant of *book,* as *white stuff* is of *snow, yellow metal* of *gold,* and *pachyderm* of *elephant*. *Tome* is properly applied to a volume forming part of a larger work, or to a big book. But it has been found in bad company so often the fastidious writer perhaps would rather be caught dead than use it even in its correct sense.

too   *Too* (like *not too,* which see) is sometimes used illogically. In A. J. Liebling's book *The Press* he quotes a statement from the New York *World-Telegram* in 1953 in which a speaker was reported as denying "charges by some followers of Adlai E. Stevenson, the Democratic candidate [for President in 1952] that the press was too lopsided in its support of President Eisenhower." Liebling's comment was "Just lopsided enough, he must have meant."

Setting off *too* with commas is old-fashioned: "They, too, depend on cash flow to finance their activities." *They too depend*.

tortuous, torturous   *Tortuous* means *twisting* or *winding,* as *a tortuous mountain road; torturous* means *giving torture,* as *a torturous stiff collar*.

toss   There is no good reason why *toss* should be putting *throw* and similar expressions out of business, but it is. See also *Overwriting*.

tot, tote Often confused in their past tenses, *totted* and *toted.* *Tote* is a dialectal expression meaning *carry:* "We *toted* our own wood for the fire." *Tot* (with *up*) means *add up:* "The accountant *totted* up the column of figures."

totally (or completely) destroyed (or demolished) Redundant for *destroyed* or *demolished.* It is true, of course, that something may be partly destroyed, but the sense of the words is absolute without a qualifier. If anything, *completely* and *totally* detract force.

to the manner (manor) born See *manner.*

touch See *finishing touch.*

tour of duty Military lingo that may best be left to military connections. A writer infatuated with inappropriate cant, however, may speak of a policeman going off duty as "ending his tour of duty." Properly, a tour of duty is an assignment to a locality or post for a considerable period, and is not applied even by the military to a watch or shift or day's work.

toward, towards Many have a distaste for *towards,* though both forms are standard. *Toward* is perhaps somewhat commoner in the U.S., *towards* in Britain. Or, at any rate, this was formerly so; the Second Edition of Webster said: "The form *towards* is now the prevailing form in Britain, whereas *toward* is more common in the U.S., except where *towards* is preferred for euphony." The Third Edition does not make this distinction, so we may conclude that the forms are now about equally prevalent in the U.S. There is a notion that *towards* goes with tangible objects (*towards a tree*) and *toward* with intangibles (*toward the fulfillment of a dream*) but this is fanciful.

to we "We, the people . . ." has a fine constitutional ring, and thus to many the phrase seems hallowed and immutable. They are therefore led to write things like "The issue should have been referred to we, the people." Ungrammatical, of course, since the preposition *to* makes it *us, the people.* Admittedly, the noble declamatory effect has now evaporated. "This is no joke to we bus drivers." *us.* In this instance the fault probably lies in an ignorant overcorrectness that makes the writer avoid objective pronouns.

track, tract A rather stupid confusion, but it nevertheless sometimes turns up in otherwise reputable surroundings. A track is what a train runs on, among other meanings; a tract is a pamphlet, usually religious and admonitory, or a piece of land.

trademark One word; not *trade mark* or *trade-mark*. Most combinations with *trade*, however, are two words: *trade name, trade practice, trade wind*. Other exceptions: *tradesfolk, tradesmen*.

TRADE NAMES When is a free ad not a free ad nor, for that matter, an ad at all? This is a question some editors find so difficult they usually do not even try to answer it, but instead yield to panic. When a trade name shows its face, they automatically strike it out, with no thought of the consequences.

The effects are often undesirable. An initial wire-service story about a woman left injured in an isolated area by a plane crash told how she gained her only nourishment by sucking Lifesavers. But this was only until some overzealous copyreader wielded his pencil on it; later versions read "candy mints."

As was brought out in protests from subscribing editors, the substitution was decidedly unhappy, and more than overbalanced the drawback of any free advertising the makers of Lifesavers might have enjoyed. Lifesavers are a product known to everyone; the name creates a specific image that *candy mints* cannot match. *Candy mints* succeeds only in swaddling the precise fact in the wool the fuzzy-minded are so fond of.

Often the identification of the make of an automobile can send a shaft of light into a sentence. It conveys something, for example, if the Sultan of Swat, who is worth his weight in rubies, is described as driving a Model A Ford. Or if a relief client is described as driving up to the welfare office in a new Cadillac to collect his check.

A group of Russians on a tour of the United States visited a Chevrolet plant, but numerous copyreaders who could not see the news for the superstitions changed it to *automobile plant*. An American visiting in Russia smuggled a copy of *Time* to an eager student there, but this became *an American newsmagazine*. Newspapers often refer mysteriously to "a national magazine." The *Atlantic Monthly* or the *Police Gazette*?

Does the casual appearance of trade names really constitute free advertising? And if so, what of it?

Newspapers often pretend they do not know the names of the papers in neighboring places. The *Dogtown Yelp* (circ. 2,964), for example, will refer to the *Metropolitan Uproar* (circ. 289,436), which is published in a city 25 miles away and relied upon by most *Yelp* readers for everything except tidings of Dogtown box socials, as "an upstate big-city daily." Who is fooled? Only the editors who foster such didoes. Readers are amused at such transparent efforts to dissemble, and marvel anew how it is possible to publish successful newspapers without invoking common sense.

For that matter, rival metropolitan dailies in the same town (if such still exist) will often act as if they have never been introduced. One will refer to the other, when such reference is unavoidable, as "a Bigtown evening paper."

Television possibly has taken its cue from this, or perhaps out of its own inspired chintzyness has evolved the prissy "another network" evasion instead of coming right out and acknowledging what the other network is. Listeners who look up the program so described are bound to find out *what* network. Actually, however, the chances are overwhelming that they never notice the network at all; what interests the program-seeker is the channel number. But if the networks concluded a pact of mutual recognition, look at all the free advertising they'd get from each other.

Advertisements regularly appear, especially in periodicals read by journalists, gently admonishing them to capitalize such proprietary terms as *Coke* (a registered designation for Coca-Cola), *Scotch* in reference to transparent tape, *Band-Aid*, *Dacron* (a synthetic fabric), *Teletype*, and many others.

Lawyers speaking for the owners of such trademarks assiduously write letters to editors in whose publications the terms have appeared in improper form—that is to say, uncapitalized, as generic terms. Usually the tone is one of persuasion or gentle admonition; sometimes, however, it is peremptory. Sometimes the innocent misuser of a trademark may wonder whether he has opened himself to sterner action than a reproof.

Trademarks are valuable property, and by failure to exercise diligence in protecting their rights in trademarks, the owners may lose them. This is the reason for the admonitory advertisements and letters. Most publications, out of consideration for trademark owners (who are often advertisers), acquiesce in using the proper form. But the owner has no recourse against a publication that uses his trademark improperly. He can only remonstrate.

Newspapers and sometimes other publications often deliberately avoid using proprietary names rather than give them free advertising. Many a stylebook, for example, prescribes *slide fastener* (a generic term) in place of *Zipper* (a trademark). But this is all in vain; the proprietary right in *zipper* was lost for want of effort to preserve it. The same thing has happened to *aspirin, milk of magnesia, linoleum,* and *shredded wheat,* among others.

tragedy What is termed a tragedy should have impressive or at least respectable dimensions: "The tragedy is that there is seldom complete agreement as to which direction change should take in yielding to progress." An inconvenience, no doubt, perhaps a stumbling block, but hardly a tragedy. *Tragedy, tragic* are sometimes misspelled *tradgedy, tradgic.*

tragicomedy Thus; not *tragic comedy.*

trained expert Redundant; see also *qualified expert.*

trans- Solid as a prefix: *transarctic, transoceanic, transphysical,* etc. But: *trans-American, trans-Mississippi, trans-Ural* (followed by capitals). *Transatlantic* and *transpacific* are solidly established, however.

transpire Its use for *occur* or *happen,* Webster's Second Edition said, is, or was, "disapproved by most authorities but found in the writings of authors of good standing." Webster's Third Edition omits the caveat and quotes several authors, including Jane Austen and Walter Lippmann, as using the word to mean *become known* (a sense equally frowned on in some critical quarters), as well as *occur* or *happen.* The battle, it appears, may be considered over. One more thing, however, remains to be considered: that *transpire* is a somewhat highfalutin displacement of *become known, happen, occur.*

transverse, traverse *Transverse* is an adjective meaning *crosswise:* "*transverse* stripes were painted on the paving"; *traverse* is a verb meaning *travel across:* "The signal transversed the vast reaches of space"; unlikely unless the signal was more erratic than we could expect. More likely *traversed.*

tread, trod   The use of *trod* (*tread's* past tense) for *tread* and of *trodding* for *treading* is a ludicrous though not uncommon gaffe: "He's trodding softly, meanwhile, on that borrowed oriental rug"; "She will trod the boards tomorrow." Next thing we know they'll be giving us:

> "Will you walk a little faster?" said a whiting
>   to a snail,
> "There's a porpoise just behind us, and he's
>   trodding on my tail."

No doubt, too, they will rush in where angels fear to trod. *Trod* does exist in the sense *follow as a chosen course*; it does not mean *step* or *walk on*, as intended in the examples.

treble, triple   Interchangeable in the sense *three times* (*treble damages*).

tri-   Solid as a prefix: *tricentennial, tricolor, triennial, trimonthly,* etc.

trigger   In an age of armament races, wars, and rumors of wars, the popularity of *trigger* as a verb displacing *cause, begin, set off* and the like is probably inevitable. Like many other words fancied as contributing drama, however specious, this one is mournfully overworked.

trio   Journalese as a collective reference to three of anything whether they have any relationship or not. See also *Useless Counting* under *Numbers.*

triumphal, triumphant   *Triumphal* means expressing or celebrating triumph; *triumphant,* feeling or experiencing triumph. *Triumphal* often applies, for example, to *procession;* a procession could be described as triumphant if its participants were exultant. Usually *triumphant* applies to people, *triumphal* to things: *the triumphant victors; a triumphal arch.*

trod   See *tread, trod.*

trooper, trouper   A trooper is a cavalryman or a mounted policeman; a trouper is an actor, or member of a troupe.

true facts   Redundant. What are not facts are not true. See *fact.*

trustee, trusty   Both are people in whom trust has been reposed, and the confusion arises generally in the plural forms: *trustees, trusties*. A trustee is a member of a controlling board, as of a college or foundation. A trusty is an inmate of a prison who enjoys special privileges because of his trustworthiness. Regrettably, it is not unknown for irresponsible trustees to wind up as trusties.

try and, try to   *Try and* is sometimes disdained by the pedantic as an error for *try to,* but so severe a critic as Fowler adjudged it an idiom that should not be disapproved when it comes naturally. Writing in general has grown vastly more informal, furthermore, since Fowler. "The candidate will try and carry the South" was criticized as misleading on the ground that it really says the candidate will not only try but also carry. This proves nothing but the lengths to which hairsplitters will go in efforts to make nonexistent points. All this, however, does not affect the good standing of *try to.*

tsk, tsk   An ad published nationally by a radio station carried an incidental reminder: "Have you registered to vote? Tch, tch—better do it now." Deviations like this must be nipped in the bud, for a tsk is a tsk is a tsk—and not a tch.

tuber   The journalese variant for *potato*. See *Variation.*

turn into   "He turned himself into the Fourth Precinct Police Station" sounds like a feat that would have humbled Houdini. We have here a phrasal verb, *turn in,* and the *in* has unfortunately been fused with the preposition *to.* It should have been "turned himself in to." *Turn into,* however, is possible, as in "We turned into a side street." If *this* be magic, make the most of it.

tuxedo   There is an idea that *tuxedo* is inferior, somehow, to *dinner coat* or *dinner jacket*. This is not so, and further, the prevalence of *tuxedo,* and especially *tux,* is now such that people know them who do not know that dinner coat and dinner jacket are the same thing. On the other hand, among the people who wear them, *tuxedo* may be growing quaint. *Tuxedo* comes from the name of a club at Tuxedo Park, N. Y. The term as applied to clothing dates from 1899.

'twas, 'twere, 'twill   See *Poesy.*

twelve noon, twelve midnight   Redundant. Noon and midnight are both twelve.

twit   A transitive verb; twitting is done to someone, and is not reciprocal. "When he courted Jane Hadley, Kentucky twitted with him; when he finally won and married her, Kentucky rejoiced with him, too." *Twitted with* is unidiomatic; *twitted him.* "They couldn't help twitting about the relationship between the city council and the city manager's office." *Joking*, perhaps, but not *twitting*, which requires a direct object: *twitting each other.*

two-by-four   Some are apprehensive that this familiar lumber will not be recognized for what it is, and pad out reference to it as "two-by-four-inch piece of lumber." *Two-by-four* suffices as a noun; "He hit me with a two-by-four."

type   There are several things to be said about the misuse of this noun as an adjective (*the intellectual type employee, athletic type persons, a nonparalytic type polio, a new type antenna, a different type Communist dictator, an adventure type show*). The first is that no one with any sensitivity to the nuances of expression uses the word in the way illustrated, in either speech or writing. Such locutions are characteristic of the untutored speech of New York's lower East Side or the Bronx, as reproduced so amusingly in the fiction of Arthur Kober. A hyphen between *type* and the modifier preceding it at least brings this construction within the pale: *the intellectual-type employee, a nonparalytic-type polio.* The trouble with this way out is that those who fancy *type* as an adjective are the type who cannot be depended on to appreciate the role of hyphens, either. *Type* with a hyphen is most acceptable in technical connections, as in *V-type engine, O-type blood, cantilever-type bridge.* Let's face it: It is necessary to say *type of* (*the intellectual type of employee, a new type of antenna*) or be set down as an ungrammatical type.

TYPEWRITER TRICKS   First, the number 1 is formed on the typewriter by striking the lower-case *l* (ell, that is), not the *I*.
  The dash is formed by striking the hyphen twice, and it is standard practice to leave no space between the strokes or at either side of the dash—nor, for that matter, at either side of the hyphen. A hyphen with a space at either side is not a proper dash. Convention requires that the period and colon be followed by two spaces, the comma and semicolon by one.

A number of useful marks may be made by using typewriter characters for other than their intended purposes, or by combining them. The exclamation point is formed by striking the apostrophe and the period one at a time while holding the space bar down.

Reasonably satisfactory brackets ([ ], used to enclose interpolated matter) can be made, if absolutely necessary and worth the trouble, by use of the underline (__) and the virgule, or slant (/). To form the upper horizontal lines, the underline must be struck on the line above that on which the bracket is being formed. A box may be made by joining a pair of such brackets.

Reasonable facsimiles of diacritical marks are also possible with the typewriter, if you are not unreasonably critical. The double quotation mark, struck over a letter, will serve as an acceptable umlaut, and the single quote will serve at least as a gesture toward the *grave* or *acute* accent, although of course it will not be possible to tell one from the other. Perhaps this mark is better made with a pen. A cedilla may be made by striking the comma under a *c*.

typhoon, hurricane Both are tropical cyclones but *typhoon* is applied only to those occurring near the Philippines or the China Sea.

—U—

uh-huh, unh-unh, etc.   See *ah, aw.*

ultra-   Solid as a prefix: *ultraconfident, ultramicroscopic, ultraviolet,* etc. But *ultra-ambitious* (followed by *a*).

umlaut   See *Diacritical Marks; Typewriter Tricks.*

un-   Solid as a prefix: *unadaptable, unbreakable, uncomputed, unnamed, unnaturalized,* etc.

UNCONSCIOUS HUMOR   It is questionable whether unconscious humor should be discouraged, since it has added so much to the levity of nations. Nevertheless, the writer who does not want to be the butt of laughter does well to scan his work critically for this quality.

"A jury of eight men and four women found the doctor

innocent of 'being a lewd and dissolute person' in his relations with three women who testified he gave them aphrodisiacs and then fondled them in an unprofessional manner." This implies that there is such a thing as a doctor's fondling women patients in a *professional* manner, and raises the question whether the man who did it would still be open to accusation.

"The girls stole cosmetics, tight sweaters, and toreador pants from stores." A sweater is not tight except in relation to the wearer; but if these girls were intent on tight sweaters, why not also tight pants?

under- Solid as a prefix: *underdevelop, underrate, undersecretary, undercapitalize,* etc.

underestimate "It would be a mistake to underestimate the Russian leadership," pontificated a newsmagazine. Well, yes; a mistake is indeed a mistake. Similarly, "The role that his wife played in this new and immense shot in the arm for the importance of his office cannot be underestimated" should read *overestimated.* "As Yalta, for example, has shown, the importance of minority opinion cannot be underestimated." *overestimated.* See also *minimize; Double Negative; undue; Reversal of Sense; reverse,* etc.

underhand, underhanded *Underhand* predominates for the style of pitching a ball and *underhanded* in the sense *crafty, deceitful,* though the forms are interchangeable.

underprivileged The term has been disparaged by an English critic as a leading example of "American pretentious illiteracy." This harsh judgment was based on the Latin meaning of *privilege, a private law.* It is stupid, the critic said, to pretend favoring equality before the law and at the same time use a word like *underprivileged,* which complains, in his view, that there is not enough inequality. *Privilege* in English, however, is established not only in the sense of exclusive right but also in that of advantage or benefit in general. This is dictionary definition in both England and America. The term *underprivileged* may have grown out of the British concept *privileged classes.* Originally those classes enjoyed certain legal rights and exemptions, but who will argue that the word is not now understood to mean, in general, *well off? Underprivileged,* then, means *not so well off.* Sometimes it is a euphemism for *poor.* The word is defined in Webster as "deprived through social or economic oppression . . ." H. L. Mencken identified *underprivileged* as a novelty that originated in the New Deal era, and apparently saw no reason to scorn it.

undersecretary One word; not *under secretary, under-secretary.*

under way, weigh; aweigh *Under way,* which was born on the foam but has become firmly settled ashore, and the title of that fine old chantey, "Anchors Aweigh," are likely to get tangled, like neglected lines. *Way,* to a sailor, generally means *power,* so that a ship under way is one under power, or not moored or anchored. *Under way,* of course, has come into general use in the sense of *getting started* or *in motion,* and there is a noticeable tendency to make it one word.

Under weigh is neither fish, flesh, nor good red herring. *Under weigh* is the spawn of confusion with *anchor's aweigh,* a shipboard report better known as the name of the Navy song. An anchor is aweigh when, in effect, it is being weighed by the ship—that is, free of the bottom and hanging by the chain. "Anchor's aweigh, sir," is what the boatswain reports to the officer of the deck. Thus *anchor's away* is meaningless.

undue Often used redundantly and, indeed, absurdly, as in "The situation does not warrant undue concern." This says that the situation does not warrant unwarranted concern, a contradiction in terms. "The situation does not warrant concern"; or, if this is not strong enough, "The situation does not warrant great [or *keen,* or any of a number of other adjectives] concern." See also *Double Negative; minimize; underestimate; Reversal in Sense; reverse,* etc.

unexceptionable, unexceptional What is unexceptionable cannot be taken exception to; what is unexceptional is not exceptional, that is, ordinary.

unhealthful, unhealthy See *healthful, healthy.*

uni- Solid as a prefix: *uniaxial, unidirectional, unicellular, unicycle,* etc.

uninterest See *disinterest, uninterest.*

unique The doctrine that *unique* is an absolute modifier that cannot be qualified may be a noble one, but it has no connection with the facts of usage. When used without a qualifier, as in "His outlook on the world was *unique*," it means *without a like or equal*. There are so few unique things under the sun that generally the word is used with a qualifier. This simply extends its usefulness without diminishing its force as an absolute when used alone. "So *unique* then was a ship carrying only tourists that port officials greeted them with alarm" and "The college shares with other private schools several points of *uniqueness*" are not open to reasonable criticism. *More unique, most unique, quite unique,* and the like are equally acceptable. Yet the fastidious reserve *unique* for the absolute sense. Unique takes *a*, not *an*.

United Kingdom See *Great Britain*.

unlike See *False Comparison*.

unpleasantry See *pleasantry, unpleasantry*.

unprecedented If, as the Bible says, there is no new thing under the sun, there is no occasion for *unprecedented*. At any rate, the word is often loosely used for *uncommon, unusual;* what is unprecedented has never happened before.

unravel, ravel Since we have *ravel, unravel* seems both unnecessary and supererogatory. But it is so thoroughly well established in the writings of the reputable we can hardly spurn it.

unveil Journalese for *announce, display, reveal, exhibit*.

up As a verb (*prices have been upped*), journalese.

up-, -up Solid as a prefix: *upbear, upend, upstate*, etc.
Solid as a suffix except after a vowel: *buildup, holdup, windup, setup*, but *close-up, shake-up*.

upcoming The word may appear to be an invention of journalists, who favor it, especially in their own trade-talk. Actually, it dates back to Middle English, but as a noun meaning *the process of coming up. Upcoming* as an adjective is distasteful to many, and perhaps best avoided when *coming* alone will do (*the coming season*). *Forthcoming* and *approaching* are also available. "Old diplomatic hands are worried about the up-coming visit of six U.S. cabinet ministers to Japan." *approaching*.

upon   Often used where idiom or simplicity call for *on*, quite likely because of some ill-defined idea it is more elegant. "As chief speech writer, he provided many of the phrases upon which the candidate campaigned." *on*. "He's cashing in upon the publicity." A clear case of defiance of idiom; *on*. "This is an opportunity to cut down the drain upon our shrinking gold supply." *on*.

There is no clearcut difference in sense between *on* and *upon*, although *upon* more distinctly connotes *on top of*. *Upon*, once favored as more formal, is falling into disuse where *on* will do, and in those places tends to sound stilted. Earl Wilson, the columnist, has seen humor in some occurrences of *upon*: "He kissed her passionately upon her reappearance"; "She walked in upon his invitation"; "She fainted upon his departure."

UP STYLE   See *Capitalization*.

upward revision   A euphemism, usually, for *increase* (particularly in prices). Sometimes also *upward adjustment*. See *Euphemisms*.

upwards of   Clumsy for *more than*. It is in the same league with *in back of* for *behind* and *close to* for *nearly*.

usable, useable   Both forms are correct, but the first predominates and is to be encouraged on the principle that simplicity is desirable.

usage, use   *Usage* relates to a customary practice, *use* to the act of employing something. Often *usage* has a technical sense; when it applies to language, as it often does in this book, it means a standard of use. It may also apply to customs, traditions, rituals, and the like: *the usages of the church*. In "the unprecedented usage of power," the writer would have been better advised to use *use*.

"He didn't like the word *no* and wouldn't accept its usage by his customers." *use*.

"This custom is no longer in usage"; "This expert recommends year-round usage of schools." *use*.

use to, used to   This expression is seldom used these days other than in the past tense, for which the form is *used to*, not *use to*: "We used to go skating every Saturday." With a negative, however, the form is *use to*, though such constructions are clumsy and best avoided: "We didn't use to build a fire unless it was bitter cold."

utopia   Takes *a*, not *an*.

—V—

vaccinate   See *inoculate, vaccinate*.

van, von   See *de, du, etc.*

VARIATION   Conspicuous variation to avoid repeating a term is not only worse than repetition, as Fowler said, but may suggest a distinction that does not exist.

The problem is often neatly solved by ellipsis:

"He played with Charlie Barnet's Orchestra and worked with Red Norvo's Sextet." Play and work are different things, but the writer was merely straining to avoid repeating the same words to express the same idea. Yet he might have said "played with Charlie Barnet's Orchestra and with Red Norvo's Sextet."

"Russia's army newspaper *Red Star* claims there are now 33 million Communist Party members in seventy-five nations. The breakdown gave Indonesia one million. France was said to have 5 million Red voters; Italy, 1.8 million card-carriers." Are Communist Party members, Red voters, and card-carriers all the same? The writer assumed this to be true, but of course it is not. The changes are rung unnecessarily. Once it has been established that *Communist Party members* is the idea under discussion, the writer might have trusted the reader's memory beyond Indonesia to: "France was said to have 5 million; Italy, 1.8 million."

In other common instances, variation is merely silly:

"About 76 per cent of Russia's doctors are women, while in the United States only 6 per cent are female." *Women* would have sounded better repeated; or "but the proportion in the United States is only 6 per cent."

"Cigarette smokers puffed a record 205 billion cigarettes in the first six months of this year, 4.4 per cent more than they lit up in the same time in 1956." Lighting up and puffing are different things, and the variation is absurd: "4.4 per cent more than in the same period in 1956."

"In cases where both parents are obese, 72 per cent of the offspring also are fat. When one parent is fat, 41 per cent of the children are overweight. When neither parent is obese, only 4 per cent of the offspring are fat." This writer danced an ungainly dance between *obese, fat,* and *overweight* on one hand, and between *children* and *offspring* on the other. What about "When both parents are fat, 72 per cent of the children are. When one parent is fat, 41 per cent of the children are. When neither parent is fat, only 4 per cent of the children are"?

One aspect of what Fowler called elegant variation might be described as the geographical fetish, since it requires that the second reference to a place be in the form of a geographical description. In Southern California, under these ground rules, it is permissible to name San Francisco once, but the second time it is mentioned it must become *the northern city.* Other samples of this aberration:

"The caravan plans a dinner in Podunk and an overnight stop in the Razorback County city" and "A three-day international convention opened today in Nagasaki on the anniversary of the atom bombing of the southern Japanese city."

There is something to be said for this practice. It conveys information to the reader about the location of the place named, in the event he happens not to know where it is. But there is also something to be said against the practice—it's an asinine way to write. Desirable information about locale or anything else should be offered for its own sake and not made a device to avoid naming the place again.

From map-making, the fashioners of this kind of prose often graduate into zoological classification:

"Children who want to enter a frog in the event may pick up an amphibian at the Chamber of Commerce office." Here pearls of another branch of knowledge are being cast before readers, but they probably will not appreciate it, the swine. Yet swine-lovers will defend them if they prefer *an overnight stop there* to *an overnight stop in the Razorback County city,* or *may pick one up* to *may pick up an amphibian.*

"A search for a mountain lion was abandoned when no sign of such a carnivore was found." *Such a carnivore* is a pompously stupid substitute for *such an animal* or even *one*. Here are some common latter-day examples of variation: *simian* for *monkey, jurist* for *judge, bovine* for *cow, feline* for *cat, quadruped* for any four-legged animal, *equine* for *horse, optic* for *eye, tome* for *book, white stuff* for *snow*.

The printed word is a powerful educative force, but it is questionable whether calling an oyster *a bivalve*, an elephant *a pachyderm*, a dog *a canine*, gold *the yellow metal*, legislators *solons*, or professors *savants* has contributed anything to public uplift.

"To use a vulgar expression, they were spitting with the wind, whereas in Italy, which has enjoyed a persistently favorable balance of payments, they were expectorating against the wind." It is surely inexcusable to use a word one considers it necessary to apologize for and then obtrusively sidestep it a moment later. See also *Leapfrog; Apologetic Quotes* under *Quotation*.

various   See *different, various*.

verbal, -ly   *Verbal* means *in words*, either spoken or written. If it is intended to convey the idea of spoken, rather than written, words, the expression wanted is *oral*, whose opposite is *written*. "He *verbally* assaulted the committee" illustrates a not altogether explicit use. We know that the assault was with words, rather than blows, but we cannot be sure whether the words were written or spoken. If the context did not show, we would probably assume the words were spoken, for *verbal* is often loosely used in this way, as in *a verbal contract*. If exactness is of any consequence, the writer should choose between *oral* and *written*, and not take a chance with *verbal*.

VERBS   It is well to repeat verbs in parallel constructions when they differ in tense and pronunciation, even though the forms are spelled identically: "The deplorable fact is that he has denounced a book that he has not and will not read." *has not read* (past tense, pronounced *red*) *and will not read* (future, with the auxiliary, pronounced *reed*). Such constructions are disjointed and distract the reader.

"The board may—and has on one occasion—adopt two books on one subject." *has adopt? The board has adopted two books on one subject once in the past and may do so again.*

"This program exists as an example of what private enterprise can and is doing." *can do and is doing*.

"The woman wearing a hat like this hasn't and probably won't grow up." *hasn't grown up and probably won't*.

"The United States will continue with a policy of a mixed force of bombers and missiles, and modernize conventional forces." *will modernize*. Although the auxiliary here is the same, the parallel verbs are so far apart *will* is best repeated.

"In all, more than 100 witnesses were heard, 1,447 exhibits shown, and 26,700 pages of testimony taken." This is satisfactory; the omitted *were* is easily assumed before *shown* and *taken*.

See also *Passive Voice; Time Elements; Sequence of Tenses; Hyphens with Phrasal Verbs* under *Hyphens; Parallelism*.

Division of Compound Verbs Many who otherwise profess cynicism are romantics in their attitude toward compound verbs (*has been, must approve, will block*). They seem to assume a connubial relationship between the halves of the verb forms, and are determined that nothing shall set them asunder.

All the commentators on this foible, starting with Fowler, seem agreed that it is the illegitimate offspring of a disreputable parent, namely, the split-infinitive phobia.

Consider "The budget was *tentatively* approved"; "The matter was *automatically* delayed"; "Experts are *now* pinning their hopes on the House."

The words in italics separate the parts of compound verbs, and objectors would wish them elsewhere. Don't ask them why. They have no reason, except perhaps that someone once told them "That's the way it ought to be."

These points are relevant:

1. In many sentences, an adverb falls naturally among the parts of a compound verb and not nearly so naturally anywhere else. Juggle the quoted sentences around and see for yourself.

2. The splitting of compound verbs is essentially a question of word order. Considerations of emphasis, euphony, and meaning—rather than prejudice—should govern here.

3. It is impossible to be consistent about keeping compound verbs together, even for those willing to ignore nuances of emphasis and the like. Sentences containing negatives illustrate this: "I will *not* concede the election" and "The decision will *not necessarily* block action." Note also questions like

"How has *your health* been?" (Again, the divisive elements are italicized.)

Fowler was inclusive, specific, and emphatic in refuting the superstition that division of compound verbs is undesirable, and went so far as to say that putting the adverb anywhere except within the parts of the verb requires special justification.

See also *Utterance by Proxy* under *Attribution*.

vermilion, vermillion Both forms are considered acceptable, but the first is conspicuously predominant. Some proper names use the second version.

VERSE Is chintzyness on the rise? It seems so, when verse is reprinted like this: "Twinkle, twinkle, little star How I wonder what you are Up above the world so high Like a diamond in the sky." Quoted poetry once was set up line by line, as it ought to be. This takes a little more space. But running the lines in tends to kill their effect as verse. See also *poetry, verse.*

very It is true that this is a four-letter word, but that hardly justifies the opprobrium that has been heaped on it in stylebooks and otherwise. Some journals, for example, interdict its use entirely, a ban they attempt to justify on the ground that *very* implies a judgment by the writer. One deep thinker in the newspaper profession adjured his reporters, when tempted to use *very*, to set down *damn* instead. This may be clever, but it is not damn (or *very*, if you prefer) smart. An outright prohibition on the use of any word that is not indecent only reflects on the judgment of the prohibitor.

What is so bad about *very?* Overuse, say its critics. But the prejudice has outlived the vice that produced it, for no objectionable number of *verys* is evident these days. This is not to say the word is never misused. But the most conspicuous misuse is seen in misguided attempts to strengthen words that are already strong. The result of fastening *very* to them is that they are weakened, not strengthened. *Wonderful* is a frequent victim. *Wonderful* is wonderful, but *very wonderful* is less so. The reader is left with the impression that the writer doth protest too much. Likewise *lovely* (*a very lovely singing star*), *splendid* (*a very splendid performance*), and *excellent* (*a very excellent dinner*). The writer who wants to damn can do it not only with damns, like the captious editor we have referred to, but by tacking *very* onto what would otherwise be veritable praise. *Very* is often invoked when the writer is straining for an effect he does not quite believe in. Consider the common tribute, *a very great man.* Palpably a very great man is less great than a great one; the writer is trying to convince himself, and by letting the cat out of the bag with *very* he loses the confidence of the reader.

Fowler cited instances in which *very* could not be correctly used with a passive participle. *A very worried official,* he said, is right, but *The Government, very worried, withdrew the motion* is wrong. It seems hardly worthwhile to go into the ins and outs of this, because it is now a dead issue. A writer's ear will tell him whether he is using *very* idiomatically. The substitution of *much* for a *very* that sounds questionable (*I was much inconvenienced*), as recommended by Fowler, jars on the American ear. But *very much* (*I was very much inconvenienced*) will solve the problem, if problem this be. See also *rather; quite.*

vest, waistcoat In general, the American and the British names for the same thing. Fancy ones, however, like Tattersall vests, are often referred to as waistcoats (pronounced *weskits*) in America.

via A great favorite with the journalese artist, who uses it to inflate *by* and in other disagreeable ways. The proper use of *via* is in the sense *by way of:* "We traveled to San Francisco from Chicago *via* New Orleans." *Via train* would be better *by train. Via the . . . route* is a journalistic concretion. Basketball writers like to tell of scores being made "via the free-throw route" when they mean "*by* free throws." Mayhem is often reported as being committed "via the knife route" instead of "*with* a knife." "An electronic device fits around the dog via a harness." *on.* "They talk via ham radio to their relatives and friends." *by* or *over.* "The museum will open its new gallery via an exhibit of fifty paintings." *with.* "Dr. Young's pigs were born via cesarean section." *by.*

vice, vise A vice is an evil ("He knew all the vices before he was 18"); a vise is a form of clamp usually mounted on a workbench ("The subassembly is held in a vise while braces are welded on it"). *Vice* for *vise* is a Briticism and obsolete in the U.S.

vice- Usually hyphenated as a prefix with nouns denoting of-

428

fices: *vice-admiral, vice-governor, vice-consul,* etc. But *viceroy, viceregal.* And *vice president* is often given thus.

vice versa   See *reverse,* etc.; *Reversal of Sense.*

vicious, viscous   Occasionally the victims of confusion in spelling. *Vicious* means *mean* (*a vicious dog*); *viscous* means *oily or sirupy in consistency;* said usually of liquids.

vilify, -ification   Sometimes misspelled *villify, villification.*

villain   Often misspelled *villian.*

virile   Means *masculine* or *manly;* it is capable of figurative extensions, but not to individuals: "They made a healthy, virile-looking couple." Regrettably, this was man and wife, not a pair of epicenes or lesbians as the descriptive seems to suggest. Fowler suggested substituting *male* as the test of suitability. Though the word is inescapably associated with masculinity, one modern sense is *decisive, forceful.* It is ludicrous to speak of anything associated with women as *virile* unless it is desired to suggest mannishness, and even then *mannish* or *masculine* would be a better choice. *Virile* comes from *vir,* Latin for *man.*

virtual, -ly   *Virtual* means *in effect though not in fact;* the virtual ruler of a country, then, would be the power behind the throne. It is often misused in the sense of *bordering on* or *near* or sometimes *veritable:* "It was a virtual cloudburst." The distinction does not extend to the adverbial form; *virtually* means *almost entirely,* or *for all practical purposes.*

visionary   Means *existing in imagination only,* hence chimerical or impractical. It usually has a derogatory connotation, and should not be used in place of *farsighted, prophetic,* or *imaginative.* "The speaker closed with an appeal to city officials in the audience to do some visionary planning." *farsighted, imaginative.*

visit with   Well established on a conversational level for *converse with;* thus it is possible to speak of visiting with someone over the telephone.

voice   *Voiced objections, voiced praise* and the like are roundabout for *objected, praised.*

von   See *de, du,* etc.

vow   As a verb, *vow* means *to take an oath*. It is rare in ordinary parlance, except that in journalese it is a favored variant of *say* or *promise*. "We'll win the next one, the coach vowed," not making a bloody sacrifice on an altar but merely being wistful. The use of *vow* where *promise* will do implies an inappropriate solemnity. The fondness for *vow* has something in common with a preference for *lone* (which see) over *sole* or *only*.

—W—

wacky   The slang term for *mentally unbalanced* or *eccentric* is preferably thus spelled, not *whacky*.

wage   See *salary*.

want   In the sense of *lack, want* is falling into disuse, and consequently sounds a trifle old-fashioned: *This shirt wants a button*.

want in, out   Acceptable for *wants* with an infinitive: *The cat wants* [to come] *in*. But generally avoided in writing; until recently considered dialectal.

War Between the States   A euphemism, favored in the South, for the Civil War. See also *sovereign*.

warn   Takes *of, about, against,* not *on:* "The Better Business Bureau warns on unscrupulous magazine sellers." *of* or *against*. See also *on*.

was, were   See *if I was, were*.

was a former   The phrase does not make sense in reference to a living person: "Like Hull and Padrutt, Johnson was a former Progressive." Once a former, always a former. *Was a former* (and *was a onetime*) can be sensibly used only of a dead man to describe a condition that ceased to exist before he died. Even then, the meaning is better expressed with different wording: "The late governor was at one time a Farmer-Laborite."

was given   The *was given* phobia appears to have had its origin in one of the strictures of Ambrose Bierce. The supposition is that such a sentence as "The soldier was given a rifle" is inadmissible because, Bierce wrote, "What was given is the rifle, not the soldier. . . . Nothing can be 'given' anything." How easy it is to go astray handing down rules *ex cathedra* is demonstrated by the fact that Bierce broke his own rule by using *was given* in the very lines he composed to forbid its use.

"The soldier was given a rifle" is a variant arrangement of "A rifle was given to the soldier." Curme writes that sentences in which the accusative becomes nominative "are often preferred in choice expression," and cites as an example "They were given ample warning."

Simeon Potter, in *Our Language*, says: ". . . in spite of loud protests from prescriptive grammarians, 'Me was given the book' has become 'I was given the book' by the most natural process in the world."

The *Oxford English Dictionary* quotes as an example of the uses of *give* "He was given the contract." When we read sentences like this, do we get the impression, even for a moment, that it was *the soldier, they, I*, or *he* that was given? The idea is obviously nonsense.

Bierce also forbade us to say "The house was given a coat of paint." But then he didn't like *coat of paint*, either; he insisted it should be *coating*.

was graduated   See *graduate, was graduated*.

wax   As a verb in the sense of *become*, sometimes erroneously modified: "His speeches belittled glamorous TV commentators who waxed authoritatively in the studio but seldom went out and actually covered a story." Well, no wonder they seldom went out; they were too busy waxing (the furniture, perhaps?). *waxed authoritative*, not *authoritatively*; *authoritative* modifies *commentators*, not *waxed*.

way back, way down, etc.   *Way* is the idiom in such constructions; not *away* or *'way*: *way back in the Twenties; way down yonder*.

ways   *Ways* is loose for *way* in such expressions as *a long way, a little way*. See also *Ad Lingo*.

we   See *I, we; Editorial we*.

weaponize Governmentese of such uncertain meaning the Merriam-Webster editors, who were widely criticized for excessive indulgence in putting together the *Third Unabridged,* did not see fit to include it. The statement "Army personnel are completing weaponization of the Redstone ballistic missile system," which appeared in a news service dispatch, drew an agonized protest from a subscribing editor. "Do you mean," he demanded, "that the missiles are being warheadized? Or that the system is undergoing agonizing reappraisalization? Or is it that the writer didn't know just what was going on and so called it weaponized?" The wire service, having no definition to offer, apologized.

WEATHER REPORTS Whether nothing can be done about the weather has become a questionable proposition since the development of cloud-seeding. There is no question, however, that something can be done about weather stories in the newspapers. First, let's sacrifice all that impressive but unintelligible mumbo jumbo about high- and low-pressure areas, well-defined frontal systems, and other technicalities of the forecasting business. That stuff may be all right for the detailed report in the back pages, for it undoubtedly is interesting to some, like every other specialty. But such complexities seem out of place in the general weather story, because the average reader does not understand them. There may be some question whether even the forecasters understand them, when you compare the forecasts with the weather.

Temperatures are commonly spoken of as *cooler* or *warmer,* although a temperature, being a reading, can only be *higher* or *lower*. An *increase* (rather than a *rise*) or a *decrease* (rather than a *drop*) is no better.

Weather writing, like all newsdom, has its clichés. One might expect that anything as changeable as the weather would inspire some variety in the terms used to describe it, but this seems a vain hope. Newspaper readers, especially in a wet season, must be unnecessarily depressed to read without variation day after day that the rainfall total has been *boosted;* that rivers are *on a rampage;* and that rain and snow are being *dumped*—like garbage, presumably. Rain is also often spoken of delicately as *dampening* (never wetting), but a rain that merely dampens hardly qualifies as a rain. Typhoons usually pack winds of such-and-such velocity. *Twenty-five-mile-an-hour winds* could be more neatly disposed of as *twenty-five-mile winds*.

The temperature, when high, gets where it is in only one way: it *soars*. On the other hand, when it drops quickly, it must *plummet*. The fog always seems to *roll in*. This sounds as if it's on wheels, instead of cat feet, as Carl Sandburg had it. The weather writers' gods, of course, are Jupiter Pluvius and Old Sol.

A faithful standby in stories related to wet weather is the comment that the rain *failed to dampen the spirits* of some person, group, or occasion. Maybe so, but where the rain fails, banalities like this are likely to succeed.

weigh, weight The confusion of *weigh* with *weight* in such contexts as "I weight only 129 pounds" is too frequent to be set down as a typographical error. *Weigh* and *weight* can each be verb or noun, which probably gives rise to the confusion.

well Generally hyphened in combination: *well-being, well-favored, well-read*. When compound modifiers with *well* come before what they modify, they are always hyphened (*a well-turned phrase, a well-aimed dart*). When they occur after (*the play was well acted, the matter was well explored, the teacher was well-read*) usage is somewhat inconsistent and arbitrary, and the only thing for it is to have recourse to a dictionary. Sometimes there is a difference in sense: an author might be described as well read if his work were popular, and well-read if he himself had read widely. Often the matter of whether to hyphen *well* used predicatively becomes a matter of hairsplitting, not worth the time of anyone who has better things to do.

well and good The two most inane expressions of recent years are *well and good* and *still and all. Well and good* apparently reflects the influence of radio and TV announcers, who seem unwilling to trust any word to convey an idea by itself, especially when they are ad-libbing, but must bolster it with a synonym. *Still and all* (sometimes rendered *still in all*, which surely means no less) has even found its way into the ordinarily well-culled pages of *The New Yorker*.

well breeding Apparently the misshapen descendant of *well bred:* "The apology showed well breeding." *Well* cannot be used as an adjective in place of *good;* "The apology showed *good breeding." Well breeding* will have to be reserved for breeders of wells, presumably well-drillers.

well known Under interdiction in some quarters on the fussy assumption it is an error for *widely known*. There is nothing to this. *Widely known* is correct, of course. So is *well known*. It is solidly established, and the expressions are synonymous.

welsh, welch *Welsh* enjoys marked preference over *welch* as the form for the word meaning to swindle someone in a bet, or to go back on a commitment. Welshmen have been known to object to the term as unjustly aspersing them. It is unlikely that anyone has Welshmen in mind when using it, however, and the *Oxford English Dictionary* diplomatically describes its origin as obscure. In any event, *welsh* in this sense is never capitalized. See also *Scotch*, etc.

welsh rabbit, rarebit The first form was the original, and is said to have been a joke at the expense of Welsh hunters. (The dish is melted cheese poured over toast or crackers.) *Rarebit* represents an effort to dignify that caught on; the form is now commoner than *rabbit*. Since it is now perhaps never consciously used with the intent to sound high-toned, but rather on the assumption that it is the correct form and *rabbit* the corruption, criticisms of *rarebit* are pedantry.

West As a part of the United States, by common consent (like *North, South, East*) usually capitalized. This is true also of references to the Western Hemisphere or to the Free World as a political entity.

wha A kittenish reviewer, after giving a generally rough time to a movie version of *Brigadoon*, asked, "Scots, wha' this?" Sometimes it doesn't pay to get cute. *Wha* in Scots dialect means *who*, not *what* or *what's*. Robert Burns wrote:

> Wha will be a traitor knave?
> Wha can fill a coward's grave?
> Wha sae base as be a slave?

Wha, indeed?

wharf See *dock*.

what The argument over the number of the verb in sentences and clauses starting with *what* shows no sign of being settled. Indecision arises when the predicate is plural, as in "Let me point out what seems to be some misplacements of emphasis."

434

Seems or *seem*? It doesn't really matter; the authorities disagree, both constructions are observable in careful writing, and thus the only sensible advice is to write what is comfortable in a given instance.

With a linking verb (chiefly forms of *to be—is, was,* etc.) *what* is generally considered singular no matter what follows: "What I saw was eight white horses."

when, where *When* and *where* in definitions ("Music is when there is a concordance of pleasing sound") mark an immature style.

There is no reason why *where* should be used for *when* or *if*: "Where the superintendent feels that continuing use of the material is important, the school board must make the final decision." The context indicated *where* did not relate to place.

"Employees of the company are given compensatory time off, or where this is not possible, they get extra pay." *when, if.*

When *where* begins a clause, a decision must always be made whether a comma should be placed before it. "It is equally true of Italy[,] where the elections next spring will have great significance."

See also *from where, whence; Restrictive and Nonrestrictive Clauses.*

whence, from whence See *from where, whence.*

when . . . then See *if . . . then*; the same criticism applies.

whether See *if, whether.*

whether or not Although some insist *or not* is redundant, the form is so well established they may as well turn their attention to weightier matters. *As to* preceding *whether* ("The question as to whether he had dinner") is useless.

which May be ambiguous in reference to the whole clause preceding, rather than the nearest noun or pronoun: "Styles of the 1920s did nothing to set off the feminine figure, which frustrated girl-watchers." *figure; this frustrated.*

Which should be preceded by a comma, or the pronoun should be *that.* This point is of little importance, however, compared with the necessity of deciding whether the comma belongs or not. See *Restrictive and Nonrestrictive Clauses; and (but) which,* etc.

while   *While* is best reserved to mean *at the same time as* and is less happily used in the senses of *and, but,* or *although.* "One brother was born June 9, 1893, at Oakland, while the other was born July 19, 1898, at San Jose" unnecessarily makes the reader hesitate, and may make him smile. *and.*

"The cannon will be based on Okinawa while the rockets are being sent to Japan" is ambiguous, because what the writer intended was *"but* the rockets are being sent to Japan." "While architecture flourished in Rome, sculpture was less cultivated" would have been understandable at once as it was meant if it had been written, *"Although* architecture flourished . . ." See also *awhile, a while.*

whimsy, whimsey   The first is noticeably the preferred spelling.

white   There is a tendency to capitalize the word in reference to race; this is absurd. A kind of status-seeking, perhaps?

white stuff   The journalese variant for *snow.* See *Variation.*

who, whom

If a boy ignores his arithmetic teacher and states that 8 times 7 are 63, he will be laughed at by his friends; but if he *obeys* his English teacher and says, *"With whom are you going to the party?"* instead of *"Who* are you going to the party *with?" he will also be laughed at.* Grammar, at least as taught by many old-fashioned teachers, is almost purely directive and bears little relation to the way English is actually spoken and written.*

In a survey by Norman Lewis, "How Correct Must Correct English Be?" (*Harper's,* March, 1949), "Who did you meet?" was given 43 per cent acceptance in an opinion poll of 468 high-school and college teachers of English, authors, editors, journalists, radio commentators, lexicographers, and a random of sampling of subscribers to *Harper's.* Kyle Crichton, associate editor of *Collier's,* commented:

"The most loathsome word (to me at least) in the English language is *whom.* You can always tell a half-educated buffoon by the care he takes in working the word in. When he starts it I know I am faced with a pompous illiterate who is not going to have me long as company."

The *Oxford English Dictionary* calls *whom* "no longer cur-

* *Language in Thought and Action,* S. I. Hayakawa.

rent in unstudied colloquial speech." *Whom* is regularly nom- inated for oblivion. Yet there remain a good many people to whom its strictly correct use, whatever that may be, is the touchstone of education. The chief among these, possibly, are the editors of *The New Yorker,* who steadily note misuses under the snide caption, "The Omnipotent Whom."

It appears that critics of the supposed misuse of *who* or *whom* are on shaky ground. *Whom,* of course, is the objective (or accusative) form. Most of the trouble with *whom* comes in relatively complex constructions that must be taken apart to determine what is subject and what is object. Most of us, es- pecially in view of the ambiguous standing of *whom,* pay little attention to which form is used.

"He summoned the officer, whom he said had just been commissioned." *Whom* is not the object of *summoned* as may appear, but rather the subject of *had been commissioned,* and should be *who.*

"She explained her presence to the Hungarian hussar, whom she hoped would fall in love with her." *Whom* is not the object of *hoped,* but the subject of *would fall,* and should be *who.*

These sentences illustrate the commonest "misuse" of *whom.* Yet when the critics of such errors must indict the translators of the Bible, together with Keats and Shakespeare, as having known no better, their preachments take on a hollow ring:

"Young Ferdinand *whom* they suppose is drown'd"; "Arthur, whom they say is killed tonight." Shakespeare.

"*Whom* say ye that I am?" Matthew 14:15.

"I have met with women *whom* I really think would like to be married to a poem." Keats.

The consensus is that either *whom* or *who* is acceptable in these constructions.

There is general agreement among grammarians that a preposition or verb following *who* does not make it *whom* even if it is the object. Thus "*Who* are you going with?" and "*Who* did you invite?" are not only correct, but preferable to *whom.* *Than whom* is an idiom: "An architect *than whom* there was none more clever."

In Boston, according to Ernest Weekley, the owls say "To- whit, to-*whom.*" And George Ade wrote, "'Whom are you?' he asked, for he had been to night school."

whodunit   Since the term is solidly established as the designa- tion for a murder mystery story, the frequent renderings *who dun it, whodunnit,* etc., are hardly excusable.

wholehearted   Not *whole-hearted.*

whopping   Long ago had all the whop whopped out of it. *Whacking* and *thumping*, as modifiers, are coming to the same end.

who's, whose   *Who's* means *who is* or *who has; whose* means *belonging to whom.* A rather ignorant but not uncommon confusion in print, much like *it's* for *its* (and vice versa). "Whose to say?" *who's* (who is).
   Whose is correctly applicable to things as well as to people: "The tree *whose* leaves were falling." *of which* is correct, but unnecessary and usually clumsy.

wide-, -wide   Usually hyphenated as a prefix: *wide-angle, wide-awake, wide-open.* But *widespread.*
   Solid as a suffix: *citywide, countywide, nationwide.*

widespread   Often erroneously divided: *wide-spread.*

widow   For *widow* vs. *wife* with *survive*, see *Obituaries.*

widow of the late   A redundancy that has been under fire for a long time. The husband of a widow must inevitably be *the late.*

widow woman   Dialectal, as well as redundant; a widow must be a woman.

wife, widow   See *Obituaries.*

will, shall   See *shall, will.*

-wise   *Wise*-words like *dollarwise, saleswise, productionwise* have been widely jeered as samples of Madison Avenue prose at its worst.
   It was only to be expected, then, that the writer of *"Budget-wise* housewives are looking for economical buys," should be taken to task, as indeed he was. But the critic was barking up the wrong avenue that time. If the victim had written, *"Budget-wise,* housewives are confused," he would have been guilty as charged, for there, indeed, is one of the excoriated species.
   Th *wise* in a true *wise*-word is a suffix meaning *in terms of* or *with respect to. Wise*-words often are used as adverbs, taking the place of prepositional phrases modifying the whole

sentence: "Sales are up, *dollarwise*" (in terms of dollars). But the *wise* in *budget-wise housewives* is the adjective that means *possessing wisdom*. What the writer had in mind were housewives who are wise in the ways of budgets. The use of *wise* in this instance cannot fairly be blamed on Madison Avenue. The use of *wise* in this way (as a word in its own right, serving as part of a compound adjective, rather than as a mere suffix) is long established and highly respectable. The saying "Penny-wise, pound-foolish," for example, is surely old enough to be virtuous. Why should *budget-wise* be any more objectionable than any other compound modifier: *large-scale* (map), *next-door* (neighbor), *money-back* (guarantee)?

True *wise*-words, on the other hand, by contrast, seem to have developed on the model of certain reputable expressions in which *wise* is a suffix having a slightly different sense, namely, *in the way*, or *manner, of*. Some of those words are *lengthwise, clockwise, likewise*, and *otherwise*. Since we have seen a false accusation against the compound adjective *budget-wise*, it may be well to administer loyalty oaths to *lengthwise, clockwise, likewise*, and *otherwise* before they are hauled up for guilt by association.

Note that *-wise* is solidly attached to *wise*-words; compounds with *-wise* (possessing wisdom) are hyphenated. It now looks, however, as if some *wise*-words have a future, at least in conversation. They shorten expression in a way that is undeniably handy, however loathsome it may seem while it is still relatively new. Certainly it is easier to say "This scheme is clumsy productionwise" than "This scheme is clumsy with respect to production" (or "when it comes to production"). Snobbery and imitation play large roles in the rejection or acceptance of such devices. Some people are delighted by the economy of *wise*-words, and after becoming aware of their possibilities, go at once and do likewise at every opportunity. There is a tendency to jump overboard: "Solano is the largest county populationwise and assessed valuationwise." *Wise?* Unwise. Others are jarred by the compression and bluntness of *wise*-words, and, even more important, are overimpressed by having read they are disdained in some quarters.

Madison Avenooers have denied inventing, using, or even hearing used among their associates the expressions blamed on their kind. Observation shows that *wise*-words, at least, were being manufactured long before Madison Avenue existed as a mythical institution, or as a fount of supposedly defiled language.

wisecrack   See *quip, quipped.*

wit and wisdom   A tiresome pairing, and in addition often inaccurately applied.

with   "Only citizens of the United States will be eligible for permits with all of them to be issued on a competitive basis."

"Smith was struck in the chest and right hip with the third shot going wild."

"The United States ranks ninth in infant mortality with Sweden having the best record."

Sentences of this ilk are as thick as thistles, and about as easy to penetrate. They can be figured out, but not without a pause after *with* to decide which way the wind is blowing. Easley S. Jones, the author of *Practical English Composition,* describes such *with*-constructions as nonrestrictive adverbial prepositional phrases.

The main points are that *with*-phrases can be legitimate, and that they must be set off by commas. Here is an example of an unobjectionable *with*-phrase, which unmistakably modifies the main part of the sentence, as it should: "The bandit raced through the corridor, with the police gaining slowly."

But many *with*-phrases are clumsy substitutes for clearer construction. On close inspection, *with* is seen to be introducing elements that ought to be clauses. *With*-phrases are used sparingly by good writers, because they seldom fit happily. Let us see whether a little carpentry will improve the sentences quoted at the beginning:

"Only citizens of the United States will be eligible for permits, all of which will be issued on a competitive basis."

"Smith was struck in the chest and right hip, but the third shot went wild."

"The United States ranks ninth in infant mortality. Sweden has the best record."

The moral: If you must use *with*-phrases, put commas in front of them. But remember that a sentence containing this construction is often a poor job in the first place. *With* is commonly used as a stylistic trick to string together elements that should stand separately, often as sentences. The natural habitat of this device is journalese.

A phrase beginning with *with* does not affect the number of a subject: "A representative of the secretary general with ten expert advisers *is* [not *are*] already there."

440

with a view to   The idiomatic form; not *with a view of.*

without   Substandard for *unless:* "He could not reach the island without he rented a boat." *unless,* or *without renting.*

with regard to   See *regard.*

with respect to   Why not *about* or *concerning?* See also *in respect to.*

with the exception of   Often redundant for *except, except for.*

with the purpose of   See *for the purpose of.*

witness   Often a pretentious substitute for the simpler and more direct *see, watch, observe. Witness* has a legal or official connotation that is out of place in its usual contexts: *witness a ball game, witness a school play.* Used in this way, the word is journalese.

woman, lady   Rudyard Kipling's cavalier verdict was that "A woman is only a woman, but a good cigar is a smoke." Many of that sex are likely to go up in smoke themselves at hearing the term *woman,* rather than *lady,* applied to them, and in their indignation might not even notice any unfavorable comparison with a cigar. The conflict between *woman* and *lady* in American usage is a curious thing to behold. In one widely accepted view, *woman* suggests commonness, if not vulgarity, while *lady* suggests breeding and refinement. It is this idea, no doubt, that has led to the rejection of *women's* in such names of organizations as *Ladies' Aid* and *Ladies' Auxiliary.*

Go up a few notches in the social scale, however, at least as far as pretensions are concerned, and you will find organization with names like *Woman's Club* and *Women's Alliance.* This choice is common among the country-club, study-group, and college-alumnae sets.

Newspapers commonly forbid the use of the word *lady* in their columns as a synonym for *woman,* holding that *lady* belongs only in titles (Lady Astor) and in references to their holders. This seems to be an unduly restrictive attitude. Anyhow, no newspaper has been known to insist that ladies' aids are women's aids. At the same time, *neighbor woman, widow woman,* and *the Smith woman* are discouraged as poor usage (see *Miss*).

Lady is in general use as a courtesy, as in the salutation *ladies and gentlemen*. Few of us, in directing a remark at a group, would say *you women* rather than *you ladies*. The upshot seems to be that *lady* remains useful when a touch of courtliness is desired, but like all tributes sounds more graceful when it is not self-applied. *Woman* is the workaday word for the female of the species, and the idea that it carries a hint of disparagement is mistaken.

wonder   The expression of wonder is a declarative statement, not a question, and does not take a question mark: "I wonder what people expect of bus drivers?" *drivers*. See also *Questions*.

WORD AS A WORD   To call attention to a word as such, use italics or quotation marks, not commas. "Magnuson suggested that he had used the word, bottle, a little perversely." The writer of this used commas a little perversely: "the word *bottle*" or *the word "bottle."*

WORD DIVISION   There is nothing esoteric about this, although apparently it is becoming a lost art. The basic rule is that words are properly divided only on syllables. The way to resolve questions about this, and they are many, is to consult a dictionary. The dots used in dictionary entries to divide syllables are often mistaken for hyphens (*gob'ble·dy·gook*). Hyphens intended as such are printed in their usual form in dictionary entries or sometimes as double hyphens (=).

Division of words in typescript is generally discouraged, especially in material intended to be set in type. Hyphens at the ends of lines in manuscript can raise unnecessary questions for the printer. The lines as he sets them will not correspond to the way they break in the manuscript, and thus he cannot always be sure whether the hyphen in a compound modifier, for example, that happens to fall at the end of the line in the manuscript is intended if the break occurs elsewhere in type.

Single-syllable words, no matter how long, cannot be divided: *through, though, would, smooth*. Divisions on one letter, as *a-round*, are improper. *English for Printers*, the instruction manual of the International Typographical Union, says: "Singular nouns of one syllable, pronounced as if they were words of two syllables when pluralized, cannot be divided: as, 'horse,' *horses;* 'inch,' *inches;* 'fox,' *foxes;* 'dish,' *dishes.*" Divisions of words ending in *-es* and *-ed* are not uncommon, however.

Divisions of figures and of names of people are to be discouraged, but are unavoidable in printing set in narrow measure.

WORD ORDER Atmospheric inversion has been blamed for smog. The inversion of sentences creates a kind of linguistic smog that puts the reader to work sorting out the disarranged words, causes his eyes to smart, and perhaps makes him wish he were reading something else. A desperate straining for variety in sentence structure is to blame. Tired of starting with the subject and adding the predicate, some writers make a mighty effort and jump out of the frying pan into the smog.

Commonly they grab a hapless auxiliary verb by the ears, yank it out of the protective shadow of its principal, and plop it down at the beginning of the sentence. Like this: "Encouraging the United States were Britain and France." The normal, painless way to say this is "Britain and France were encouraging the United States"; or, passively, "The United States was being encouraged by Britain and France."

The usual word order has been varied by moving *encouraging* forward, but the variety may have been gained at too high a price. Americans, unlike Germans and ancient Romans, are not used to holding some element of a sentence in suspension until the other pieces of the puzzle come along, and there is no reason why they should get used to it. Inversion, of course, is not wrong; it is just pathetically overdone, particularly in newswriting.

Versifiers have an excuse for this kind of thing, when they find it necessary to place the word with the desired rhyme at the end of the line, regardless of how the chips fall. But they at least can plead poetic license.

When a fellow who wrote "Hiring the men will be ranchers in the vicinity" was asked whether he had a license to mangle prose, he only reddened and fell silent. It was noticed, however, that he amended the sentence to "The men will be hired by ranchers in the vicinity."

Stuff like "Damaged were the cars of two motorists" and "Suffering minor injuries in the crash was his wife, Viola" and "Caught in the school during the explosion were twenty girls" is gawky and inexcusable. These examples call to mind the line from Wolcott Gibbs' classic satire on *Time:* "Backward ran sentences until reeled the mind." No word-mincer, Gibbs.

Sometimes writers start sentences with auxiliary verbs only because they think there is no other way out when introducing a series of names: "Passing their intermediate tests were George Simms, Ernest Worth, Alben Smith, Nelson Raddle, and Alex Jones." But there *is* another way out: "Those who passed their intermediate tests were . . ." ("Intermediate tests were passed by . . ." is possible, but would be a clumsy use of the passive.)

It should be kept in mind that emphasis is given a word that is taken out of its normal position. When a sentence is disarranged for no other reason than to gain variety in its structure, the effect may be awkward. The reader gets an impression of emphasis where emphasis makes no sense. Better methods are available for structural variety, such as beginning with subordinate elements, e.g., clauses introduced by *when, although,* or *nevertheless,* prepositional phrases, infinitives, participial phrases.

The uprooted word is not always an auxiliary verb; it may be an adjective, as in "Responsible for all cultural questions is a key member of the city administration." There is still no good reason for standing a sentence like this on its head. Fowler called the abuse of inversion one of the most repellent vices of modern writing.

Misplaced Modifiers   FOR SALE: *Piano, by a lady going to Europe with carved legs.* The authors of books on grammar are so fond of quoting examples like this that we might expect such errors to be extinct by now.

"Details are slipping out of plans for the first Soviet-bloc beauty contest." *Details of plans for the first Soviet-bloc beauty contest are slipping out.*

"Hospital attendants said the baby had a history since birth of heart disease." . . . *a history of heart disease since birth.*

"They held at gunpoint the woman in her home for four hours." *They held the woman at gunpoint . . .*

"The group opposed a proposal calling for a written definition of the positions on disarmament of the great powers." *of the positions of the great powers on disarmament.*

"The Israelis were accused of firing on the Egyptian post of Deir el Balat for ten minutes without causing casualties." A reproach for poor marksmanship?

Here are two more examples that fit in with the others, although the misplaced elements are not prepositional:

"He said every chance would be given to complete satisfactorily the negotiations." This is too Teutonic for the American ear. *to complete the negotiations satisfactorily.*

"An applicant for a federal job should have a chance to explain informally derogatory information." *to explain derogatory information informally.*

From these examples we may deduce some principles: (a) an adverbial modifier, such as a prepositional phrase or an adverb, should not intervene between a verb and its direct object (*held at gunpoint the woman; explain informally derogatory information*); (b) an *of*-phrase modifying a noun should stand as close to it as possible (*positions on disarmament of the great powers*). But there is an exception to (a) when it would mean moving the modifier too far from the verb: "I have been following Mr. Ellis' pronouncements on why he is a better candidate than his opponent very closely." *following very closely Mr. Ellis' . . .*

See also *Modifiers; Split Infinitives; Time Elements; as is, as are; Division of Compound Verbs* under *Verbs; Variation; Leapfrog.*

work for   See *affiliated with.*

worse to worst. . . .   See *Misquotation.*

worsen   A suspicion is abroad that *worsen* is not all it should be, even in the sense *get worse*, to say nothing of *make worse*. But the *Oxford English Dictionary* describes it as having been reintroduced to literature about 1800 to 1830 by writers like Southey and De Quincey, and Fowler also approved of it.

worthwhile   One word; not *worth-while* or *worth while.*

would, should   See *shall, will*, etc.; *Sequence of Tenses.*

would have   Often used quasi-literately in conditional clauses where *had* belongs: "If a doctor would have been on the premises, a death certificate would have been signed." The first *would have* should be *had;* the second is correct.

wraps   In reply to a reader who wrote in asking about the sentence, "Will they really put the wraps on the senator?" *Newsweek* explained: "*Wraps* is a sports term meaning: 'A turn of the reins around the jockey's hands to restrain a horse, hence, restraint.'" All very interesting, but the expression is constantly used and interpreted in a less esoteric fashion, to wit, in the sense of *wrappings*. Most readers probably visualized the senator as muffled or gagged, rather than drawn up short. *Newsweek* itself uses *wraps* in this way: "The army demonstrated its latest antitank weapon and removed some of the secrecy wraps that have surrounded the project for several years."

wrassle, wrastle   See *rassle.*

wreathed in smiles   It may be that this expression is itself ready to be wreathed—and interred.

—X—

Xmas   *Xmas,* popular assumption to the contrary, is not an irreverent, commercialized form, nor a space-saving form invented by headline writers, but rather a reverent form that originated in the early Greek church. X, the first letter of Christ's name in Greek, has often been used as a holy symbol. No etymology will remove the taint of derogation that many people see in *Xmas,* however.

—Y—

ye   Pedants complain that there is no such thing as *ye,* pronounced as it looks, in such names as "Ye Olde Tobacco Shoppe." *Ye,* they explain, is the result of confusing an old printing character that stood for *th* with *y.* What of it? Indians in America are so called because of a misapprehension by Columbus that no one has succeeded in correcting in nearly five centuries; in fact, no one even tries any longer. Names that are artificially aged by such devices as *ye,* however, have a synthetic flavor.

year round   The idiom; not *year around.*

yellow metal   The journalese variant for *gold.* See *Variation.*

Yiddish   See *Hebrew.*

you   There is a prejudice, the heritage of the superstition that informal writing is somehow inferior, against addressing the reader directly. ("You have heard the legend about King Canute.") Yet by far the greater part of what is published today is informal, even conversational, in tone, and when this is so there is no reason why the writer should not recognize the reader as a person instead of regarding him as a disembodied abstraction. It has been conclusively shown that interest and sympathy are created by establishing a personal link between the writer and the reader, and addressing him as a person is one way to do it.

You for *one* is acceptable, and indeed preferable if the writer wants to strike an informal, conversational tone: "You can see the ocean from here on a clear day." *One* (which see) is stiff and even stuffy.

you-all Defenders of *you-all* as used in the South are prone to assertions that are not borne out by observation. One such assertion is that *you-all* is always used as a plural, never as a singular.

"All the South has one word in common and that is the you-all [y'all or yawl] that Yankees usually mess up. It is used only in a collective sense and takes a plural verb," wrote James Street in *James Street's South*. Arthur Gordon is cited to similar effect in *Webster's Unabridged*, which says *you-all* may be used in addressing one person as representing another or others.

Southerners have been known to cite such examples as "Tell your family I want you all to come" and the Biblical "The grace of our Lord Jesus Christ be with you all" in justification of the Southern *you-all*. They also regard the hyphen connecting *you* and *all* as a damyankee intrusion.

But such examples are unexceptionable in any context; *you all* in these instances is used to emphasize inclusiveness. The Southern *you-all* is used where *you* alone suffices. Originally, perhaps, *all* was tacked on to give an emphatic plural feeling to *you*, just as *you* sometimes becomes *youse*.

your *Your* for *the* or *a* (or when no article at all would be required) is a peculiarity of speaking, primarily: "New York is still your [the] literary capital of the United States." It may be objected that Shakespeare had one of the gravediggers in *Hamlet* remark, "Your water is a sore decayer of your whoreson dead body," but then it must be allowed that the gravediggers were clowns.

your's   No such form; *yours*: "The idea was yours."

youth   Attempts have been made to set an age limit for this term, as a discouragement against applying it to those who are no longer young. Such limits are difficult to enforce, however, since it is evident that youth, like beauty, is in the eye of the beholder, and perhaps even more so in the mind of the possessor. We all know elderly men and women who refer to each other as *boys* and *girls*. *Youth* as applied to individuals means only males (*four youths were sauntering down the walk*); as a general term (*the youth of the nation*) it includes both sexes. See also *elderly*.

Yugoslavia, Jugoslavia   *Jugoslavia* was commonly seen a few years ago, and both forms are correct. There is now overwhelming preference for *Yugoslavia*.

—Z—

zoom   The original meaning (and one still in use) was to make an aircraft climb briefly at an angle sharper than it would be capable of in sustained flight. On this is based the insistence in some quarters that applications of *zoom* must always imply an upward direction. The word also has an imitative sense, however, that all dictionaries now recognize, and used thus has no relation to direction: "The car zoomed down the incline"; "The jet zoomed across the Atlantic."

Bibliography

The American College Dictionary. New York: Random House, 1957.

CURME, GEORGE O., *Syntax*. New York: D. C. Heath and Company, 1931.

DAVIES, HUGH SYKES, *Grammar Without Tears*. New York: John Day Company, 1953.

EVANS, BERGEN, AND CORNELIA EVANS, *A Dictionary of Contemporary American Usage*. New York: Random House, 1957.

FLESCH, RUDOLF, *The Art of Plain Talk*. New York: Harper & Row, Publishers, 1946.

——, *The Art of Readable Writing*. New York: Harper & Row, Publishers, 1949.

FOWLER, H. W., *A Dictionary of Modern English Usage*. London: Oxford University Press, 1926.

FOWLER, H. W. AND F. G. FOWLER, *The King's English*. London: Oxford University Press, 1906.

GOWERS, SIR ERNEST, *Plain Words, Their ABC*. New York: Alfred A. Knopf, Inc., 1954.

HAYAKAWA, S. I., *Language in Thought and Action*. New York: Harcourt, Brace & World, Inc., 1949.

JONES, EASLEY S., *Practical English Composition*. New York: Appleton-Century-Crofts, 1956.

MONTAGUE, C. E., *A Writer's Notes on His Trade*. London: Pelican Books, 1952.

New College Standard Dictionary. New York: Funk & Wagnalls Co., Inc., 1961.

Oxford English Dictionary. London: Oxford University Press, 1888 *et seq.*

BIBLIOGRAPHY

Oxford Universal Dictionary. London: Oxford University Press, Third Edition, 1955.

PARTRIDGE, ERIC, *Usage and Abusage*. New York: Harper & Row, Publishers, Second Edition, 1942.

PERRIN, PORTER G., *Writer's Guide and Index to English*. New York: Scott, Foresman & Company, Third Edition, 1959.

POTTER, SIMEON, *Our Language*. London: Penguin Books, 1950.

QUILLER-COUCH, SIR ARTHUR, *On the Art of Writing*. New York: G. P. Putnam's Sons, 1961.

STRUNK, WILLIAM JR., and E. B. WHITE, *Elements of Style*. New York: The Macmillan Company, 1959.

VALLINS, G. H., *Pattern of English*. London: Penguin Books, 1957.

Webster's New International Dictionary. Springfield, Mass.: G. & C. Merriam Company, Second Edition, 1958, Third Edition, 1961.

Webster's New Collegiate Dictionary. Springfield, Mass.: G. & C. Merriam Company, 1963.

Webster's New World Dictionary. Cleveland: The World Publishing Company, 1960.

Word Study (a periodical). Springfield, Mass.: G. & C. Merriam Company.